MODERNISM, MEDIA, AND PROPAGANDA

MODERNISM, MEDIA, AND PROPAGANDA

BRITISH NARRATIVE FROM
1900 TO 1945

MARK WOLLAEGER

PRINCETON UNIVERSITY PRESS

PRINCETON AND OXFORD

Copyright © 2006 by Princeton University Press

Published by Princeton University Press, 41 William Street, Princeton, New Jersey 08540
In the United Kingdom: Princeton University Press, 3 Market Place, Woodstock,
Oxfordshire OX20 1SY

All Rights Reserved

Library of Congress Cataloging-in-Publication Data

Wollaeger, Mark A., 1957–
    Modernism, media, and propaganda : British narrative from 1900 to 1945 / Mark
Wollaeger.
        p.   cm.
    Includes bibliographical references and index.
    ISBN-13: 978-0-691-12811-5 (alk. paper)
    ISBN-10: 0-691-12811-1 (alk. paper)
    1. English fiction—20th century—History and criticism.   2. Modernism (Literature)—
Great Britain.   3. Propaganda—Great Britain—History—20th century.   4. Motion
pictures in propaganda.   I. Title.
    PR888.M63W65   2007
    820.9'112—dc22   2006009788

British Library Cataloging-in-Publication Data is available

This book has been composed in Sabon

Printed on acid-free paper. ∞

pup.princeton.edu

Printed in the United States of America

10   9   8   7   6   5   4   3   2   1

For Corey and Mia

CONTENTS

LIST OF ILLUSTRATIONS

PREFACE

IN A 1941 RADIO address, George Orwell asserted that "propaganda in some form or other lurks in every book, that every work of art has a meaning and a purpose—a political, social and religious purpose—and that our aesthetic judgements are always coloured by our prejudices and beliefs."[1] Change "propaganda" to "ideology" and this familiar thought would fit easily into any recent introduction to literary studies. But Orwell's invocation of propaganda is characteristic of his historical moment, for after the so-called propaganda boom of the 1930s, the proliferating array of discourses through which ideology was disseminated, spreading in waves across the globe, became as much a matter for public concern as the ideological messages themselves. A relatively innocuous word in the late nineteenth century, propaganda most often designated persuasive information or mere boosterism; by midcentury it had acquired the sinister connotations so familiar in today's world of government-sponsored fake news, doctored facts, and transnational public relations firms. The political consequences of these developments are familiar, the aesthetic less so. By the forties Orwell and others had begun to wonder whether there was a place within an increasingly manipulated public sphere for forms of aesthetic experience that preserved some degree of autonomy. Was there a place, in other words, for modernism?

Orwell's address offered what became the standard account of the fate of modernism in the interwar years. Under the pressure of global politics and economic depression, writers and artists in the thirties increasingly began to choose political engagement over the previous decade's emphasis on aesthetic experimentation and technique. Orwell's focus on the thirties makes sense, and not only because historians so often think in terms of decades. Within that highly politicized climate of opinion, art was often defined in relation to propaganda: for some, art was precisely what propaganda was not; others followed the artist Eric Gill in declaring that all art is propaganda.[2] But Orwell's literary history tells only the latter end of a story that began at the turn of the twentieth century, when modernism and modern propaganda emerged as mutually illuminating responses to modernity.

Charting relations between modernism and propaganda from 1900 to 1940, *Modernism, Media, and Propaganda* offers a missing chapter in the history of British modernism. I argue that through its real and imagined proximity to propaganda, modernism came to know what it was in contrast to what it definitely was not and must not become. Contrary to the polarized view that dominated the late thirties, propaganda operated less as an index of absolute difference than as a proximate other, an other so different and yet so close that it had to be acknowledged in order to be rejected.[3] Propaganda, to put it another way, is the alter ego of modernist distanciation.

At the time of Orwell's radio address, "modernism" had not yet become the widely accepted umbrella term for the aesthetic innovations that flourished in England in the first decades of the twentieth century; more common was Orwell's reference to aestheticism as a lasting legacy that, post Oscar Wilde, dared not speak its name. "Propaganda," in contrast, was firmly established as a covering term for the discourses of political persuasion that were making art for art's sake seem increasingly out of touch with the urgent matters of the day. And yet it was difficult to map "the frontiers of art and propaganda," to cite the title of Orwell's address, because "aestheticism" was as contested a term then as "modernism" is now, and "propaganda" presented even more problems. Orwell's ambivalence and confusion are exemplary. Like most critics on the left, Orwell welcomed the unmasking of aestheticism's pretension to political transcendence, but he also lamented that the counterpressure of propaganda had led many young artists into forms of "mental dishonesty" that were impervious to contradiction or qualification. Equally telling is Orwell's uncertain account of just what propaganda is. His debunking of aestheticism serially equates propaganda with "meaning," "purpose," "prejudices," and "belief." If any animating belief or rhetorical design is tantamount to propaganda, then all art *is* propaganda, but Orwell was not alone in refusing to cede the distinction between the aesthetic and the ideological. The difficulty of definition—the sense that propaganda was becoming a kind of ether, everywhere and nowhere at once—is an important legacy of the modernist period and a key context for understanding British narrative.

The lack of critical attention to this topic may derive from an intuitive sense that modernism and propaganda must be antithetical in ways that do not require much elaboration. According to Jacques Ellul, propaganda gives citizens increasingly deprived of traditional forms of support, such as church, family, or village life, precisely what they need: personal involvement in public events and a justification for otherwise useless feelings of anger and resentment.[4] Finding a use value for negative affect, often by channeling alienation into safely xenophobic forms, propaganda rushes into the vacuum produced by deracination and rising skepticism in order to organize psyches hungry for belief. In contrast, modernism arguably elicits resentment by equating civilization with its discontents and so adds to the surplus of negativity in modernity's affective economy.

All this is true enough, as far as it goes, but the assumption of an anti-thetical relation between modernism and propaganda has blocked recognition of their symbiosis.

Recent studies of modernism have revised Orwell's account of the thirties' challenge to modernist insularity by arguing that modernists and their texts were always more actively engaged with their cultural surroundings than earlier historians of modernism were inclined to admit. The subtitle of Michael North's *Reading 1922*, "a return to the scene of the modern," succinctly summarizes the goal of what has been called the New Modernist Studies.[5] Not simply disengaged mandarins—though of course they were often that too—James Joyce, we know now, was keenly interested in advertising, T. S. Eliot and Ezra Pound in self-promotion and popular culture, Virginia Woolf in techniques of mechanical reproduction.[6] But if the project of rethinking the cultural bearings of modernism has left the topic of propaganda relatively untouched,[7] Ellul's sociological analysis begins to get at the deeper logic by which propaganda and modernism were defined adversatively but constituted symbiotically.

Propaganda, Ellul observes, provides the social glue that modernity otherwise tends to dissolve, but he points out as well that propaganda also contributes to the alienation it exploits. Conversely, if modernism amplifies civilization's disenchantment with itself, it also operates as a form of solace. Propaganda and modernism can so easily switch places in these formulations, with propaganda generating the discomfort that modernism eases, because the two emerged concurrently as interrelated languages of the new information age. Propaganda has always existed, but modern propaganda, operating through techniques of saturation and multiple media channels, developed contemporaneously with literary modernism.[8] Ford Madox Ford, one of modernism's most influential theorists, spoke for many when he complained in 1911 that the English were "overwhelmed every morning with a white spray of facts" from the newly dominant popular press,[9] and the alienating effects of information overload were soon exacerbated by photojournalism and the wireless. Mass media thus became both cause and cure: the propagation of too much information by the media created a need for the propagandistic simplifications disseminated by the media as well as a receptive audience for modernism's deep structures of significance. Provisionally holding at bay obvious differences, we can recognize that both modernism and propaganda provided mechanisms for coping with information flows that had begun to outstrip the processing capacity of the mind; both fabricated new forms of coherence in response to new experiences of chaos.

The rise of professionalism and specialization early in the century underscores the connection between these rival discourses. As public affairs became too complex for the average person to grasp, citizens became increasingly dependent on specialists. The professional propagandist emerged as one such specialist, the modernist writer as another.[10] T. S. Eliot took Joyce's "mythic method" as a model for *The Waste Land* because *Ulysses* provided "myths" that gave "a shape and a significance to the immense panorama of futility and chaos which is contemporary history."[11] When British propagandists in World War I needed consoling myths to send abroad, they turned to Ford, whose propaganda books, written expressly for the government, redeploy the modernist techniques he perfected earlier that year in *The Good Soldier*. Even the issue of ambiguity, which (paradoxically enough) seems to provide a bright line of separation, becomes more complex with the realization that the erosion of the distinction between information and propaganda, first theorized in the 1950s, was accelerated in World War I by the British Ministry of Information, which cultivated ambiguity as much as modernists did.

Neither uniformly antithetical nor identical, then, modernism and propaganda were sometimes agonistic, sometimes allied, and sometimes nearly indistinguishable. In practice, some modernists self-consciously assisted state efforts to mold public opinion; others theorized that art by its very nature seals itself off from propaganda; and others actively contested the cultural work performed by propaganda. For every conflation of art and propaganda, á la Eric Gill, there was a Clive Bell, whose influential account of "significant form" in *Art* (1914) theorizes aesthetic autonomy as a defense against the persuasive appeals of everyday life through the isolation of "aesthetic emotion."[12] Gill and Bell in effect articulate antithetical responses to a constellation of shared insights. Both modernism and propaganda raise the problem of the separation of form from content; both try to make meaning effective through ambiguity. And just as many modernist movements saw the need to reinvest an overly rationalized society with new emotion, it became crucial for World War I propagandists to rethink political emotion as a matter for culture, not just for politics per se.

Exploring the ambiguous terrain Orwell maps in his radio address, *Modernism, Media, and Propaganda* studies examples of the mutual imbrication of propaganda and modernism from across the spectrum while paying particularly close attention to highly charged limit cases. Through detailed readings of canonical texts situated in relation to multiple discourses of propaganda, I argue that modernist narrative performed its cultural work within a kind of psychosocial contact zone, a highly contested liminal space defined at one extreme by aesthetic subjectivity construed as an unsullied sanctuary for being, and at the other by propaganda as an encompassing array of manipulative discourses.

Received understandings require that I challenge the notion that modernism and propaganda are best understood as simple opposites—or worse, that they are not related at all—but I do not wish to equate them. There is good reason, after all, for most readers to associate propaganda with techniques of political deception and persuasion designed to influence a mass audience. Leni Riefenstahl's *Triumph of the Will* (1934) or other Nazi era images might spring to mind, or perhaps Soviet posters extolling the worker. Where propaganda operates through the deceptive transparency of simplification, traditional accounts of modernism have emphasized its withdrawal from mass culture through the cultivation of ambiguity, aesthetic autonomy, arcane mythopoesis, and private symbolism. Where popular fiction might pursue arguments—"Beef up national defense or Germany will invade"; "Spurn the devil's overtures or you will go to hell"—modernist narrative often seems more interested in finding a still point beyond the fray.[13] The example of Virginia Woolf, however, complicates these familiar distinctions.

Woolf's anxieties while struggling with "The Pargiters" (later to become *The Years*) provide an apt case of threatening adjacency: "I was vagrant this morning & made a rash attempt, with the interesting discovery that one cant [*sic*] propagate at the same time as write fiction. And as this fiction is dangerously near propaganda, I must keep my hands clear."[14] Elsewhere Woolf tends to identify Victorian moralizing with propaganda and modern literature with a world free from what she calls "the burden of didacticism." In her essay "The Leaning Tower," for example, she distances herself from a literary tradition she associates with Jane Austen's "dominion of hedges," or the propagation of class hierarchies, and hopes that a future poet living in a classless society might use a new vocabulary to transcend "propaganda."[15] On one hand, then, Woolf's fear of "propagating" while writing "The Pargiters" is consonant with the familiar narrative of modernism as a rejection of the Victorian era: to write propaganda is to risk reverting to Victorianism. In a comparably elastic use of the term, Ford makes a similar connection between Victorian narrators and propaganda when he proscribes "propaganda" in his critical writings on the grounds that the author "may not indulge in the expression of any prejudices or like any one of his characters more than any other."[16] On the other hand, Woolf's use of the verb "propagate" to mean "propagandize" suggests the degree to which she, also like Ford, was equally inclined to associate propaganda with the new, that is, with modernity's new flows of information. Around the same time, Woolf noticed fascist symbols linked to Walter Mosley appearing on London walls and was dismayed by her sense that norms of persuasion were changing; in a letter to a fellow writer she complains that "people must have things written in chalk and large and repeated over and over again."[17] Repetition may be a key to propaganda and (as Leopold Bloom reminds us) advertising, but it is also a hallmark of modernist style, in which strategic repetition takes up the burden of signification formerly shouldered by narrative. "Dangerously near" as Woolf writes "The Pargiters," propaganda comes to seem her secret sharer.

By focusing on the complexities of this symbiotic relation, *Modernism, Media, and Propaganda* aims to chart new territory while also revisiting familiar topics in literary studies (art and propaganda, war and literature, ideology and rhetoric) and key antinomies in modernist studies (irony versus sincerity, singularity versus mechanical reproduction, authenticity versus the inauthentic, formal mastery versus contingency). Drawing on the concept of a media ecology, I treat modernism and propaganda as proximate information practices operating within a system of interrelated practices. My analysis therefore attempts to grasp a broad range of cultural productions as part of a shared environment, from early film and canonical texts of high modernism to classical Hollywood cinema and mass cultural ephemera, such as picture postcards and posters. In recent years, both Victorian and modernist studies have devoted increasing attention to the fact that new communications technologies (from photography and telegraphy to sound technologies, radio, and film) were transforming the nature of everyday life as radically as were new forms of transportation.[18] But if modernist studies has started to develop Raymond Williams's claim that any account of the modernist moment must start from "the fact that the late nineteenth century was the occasion for the greatest changes ever seen in the media of cultural production,"[19] literary criticism has not yet grasped the degree to which the pervasive propaganda made possible by new media—not just the media themselves—contributed to the shaping of modernism.

My contribution to the rapidly expanding body of new approaches to modernism is best explained by the sense in which *Modernism, Media, and Propaganda* both is and is not a book about World War I. During the Great War, Britain invented the greatest propaganda campaign the world had ever seen. So effective was the British strategy that Adolf Hitler and Joseph Goebbels reportedly modeled the Nazi propaganda machine on the influential British prototype.[20] In that sense, this book necessarily *is* about the Great War, and I aim to contribute to a recently revitalized field.[21] The British propaganda campaign was unique in secretly using established imaginative writers and well-known intellectuals who wrote under their own names but published through commercial and university presses that were subsidized by the government. In his pioneering work *The Great War of Words*, Peter Buitenhuis suggests that the delayed revelation of writers' participation contributed in the thirties to the collapse of a shared rhetoric, loss of faith in the word, generational conflict, and the emergence of a more ironic idiom.[22] Buitenhuis is undoubtedly correct to link British propaganda to broader cultural effects, but the campaign's most important effects were apparent well before its cover was blown: the transformation of factual enumeration into a form of rhetoric divorced from empirical grounding, and the formation of what Walter Lippmann called a "pseudo-environment" of mediated images.[23] What's more, these developments were not so much caused by World War I but accelerated by it.[24] This last point suggests the sense in which *Modernism, Media, and Propaganda* is *not* about the war.

It is a truism to say that cultural phenomena are always historically overdetermined, but I want to complicate the story of war and modernism in one specific way. Rather than making modernism possible through various forms of cataclysmic discontinuity, whether the destruction of shared values or the ironizing of outmoded ideals, the Great War accelerated the transformation of a media ecology already undergoing rapid change under the pressure of new media and increasing flows of information.[25] Modernism, already emerging by the turn of the century, developed in dialogue with a cultural array that began to change yet more rapidly in response to the war.[26] By drawing on contemporary media theory, my readings of British narrative over the first four decades of the twentieth century tend to corroborate Friedrich Kittler's hypothesis that the status of the word was forever changed over the turn of the century by the emergence of new techniques of information storage that ended language's monopoly over the recording of experience.[27] At the same time, by reading British narrative against specific discourses of propaganda, I depart from Kittler's deterministic claim that military necessity is the prime mover of media history.[28] My discussions of Woolf and Joyce consequently focus as much on colonial propaganda as they do on war propaganda. As I argue in chapter 2, Woolf may have played a prank on a dreadnought, but her early modernism is indebted less to military history than to the history of international exhibitions.

Understanding World War I as a pivotal chapter in the formation of a modern media ecology, my analysis shows that propaganda and a broad range of recognizably modernist works have common roots in the emergence of an information society. With the war placing huge new demands for information control on the government, the bureaucratization of propaganda during the war constituted a major step in the information revolution that was well underway before the advent of microprocessors popularized the notion of an information society. As James R. Beniger has shown, the concept of an information society is best understood as a revolution in the management of information that began late in the nineteenth century as a response to a "control crisis" caused by the Industrial Revolution.[29] Effective management of the increasingly rapid flow of goods early in the nineteenth century required a correlative transformation of communications systems and information processing and new ways to control demand and consumption. In the twentieth century, responses to the growing control crisis included techniques for rationalizing the production process, such as Frederick Taylor's principles of scientific management, and for managing demand, such as advertising and market research. The most effective response, however, was modern propaganda.

Alexander Welsh has studied a literary response to the information explosion in the Victorian era, arguing in *George Eliot and Blackmail* (1985) that when blackmail became the age's chief information pathology—that is, an aberration that made visible the normal operation of the system—blackmail plots turning on the control and release of hidden information became increasingly prominent in Victorian fiction.[30] The chief information pathology of twentieth century was propaganda, but propaganda, unlike blackmail, did not generate a single generic counterpart. *Modernism, Media, and Propaganda* explores multiple responses to propaganda's relativization of facts, its creation of a pseudo-environment, and its aspirations to mastery. By situating specific features of modernist narrative, such as the artificial innocence conjured by its narrators and the oscillation between extreme forms of objectivity and subjectivity, in relation to specific discourses of propaganda, my argument intervenes in longstanding debates about the politics of modernism. Theodor Adorno has taught us that aesthetic complexity and oblique perspectives on the real can operate as forms of critique, but the refusal of direct engagement finds expression in historically specific forms whose political effects vary with circumstances of reception.[31] Revisiting the scene of the modern, *Modernism, Media, and Propaganda* brings into focus multiple literary responses to modern propaganda by reading canonical fiction within the welter of competing media that, for many writers, were rendering the literary word both less powerful and more important than ever before.

The introduction, "Modernism and the Information-Propaganda Matrix," addresses key theoretical and historical coordinates while tracing the notorious difficulty of defining propaganda through a variety of moderns, from George Orwell and Virginia Woolf to Edward Bernays and Jacques Ellul. The introduction also offers a condensed history of the development of the British propaganda machine during World War I in order to show how the British campaign reveals in miniature the formation of the modern media ecology within which modernists struggled to find a cultural foothold. Although early on the campaign relied on relatively highbrow writers, by turning increasingly to film and other mass media British officials acknowledged the waning cultural authority of literature and ultimately accelerated the decline of literature's influence.

But even as the British campaign tells the story of the depriviliging of the literary word, within *Modernism, Media, and Propaganda* literature largely retains its privileged position. The introduction thus concludes by rereading *Heart of Darkness* through Conrad's 1916 propaganda essay for the Admiralty in order to demonstrate the yield of my approach for those interested in the history, authors, and works of modernist narrative, and beyond them, in the fate of modernism in other media, especially film.

Chapter 1, "From Conrad to Hitchcock: Modernism, Film, and the Art of Propaganda," anticipates my project's historical sweep and its intermedial approach to the conjunction of modernism and propaganda by continuing the introduction's discussion of Conrad in light of Alfred Hitchcock's film adaptation of *The Secret Agent* (1907) as *Sabotage* (1936). To explore Hitchcock's reworking of Conrad's novel is to trace the evolving relationship between literature and film during the rise of modern propaganda. Having meditated on propaganda in *Heart of Darkness*, Conrad returned forcefully to the topic in *The Secret Agent*: the failed bombing of Greenwich Observatory acknowledges the emergence of a new form of propaganda; Ossipon's ineffective propaganda pamphlets operate as a negative image of the rhetorical power to which the novel aspires; and the Professor's chilling commitment to anarchist violence embodies Conrad's ambivalent fantasy of the power he would like to wield in the marketplace. If violence was once considered persuasion by other means, by the turn of the twentieth century political violence designed to shift public opinion had come to be known as "propaganda by the deed."[32] Hitchcock's response to *The Secret Agent* during the propaganda boom of the thirties transposes Conrad's problem of readership into a cinematic exploration of film's capacity to master its audience.

Returning to the prewar years, chapter 2, "The Woolfs, Picture Postcards, and the Propaganda of Everyday Life," explores the diffuse forms of propaganda that preceded (and were transformed by) the more professionalized propaganda of World War I and World War II. Woolf was acutely sensitive to the pressures of what Ellul termed "integration propaganda" in her first novel, *The Voyage Out*, in which her heroine's failed efforts to disentangle herself from interlocking ideologies woven into the texture of everyday life mirror Woolf's struggle to define a space for herself as a woman novelist. The chapter reads *The Voyage Out* in relation to the patriarchal hailing of colonial postcards, imperial exhibitions, and Leonard Woolf's first novel, *The Village in the Jungle* (1913), in order to resituate Virginia's dissident modernism within the mass cultural and literary forms soon to be appropriated by the British propaganda campaign.

Chapter 3, "Impressionism and Propaganda: Ford's Wellington House Books and *The Good Soldier*," is the first of two chapters that directly engage with World War I propaganda. This chapter closely studies the relationship between Ford's two propaganda books and his modernist masterpiece, *The Good Soldier*, and argues that his doctrine of impressionism offers a theory of spin *avant la lettre*. By fusing facts and human feeling in the impression, Ford aims to reinvest "dead facts" with coherent value, but in doing so his theory embraces the subtle subjectification of history on which propaganda depends. At the same time, Ford's modernism and propaganda can be distinguished with respect to the way the former complicates the processes of identification on which the latter relies. Chapter 4, "Joyce and the Limits of Political Propaganda," continues to focus on modernism and state-sponsored manipulations of information by analyzing the ways in which *Ulysses* engages with the rising political and aesthetic influence of the poster. De-composing notions of Irish national identity propagated by British recruiting posters distributed in Ireland, Joyce invents new forms of cosmopolitan subjectivity in response to nationalizing discourses of propaganda. If Ford's modernism is closely allied with and yet distinct from propaganda, Joyce widens the gap by showing how modernist explorations of the flux of consciousness can contest the internalization of authority that propaganda promotes.

Chapter 5, "From the Thirties to World War II: Negotiating Modernism and Propaganda in Hitchcock and Welles," operates as an extended epilogue by returning to Hitchcock in order to set his early Hollywood career against the early career of his American counterpart, Orson Welles, whose theater work in the Federal Theatre Project was caught up in what he called "the propaganda play." If Hitchcock was the first British auteur, Welles soon became Hollywood's preeminent master-stylist, and their career paths trace the afterlife of issues that run through the previous four chapters: the connection between the rise of propaganda and modernism's self-conscious exploration of competing media; artists' ambivalent attraction to the power and efficacy of propaganda at a time when an increasingly fragmented audience was becoming more difficult to reach; the social function of formal innovation; and the challenge of articulating a space for art within the pseudo-environment fostered by propaganda. The chapter analyzes both familiar works, such as *Spellbound* (1945) and *Citizen Kane* (1941), and works that were lost for over forty years, Welles's *It's All True* (partially reconstructed in 1994) and Hitchcock's *Aventure Malgache* and *Bon Voyage* (released by the British Ministry of Information for the first time in 1994). Both Hitchcock and Welles failed as propagandists, and their failures tell a story about the political fortunes of modernism at midcentury. The modernist desire for cultural renewal may seem sadly naive in light of the subsequent ascendency of propaganda, but the divergent fates of Welles and Hitchcock suggest that neither the rejection nor institutionalization of modernism need negate its powers of disruption. Their failed propaganda projects indicate that even near the end of its heyday modernism was able to disrupt a cultural formation whose origins are mixed up with its own, but whose legacy casts a darker shadow.

It only dawned on me after I was well into this project that *Modernism, Media, and Propaganda* explores the flip side of my first book, *Joseph Conrad and the Fictions of Skepticism*. In the preface to that book, I expressed my intention at a later date to shift my focus from relations between philosophical skepticism and literary form in order to do more work on social and political contexts for skepticism in the modernist period. Just what it would mean to undertake such a project I did not disclose at the time, for I had no idea. I did, however, share Dominick LaCapra's conviction that it is only by grasping the relationship between text and context as "a genuine problem" that historical criticism "will be able to counteract the dogmatic assumption that any given context . . . is *the* context for the adequate interpretation of texts."[33] As I found myself increasingly drawn to diverse cultural forms while working through new ways to contextualize modernism, I also came to see that when the problem of text and context involves a wide range of media, a thorough rethinking of contextualization also requires fine-grained attention to the distinct signifying practices and modes of address of different media. So my commitments required not only a lot of new reading but also new ways (for me) of reading closely.

Perhaps I took a little too much pleasure in learning more about various extraliterary matters than was strictly necessary, though I do not regret my attention to anarchism or Hans Haacke's installations. At all events, more years than I would have thought likely have passed since I formulated the first glimmer of an idea for this book. Much in my life has changed in the interim. I moved from one institution to another, and stepped entirely out of a third. My investment in the pleasures of reading literature, however, has remained steady, which means that despite my intermedial analysis, this book devotes more attention to detailed readings of literary texts than has become customary in recent culturalist criticism; and while I would not have thought so for a good deal of the time, it turns out that the notion of contextualizing skepticism has guided my efforts all along. The moment of crystallization came when I found myself trying to think through the fog of wars in the Persian Gulf, Afghanistan, and Iraq and realized that I was thinking in terms of slippages, suppressions, and distortions both exemplified and analyzed by Conrad in *Heart of Darkness*. What does modernism have to say to us, I wondered, in a cultural moment when the notion of a pre-Orwellian world of lucid information has come to seem a pipe dream? Now, years later, I imagine my children asking me at some future date why I devoted so much attention to the intricacies of modern British novels. In answer, I will offer them this book. For by revisiting modernism in light of the history of modern propaganda, I hope to amplify the resilient challenge of the modernist sensibility—interrogative, ambitious, hopeful—within the highly propagandized space of twenty-first-century modernity.

ACKNOWLEDGMENTS

WHAT GREATER PLEASURE, after a long haul, than offering thanks for the generosity of friends, family, and supporting institutions? At Stanford as an undergraduate I was very fortunate to have found myself working with Ian Watt. I was much like John Dowell at the time: I just drifted into his office, not knowing enough to be intimidated, and once I demonstrated a readiness to write myself into a more determinate relation to the world, he let me become a regular interlocutor. I wish he had lived long enough to read this book. Professor Watt had a keen mind for intellectual and cultural history—he was writing thick descriptions of literary texts before Clifford Geertz coined the term—and took great satisfaction in a review that referred to his work as "remorselessly empirical." I took that disciplinary bias with me when I crossed the country in 1980 to attend graduate school at Yale. On my arrival, I hadn't even heard of the three D's—Derrida, DeMan, and Deconstruction—and instantly felt gormless and provincial. Months of mental anguish ensuing, I frequently found myself falling into the abysses, gaps, and rifts that riddled the unstable ground of Yale Theory. Eventually I discovered that my preference for Edward Said over Derrida was nothing to be ashamed of, and that the "free play of signification" (catchphrase of the day) and the worldliness of texts were not necessarily mutually exclusive. Teaching at Yale, I began to explore workable syntheses of historical and theoretical approaches, always with an emphasis on close reading, and in the early nineties, not long before I left for Vanderbilt, deconstruction that discovered history began to call itself the New Historicism. At Vanderbilt, devoting a great deal of thought to teaching graduate students how to teach writing, I ended up settling my accounts with New Historicism while gradually developing a more situated sense of rhetoric. Administration, teaching, and scholarship have thus linked up nicely, each contributing in its own way to this book.

Material support from Vanderbilt and other institutions, I am glad to say, has been plentiful. A Senior Faculty Leave at Yale University helped germinate the first seeds for this project; a Research Scholar Fellowship from Vanderbilt opened space for further growth; and a Summer Stipend and a Fellowship from the National Endowment for the Humanities (2001, 2005–6) made possible a great deal of writing. I am also grateful to the Lilly Library at Indiana University for a Helm Fellowship to study the papers of Orson Welles and to Vanderbilt's University Research Committee for a travel grant to work at the Public Record Office at Kew,

England. I also want to thank the English Department and the Dean's Office at Vanderbilt for their various efforts to support my scholarship through funding and creative scheduling.

This work would not have been possible without the patient help of many libraries and librarians. The staffs at the Public Record Office at Kew and the Imperial War Museum in London were always extremely helpful, as were the British Film Institute, the National Library in Ireland, the British Library, the Lilly Library at Indiana University, Trinity College Library (Dublin), and the Bodleian Library at the University of Oxford. Special thanks go to William Massa, who helped me with the Historical Postcard Collection and the African Postcard Collection at Manuscripts and Archives, Yale University Libraries; all postcards and posters reprinted here are from Manuscripts and Archives. Also invaluable have been the Interlibrary Loan staff and the reference librarians at Vanderbilt's Central Library.

Many individuals read and responded to drafts of various chapters or pieces that became chapters: Marshall Brown, Jay Clayton, Beth Conklin, Jerry Christensen, Carolyn Dever, Ian Duncan, Jed Esty, Susan Stanford Friedman, Roy Gottfried, Adam Grener, Kurt Koenigsberger, Bill Kupinse, Victor Luftig, Ellen Levy, Pericles Lewis, Peter Mallios, Jesse Matz, Michael Mirabile, Richard Pearce, Gayle Rogers, Max Saunders, Mark Schoenfield, Bob Scholes, Jen Shelton, Garrett Stewart, Karin Westman, Andrea White, and Paul Young. Lively audiences during my annual conference rotation have helped enormously over the years, so thanks to the Modernist Studies Association, the Society for the Study of Narrative Literature, and to the Modern Language Association. Thanks also to the Virginia Woolf Society, the Joseph Conrad Society of America, the International James Joyce Foundation, and the International Society for the Study of Irish Literature. I am particularly grateful to Ellen Levy, whose generosity and editorial acumen improved everything she read; to Jesse Matz, whose conversations about Ford and impressionism were invaluable; to Jed Esty, for his theoretical insight and encouragement; to Beth Conklin, for insight, support, and healing powers; to Paul Young, who provided critical intellectual companionship and moral support over the last year of the project, and whose film expertise saved me from more than one mistake; and to Jonathan Munk, whose copyediting eliminated many others. All the remaining mistakes are mine to brood over alone. My editor at Princeton University Press, Hanne Winarsky, has been continually enthusiastic, and my production editor, Debbie Tegarden, has always been responsive and efficient.

I have been blessed with excellent students and supportive colleagues at Yale and Vanderbilt. The junior faculty work-in-progress reading group at Yale was more stimulating than anyone has a right to expect, and I learned a great deal in a year-long seminar at the Robert Penn Warren Center for the Humanities at Vanderbilt. To all my undergraduate and graduate students: thanks for your patience, enthusiasm, and critical response. I have also been fortunate in my research assistants at Vanderbilt: Tommy Anderson, Natalie Champ, Josh Epstein, Ben Graydon, Charlie Parks, Gayle Rogers, Dan Turner, and Honor (Miki) Wallace. Gayle in particular enriched my thinking about Hitchcock in the forties, and Ben's meticulous attention to detail in the waning weeks was a godsend. For ten years, Dori Mikus eased the burden of administration with her secretarial skills, boundless energy, and unfailing good spirits.

Parts of several chapters have been published before in earlier versions, and I am happy to acknowledge permission to rework these materials here. Some of the Conrad discussion in the introduction was first published in "Conrad's Darkness Revisited: Mediated Warfare and Modern(ist) Propaganda," in *Conrad in the Twenty-First Century*, ed. Carola M. Kaplan, Peter Lancelot Mallios, and Andrea White (New York: Routledge, 2005); chapter 1 draws on "Killing Stevie: Modernity, Modernism, and Mastery in Conrad and Hitchcock," *Modern Language Quarterly* 58, no. 3 (August 1997): 323–50; chapter 2 revises and integrates two articles, "Virginia and Leonard in the Jungle: Intertextuality, Sexuality, and Authority in *The Voyage Out*, *The Village in the Jungle*, and *Heart of Darkness*," *Modern Language Quarterly* 64, no. 1 (March 2003): 33–69, and "Woolf, Picture Postcards, and the Elision of Race: Colonizing Women in *The Voyage Out*," *Modernism/Modernity* 8, no. 1 (January 2001): 43–75; chapter 4 incorporates parts of "Bloom's Coronation and the Subjection of the Subject," *James Joyce Quarterly* 28 (Summer 1991): 799–808, and "Posters, Modernism, Cosmopolitanism: *Ulysses* and World War I Recruiting Posters in Ireland," *Yale Journal of Criticism* 6, no. 2 (1993): 87–131. All these materials appear in thoroughly revised form.

I am also grateful to Rank Film Distributors for permission to quote from the full treatment for Hitchcock's *Sabotage*; to the Trustees of the Imperial War Museum in London for allowing access to the Papers of Lord Sidney Bernstein and to the copyright holders for permission to quote from that collection; to the Lilly Library for permission to quote from unpublished materials held in the Orson Welles Collection; and to Commerce Graphics for permission to use Berenice Abbott's "Interference of Waves" on the dust jacket.

Finally, I thank my children, Corey and Mia, whose love, intelligence, and wit sustain me. This book is for them.

MODERNISM, MEDIA, AND PROPAGANDA

INTRODUCTION

MODERNISM AND THE
INFORMATION-PROPAGANDA MATRIX

COMMON SENSE, that mysterious repository of unarticulated assumptions, may suggest that modernism and propaganda have little to do with each other. The case of Ford Madox Ford indicates otherwise. Ford is central to the larger argument of this book (and therefore receives extended treatment in chapter 3) because his passionate engagement with both literary aesthetics and the contemporary media environment reveals the sense in which modernism and propaganda are two sides of the same coin of modernity. Setting out to define literary impressionism (which is to say, modernism) early in 1914, Ford proclaimed that an impressionist "must not write propaganda."[1] But within weeks of completing his modernist masterwork, *The Good Soldier* (1914), Ford began writing two books, *Between St. Dennis and St. George* (1915) and *When Blood Is Their Argument* (1915), for the propaganda operation run by C.F.G. Masterman out of Wellington House. With respect to style and narrative technique, the three books are indistinguishable. The conjunction of propaganda and modernist style is not in itself surprising. Just as Dziga Vertov's film *Man with a Movie Camera* (1929) is at once a brilliant city symphony and a piece of Leninist propaganda, so Picasso attacked fascism through the cubist abstraction of *Guernica* (1937).[2] But by grounding his theory of impressionism in a refusal to propagandize even as he wrote propaganda grounded in impressionist technique, Ford betrays a deeper connection between modernism and propaganda. Understood in relation to his belief that modern writers had a civic duty to repair a dysfunctional culture of information, Ford's modernism and propaganda begin to look less like strange bedfellows than like conjoined twins.

Ford, like George Orwell and Joseph Conrad, wrote both as a novelist and as a propagandist, but whereas Orwell felt compelled to theorize the relationship between art and propaganda, and Conrad, like Virginia Woolf, felt threatened by their cultural adjacency, Ford largely shrugged off perceived tensions. With information overwhelming the processing capacity of consciousness, Ford's impression is designed to resist the onset of the posthuman by reinvesting facts with feeling. That is, where T. S. Eliot posited a dissociation of sensibility that began in the seventeenth century with the English Revolution, Ford, more attuned to recent media history, described a split between factuality and the human caused by the surfeit of quantitative data spewed out by the mass press, reference books, and sociology. In Ford's theory, the impression mediates between the human sensorium and a body of facts that otherwise cannot be held together by the mind; propaganda steps in later to manipulate the reunified individual into the greater unity of a collective cause. Rehumanized to appeal to the modern citizen's overtaxed powers of synthesis, the impression is Ford's less direct method for controlling reader response. Propaganda, in this understanding, is acceptable so long as it does not advertise itself as such. The British Ministry of Information (MoI), as I shall describe in this chapter, held a similar view.

This is not to say that the shared subjectification of the fact in impressionism and British propaganda elides all distinctions between the two. Even in Ford, who wrote for the government, friction persists despite the close meshing of gears. Rather, the ease with which Ford moved between impressionism and propaganda indicates how important it is to grasp what modern writers thought propaganda was. To some it recalled the dead hand of Victorianism; to others it heralded a new age (now recognizable as our age) of informatic indeterminacy. By tracing the concept's significance through a range of modernists, and by looking closely at the distinctiveness of the British propaganda campaign, this chapter seeks to show how modernism and propaganda were constituted within an information-propaganda matrix.

MAKING SENSE OF PROPAGANDA: FROM ORWELL AND WOOLF TO BERNAYS AND ELLUL

Understanding what "propaganda" meant to modernists requires us to see the word's problematic status in light of its complicated history in the twentieth century. Specialists in propaganda studies today disagree so much about terminology that some have argued that "propaganda" is useless as an analytic tool and use "persuasion" instead; but "persuasion," others counter, covers too much ground. In mainstream discourse, "propaganda" is regularly used to dismiss purportedly documentary accounts for their deceptive inaccuracy or deliberate bias, as if "propaganda" were the accepted name for the capacious category of politically motivated falsehood. But slinging the term rarely settles the case: one person's propaganda is another person's information, and the distinction between the two is often difficult to draw.

"Propaganda" has not always been so difficult to define. The English word derives from a Latin term that originally referred to a committee of Cardinals, or Congregation of Propaganda, established by Pope Gregory XV in 1622 to propagate Roman Catholicism. The word was later extended to designate "any association, systematic scheme, or concerted movement for the propagation of a particular doctrine or practice" (*OED*). But with the professionalization of advertising in the late nineteenth century, and the emergence of public relations specialists and the rapid development of mass media in the twentieth century, "propaganda" became increasingly difficult to pin down. Although the word began to acquire some negative connotations over the nineteenth century owing to government distrust of secret organizations designed to sway public opinion, the *OED* does not record until 1908 the now-common definition of "propaganda" as tendentious persuasion by interested parties. At that time, with so much of modern society dependent on the rapid exchange of information, "propaganda" usually denoted persuasive information or mere boosterism. The information propagated might come from interested sources, but its integrity or reliability was not necessarily suspect. That would change over the first half of the twentieth century, when two world wars helped link "propaganda" to lies and deception without completely erasing the notion that "to persuade" might simply mean "to inform."

By the forties, when the propaganda techniques pioneered by the British had been refined and deployed around the world for over two decades, propaganda seemed inescapable, and the sinister connotations it had began to gather by the twenties were firmly established. For the Western world, Soviet domestic propaganda had begun to blur distinctions between propaganda and education, and the Nazi campaign added associations with obfuscation and systematic deception. With the surge in global propaganda in the interwar years, artists felt the pressure acutely. Themselves engaged in acts of communication within a media ecology that was changing rapidly, artists were forced to compete not only with increasingly pervasive new media but with organized efforts to use those media to manage the public. When in 1918 Ezra Pound referred to poets as "the antennae of the race," he was already tuned in to the new medium of radio, which he himself exploited as a propagandist during World War II.[3]

But modernists responded to propaganda and the media that made it possible in diverse ways. D. H. Lawrence, for instance, was in one sense a born propagandist. He wrote entire books of doctrine urging readers to live their lives differently, and his fiction sometimes turns away from his characters to advocate alternative modes of being. Perhaps for that very reason, recruiting tactics during World War I enraged him. In December 1915 he spent some time in Battersea Town Hall at a recruiting station.

He was there because when British recruitment fell off drastically in the spring of 1915, Lord Derby, the newly appointed Director-General of Recruitment, devised a program under which men of military age would come forward "to attest" their willingness to serve if required. The so-called Derby Scheme was intended as a compromise between conscription and volunteerism. And so Lawrence, confident that his poor health would earn an exemption and needing to attest before he could apply for a passport to America, went to the town hall to proclaim himself ready and willing.[4] But the next day Lawrence wrote to Ottoline Morrell that after waiting for several hours he left before securing an exemption because he "*hated* the situation almost to *madness*." Lawrence was not put off by the recruiting officials or the potential recruits: "waiting there in the queue, I felt the *men* were very decent, and that the slumbering lion was going to wake up in them: not against the Germans either, but against the great lie of this life." Taken out of context, Lawrence's remarks simply repeat one of his familiar metaphysical points: men fail to live in truth because they do not live in harmony with their leonine passions. Yet the context of recruitment suggests that Lawrence's visceral hatred—in the letter he underscores "hated" five times—was catalyzed in this instance not so much by the men's capitulation to the bogey of mental consciousness as by their "spectral submission" to the untruth associated with war propaganda. The real enemy is not Germany but, as Stephen Dedalus puts it in *Ulysses*, the priest and king within. And like Stephen, Lawrence declares that he will not serve: "I had triumphed, like Satan flying over the world and knowing he had won at last."[5]

Somewhat less satanic, George Orwell and Virginia Woolf both devoted relatively measured attention to propaganda. Woolf thought about the problem more than she wanted to, while Orwell devoted more attention to propaganda than any British writer of his generation. Although both were ambivalent, both sometimes wrote as propagandists, and their explorations of the blurred boundaries between art and propaganda shed light on problems of definition that were newly emerging as matters for public debate.

Orwell's various writings reflect the polarized thinking of the thirties even as they suggest why it is difficult to generalize about relations between art and propaganda. In a 1941 BBC radio broadcast, "The Frontiers of Art and Propaganda," Orwell tries to draw some conclusions from the propaganda wars of the previous decade. For Orwell, art since the 1890s took for granted the notion of art for art's sake, even after the slogan itself was driven underground by the trial of Oscar Wilde. Writers still emphasized "technique" throughout the twenties, but in the thirties Nazism and the global economic depression made it impossible to preserve the "intellectual detachment" required by aestheticism: "any thinking person had to take sides, and his feelings had to find their way not only into his writing but into his judgements on literature."[6] Orwell has mixed feelings about this development. Although he is happy to wave goodbye to the notion that literature ever could wholly detach itself from politics, the politicizing of literature, now "swamped by propaganda," also caused "countless young writers . . . to tie their minds to a political discipline"—"official Marxism"—that "made mental honesty impossible" (*Collected Essays* 2:123, 126). Orwell draws the reasonable lesson that writers can neither remain wholly detached from their times nor sacrifice their "intellectual integrity" to political exigency (ibid., 2:126). Unsure how to reconcile "aesthetic scrupulousness" and "political rectitude," Orwell can only conclude that the decade's events at least "helped us to define, better than was possible before, the frontiers of art and propaganda" (ibid., 2:126–27).

Relatively inconclusive here, Orwell remains illuminating as a guide, in part because he refuses pat solutions to real problems, in part because he wrote both as an artist and as a propagandist. Orwell reflected at length on his dual identity in his diaries—and on whether his roles could even be separated. As a novelist, Orwell probed deeply into propaganda's colonization of everyday life. *1984* is the most powerful novelistic indictment of propaganda ever written in English, perhaps in any language. But the most frightening and prescient element of the novel is not so much the state's "rectification" of the news or the invention of Big Brother, for which the book remains famous. With Big Brother, Orwell simply anticipated Michel Foucault's extension of Jeremy Bentham's nineteenth-century fantasy of the panopticon from the prison to the whole of society, and "rectified" news, sad to say, was already a fact of life as Orwell was writing in 1948. More shocking is Orwell's implicit claim that modern propaganda is able to restructure desire to such an extent that the very concept of internalizing authority breaks down. By the end of *1984*, the distinction between private and public no longer exists: Winston Smith truly loves Big Brother. Authority cannot be internalized when authority has always and already occupied the inner life of the mind. Or to borrow Stephen Dedalus's formulation again, how can the priest and king within be killed if to do so means extinguishing consciousness itself?

Orwell nevertheless felt that propaganda had its uses: the object of his critique in *1984* is not propaganda per se but the totalitarian system it serves. In *Homage to Catalonia* (1938), Orwell expresses disgust over the fact that propaganda during the Spanish Civil War is being produced by noncombatants sheltered from actual bullets, but within five years Orwell (who *did* fight against fascism in Spain) was writing propaganda for BBC radio and confiding in his diary: "All propaganda is lies, even when one is telling the truth. I don't think this matters so long as one knows what one is doing, and why" (ibid. 2:416, 411).[7] Nietzsche never put it better. Nor did Orwell restrict himself to anti-Nazi propaganda. In August 2003 the Public Record Office in England released a list of "crypto-communists" that Orwell compiled in 1949 for the Information Research Department, a propaganda bureau that operated out of the Foreign Office. The important point for my purposes is not that a leftist would collaborate with the government to root out suspected communists. Although the notion of Orwell as a McCarthyite is alarming, there is no evidence that his handing over of the list did anyone any harm, and Orwell was not alone in believing that the Soviet Union had betrayed the left and that many British Marxists had in effect become Soviet nationalists.[8] More significant is that Orwell, anticipating the analysis of Jacques Ellul, had correctly seen that modern governments cannot survive without propaganda. Rather than decry the decay of organic communities, he decided to help hold things together against the perceived threats of Marxism, fascism, and Nazism.

Orwell's ambivalence toward propaganda opens onto complex attitudes shared by many of his fellow writers and citizens in the early twentieth century. Orwell believed that literature should participate in politics, but he did not want to dispense with distinctions between the aesthetic and the ideological. His famous essay "Politics and the English Language" is based on the premise that the operations of language should not be subordinated to political exigencies and on the belief that language can shake off ideology.[9] And yet, as Orwell knew, this was easier said than done.

Virginia Woolf found herself in a similar bind in the thirties. Feeling the unwelcome pressure of propaganda while writing "The Pargiters," Woolf decided that even though "this fiction is dangerously near propaganda," she could not "propagate at the same time as write fiction."[10] But if she was dismayed with a new era in which "people must have things written in chalk and large and repeated over and over again,"[11] she was more than willing to enter the fray: with *Three Guineas* (1938) Woolf earned the title of "the most brilliant pamphleteer in England" from the *Times Literary Supplement* (*Diary* 5:148).[12] Not that Woolf would have appreciated being called the most brilliant *propagandist* in England. Keenly attentive to National Socialist propaganda, Woolf had come to see "propaganda" as a dirty word.

As I noted earlier, it was not always so. Before World War I propagandists began to professionalize the manipulation of public opinion, the Orwellian connotations of names such as Britain's MoI or the U.S. Committee on Public Information (CPI) did not yet exist: "propaganda" was typically used as "information" always had been, in a largely neutral sense. During World War II, British officials still tended to use the words "information," "propaganda," and "publicity" interchangeably among themselves,[13] but the popular view had long since changed, and the public was primed to accept Orwell's now common assumption, canonized by *1984*, that any official linkage between information and government is intrinsically sinister. As cultural pressures began to force a semantic shift, some intellectuals in the interwar years felt compelled to discount the common notion that there could be good and bad propaganda. Feeling the effects of what A. J. MacKenzie termed "the propaganda boom" of the thirties,[14] Frederick E. Lumley undertook in *The Propaganda Menace* (1933) to disentangle propaganda from education and cultural boosterism by arguing that the word should be reserved only for "promotion which is veiled in one way or another" as to its origin, interests, methods, content, or results; "whatever promotional work has passed and now passes under that name had better be called something else in the interests of clear thinking."[15] Edward Bernays, it turns out, had already attempted to address the problem.

Nephew to Sigmund Freud and founder of public relations as a profession, Bernays realized the commercial potential of engineering public opinion while working as a propagandist for the CPI, better known as the Creel Commission.[16] His first two books record his struggle to distinguish between the honorable work of public relations and its disreputable progenitor, propaganda. *Crystallizing Public Opinion* (1923) opens as if Bernays intends to distance himself from the word by undertaking to explain the significance of "a new phrase": "counsel on public relations."[17] In fact, Bernays himself had coined the title in order to give his new enterprise an aura of professional standing. Detecting a connotative shift underway, Bernays admits that the average person probably thinks of the public relations counsel as someone who "produces that vaguely defined evil, 'propaganda'" (*Crystallizing Public Opinion*, 11–12). But rather than clear away a misconception, he simply continues: "And yet . . . there is probably no single profession which within the last ten years has extended its field of usefulness more remarkably and touched upon intimate and important aspects of the everyday life of the world more significantly than the profession of public relations counsel" (ibid., 12). Bernays's odd sense that the extended reach of public relations ought to quell fears about the vague evils of propaganda may explain why he remained stubbornly immune for so long to the increasingly negative connotations of the word. When Bernays published his second book on public relations in 1928, he titled it *Propaganda* and proclaimed without qualms that "propaganda is the executive arm of the invisible government."[18] Yet *Propaganda* also suggests that Bernays was beginning to acknowledge the need to disentangle his profession from the title of his own book. He therefore devotes over two and a half pages to a tissue of quotations from Funk and Wagnalls that emphasizes the neutrality of the term by recalling its original meaning: " 'Propaganda' in its proper meaning is a perfectly wholesome word, of honest parentage, and with an honorable history. The fact that it should to-day be carrying a sinister meaning merely shows how much of the child remains in the average adult" (Bernays, *Propaganda*, 22). Grow up, in other words, and stop calling your sibling a bastard. Bernays is only too happy to seize on the dictionary's puritanical allegiance to etymology in order to bolster the position Lumley would soon attack, that whether "propaganda is good or bad depends upon the merit of the cause urged, and the correctness of the information published" (ibid., 20). He is therefore unconcerned that by his own count half the stories on the front page of the *New York Times* amount to propaganda. And yet within a few pages Bernays decides that "new activities call for a new nomenclature," and, harking back to *Crystallizing Public Opinion*, reminds the reader that "the propagandist who specializes in interpreting enterprises and ideas to the public . . . has come to be known by the name of 'public relations counsel' " (ibid., 37). Only a few pages later Bernays suggests that those who conflate public relations and propaganda are missing an important distinction: "the stage at which many suppose [the public relations counsel] starts his activities may actually be the stage at which he ends them" (ibid., 43). In other words, public relations enables propaganda without actually engaging in it.

Insofar as common parlance today tends to equate public relations with spin and propaganda with lies, Bernays can be said to have won the battle over nomenclature. But Bernays's tortured distancing of himself from the term, Woolf's insight into changing norms of persuasion, and Orwell's sense of the modern state's dependence on propaganda begin to get at the more complex understanding that emerges in the following decades, particularly in the work of Jacques Ellul.

Ellul's importance in propaganda studies derives from his focus on propaganda as a sociological phenomenon made necessary by the nature of modern society rather than as the political weapon of a particular regime or organization. Ellul's landmark book *Propaganda* (1962) draws on Bernays, and his definition of "sociological propaganda" as "the penetration of an ideology by means of its sociological context" echoes Bernays's account of "the new propaganda," which "sees the individual not only as a cell in the social organism but as a cell organized into the social unit."[19] The concept of sociological or "integration" propaganda permits Ellul to set aside extreme solutions to problems of definition, namely, the notion that everything is propaganda because ideology permeates all spheres of existence and the rejection of the term altogether in favor of a yet broader term, such as "persuasion." Slower and more diffuse than political propaganda, integration propaganda operates through political, economic, and cultural structures, and produces "a progressive adaptation to a certain order of things, a certain concept of human relations, which unconsciously molds individuals and makes them conform to society" (Ellul, *Propaganda*, 64). Integration propaganda thus includes not just the usual state-sponsored suspects—political broadcasting, censorship, atrocity stories, and the manipulation of news—but also more diffusely constellated organizations and institutions, such as advertising, public relations, and popular films, whose interactions effectively reinforce official political propaganda without necessarily setting out to do so. Ellul is clearly open to the charge that insofar as nearly everything counts as propaganda, he empties the category of meaning. But it is equally clear that it makes sense to use "propaganda" as a covering term to articulate the notion that in highly rationalized societies, diverse forms of modern communication function together to ensure the reproduction of the system.[20]

In many ways Ellul's theory overlaps with Max Horkheimer and Theodor Adorno's earlier account of "the culture industry" in *Dialectic of Enlightenment* (1947). Both theories focus on mechanisms of integration and control grounded in principles of rationality that ultimately subvert themselves. For Horkheimer and Adorno, "the tireless self-destruction of enlightenment," or its regression into myth, is rooted in rationality's fear that its power of critique will unground the existing order.[21] Ellul's investigation of propaganda grows out of his critique of instrumental rationality in his more frequently cited *The Technological Society* (1954). For Ellul, technique is at the heart of modern society (not technology; the English title misleadingly translates the original French, *La technique*).[22] By "technique" Ellul means any standardized ensemble of means used to attain a given end, and he understands propaganda as a necessary corollary of a society dominated by technique. Recalling Max Weber's theory of rationalization, Ellul argues that while technique began with the machine, the progressive extension of technique into all domains of existence produces a civilization committed only to efficiency as an end in itself. Propaganda is necessary in such a world, for "propaganda is called upon to solve problems created by technology, to play on maladjustments, and to integrate the individual into a technological world" (Ellul, *Propaganda*, xvii). Like Horkheimer and Adorno, Ellul understands modern propaganda as a species of mythopoesis that papers over contradictions opened up by the homologous forces of rationalization, technique, and enlightenment.

But in comparison with Horkheimer and Adorno's culture industry, Ellul's model of relations among ideology, cultural production, and modernity offers a sharper analytic tool. First, Ellul's theory is more dynamic and less monolithic. The culture industry articulates a top-down model in which power is uniformly diffused throughout culture and in-exorably subordinates the individual to the social totality through the agency of media controlled by capital. Thus all preexisting forms of en-tertainment and art are "taken over from above"; the resulting enter-tainment "prescribes each reaction"; content is transformed into style; and the stylistic transformation of "all branches of intellectual produc-tion" dictates "obedience to the social hierarchy."[23] For Ellul, in con-trast, individuals become consumers not because advertising and mod-ern media (epitomized by cinema and radio) manufacture desire but because the desires and needs of the individual help generate the mecha-nisms that lead to their integration. Individuals collaborate in their sub-jection, in other words, because processes of rationalization, more broadly construed than in Horkheimer and Adorno, create needs that only propaganda can fulfill. Thus if both Ellul and the Frankfurt school critics offer grim visions of domination, the former's approach preserves the possibility of agency by positing of a zone of interaction between in-dividuals and apparatuses of integration. Modernism performs its cul-tural work, I argue in succeeding chapters, within this liminal space, a kind of psychosocial contact zone defined at one extreme by subjectivity construed as a sanctuary for being, and at the other by propaganda as an encompassing array of manipulative discourses. Second, whereas in Horkheimer and Adorno the difference between culture and propaganda disappears through the agency of media controlled by the culture industry—power, that is, alchemically transforms all cultural produc-tions into propaganda—Ellul recognizes that cultural desires precede and motivate the invention of new technologies, such as new media, and that new technologies then reshape those cultural desires. In short, El-lul's model is more genuinely dialectical than Horkheimer and Adorno's "dialectic of enlightenment." Thus where the concept of the culture in-dustry asserts a media determinism in which specific media necessarily produce particular effects (e.g., "to posit the human word as absolute . . . is the immanent tendency of radio"),[24] Ellul sees the growing dominance of mass media as contributing to a more fundamental dynamic, in which the explosion of information requires the development of propaganda. This difference requires further explanation, for it goes to the heart of how Ellul's theory brings into focus the ways in which modernism and propaganda, as incipient languages of the new information age, are re-lated yet ultimately divergent mechanisms for processing information within modernity's new regimes of rationalization.

In *Propaganda* Ellul repeats an argument he made more forcefully in an earlier essay, "Information and Propaganda" (1957): by the mid-twentieth century it has become virtually impossible to distinguish be-tween information and propaganda. Ellul's critics often misread him to mean that the two are theoretically indistinguishable, but his point, in the words of Stanley Cunningham, is that modern propaganda is

> characterized by a very close alliance with or incorporation of some central, highly prized epistemic values: information and knowledge; truth and facts; certainty and objectivity. It is further enhanced whenever these epistemic values are embedded within such culturally esteemed practices as debate, discussion, and scientific research; or when it is associated with such para-epistemic dispositions as thoughtfulness and reflection, and with the social values of openness, cooperation, courtesy, and civility—all of which add up to give a total impression of fair play and reasonableness in persuasive discourse.[25]

Within this information-propaganda matrix, those most confident of their ability to tell the difference—intellectuals and professionals—are the most likely to be mistaken. Thus where Horkheimer and Adorno conjure the threat of elite capitalists gathered behind the curtain to orchestrate mass deception, Ellul describes the more alarming scenario in which the hidden persuaders (to cite Vance Packard's popular version of the Frankfurt school's conspiratorial vision)[26] are as blinded by information as those they would manipulate.[27]

Much of the resistance to Ellul's theory derives from his counterintuitive claim that "intellectuals are most easily reached by propaganda, particularly if it employs ambiguity" (*Propaganda*, 113). Horkheimer and Adorno implicitly exempt readers able to follow their complex dialectical critique (not to mention the writers capable of overcoming the reification of language that their analysis insists is universal) from the exhausted capitulation routinely suffered by their less nimble compatriots, for whom the culture industry is the only game in town. But for Ellul, information overrides intellect: "the more informed public or private opinion is, the more susceptible it is to propaganda," because more informed is not the same as better informed: "information not only provides the basis for propaganda but gives propaganda the means to operate; for information actually generates the problems that propaganda exploits and for which it pretends to offer solutions" (ibid., 113–14). If the intellectual reader resists this blow to academic self-regard, Ellul is no easier on everyone else: "The majority prefers expressing stupidities to not expressing any opinion: this gives them the feeling of participation" (ibid., 140). So much for talk radio in the United States. Addressing the elite and the masses together, Ellul continues:

> Developments [in the modern world] are not merely beyond man's intellectual scope; they are also beyond him in volume and intensity; he simply cannot grasp the world's economic and political problems. Faced with such matters, he feels his weakness, his inconsistency, his lack of effectiveness. He realizes

that he depends on decisions over which he has no control, and that realization drives him to despair. Man cannot stay in this situation too long. He needs an ideological veil to cover the harsh reality, some consolation, a *raison d'être*, a sense of values. And only propaganda offers him a remedy for a basically intolerable situation. (Ellul, *Propaganda*, 140)

Thus a claim I advanced in the preface can be refined here: propaganda finds a use value for negative affect by channeling what might be called informatic alienation into socially "productive" forms, such as myths, stereotypes, and xenophobia.

Admittedly, Ellul's account exaggerates the effectiveness of propaganda—like Horkheimer and Adorno, he has no interest in empirical studies—as well as the degree to which propaganda usurps the role of all competing belief systems. The strong affect driving Ellul's argument, particularly noticeable in "Propaganda and Information," betrays an historical source when Ellul, discussing the role of memory in the conversion of information into knowledge, observes that "quite recently . . . we watched our intellectuals seriously assert the exact opposite of what they had said a few months before—not even alluding to their former stand and demonstrating that there is frequent loss of memory."[28] The historical referent goes unnamed, but Ellul's acid irony is motivated by the 1956 Soviet Party Congress in which Nikita Krushchev, finally acknowledging Stalin's crimes and denouncing his despotism, in effect admitted that official Soviet history had been composed of propaganda unburdened by any fidelity to fact.[29] Writing as a quasi-Marxist just as the word "disinformation" was coined to name the blurry semantic space in which distinctions between information and propaganda were once discerned, Ellul no doubt felt betrayed into theorizing his own gullibility. But the depth of Ellul's animus may also derive from the fact that he was a theologian as well as a cultural critic: sometimes he implies that humankind has fallen from a state of mythic premodernity—a state of psychic and social wholeness—into the modern hell of propaganda. Ellul himself thus writes as a modernist: his sustained analysis of the snares of modern existence amounts to a descent into the underworld, where he unearths, as Joyce does in Nighttown, the interlocking network of desires and social determinants that makes it hard for modern citizens to declare that they will not serve.

At this juncture, the interface between propaganda and information and between information and modernism becomes apparent. One might say that if the alienated, frustrated, and confused protagonists of modern British narrative are symptoms of modernity, propaganda is the solution. From the eddies and repetitions within "the prolonged present" of Gertrude Stein's characteristic narrative voice to the present-tense monologues of Woolf's characters in *The Waves* (1931), modernism's innocent eye or knowing ignorance, so intent on disavowing knowledge in favor of being, may be understood as a mechanism for coping with flows of information that exceed human comprehension. If Woolf's waves conjure the ruling power of Britannia, a covert power everywhere present but nowhere seen,[30] the italicized interchapters through which the waves roll insist equally on the natural fact of tides, seasons, and the rotation of the earth, offering a counterpoint to the turbulent ideological moment of the novel's composition and reception. According to this logic, lyric immediacy and modernist mythologies, like imagistic concentration and encyclopedic capaciousness, are the systole and diastole of an information ecology that demands either arbitrary exclusion ("We must exclude someone from our gathering, or we shall be left with nothing," says a missionary in *A Passage to India*) or impossible comprehension (the "Akasic records of all that ever anywhere wherever was" invoked by Stephen in *Ulysses*).[31]

If propaganda has always existed, reliable information has always been hard to come by in wartime; hence the proverbial fog. But the acuteness of the problems posed by the information-propaganda matrix is a distinctly twentieth-century phenomenon. The saying "to lie like a bulletin" dates from the Napoleonic Wars, and the well-known tripartite typology of deception—lies, damned lies, and statistics—dates from the late nineteenth century.[32] But with World War I, when newly invented propaganda techniques first harnessed the considerable power of the advertising industry to the political aims of the nation-state, the most telling saying emerged: the first casualty of war is truth.[33] Truth has died many deaths over the twentieth century, but the role played by the British propaganda campaign in World War I is fundamental to understanding the new media ecology faced by modernist writers and its effects on attitudes toward truth, factuality, and rhetoric. For when Woolf and Orwell struggle to articulate a space for the aesthetic in the culture wars of the thirties, they are attempting to find their bearings in a media environment whose rate of change, already an overwhelming fact of existence prior to 1914, had been accelerated by war.

PROPAGATING FICTIONS: WELLINGTON HOUSE, MODERNISM, AND THE INVENTION OF MODERN PROPAGANDA

Although historical accounts of modernism have devoted a lot of attention to World War I, the innovative British propaganda campaign rarely enters the calculus. The plan was unique among its European counterparts in that it emphasized facts over overt persuasion, disguised the official origins of its propaganda, and placed literature at the heart of its efforts—at least at the beginning.

On September 2, 1914, just under a month after the outbreak of war, C.F.G. Masterman, the former Liberal MP charged by Prime Minister Herbert Asquith with initiating the British propaganda campaign, tapped into the tremendous cultural prestige of British letters by secretly inviting to his office in Wellington House twenty-five of England's most influential writers. The invitees included William Archer, J. M. Barrie, Arnold Bennett, Robert Bridges, G. K. Chesterton, Arthur Conan Doyle, John Galsworthy, Anthony Hope Hawkins, Thomas Hardy, George Trevelyan, H. G. Wells, and Israel Zangwill. Rudyard Kipling and Arthur Quiller Couch could not attend but sent messages offering their services.[34] With the exception of Hardy, all those in attendance chose to help, and many others, including Ford Madox Ford and Joseph Conrad, joined the campaign later. It is not at all surprising that so many writers supported the war: though the Liberal Party traditionally had been far less inclined to wage war than the Conservatives, early support for the fight against Germany tended to cut across party affiliation. Positioning themselves as concerned citizens, the authors recruited into service published commissioned books under their own names through well-known commercial and university presses that were secretly subsidized by the government. The plan was so effectively secretive that most members of Parliament remained unaware of its operations for two years, and the public did not learn of the writers' participation until the early 1930s.[35] Although Masterman's publishing enterprise has been narrated in traditional literary histories, its full significance has not been fully understood or explored, particularly with respect to British modernism.

It is hard to overestimate the cultural influence wielded by Masterman's gathering of writers. "The novelists, poets, short story writers, critics, and dramatists at Masterman's meeting," as Gary Messinger observes, "were all part of an Edwardian literary establishment that had no competition from radio or television and whose representatives enjoyed tremendous prestige throughout the world among both elite and mass audiences": "Not only through their writings, but also through the earnings they amassed, the access they were given to the social networks of the politically and economically powerful, and the letter-writing correspondence they maintained with numerous loyal readers, these men were as influential a group of writers as the world has ever produced."[36] As influential as these men were, however, literature's role shrunk over the course of the war, for Masterman and his successors soon realized that film and other mass media were beginning to overshadow the cultural influence of literary intellectuals. The evolving British strategy thus charts the emergence of what in retrospect looks like a modern media environment. More than a microcosm, however, the campaign also accelerated the pace of change. Propaganda's influence on the truth value of facts or, to put it another way, on the tension between the seeming immediacy of facts and the subtle ways in which facts are already and always mediated, registers across a wide range of modernist texts. The following historical narrative is therefore intended to lay the ground for subsequent discussions of the way modernists struggle to position themselves in relation to a media ecology whose transformation of factuality into rhetoric was contributing to the formation of what Walter Lippmann called a "pseudo-environment" of mediated images.[37]

The most benign view of British propaganda is that it was designed primarily to disseminate factual accounts to counter rumors, gossip, incomplete stories, and fabrications already in circulation. To the extent that German propagandists, confident of a quick victory, sometimes resorted early in the war to lies or misrepresentations concerning enemy losses, landmarks destroyed, or territory captured, counterpropaganda could respond effectively simply by means of factual enumeration. As Lord Robert Cecil observed in a confidential memo, "in war-time it is the facts that count, not words. All we can do to help by propaganda is to let foreigners know what is actually happening."[38] Masterman too was committed to facts, and, judging from available documents, it seems that many British officials sincerely believed that factual enlightenment and persuasion amounted to much the same thing. Ivor Nicholson, who was in charge of pictorial propaganda, claimed after the war that the British never circulated "a deliberate untruth" and that "infinite pains were taken to sift information."[39] Facts would speak for themselves, and the world would recognize the truth of Allied accounts and the virtue of Allied aims.

The British factual emphasis developed in response to the pressures exerted by Germany's already well-established campaign. When war broke out on August 4, 1914, Germany had been using official propaganda bureaus, openly identified as such, to ply the world with its version of political tensions in Europe for decades. By the fall of 1914, many European neutrals resented the endless stream of German pamphlets. Masterman therefore decided to rule out direct appeals to neutral countries: "Strict secrecy has been observed as to any connection of the Government with the work," he reported: "every recipient of material distributed gratuitously should receive it from an unofficial source" and the material itself would not "bear any sign of having been produced under the auspices of the Government."[40] Officially named the Propaganda Bureau, Masterman's project soon came to be known by the building in which it was housed, Wellington House, a cover name Masterman made quasi-official in the title of subsequent parliamentary reports in order to camouflage his operation's status as the state's central organ of propaganda. By the end of the war, it was generally agreed that British propaganda completely dominated the field, and most historians today believe that the British campaign played some role in persuading the United States to enter the war, contributed materially to shortening the war by undermining German morale, and was a significant influence on the punitive nature of the Treaty of Versailles.[41]

When Masterman assembled his writers, the first order of business was to organize an "Authors' Declaration" in support of the war in response to a letter recently published by German academics; the declaration appeared in *The Times* on September 18. But his long-term plans were more important. Knowing that the United States was particularly hostile to overt appeals from its former colonial overlord, Masterman had Gilbert Parker consult the American *Who's Who* and compile a list of prominent people who would receive the books with a note from Gilbert or the author, as if from one private individual to another. The same tactic was used with other neutral countries. Commercial publishing houses cooperating included Hodder and Stoughton and T. Fisher Unwin; Oxford University Press also helped out by publishing several volumes, most notably *Why We Are at War* (1914) by the Oxford Historians. Arnold Toynbee wrote several books for Wellington House, as did Lewis Namier, Hugh Walpole, and Arthur Conan Doyle; Mrs. Humphrey Ward, Hilaire Belloc, Gilbert Murray, and G. M. Trevelyan contributed at least one each. Extending its reach beyond English writers, Wellington House also solicited and translated works by foreign authors, including *Who Wanted War* (1915), co-authored by Émile Durkheim, and *The Trail of the Barbarians* (1917), written by Pierre Loti and translated by Ford Madox Ford.

Samuel Hynes has called the exclusiveness of Masterman's initial gathering a "crucial mistake" and suggests that the meeting was in part responsible for one of the dominant myths of World War I, "the concept of the Old Men, as the makers of the war and enemies of the young."[42] Looking back, Hardy, who was seventy-four in 1914, also intuited a generational divide: "the yellow September sun shone in from the dusty street with a tragic cast upon them as they sat round the large blue table, full of misgivings, yet unforeseeing in all their completeness the tremendous events that were to follow."[43] It is certainly true that the gathering did not include the rising generation of writers who were beginning to shape British modernism. Bloomsbury writers such as Lytton Strachey and E. M. Forster were not invited, nor were loose cannons such as D. H. Lawrence or pacifists such as Bertrand Russell. (On the contrary, Russell was dismissed from Trinity College in 1916 and later imprisoned for six months for his antiwar activities.)[44] Virginia Woolf was not yet on the map as a novelist, but no women were involved until the original twenty-five writers were joined later by twenty-five more, including Jane Ellen Harrison, May Sinclair, Flora Anne Steel, and Mrs. Humphrey Ward. Yet if Masterman's strategy was a mistake, it was so only to the extent that by rallying support for the war on idealistic grounds he ultimately contributed to the disillusionment of the postwar years. Beyond the fact that the British campaign worked exceptionally well, the meeting and subsequent campaign were clandestine (apart from the Authors' Declaration) and therefore could not have contributed directly to the generational agon that poets such as Siegfried Sassoon and Wilfred Owen helped to shape well before the existence of Masterman's campaign was revealed.

More important is the fact that the gathering marked the last moment in which literature would ever hold such cultural prestige in England. When Masterman wrote his influential critique of Edwardian culture and society, *The Condition of England*, in 1909, some of his primary "documentary" sources were literary: H. G. Wells's *Tono-Bungay* (1908) carried as much authority as William Booth's protosociological study *In Darkest England* (1890). In the long wake of World War I, however, the documentary role of fiction would be taken over by film and the rising disciplines of ethnography and sociology. By putting novelists to work as propagandists, Masterman not only helped to blur "the dividing-line between Journalism and Literature," a topic started in E. M. Forster's *Howards End* (1910) as "a conversational hare" at a Schlegel sisters' luncheon,[45] he contributed to the novel's absorption into the capacious and ill-defined category of journalistic fictionality. Woolf registers the pressure of journalism in her essay "Modern Fiction" when she criticizes Edwardian novelists such as Arnold Bennett and John Galsworthy for writing too much like newspapermen. Compared to "the luminous halo" of existence caught in the web of modernist textuality, fiction attentive to the way Bond Street tailors sew buttons, she implies, reads like copy torn from the society pages.[46]

Within days of his literary gathering, Masterman acknowledged the power of popular journalism by scheduling a meeting with influential editors and journalists. At Masterman's urging, representatives from, among others, the *Daily Chronicle*, *Daily News*, *Pall Mall Gazette*, *Daily Telegraph*, *Standard*, *Daily Mail*, *British Weekly*, *Times*, *Westminster Gazette*, and *Spectator* agreed to work with the government to coordinate the release of official news in exchange for assurances that censorship would be minimal.[47] Later in the war, Lloyd George, having replaced Asquith, recognized that he could coopt the press even more effectively by appointing prominent publishers to key administrative positions. Thus Lord Northcliffe, founder and publisher of the *Daily Mail* and the *Daily Mirror*, ran the Committee for Propaganda in Enemy Countries out of Crewe House, and Lord Beaverbrook, who held controlling interest of the *Daily Express*, ended up running the MoI; Northcliffe got some help from one of Woolf's targets, Wells, and Beaverbrook was aided by Woolf's favorite target, Bennett, whom he hired in 1918.[48]

From the start, then, literature's prominent role in the campaign was shadowed by the mass appeal of journalism, and it was not long before competing information flows from other media began to crowd out literature. When the campaign began, England was uniquely positioned to control the global flow of information—by the turn of century, British firms owned three-quarters of the world's 200,000 miles of underwater cables[49]—but Britain's material advantage would have counted for little if Masterman had not overcome his elitist inclination to appeal to the masses only indirectly through an older generation of opinion-shapers.[50] As Masterman laid aside his anxious mistrust of the crowd and began to distribute not just books and pamphlets but also films, picture postcards, illustrated magazines, and photographs, Wellington House eventually became only one branch—the literature division—of a dynamic, increasingly complex organization.

But the need to win over neutral opinion abroad and to recruit people into the new citizen army never produced a fully unified bureaucratic structure. Government propaganda was both supported and contested by private organizations on the home front, and as internal rivalries among various government propaganda agencies grew, several attempts were made to centralize control through increasingly comprehensive bureaucratic structures. In February 1917 Wellington House was absorbed into the new Department of Information (DoI), briefly run by the novelist John Buchan, and in March 1918 the DoI became the MoI.[51] But even these reforms failed to produce a fully coordinated government monopoly. The DoI and later the MoI were supplemented by the Press Bureau of the Foreign Office, the Home Office Neutral Press Committee, the War Aims Committee, and a subdivision of Military Intelligence (M.I.7[b]). The Admiralty, which solicited an essay from Conrad, was also producing its own propaganda, as was the Intelligence Department of the War Office. Citizens' groups, moreover, were very active.[52] The Central Council for National Patriotic Organizations aimed to whip up martial spirits, and the Union of Democratic Control, which opposed British war policy and included prominent figures such as Norman Angell, J. A. Hobson, Bertrand Russell, and Lowes Dickinson, held public meetings and published numerous propaganda pamphlets of their own. George Bernard Shaw's *Common Sense about the War*, which equated British and German war aims on economic grounds, made such a splash that Ford was specifically charged with responding to it. Wellington House and its later incarnations thus had to fight to maintain a monopoly over British propaganda.

If intragovernmental infighting and home-front competition prevented the formation of a highly integrated culture industry, a shared commitment to plying the British perspective through as many media channels as possible nevertheless created the most effective propaganda machine the world had ever seen. The MoI developed a Photographic Section that controlled the taking, reproduction, and distribution of war photographs at home and abroad.[53] Picture postcards had been enjoying a boom since the late 1890s (a phenomenon to which I will return in connection with Virginia Woolf in chapter 2), and in his *Third Report on the Work Conducted for the Government at Wellington House*, Masterman reported that "100,000 postcards prepared by us, containing greetings from the British soldier to the Russian soldier, were sent to the Russian armies at the time of the Russian Easter. We also printed 20,000 cards for Italy, showing General Cadorna and Lord Kitchner in medallions surrounded by flags of the Allies."[54] Maps and diagrams were also among Wellington House's publications; in November 1917, W. M. Dixon, a Glasgow professor who took over American propaganda from Gilbert Parker, proudly reported that when President Wilson "referred to a map which threw a flood of light upon the Balkan situation," the "map was one of our publications."[55]

Hindsight, however, reveals that the most important news in Masterman's *Third Report* concerns film. In early 1916 Wellington House was still in charge of cinematic propaganda, and Masterman highlights the spectacular success of a full-length feature entitled *Britain Prepared*.[56] Masterman had good reason to be proud. At the start of the war, the British, like the French and the Germans, were using hot air balloons to drop propaganda leaflets in enemy territory, a practice first developed a century earlier in the Napoleonic Wars. By war's end, not only had the British graduated to hydrogen balloons, but film propaganda was being shown in cinema houses and through Cinemotor, a mobile film unit whose large trucks gave "improvised open-air cinema shows" in rural areas and near the front.[57] Cinema trade groups approached the War Office early in 1915 to offer their services, and though Masterman was quick to grasp film's potential, the War Office Cinematograph Committee was not formed until October 1915, when a trade group, echoing Masterman, finally convinced the War Office that the political value of war films outweighed any possible costs.[58]

Strategic concerns, class prejudice, and multiform anxiety about the newness of the medium were the root causes of the military's reluctance to embrace film. In the wake of the Russo-Japanese War (1904–5), military leaders felt that Japan's strict censorship had helped their cause and were determined to follow a similar policy. Originally raised in response to the press, these concerns carried over to the new medium: "the services were completely convinced that every sort of secret would escape," and fears were not entirely misplaced: it later turned out that "one or two enemy agents were caught disguised as dealers in film."[59] Cinema houses, moreover, were viewed with great suspicion by the government. Cinema was known as the poor man's theater; most seats cost less than four pence, far less than competing forms of entertainment, and working-class attendance soared. During the war even more people attended, and by July 1916 "the public was . . . spending as much on cinema as on all other plays, shows, concerts, and organized sporting events put together."[60] With a working-class public sphere emerging across England, local governments took steps to regulate cinemas by adding provisions to the 1909 Cinematograph Act, the first act of Parliament specifically concerned with the cinema, and Parliament stepped in again in 1916 with new entertainment taxes. Anxieties about what might be going on under the cover of darkness elicited further provisions to protect children from pedophiles. But in a contradiction characteristic of class myopia, anxieties about the cultural agency of film did not stop government elites from dismissing the medium as a trivial diversion for the working class. Some field officers even objected to their being filmed on the grounds that it was beneath them.

Despite these obstacles, *Britain Prepared* became Wellington House's first film and established the dominant approach to the great majority of British propaganda films for the duration of the war.[61] A three-hour silent film with few titles, *Britain Prepared* shows scenes of the British navy, munitions work, and the army in training. Extremely well received by audiences, the film adopted a purely factual approach by giving people starved for authentic war footage a sense of what the country was doing to win. With the dominance of sound films in the thirties and forties, propaganda films became increasingly ideological by using voice-over narration to frame the images spectators viewed. But *Britain Prepared* and other British World War I films are remarkably free of that style of persuasion, nor do they in any way anticipate the manipulative editing that Soviet film invented in the twenties. Instead, the stream of visual "facts" is presented from a British point of view—literally, of course, but also in the sense that the films evince "a respect, a sympathy even, for the men and women whose experience of war was recorded on film."[62]

Eventually, as the British campaign evolved beyond Wellington House, it was recognized that film had to become a major component of the war effort. A few fiction films were made, but, consonant with Masterman's founding emphasis on facts, most films, such as *The Battle of the Somme*, which gave the public its first taste of battle footage, adopted a documentary approach before the term even existed.[63] As film historians often note, John Grierson's documentary film movement in the twenties and thirties was made possible by government propaganda films, which eventually included official newsreels, films about life on the home front, the British Royal family, and neutral and allied countries. By January 1918 Edward Carson, undersecretary of state in the Home Office and newly entrusted with general supervision of propaganda activities under the MoI, could state what had become obvious: "no more potent medium of Propaganda than the Cinematograph existed."[64] By World War II film was deeply entrenched in government propaganda bureaus throughout Europe and America.

In addition to heightening the cultural prominence of new media, Wellington House and its successors contributed to the epistemological decline of the fact. Never the stable units of self-evident truth seized on by British empiricism, facts became even less trustworthy in the media ecology of the early twentieth century. Facts were of course under assault from multiple directions. The rise of positivism and modern science in the nineteenth century, always shadowed by its dialectical counterpart, idealism, inevitably elicited responses that challenged the notion that facts were the only possible objects of knowledge. If "the experimental method" of Zola's naturalism paradoxically attempted to reclaim truth from science in the name of science "by bringing together [in fiction] the greatest number of human data arranged in their logical order," the French symbolists, carrying romanticism forward into the twentieth century, tried to reverse the polarity of real and unreal by exalting ineffable mysteries over "the accidents of daily life."[65] And despite Freud's insistent claims for the empirical truth of psychoanalysis, in his case studies facts became little more than surface clues to the deeper realities of the psyche. Jim's anguished lament while on trial in *Lord Jim* indexes the historical moment: "Facts! They demanded facts from him, as if facts could explain anything!"[66]

With an influence felt in multiple cultural domains, British propaganda's commitment to empirically verifiable information contributed enormously to the increasingly equivocal status of facts. To a significant degree the British were true to their ideals, but their propaganda techniques indicate that they also knew that information flows best when channels are properly greased, that factual accounts must be tailored to suit different audiences around the world, and that the power of facts to make an impression varies according to the media through which they are disseminated. Indeed, the single most effective piece of propaganda disseminated during World War I, Lord Bryce's *Report of the Committee on Alleged German Outrages*, published in May 1915, gave Germany ample grounds for its clever glossing of the Allies' information services as "All-lies." Though based on dubious research, the Bryce Report bore all the signs of detached objectivity: depositions, extensive appendices, and photographs of German soldiers' diary pages. Whereas Belgian committee reports refer to "the chivalrous and heroic resistance of the Belgian nation" against Germany's "devastating and murderous hordes," the language of the Bryce Report remains scrupulously legalistic and matter-of-fact.[67] In 1922 a Belgian commission could not substantiate any of the gruesome reports of children's hands having been lopped off or of citizens having been buried alive. But for the duration of the war, Wellington House made mutilated Belgian children as real as actual German brutalities by translating the Bryce Report into thirty languages and circulating it throughout the world.[68] In hindsight, the report shows how factuality was becoming detached from empirical grounding and transformed into a form of rhetoric. At the time, it firmly established one of the dominant myths of World War I: English civilization was fighting a war against German barbarism.

Initiating forms of deceit whose progeny remain with us today, the British manipulation of facts throws into relief the epistemological peculiarity of what Mary Poovey has termed the "modern fact." Poovey offers an historical account of how "facts" came to be conceived as both prior to systematic knowledge—as raw untheorized data—and inextricable from the theories they support. Tracing the emergence of this duality back to the seventeenth century, Poovey argues that the ambiguity of facts as both preinterpretive and wholly derived from theory is fundamental to modern epistemology.[69] In this context modernism and twentieth-century propaganda look like late chapters—or paired interchapters—in the history of the modern fact. Propaganda exploits the internal bifurcation of modern facts by amplifying their rhetorical appeal even while insisting on their value-free neutrality. The supposed independence of facts, their imperviousness to the assimilative power of systematic knowledge or suasion, made it easier for British officials to declare their fidelity to the veridical while subtly integrating facts into patterns designed to manipulate public opinion.[70] Although facts claim to speak for themselves—or rather, the purveyors of facts *claim* that facts speak for themselves—their framing and selection often amount to a species of ventriloquism in which the subjectivity of the editor qua propagandist speaks from behind a screen of enumerated facts. Modernism also troubles notions of objectivity, but not so much by spinning facts into spurious coherence as by pressuring one extreme into another. On one hand, some strands of modernism dwell so insistently on the image (Pound's "intellectual and emotional complex") or sensory data (Woolf's cascade of atoms falling on the brain) that the objective percept may seem to dissolve within the activity of perceiving. On the other hand, the modernist investigation of subjective perception can produce a stream of seemingly arbitrary data, the bric-a-brac of everyday life or, in Wyndham Lewis's more colorful critique of *Ulysses*, "a monument like a record diarrhoea."[71]

Georg Lukács's well-known critique of modernism turns on just this issue, which he analyzes as the rise of subjectivism and the consequent loss of an objective perspective on material reality. Lukács argues that modernist fiction loses its critical perspective by failing to invest naturalist details with a sense of typicality grounded in apprehension of the social whole. Without a socially derived hierarchy of values guiding the selection and disposition of realistic detail, modernism succumbs to an arbitrariness that de-composes objective reality into the stasis of allegorical abstraction and solipsism. In essence producing a Marxist version of Lewis's critique of Joyce's surrender to temporal flux and the undifferentiated flow of meaningless detail, Lukács understands Joyce's modernism as simultaneously a fall into naturalism's empty objectivity and an escape into subjectivity through the negation of history.

But where Lukács sees modernism's assimilation of realistic detail into abstract structures of significance as a retreat from social engagement, I want to argue that the metaphoric structures subtending modernist fragmentation provide an aesthetic alternative to the stifling social integration urged by propaganda, an alternative that need not be considered a surrender to subjectivism. For Lukács, modernism's preference for metaphoric linkage over metonymic typicality amounts to a retreat from objective to subjective totalities. Yet if modernism, as Lukács notes, often seems obsessed with the phenomenological intensity of sheer factuality at the expense of objective laws governing historical experience, one need not simply reject his Marxist faith in the existence of such laws in order to acknowledge the social dimension of the modernist aspiration to discover principles of order occluded by a surfeit of naturalistic detail. To some extent, Lukács simply refuses to acknowledge the kind of ordering undertaken by many modernists; he sees the fragments, not the patterns. Yet we are also dealing here with incompatible epistemologies: even when acknowledged, modernism's metaphoric structures will be dismissed as escapist projections if significant structures cannot be made but only revealed. But far from being a kind of solipsistic projection, the construction of coherence is a fundamentally social response to the early century's fracturing of factuality. Propaganda, I have argued, drives a wedge between the objective and subjective poles of what Poovey calls the "modern fact." Inasmuch as the illusory autonomy of the modernist fragment corresponds to the supposed neutrality of the modern fact, modernism participates in the same dynamic. Both the fragment and the fact seem to stand on their own as indices of the real and yet both are constituted within larger systems of meaning that invest them with significance. *Ulysses* offers a telling example of the historical embeddedness of the play between fragmentation and wholeness in modernism.

As Leopold Bloom wanders the streets in the "Lestrygonians" episode, the term "throwaway" first appears as a nonce word to describe a flier—an ad for an American evangelist—placed in Bloom's hand by a young man from the YMCA. The word seems as disposable as the thing it designates. But after Bloom crunches up the flier and tosses it into the Liffey, "throwaway" begins to accrue ever more complex meanings within a symbolic structure that links the flier with, among other things, Bloom, a thoroughbred named Throwaway in the Gold Cup race, adultery, Odysseus's ship, racial difference, empire, advertising, and Elijah. Increasingly available in retrospect, such chains of connection may be experienced at first as random fragments. Joyce, however, feared he might have oversystematized *Ulysses*, and in this instance the playful expansion of signification out from "throwaway" provides multiple perspectives that all converge on the fundamental story of Bloom, the Jewish outsider and disposable husband who, like the dark horse Throwaway, ends up winning the race. To call this web of connections, as Lukács would, a form of abstraction that destroys "the complex tissue of man's relations with his environment" is to overlook how the activity of navigating Joyce's connections between the pattern and the detail mirrors the social challenges Bloom faces as he makes his way through the competing ideological appeals woven into the texture of Dublin's everyday life.[72] The flier he throws away, after all, is attempting to convert him to Christianity.

Particularly prominent in Joyce, tension between the relative autonomy of the realistic detail and the integrative power of modernist form is felt throughout modernism. It also produces the sense of adjacency that Woolf and Conrad find so threatening: however different in intention, integration is a shared aim of modernist form and propaganda. As I will discuss in the next chapter, *The Secret Agent* is located precisely at the rift between the isolation of brute facts and the revelation of connectedness: amid the "nameless fragments" of Stevie's shattered body, Chief Inspector Heat finds a name tag that ultimately reorganizes Conrad's text around tropes of innocence, incorporation, and death. Itself chronologically disjunct, a narrative that makes fragmentation its main subject draws itself together through the agency of metaphor in order to comment on the fate of the easily manipulated within urban modernity.

For Conrad, the lived experience of fragmentation and the hunger for coherence could be narrated only as an uneasy mix of dark comedy and tragedy. Analytic commentaries traced similar fault lines. The early century saw not only increasing attention to the fragmenting of perception under modernity, as in Georg Simmel's "The Metropolis and Mental Life" (1903), but also new attention to the totalizing fictions generated by societies eager to hold themselves together. Walter Lippmann was the first major thinker to grasp the connection between integration propaganda and the felt unreality, or fictiveness, of modern life. In 1922 Lippmann's *Public Opinion*, one of the founding books of modern media studies, posited the emergence of a "pseudo-environment" built up by the propagation of stereotypical images and the interactions among them in the mass media.[73] As with Bernays, Lippmann's analysis was catalyzed by working as a propagandist. In June 1918 the Military Intelligence Branch (MIB) of the U.S. Army approached Lippmann to help offset the crude propaganda being produced by the CPI. Like Masterman, Lippmann believed in factual propaganda and aimed for "a frank campaign of education addressed to the German and Austrian troops, explaining as simply and persuasively as possible the unselfish character of the war, the generosity of our aims, and the great hope of mankind which we are trying to realize."[74] Despite such idealism, or perhaps because of it, Lippmann became deeply disillusioned by the ease with which facts could be distorted and used to manipulate public understanding. Out of this disillusionment came *Public Opinion*, a profound critique of democracy that anticipates Ellul's fears that average citizens were losing the capacity to understand their world.

The book's enduring contribution to media theory is the notion that human behavior under modernity is increasingly based not on "direct and certain knowledge" but on "pictures in our heads." Lippmann links the increasingly mediated nature of existence with the circulation of stereotypes disseminated by film and photography and then re-evoked by newspapers. The resulting pseudo-environment is then manipulated by propagandists. "What is propaganda," he writes, "if not the effort to alter the picture to which men respond, to substitute one social pattern for another?"[75] Lippmann thus provides a historically specific antecedent of what Jean Baudrillard has called the "simulacrum," but where Baudrillard is largely content to point out the strangeness of the copy without an original, Lippmann laments that the eclipse of a less mediated relation to contemporaneity is undermining the foundations of democracy.[76]

The recession of the real within a pseudo-environment is of course overdetermined.[77] By the late nineteenth century, a nostalgia for the real-as-the-immediate was already manifest in diverse ways,[78] and in the early twentieth century the hunger for immediacy became yet more urgent in stream-of-consciousness techniques and imagism. According to what Jay Bolter and Richard Grusin call the "logic of remediation," desire for the immediate will inevitably result in hypermediation, and modern narrative provides a telling example.[79] Counterpointing the imagist emphasis on presentation, modern narrative's scenic immediacy is often nested within elaborate narrative architectonics that are designed to reconstruct the meaning of events whose meanings were once thought to be immanent. In consequence, a screen of language seems to rise between the reader and narrative events. The flow of Clarissa Dalloway's thoughts, sometimes crisply focused, may dissolve, like Septimus Smith's, into words that resist transparency, or Lawrence's passionate bodies, often vividly rendered through gesture and dialogue, may disappear behind the "pulsing, frictional to-and-fro" of Lawrentian style.[80] The event itself may come to seem (as of course in narratological terms it is) an effect of its telling. The pseudo-environment's derealizing effect also contributed to the modernist investment in authenticity. Artificial authenticity in service of "true facts" formed the backbone of British propaganda, and the turn of the century's increasingly urgent fantasy of unmediated connection to the real understood as the elemental or the factual marks one pole in a dialectic between perceptions of the real and the unreal that was significantly heightened by Wellington House in World War I.

Lippmann recognized that the surge of propaganda, operating through multiple media channels, exacerbated the derealization of the event and accelerated the emergence of a pseudo-environment by filling heads with pictures. Brought together as historical context and analytic lens, the legacy of the British propaganda campaign and the theories of Lippmann and Ellul offer a new perspective on British narrative in the first half of the twentieth century. To anticipate the literary yield of this approach, I will close this introductory chapter with a close reading of *Heart of Darkness* in relation to Conrad's propaganda essay for the Admiralty, "The Unlighted Coast."

Modernism and the Media of Propaganda: *Heart of Darkness* and "The Unlighted Coast"

Conrad addressed the threatening adjacency of propaganda long before the Great War was glimpsed on the horizon. Indeed, *Heart of Darkness*, published in the opening moments of the twentieth century, anticipates the complex entangling of modernism, new media, and propaganda that is the subject of this book. Sixteen year later he wrote a propaganda essay for the Admiralty, "The Unlighted Coast," that rethinks *Heart of Darkness* within the new information ecology of global war. Read through the retrospective lens of the propaganda essay, *Heart of Darkness* suggests that the symbiosis of information and propaganda analyzed by Ellul was already emerging at the turn of the century, and that Lippmann's concept of the pseudo-environment gave a name to existing media effects that propaganda exacerbated.

Heart of Darkness was first serialized in *Blackwood's* (1899–1900) just as J. A. Hobson was commenting in *The Psychology of Jingoism* on the "spectatorial passion" for war exploited by the popular press.[81] Always interested in the historical truth of his fictions, Conrad already sensed that the mass distribution of conflict as entertainment raised questions about the relationship between his own writing and propaganda. *Heart of Darkness* gets at both sides of the equation: the eroding distinction between truth and lies in Marlow's ambivalent loyalty to Kurtz, for whom Marlow lies in order to preserve a different order of truth, and the emergence of the professional propagandist in Kurtz, a man whose seductive eloquence, as one character remarks, would make him a terrific candidate to lead *any* political party. All readings of *Heart of Darkness* must make sense of the pivotal relation between Marlow and Kurtz, and seeing this relation in light of Ellul's information-propaganda matrix helps illuminate the underpinnings of Marlow's ambivalent discipleship.

In part Marlow sees Kurtz as a symbol of the capacity for belief he himself desires. The death of his helmsman, killed by a spear, is pivotal. The helmsman had carried out the most valuable service in Conrad's world: like the aptly-named Singleton in *The Nigger of the "Narcissus,"* he had steered. With his Palinurus gone, Marlow's mind turns instantly to Kurtz, a figure who might provide the guidance formerly supplied by the helmsman. But what Kurtz supplies is the consoling coherence that is the special province of propaganda. The helmsman's death makes Marlow realize that he had "never imagined [Kurtz] as doing, you know, but as discoursing," and his famous description of Kurtz's "gift of expression"—"the pulsating stream of light or the deceitful flow from the heart of an impenetrable darkness"—speaks directly to today's truism that one person's information is another's propaganda.[82] It makes sense, then, that in a compressed moment of calculation and instinctive reaction, Marlow later turns away from the Russian adventurer's account of the Africans' ceremonial deference to Kurtz to find comfort in the heads on stakes with which Kurtz has ringed his compound: "pure, uncomplicated savagery was a positive relief," he explains (*Heart of Darkness*, 58). A staple of propaganda, atrocity stories have always counted on the appeal of uncomplicated savagery. If a loss of moral compass is implied by the helmsman's death, in Kurtz Marlow seeks clarity at the expense of moral value.

Propaganda mediates other relations as well. Kurtz's Intended, like Marlow's aunt, remains serenely impervious to the painful contradictions Marlow experiences in the Congo because the "rot let loose in print and talk just about that time" (ibid., 15–16) inoculates her against thinking too hard about the actual fate of emissaries of light sent into the darkness. Like British journalists who preemptively censored themselves during the war, Marlow helps keep the Intended safely cocooned in propaganda by suppressing information: he lies about Kurtz's last words in order to give her the romantic ending life withheld, and he tears off the savage postscript to Kurtz's report on the suppression of savage customs—"Exterminate the brutes!"—in order to prevent the degradation of Kurtz's original intentions from seeing the light of day. In many ways, of course, Marlow is Conrad's agent for debunking the myths that Kurtz's Intended and Marlow's aunt drink in. Thus if Marlow indulges in primitivist stereotypes by seeing Africans who paddle up in canoes as emblems of the receding real—"they had bone, muscle, a wild vitality, an intense energy of movement that was as natural and true as the surf along their coast" (ibid., 17)—he also undercuts such stereotypes when he acknowledges that the cannibals on board his steamer show more "restraint" than the armed white men alongside them (ibid., 43).

Such subversions notwithstanding, Marlow is far from immune to popular myths. His celebrated denunciation of "the conquest of the earth" as "the taking it away from those who have a different complexion or slightly flatter noses than ourselves" is undermined not only by the equivocal language of idolatry in which it culminates—that is, Marlow's praise for a belief "you can set up and bow down before, and offer a sacrifice to"—but also by the peroration on the virtue of British "efficiency" that introduces it (ibid., 10). Marlow's "devotion to efficiency" betrays no ethical coordinates. A highly political term at this time and a touchstone for British politics for decades to come, efficiency is also a key concept for Ellul, who argues that technological society fetishizes efficient means at the expense of considered ends.[83] One wonders how much of Marlow's horror at the Company Station derives from humanitarian outrage over the treatment of enslaved African workers and how much from disgust at "a wanton smash-up" in which workers became "inefficient, and were then allowed to crawl away and rest" (ibid., 20). Holding in suspension the values implicit in Marlow's diction and a critique of those values, Conrad's complex ironies register to the degree to which the propagandistic "rot let loose in print" at this time—the very stuff of Lippmann's pseudo-environment—was not easily shrugged off, even by a skeptical humanist like Marlow.

Thus if *Heart of Darkness*, in Lionel Trilling's influential words, is "the paradigmatic literary expression of the modern concern with authenticity,"[84] it is equally expressive of the modern concern with propaganda. For Marlow's anxiously incomplete disavowal of Kurtz suggests that the desire for authenticity emerges as a dialectical response to the perceived inauthenticity of propaganda. On one hand, Marlow is disgusted by the conspiratorial brickmaker at the Central Station, whom he sees as a "papier-mâché Mephistopheles" (ibid., 29); clearly he would prefer a real one. On the other hand, he finds the African canoers "a great comfort to look at," not only owing to their "vitality" but because they made him feel he "belonged still to a world of straightforward facts" (ibid., 17). The conjunction of primitivism and the factual is crucial here. For if Kurtz becomes a symbol of authenticity, he does so owing to the contrast Marlow imagines between Kurtz's voice—elemental, primitive, true—and idealistic journalistic claptrap that, like the mental universe Marlow attributes to leisured women, is "too beautiful altogether" to survive the counterpressure of facts (ibid., 16). Kurtz is going to be the one real thing in the pseudo-environment Marlow navigates on his way upriver. In the end, however, Marlow does not quite commit himself to a world of vital bodies and dependable facts but to a complexly confused idea about Kurtz in which the distinction between propaganda and authenticity is both crucial—affectively and ideologically—and unstable.

Marlow's dilemma mirrors Conrad's. For a writer who desired, in the famous words of the preface to The Nigger of the "Narcissus," "by the power of the written word, to *make* you hear, to *make* you feel . . . to *make* you see," propaganda must have seemed enviably plugged into the popular imagination.[85] Acutely aware that his fiction often left him suspended between elite and popular audiences, Conrad persuaded himself that The Secret Agent, a grimly ironic melodrama that turns on the gruesome death of an innocent young man, could win him a broader audience. In Heart of Darkness his complicated relation to the persuasive power of propaganda, sharply focused in Marlow's loyalty to Kurtz, first comes into view as a writerly matter in Marlow's ambivalent response to the Company's chief accountant, who is at once a hollow man and a kind of "miracle." "Bent over his high desk," the accountant is a writer devoted to facts, and Marlow occasionally seeks shelter in his office from "the chaos" of the station (ibid., 21). Soothed by the "apple-pie order" of the accountant's books, Marlow ends up situated smack in the middle of Poovey's modern fact. The accountant's precise numerical entries, along with his immaculate collars, cuffs, and hair, constitute part of what Marlow considers his achievement of character: "in the great demoralization of the land he kept up his appearance. That's backbone" (ibid., 21). But the accountant's bookkeeping cannot be divorced from the violence of the colonial system he facilitates: "When one has got to make correct entries," he tells Marlow, "one comes to hate those savages—hate them to the death" (ibid., 22). Marlow's fascination registers the incongruity between the accountant's writing and "the grove of death" in which inefficient workers fade away, but the intense appeal of the accountant's devotion to order blinds Marlow to the incoherence of his own assertion that the exoskeleton of the accountant's starched clothes amounts to "backbone." Marlow's blindness does not entirely negate the latent critique of the accountant implied by Conrad's irony. It would be nice, Conrad seems to be musing, if facts could remain independent of the systems of meaning that generate them, if they could be free from ideological taint or spin, but as he remarks in another context, "a book is a deed, [and] the writing of it is an enterprise, as much as the conquest of a colony."[86]

The accountant's ruthless dedication to information for its own sake holds out the promise of pure fact as a bulwark against the false abstraction of imperial rhetoric, just as Kurtz's single-minded commitment to "some sort of belief," however vague, seems to Marlow a welcome alternative to the cynical hypocrisy of the Company (ibid., 69). And yet the accountant's murderous myopia suggests that the valorization of efficiency poses as much of a threat to society as Kurtz's electrifying rhetoric, for the bracketing of values by efficiency creates the hollow men that charismatic leaders such as Kurtz exploit. The Russian adventurer is "filled" with the glory of Kurtz's eloquence to such an extent that Marlow considers him "the most dangerous thing" (ibid., 55) he encounters on the trip—before promising to honor the Russian's request to cover up anything that might injure Kurtz's reputation in Europe. Marlow's telling of the story to the men on the *Nellie* breaks that promise, but not before he tears off Kurtz's scrawled postscript to become, for a time, a public relations agent *avant la lettre*.

In some fundamental sense much of modernism can be read as an attempt to clear a space within the pseudo-environment for more authentic modes of communication. Insofar as Marlow's narration on board the *Nellie* is an attempt to rescue authenticity from lies in which he has had a part, *Heart of Darkness* holds a special place in this history. But in a world heading toward a flood of propaganda in 1914, the desire "to make you see" is always in danger of being coopted by forces beyond one's control, just as in the Congo Marlow, despite his qualms, anxieties, and resentment, is always working, moment by moment, for the same trading company that pays the Africans in worthless coils of copper wire. If Kurtz's death constitutes Conrad's disavowal of propaganda's powers of persuasion, his lingering appeal, mirroring the appeal of the accountant, testifies to the ambivalence of Conrad's engagement with the eroding distinction between information and propaganda that characterizes the early twentieth century.[87]

Conrad was suddenly returned to the problem in the fall of 1916 when the Admiralty decided that the Mercantile Navy needed publicity. On November 6 Conrad sailed out for ten days on the *Ready*, a brigantine disguised as a merchant vessel. A month later he wrote "The Unlighted Coast," an essay that recounts being off the coast of England during the black-out. The essay also suggests that the first person to re-think *Heart of Darkness* in light of the subsequent history of propaganda was Conrad himself. Reminiscent of the novella's scene of the *Nellie* anchored in the dying light on the Thames, the situation evidently was enough to return Conrad to the story in which he represented England as "one of the dark places of the earth" (ibid., 9). Shared generic conventions reinforce numerous verbal and thematic links between the essay and *Heart of Darkness*. Both are instances of late imperial romance in which the historical conditions that motivate Conrad's romance are equally responsible for his modernism.[88] In "The Unlighted Coast" Conrad's modernism emerges from a modernization of romance that is forged under the pressure of trying to figure out what it might mean to write propaganda from within the blank darkness he encounters at sea. Deprived of obvious coordinates—the heroism of one's own side, say, versus the ignominy of the enemy—Conrad is left with the truth of his impressions. For Ford, reconciling the truth of the impression with propaganda was not a problem; but for Conrad, focusing on impressions in "The Unlighted Coast" ultimately means turning toward the medium of his message—toward the place of the written word in wartime—and toward competing media that were transforming the status of his own. In *Heart of Darkness* Conrad worries over his ability, in Marlow's words, "to convey the life-sensation" proper to his story (ibid., 30). War deepens the problem in "The Unlighted Coast": Conrad's fear that language may fail, that it may be "but talk round the war," becomes so acute that his meditation on the possible supersession of the word interferes with his ability to write propaganda.[89]

Conrad's only World War I story, "The Tale," finished a few weeks before he began his propaganda activities for the Admiralty, anticipates the kind of self-reflexive intermedial turn taken by his propaganda essay. Framed by an awkward conversation between a naval commander home on leave and his wife or lover, the story recounts how the commander comes across a neutral ship he suspects of resupplying German submarines. He has no proof, however, and most of the story details his intensive scrutiny of the neutral ship's master, who claims to have been lost in the thick fog for days. The commander weighs every word of the interview and every nuance of facial expression, straining his interpretive abilities to decide whether the master is lying. Though his subordinate cautions against rash judgment, the commander finally decides to test the master's claim that he is lost by demanding that he clear out of the area on a heading that will ground his ship on "a deadly ledge of rock."[90] After the ship steams off to its destruction, the commander confesses that he does not know whether he has doled out "stern retribution" or committed murder ("The Tale," 80). More like a disillusioned postwar story than a story written during wartime, "The Tale" insists on the impossibility of resolving the questions it poses: "I shall never know," the commander admits. Readers cannot know either: our attention to the ambiguous text replays the commander's scrutiny of the master's face, and we are left simply with a tale told in a darkened room about an experience shrouded in fog and darkness. By calling the story "The Tale" rather than, say, "The Fog of War," a phrase dating from the Napoleonic Wars, Conrad not only avoids the obvious cliche but throws into relief the medium of storytelling, as if the very topic of war could only drive him back to the fundamental resources of his art.[91]

Much the same happens in "The Unlighted Coast," but what works as fiction does not necessarily work as propaganda. Deeply skeptical by nature, Conrad was not a natural propagandist. Disinclined to credit overblown language touting British heroism, he was also largely immune to the anti-German propaganda sweeping the nation, and "treated the shrill, simplistic exhortations of the press with contempt."[92] Although always eager to pledge allegiance to his adopted country, Conrad was more invested in Englishness as part of his authorial identity than he was in British citizenship. Conrad certainly wanted England to win the war, but his deepest concern always lay with the Polish question: would the war result in the reestablishment of an independent Polish state?[93] Still, he planned to write more than one essay for the Admiralty, perhaps because his son Borys, who later fought at the Somme, was stationed near the front, perhaps because he thought his participation might bolster his influence on Polish matters. "The Unlighted Coast" ended those plans. But more important than Conrad's failure is how he fails. For Conrad's failure as a propagandist is his success as a modernist.

To be sure, Conrad's task for the Admiralty was made all the more difficult by the uneventfulness of the trip. From on board Conrad telegraphed to his agent J. B. Pinker that he had high hopes of "bagging Fritz," but according to an independent account, the *Ready* (traveling under a nom de guerre supplied by Conrad, the *Freya*) encountered only three submarines, the first two turning out to be British, and the third disappearing with destroyers in pursuit before the *Ready* could get involved.[94] Lacking an obvious story of uncommon valor on the part of the British or the even more popular alternative of a German atrocity, Conrad dwells on two things: his impressions of the darkness while cruising the coastline at night, and his interview with a young seaman who had had a relatively inconclusive close encounter with a zeppelin. The German airship had emerged in classic Conradian fashion from a dense fog, was shot at twice, and departed to points unknown, perhaps to Norway, where newspapers reported sometime afterwards a damaged zeppelin had alighted. Conrad seems most struck by the encounter as a rare interruption of what he takes to be the crushing monotony of night patrol at sea: for the most part, he is sure, nothing happens. While the essay expresses admiration for the clear-sighted planning and efficiency of the patrol, it was unlikely to produce recruits or trigger a surge of patriotism and consequently was not published until after Conrad's death. The Admiralty even seems to have lost its copy.

But just as Marlow is ultimately more interesting than Kurtz, so too the essay's frame is more interesting than the "Zeppelin-strafer" ("The Unlighted Coast," 52). Conrad revisits two favorite tropes, darkness and silence, in a self-consciously revisionary way. The first sentence reveals what most engaged his imagination—"I came ashore bringing with me strongest of all, and most persistent, the impression of a great darkness"—and he immediately distinguishes this darkness from the "brooding gloom" over London in *Heart of Darkness* by assuring the reader that he does not mean darkness in "a symbolic or spiritual sense" (ibid., 48). This darkness is rather the literal fact of England under black-out. And yet Conrad does not remain in the realm of fact for long: the multiple temporalities of *Heart of Darkness*, in which Marlow spins the historical fantasy of a Roman commander of a trireme and "a decent young citizen in a toga" facing the darkness that was England (*Heart of Darkness*, 10), return in the very sentence that insists on darkness as a "fact." What also returns is a foundational trope of imperial romance. For it is a darkness "such as wrapped up early mariners' landfalls on their voyages of exploration"; "surely neither Caesar's galleys nor the ships of the Danish rovers had ever found on their approach this land so absolutely and scrupulously lightless as this" ("The Unlighted Coast," 48, 49). With this gesture the premodern is uneasily superimposed over the modern: the zeppelin will emerge from the fog as a phantasm of modernity within an older darkness understood as the epitome of romance. This darkness, blacking out the familiar landmarks and geography of the English coast, recreates the "blank spaces" on the map that make adventure possible (*Heart of Darkness*, 11).

What makes Conrad's imperial romance *late* imperial romance is his acute awareness that with colonialism and modern travel completely mapping the world, "the glamour's off" (ibid., 11). Reinvented for nineteenth-century fiction by Sir Walter Scott, modern romance represents modernity's uncanny vision of the worlds it has superseded.[95] By the late nineteenth century, however, it seemed virtually impossible for romance writers to appropriate unexplored locales for the staging of imperial adventure at the lawless boundaries of civilization. In his late essay "Travel," Conrad laments that the profusion of new travel books is "more devastating to the world's freshness of impression than a swarm of locusts in a field of young corn."[96] He goes on to praise the books of the "real travellers" of former times, regretting that "the time for such books of travel is past on this earth girt about with cables, with an atmosphere made restless by the waves of ether, lighted by that sun of the twentieth century under which there is nothing new left now, and but very little of what may still be called obscure" ("Travel," 88). To recover traces of what might have existed prior to the global reach of new media and colonialism, late imperial romance had to effect an "imaginary unmapping" of the world in order to escape from the grid of the rational and the known.[97] Hence Conan Doyle's dinosaurs on an undiscovered plateau in South America in *The Lost World* (1911), one of many early-century novels that allude directly to Conrad's blank spot on the map, and Conrad's darkness, in which a submarine might slide silently beneath a Roman galley, or Marlow might witness a spiritual drama of loss and redemption in the dark continent, or Nostromo and Martin Decoud might drift away in *Nostromo* from the "material interests" of Sulaco into the existential void of the utterly black Golfo Placido.

Yet if such blackness evokes premodernity, it also paradoxically discloses the inescapably modern. While the "placid sea gleaming faintly" in "The Unlighted Coast" recalls the atavistic space of *Nostromo*'s Golfo Placido, the silence within that darkness is also modernized. No longer conveying "the usual meaning . . . to a human mind," "that of being cut off from communication with its kind," this silence is not empty but full. For two messages arrive on board, one a report about a submarine sighting, the other about floating mines, both picked up by wireless. The unlighted coast, "emitting no sound waves, no waves of light, was talking to its watchers at sea; filling the silence with words" ("The Unlighted Coast," 49).[98] Conrad, who helps decode the messages, is fascinated by "the talk that flows on unheard" (ibid., 50).[99] In contrast to the usual empty banter of the "war talk we hear on the lips of men," "the grouped-letters war talk" is "full of sense, of meaning, and single-minded purpose; inquiries, information, orders, reports." It is, in short, a perfectly transparent language: "words in direct relation to things and facts."

The darkness and silence of "The Unlighted Coast," operating at once as a form of negation and plenitude, throw into relief the link between Conrad's modernism and his foregrounding of competing media. Fredric Jameson locates Conrad's modernism in his "will to style," which at once expresses and compensates for the rationalization and fragmentation of life under modernity. Arguing that the senses begin to split apart and become autonomous under late capitalism, and that the hallucinatory quality of Conrad's impressionistic style conjures a utopian realm of sensuality beyond rationalization even as it embodies rationalization, Jameson observes that "the realm of nonperception" Nostromo and Decoud experience in the blackness of the Golfo Placido is "a heightened form of perception in its own right, a realm of heightened yet blank intensity."[100] Jameson tells half the story here. What's missing in his otherwise incisive account is media's role in producing the historical conditions that his analysis presupposes.

Because Jameson draws his examples of perception as an end in itself almost exclusively from Conrad's representations of exotic spaces, his account cannot register Conrad's growing awareness of the pressure of competing media on his fiction. Conrad clearly understood new media as a defining feature of modernity. By the same logic, he typically linked romance with the negation of such media. Locating rationalization in the communication networks of the city and a compensatory immediacy of sensation at the colonial periphery, Conrad remains true to the conventions of imperial romance by erasing the network of cables and "waves of ether" that were rapidly shrinking the world. Accordingly, in the remote Malaysia of "Karain" and the never-never land of *Lord Jim*'s Patusan, which lies "three hundred miles beyond the end of telegraph cables and mail-boat lines" (*Lord Jim*, 282), the senses are typically reintegrated through synaesthesia and the sensory phantasmagoria that Jameson sees as fundamental to Conrad's impressionist style.[101] In the metropolitan world of *The Secret Agent*, however, sensory data operate not as a restorative balm but as discrete analytic units. Thus if oral accounts of Jim's desertion of the *Patna* in *Lord Jim* chase him around the South Pacific like bad debts in pursuit of a gambler, the flow of information in *The Secret Agent* often functions independently of human agents. Following news of Stevie's death, for instance, Verloc's words of self-justifying consolation are described as "waves of air of the proper length, propagated in accordance with correct mathematical formulas" that lap against Winnie's "head of stone."[102] Initially overhearing scraps of conversation between Verloc and Chief Inspector Heat and then confirming the death by looking in the newspaper, Winnie receives the news in a way that maps the passage from *Lord Jim*'s oral world into an impersonal system that facilitates the flow of information even as it makes reciprocal communication impossible.

How Conrad's sensitivity to the changing media ecology shapes *The Secret Agent* is part of the story I will tell in the next chapter. Here I want to focus on how the influence of new media affects Conrad's efforts as a propagandist. Under the pressure of historical change, "The Unlighted Coast" retrospectively illuminates Conrad's latent engagement with new media in *Heart of Darkness*. Explicitly linked to the wireless, "war talk" that is not propagated by "the lips of men" in Conrad's essay also recalls the primary narrator's description of Marlow's story, told in pitch darkness, as a "narrative that seemed to shape itself without human lips" (*Heart of Darkness*, 30). Ivan Kreilkamp has linked these words to the phonograph, arguing that Conrad's treatment of voice places *Heart of Darkness* within the same problematic of disembodiment and fragmentation raised by the phonograph's recording and reproduction of the human voice.[103] These two technologies—the phonograph dating from 1877, the wireless invented twenty years later but not licensed to the public in Britain for another twenty—mark two moments within the broader evolution of the media ecology that had begun to change the status of the word during the later nineteenth century. It was during this period, Friedrich Kittler has argued, that "cinema, phonography, and typewriting separated optical, acoustic, and written data flows," all of which were formerly recorded and stored by the word; with these new technologies mimetically reproducing the real-time experience of sights and sounds, writing loses its "surrogate sensualities" and is increasingly understood as a closed symbolic system composed of twenty-six standardized letters.[104]

In this context, Conrad's response to the wireless in "The Unlighted Coast" reads like a meditation on the aesthetic consequences of technological change. His characterization of coded wireless messages as "grouped-letters war talk," in other words, evoking not only the transparent language of fact but also the alphabetic opacities of Mallarmé, resonates with literary accounts that locate modernism at the confluence of naturalism and symbolism even as it acknowledges the formative role of new media that such accounts (and Jameson's "will to style") typically overlook.[105] Attention to media, moreover, brings into focus the distinctive quality of Conradian romance in the propaganda essay. For in contrast to *Nostromo*, darkness in "The Unlighted Coast" not only performs the usual function of erasure; it also operates as a kind of ether for the new medium of the radio—the unheard messages propagating through darkness simultaneously create in literature the romance they were erasing in historical experience by producing a new space of mystery. That mystery, moreover, has a suggestively literary quality, for when Conrad exalts the clarity of the wireless messages—"words in direct relation to things"—he simultaneously recodes his own language by indulging in the essay's only literary allusions. The usual war blather from "the lips of men" obscures "the one and only question: To be or not to be—the great alternative of an appeal to arms. The other, grouped-letters war talk, almost without sound and altogether without fury, is full of sense, of meaning, and single-minded purpose" ("The Unlighted Coast," 50). Trite as they are, the allusions to Shakespeare reassert the power of literary language by thickening Conrad's account of the ideal transparency of the wireless messages. A strategic military resource in World War I, the radio would become a major medium of propaganda by the next world war. For Conrad, however, the new technology catalyzes a sense of wonder that ends up transforming his propaganda into a self-reflexive account of the media through which propaganda might be conducted. Within the modernist matrix of the essay, propagandistic intent is not so much negated as arrested; in the words of the preface to *The Nigger of the "Narcissus,"* propaganda is held up for what it is in "the light of a sincere mood" (147).

Becoming a matter for self-conscious reflection in "The Unlighted Coast," the cultural agon between modernism and propaganda that emerges in *Heart of Darkness* would find multiple, provisional resolutions in the coming decades. In a way that illuminates our own predicament in front of a darkened television screen, awaiting new streaks of tracer fire over the next target in the war on terrorism, Conrad's darkness, simultaneously suppressing and producing information, evokes the space of contestation in which the frontiers of modernism and propaganda, and propaganda and information, are always being negotiated. The next chapter maps this territory intermedially by remaining with Conrad, now in relation to Alfred Hitchcock's film adaptation of *The Secret Agent* (1907) as *Sabotage* (1936), and in relation to the problem of audience—how does one reach and master the audience?—that drew Hitchcock to Conrad in the first place.

Chapter One

FROM CONRAD TO HITCHCOCK:
MODERNISM, FILM, AND THE ART
OF PROPAGANDA

WHEN CONRAD WROTE *The Secret Agent* in 1907, literature as an institution still considered itself England's dominant medium of expression. C.F.G. Masterman, man of letters and former Liberal MP, endorsed that view seven years later: charged with designing a propaganda campaign from the ground up in early September 1914, Masterman summoned to his office at Wellington House twenty-five of England's most famous writers, including J. M. Barrie, Arnold Bennett, Robert Bridges, G. K. Chesterton, Arthur Conan Doyle, John Galsworthy, Thomas Hardy, George Trevelyan, H. G. Wells, and Israel Zangwill. Where else would Masterman have turned? The Edwardian world of letters as yet had "no competition from radio or television and . . . enjoyed tremendous prestige throughout the world among both elite and mass audiences."[1] By the time Alfred Hitchcock adapted Conrad's novel for the screen as *Sabotage* in 1936, however, film was well on its way to assuming the cultural dominance it enjoys today, and the history of British propaganda reflects this shift.

By the end of World War I, the cinematic propaganda that Wellington House initiated in 1916 had become a major enterprise within the Ministry of Information (MoI), and by World War II, government propagandists no longer hired writers to supply material for print but to write for radio and cinema. George Orwell worked for BBC radio; Noel Coward wrote *In Which We Serve* (1942); and E. M. Forster wrote the voice-over narration for Humphrey Jennings's film *A Diary for Timothy* (1945). Moving from fiction to film, this chapter anticipates *Modernism, Media, and Propaganda*'s historical sweep by analyzing the ways in which Conrad and Hitchcock in *The Secret Agent* and *Sabotage*, respectively, aimed to secure their audience's attention within the rapidly changing media ecology that made possible the rise of modern propaganda. The analysis turns on the notion of mastery, a concept as important to Conrad and Hitchcock as it is to discourses of modernism and propaganda.

In 1907 Conrad already sensed that the cultural power of literature was threatened. Like imperial rhetoric, which becomes more jingoistic as actual imperial power declines, media tend to demand recognition for themselves as *the* medium when competing media challenge their cultural privilege. Whether on the rise or in decline, media compete by appropriating the effects of their competitors or by developing what is peculiar to themselves. In the modernist period, some media did both. Clement Greenberg hailed media purity as the hallmark of modernism—modern painting must be about paint and the flat surface of the canvas, literature must be about the word—but it is equally true that with artists of all stripes crowding into the European capitals, media began to poach on each other as never before.[2] Thus even as new emphasis on the materiality of the word marked the modernist moment, literary modernism also began to experiment self-consciously with montage and other filmic techniques. And even as some early film theorists championed the idea of pure cinema, early cinema, eager to acquire the authority that literature was losing, defined itself against theater, radio, telegraphy, and telephony.[3] With media hierarchies changing, both Conrad and Hitchcock were particularly sensitive to their own medium's tendency toward the repression of competing media. Both explored media-specific modes of address in order to compete successfully with other media, and they did so not only as artists but as propagandists hired by the British government.

Like Conrad, whose essay for the Admiralty was published only posthumously, Hitchcock tried his hand at official government propaganda, returning to London from Hollywood in 1943 to direct two shorts, *Bon Voyage* and *Aventure Malgache*, for the British MoI. Also like Conrad, Hitchcock's official propaganda was not very successful. But while neither was able to respond effectively when the government came calling, each was deeply engaged with propaganda in unofficial ways. If *Heart of Darkness* reveals Conrad's insight into the ambiguous relationship between information and propaganda in the emerging age of propaganda, *The Secret Agent* takes up the topic explicitly in the socialist propaganda of Ossipon and the anarchist propaganda of the Professor. Eager to move "the mass of mankind" swarming through London's streets, the Professor holds Ossipon's pamphlets in contempt and believes that only bombings, or what contemporary anarchist discourse called "propaganda by the deed," can destroy the existing order.[4] For the Professor, only violence is an adequate form of propaganda. Similarly inclined to use violence to make an impression, Hitchcock adapted Conrad's novel for the screen just as the second phase of twentieth-century propaganda—the propaganda boom leading up to World War II—was kicking into high gear. *Sabotage*, along with his political films of the early forties, such as *Foreign Correspondent* (1940) and *Saboteur* (1942), prepared him for the role of official propagandist he later assumed for the MoI. Although Conrad's attraction for Hitchcock was overdetermined, the key to unraveling the seeming inevitability of their convergence lies in a drive for mastery they shared with professional propagandists.

Deeply invested in discipline, Conrad, master mariner turned novelist, always addressed Henry James as "cher maître," signaling mastery as his anxious authorial ideal. Hitchcock ultimately earned the title Master of Suspense, a mark of his control over his audience and on his sets. *The Secret Agent* and *Sabotage*, usually linked in film criticism by a narrative of adaptation, are also linked by the historically specific forms taken by their desire for mastery.[5] For both Conrad and Hitchcock, the effort to exact a particular kind of attention from their audience folds back into the work in the form of an aesthetic of formal perfection and controlled violence. The will to perfection need not entail violence, of course, but in Conrad and Hitchcock the integrity of the body is sacrificed to an ideal of style as discipline, a strand of modernism that Richard Poirier has traced back through Eliot and Joyce to Pater.[6] But where Poirier focuses on style as a form of Paterian *ascesis*, or self-discipline, this chapter explores an aggressively punitive discipline linked to authorial efforts to master the audience.

Conrad was highly sensitive to the power of the written word in relation to the expanding cultural presence of competing media, and *The Secret Agent* measures its rhetorical power against advertising, journalism, posters, propaganda pamphlets, and the persuasive force of violence. Heightening and radicalizing issues that Conrad first confronted in *Heart of Darkness*, *The Secret Agent* suggests that Conrad was haunted by the problem of how to define the frontier between art and propaganda. The novel is particularly concerned with the ethics of propaganda—or rather the absence of ethics, for *The Secret Agent* positions propaganda (along with advertising and political discourse more generally) as an exemplary instance of the growing dominance of rhetoric ungrounded by ethics in the opening decade of the century. Conrad presents young Stevie Verloc as the ideal target of such rhetoric. Literalminded and highly suggestible, Stevie is horrified and moved to action by the violent language of the anarchist Karl Yundt, and later is easily persuaded by his stepfather to carry out a bombing. As it turns out, propaganda by the word is as responsible for his death as propaganda by the deed. When Conrad returned to the novel in 1919 to recast it as a play, he threw even greater emphasis on Stevie as a victim of propaganda by describing him as "a perfect slave to verbal suggestion."[7] Hitchcock saw Conrad's dramatization in 1922, and later looked at *The Secret Agent* from the vantage of the thirties, when the rallying cry that "all art is propaganda" had emerged from the politically engaged left to contest the resilient claims of aestheticism. Drawn to Conrad's exploration of the rhetorical power of propaganda and to the modernist self-reflexivity of his engagement with media, Hitchcock hoped to use his film adaptation of *The Secret Agent* to secure the attention of Hollywood producers and escape from the relatively backward British film industry. Hitchcock, in other words, aimed to redeploy Conrad's novel, itself consumed by the problem of persuasion, as propaganda for himself in order to earn a ticket into the greater resources of the American studio system. Ironically, Hitchcock later used propaganda as his ticket back out of the studio system, but that is the story of my last chapter.

Hitchcock had many reasons for turning to Conrad, but from the historical vantage provided by the former's ultimate mastery of the mass audience, *The Secret Agent*'s articulation of a controlling authorial presence reads like a blueprint for Hitchcock's self-construction as England's first auteur. Keen to translate Conrad's investigation of literary persuasion into his own medium, Hitchcock introduced some key changes: instead of owning a shady bookstore, the double agent Verloc runs a movie house; in place of Conrad's Assistant Commissioner, whose grasp of the plot most nearly approximates full authorial consciousness, Hitchcock invests Verloc with the surrogate power of a director; and instead of meditating on the dwindling efficacy of the word, as Conrad does, Hitchcock explores the power of film to seize control of an easily distracted audience. Appropriately, then, Conrad's failed propagandists are either writers, like Ossipon, or masters of enunciation, like Verloc, whose uncanny ability to project his voice can startle a policeman at one hundred feet. Equally fitting, Hitchcock's Verloc, also a failed propagandist, can be considered a film director whose first act of sabotage blacks out his own movie house.

One other small change, otherwise inexplicable, points to Hitchcock's awareness of *Sabotage*'s place on a world stage preoccupied with propaganda: Adolf Verloc is renamed Karl. Raymond Durgnat points out that for Conrad in 1907 anarchist threats were already becoming a thing of the past and that for Londoners in 1936 the threat of aerial bombing in the event of a second European war had become a widely publicized concern. *Sabotage* thus "catches a dreamlike overlap between memories of the anarchists, depositing bombs, and the blackouts and terrors which were later to materialize in the blitz."[8] An undercover policeman, Ted Spencer, refers explicitly to such fears when refusing refunds to the Verlocs' cinema patrons during the power outage caused by Verloc's sabotage: "if a plane were to come along and drop a bomb on you," Ted argues, that would be "an unfriendly act," but the black-out is merely "an act of God" (a nice dramatic irony, given Verloc's role as Hitchcock's surrogate). Later, one of Hitchcock's Scotland Yard officials speculates that another of Verloc's acts of sabotage was designed to distract attention from events abroad, "just as a man in a crowd will step on your foot while someone else picks your pocket." The unnamed referent here is Hitler, who had taken power as führer in 1934 and in violation of the Treaty of Versailles had reintroduced conscription in 1935. But Hitchcock had to remain coy, for British officials were unwilling to risk offending the Führer, even if only by contesting Leni Riefenstahl's benign images of Nazism in *Victory of the Faith* (1933) and *Triumph of the Will* (1934). Very likely, then, it was film censors sensitive to England's policy of appeasement who dictated that Adolf become Karl.

If censors were keenly aware of the international audience for British films, so was Hitchcock, but for very different reasons. Hitchcock had one eye on Hollywood producers, for they were the audience that could reward him with a contract, and the other on the generic spectator, the person whose rear end he wanted to keep in the seat. Conrad pondered his audience at least as much as Hitchcock did, though with far less confidence. Among British directors, Hitchcock's star rose quickly, and his films rarely had trouble finding an audience. Conrad, in contrast, did not write a popular book until he had been publishing for almost twenty years. Today we think of Conrad as a difficult novelist, a modernist whose uneven works strain against novelistic conventions, a writer's writer. But Conrad needed to be a reader's writer as well. His sailing career drying up with the advent of steam and lacking a patron or his own printing press, Conrad could not afford to turn his back on the mainstream audience as Joyce, Woolf, and Forster could. Experimental by temperament yet in need of readers to support his family, Conrad thought he had contrived a compromise in *The Secret Agent*. His readership felt otherwise. But if *Sabotage* provides a reliable guide, Hitchcock saw deeper into Conrad's story than most of Conrad's readers did. He recognized that Conrad's problem of audience was the leading edge of issues he himself was confronting in the thirties.

MANIPULATION AND MASTERY: FILM, NOVEL, ADVERTISING

In the period between *The Secret Agent* and *Sabotage*, the "art of the novel," as described by Henry James in his prefaces and codified by Percy Lubbock in *The Craft of Fiction* (1921), cultivated its distance from the mass market. At the same time, England's struggling film industry sought to define its authority in relation to both the novel and drama. The pressures to adjust to the changing market for artistic production,

or else to create a fit audience, though few, register in the correspondence of virtually any modern author, indicating that behind the seemingly serene mastery of James and Hitchcock and the would-be mastery
of Conrad lie anxious efforts to secure the attention of an audience increasingly difficult to define, even to locate. Like James, Conrad attempted the theater in his effort to tap into a wider audience, and like
James, he failed. Conrad's dramatization of *The Secret Agent* at London's Ambassadors Theatre in 1922 ran for only ten nights; Hitchcock
was among the few theater-goers to catch it. But well before the failed
dramatization, traces of Conrad's frustrated attempt to bridge the
widening gulf between an elite and middlebrow readership were inscribed in the novel on which the play is based.

The conjunction of violence and mastery in Conrad and Hitchcock
emerges in response to a generalized crisis of attention that Jonathan
Crary has identified as a defining feature of modernity from the 1870s
onward.[9] Building on an account of modernity that achieved its most influential form in Walter Benjamin's analysis of urban shock in Baudelaire, Crary argues that an empirical interest in the physiology of attentiveness and distraction underlies a great deal of late-century work in the
human sciences, including the research of Freud, William James, and
Ernst Mach; the problem of attention is also fundamental to new theories of scientific management and to the manipulation of stimulation on
a mass scale attempted first by the rapidly developing advertising industry and later by government propagandists and public relations specialists. Crary invokes this context to analyze impressionist painting's self-
conscious awareness of the positioning of the embodied spectator, whose
ability to perceive the painted image depends on his or her distance from
the canvas. Literary modernism inscribes this dialectic of attentiveness
and distraction in a variety of ways: in the minute rendering of sensory
response during Leopold Bloom's Dublin odyssey, for instance, and in
the poster-like typographic experimentation of futurism and Wyndham
Lewis's *Blast*. Modernist efforts to manage reception, from Joyce's dissemination of proper protocols of reading in guide books and schema to
T. S. Eliot's notes to *The Waste Land*, also reflect a felt need to ensure
and craft audience attention.[10] Even more fundamentally, the violent assault of modernism—its effort to scandalize the bourgeoisie and to shatter existing artistic conventions—reads as a tactic to secure attention
within the crowded space of aesthetic experimentation early in the century, and to compete within a mass culture partly formed on shocks and
their replication. Thus modernism's often noted refusal to court the
reader's expectations paradoxically operates not only to secure attention
but to secure a particular *kind* of attention: read me on my own terms or
I will not allow you to enjoy or even read me at all.

As a medium, film was ideally suited to triumph in a period when the cumulative shock effects of metropolitan life threatened to overwhelm the competing appeals of less effectively assertive cultural productions.[11] Since the recording apparatus of the cinema necessarily focuses on the contingent, on the immediacy and flux of everyday life, film was readily assimilated into the modernist aesthetic of the ephemeral described by Baudelaire in "The Painter of Modern Life" (1859-60). In his *Theory of Film*, Siegfried Kracauer correlates film's mesmeric hold on the viewer with the involuntary physiological and psychological responses elicited by its representation of motion, "the alpha and omega of the medium."[12] Much of the early attraction of film derived from the novel shocks to the senses provided by seeing a locomotive barreling toward the camera, or by the disorienting shifts of perspective produced by simple editing; even more confusing (yet appealing) was the experience of seeing montage for the first time. Advances in computer animation are returning film to its prenarrative origins—hence the increasing popularity of films whose interest is wholly constituted by state-of-the-art special effects. But at the turn of the twentieth century the intrinsic estranging effects of film were more pronounced, owing to the novelty of its representational mode, which had not yet been domesticated by the dis-integrative effects of modernism more generally.

In Britain, conscious efforts to tame the new medium took two very different, though related, forms: increased government regulation came first, then cooptation by government propagandists. Indeed, it is not too much to say, given the British response to film, that film occupies a privileged position within the conjunction of modernism and propaganda. At once emblematic of the primacy of the impression, fragmentation, and mechanical reproduction, film also was recognized for its power to absorb and transform its audience. By the second decade of the twentieth century film was generating both excitement and considerable cultural anxiety. Much of the anxiety attached to the darkened cinemas themselves, which many feared as places of moral corruption. The Cinematograph Act of 1909 was passed in response to fears that unlicensed cinemas posed the threat of fires owing to the highly combustible nitrate stock used at the time (which almost keeps Hitchcock's Stevie off a bus in *Sabotage*), but the act was soon turned to other ends. Under the act, film exhibitions were banned except in licensed premises, and the power to grant licenses for up to a year was given to county borough councils, which could attach conditions to the licenses. As concerns about the moral effects of cinema grew, the 1909 act was often revisited in order to regulate the rapid growth of interest in film. By 1912 questions were being asked in Parliament about possible correlations between cinema attendance and juvenile delinquency, and in January 1913 "the British

Board of Film Censors was formed by the various persons and trades connected with cinematography . . . to exercise the control necessary to secure the publication and exhibition of such cinematograph films as are entirely free from objectionable features." Increasingly the 1909 act was invoked to add new conditions for licenses. In late 1915, for instance, the Theatres and Music Hall Committee of the London County Council, concerned about rising fears of sexual predators in the cinema, introduced several stipulations, most notably the requirement that licensed cinemas must assign a suitable staff member to serve as a special children's attendant. Attendants were to wear badges, escort unaccompanied children to a special seating area, and instantly report any cases of molestation to the manager. The committee also felt that "certain types of films have had a demoralising and injurious influence on children," and although it felt competent to describe the kinds of entertainments most likely to cause problems, namely, "those depicting details of thefts and burglaries and scenes of crime and horror, such as (1) a woman going mad; (2) a woman in drunken madness killing her own child; (3) a mad woman in a padded room and (4) a person being chloroformed," it finally conceded that drafting detailed rules to cover all possible threats to public morality would be too difficult and settled instead for a general stipulation: "That no films be displayed which are likely to be subversive of public morality."[13] Presumably this put paid to films that depicted drunken women sedating and killing their children before going mad and being confined. Nonetheless, over the next several years many licenses were refused or revoked. The threat to morality even came to be associated with the very nature of the cinematic impression, whose optical instability (in the form of bad prints, inadequate equipment, and the constitutive flicker of the medium) was explicitly associated with moral instability.[14]

But even as the cinematic impression elicited concern, British champions of film were touting the medium's untapped potential for social good. In 1914 the cinematographer for Scott's ill-fated expedition to the South Pole in 1912, Herbert Ponting, heralded the "kinematograph" as "the greatest educational device ever conceived by the genius of man and with the most potent influence for education ever placed within his hands."[15] Writing only a month after the outbreak of war, Ponting was concerned solely with education, not propaganda, but his fear that the British education system was falling behind its counterparts in America and Germany sounded a note that would eventually be heard in Wellington House, where the distinction between education and propaganda was rarely made. As I recounted in the introduction, despite Masterman's readiness to employ the new medium, the army at first resisted it. The War Office Cinematograph Committee was not formed until the

War Office was approached in October 1915 by a trade group, which, seconding Masterman, pointed out that shots of battle footage or scenes of war-readiness could put to political use.[16] By January 1918 the production of cinematic propaganda had become a major concern, and Sir Edward Carson, who had been asked by the prime minister to take over the general supervision of propaganda, declared in a meeting that "no more potent medium of Propaganda than the Cinematograph existed."[17]

If one were to judge from *Sabotage* alone, the government had good reason to call on Hitchcock's services as a propagandist in World War II, for the film, as we shall see, is deeply interested in mastering its audience. By the same token, however, Hitchcock's last major British film also reads as a significant instance of modernist narrative, for the violence latent in the modernist will to mastery finds exemplary expression in the bombing death of an innocent boy. Discussions of *Sabotage* typically focus on a montage sequence late in the film in which Mrs. Verloc, having discovered that Verloc is responsible for the gruesome death of her younger brother, Stevie, stabs her husband to death. Mrs. Verloc begins to go through the motions of serving Verloc some roast beef, but as she handles a carving knife, Hitchcock's editing brilliantly evokes the halting emergence of her desire for revenge and Verloc's dawning recognition of danger, all without a word of dialogue.[18] As strong as this sequence is, I want to shift attention to Hitchcock's equally effective treatment of Stevie's last moments in order to explore the way shock functions in different media. In both novel and film, the shock effects derive from a need to compensate for the felt absence of the audience by asserting greater control over the artistic materials. Yet the function of shock, as we will see, changes from Conrad to Hitchcock to Hollywood.

A complex allusion to *The Secret Agent* in *Sabotage* underscores the problem of attention to which both respond. More than a bit of intertextual play, the allusion evokes a material history of spectatorship in which the manipulative ambitions of Hitchcock's film are linked to Conrad's novel (and to the wiles of advertising) through an ad for toothpaste. On his way out the door with some film tins, Stevie is stopped by the police inspector, Ted, who is seated with Mrs. Verloc in the Verlocs' empty cinema, empty chairs ranged around them. Only Verloc knows that hidden in one of Stevie's tins is a time bomb. Ted observes that the boy is returning *Bartholomew the Strangler*, a popular thriller descended from the sensation novel. "Have you seen it?" the inspector asks. "Only fourteen times," Stevie responds. Identified with the spectator, Stevie then heads out through a street fair, and as he wanders among the stalls, a vendor catches his attention and swiftly forces him, with the help of the gathered spectators, into a chair. Trapped in the vendor's chair, Stevie is forced to listen to a sales pitch for toothpaste as the vendor slathers his hair with oil and his teeth with paste: "Now I ask you," barks the vendor, "what causes teeth to fall out? . . . The process of decay, inevitable in all human organisms. But decay can be arrested, instantaneously arrested, and by what?" Owing in part to this delay, Stevie will find an ironic answer to the vendor's question in the form of a sudden death. Although it sometimes resembles a W.C. Fields routine, the vendor's spiel is clearly adapted from Conrad's sardonically portentous passage about entropy in *The Secret Agent*. There, Winnie Verloc's mother, on her way to a retirement home in a horse-drawn carriage, reflects stoically that "everything decays, wears out, in this world. . . . As regards Winnie's sisterly devotion, her stoicism flinched. She excepted that sentiment from the rule of decay affecting all things human and some things divine" (*The Secret Agent*, 161–62). In Hitchcock's mocking homage to the novel, Conrad's cosmic decay becomes tooth decay, but the scene's implication in Stevie's destruction—the delay keeps him from dropping off the tins in time—nevertheless recalls Conrad's unmistakable suggestion that Winnie's journey through London with her mother is really a journey toward death.

Hitchcock's sly allusion asks what it takes to "arrest" a viewer or reader. The body tends over the long haul to have its own dismal agenda, but in the meantime, if teeth can be kept in the head, perhaps rear ends can be kept in seats. *Sabotage* devotes an unusual amount of attention to chairs—around the dinner table, where Stevie's empty chair will take on a haunted feel; in the Verlocs' cinema, where we frequently see people responding to movies; and at the street vendor's stall. In a visually powerful moment after Stevie's death, Hitchcock reinvokes the significance of being seated when Verloc kneels down to suggest to his seated wife, Stevie's sister, that perhaps they might replace Stevie by themselves having "a kid" (the resonance of "kid brother" competes with undertones of "sacrificial lamb"); she instantly walks away in disgust, and Hitchcock holds the shot on Verloc, now kneeling alone before her suddenly empty chair (figure 1.1). Verloc's failure to keep his wife in her seat underscores the relative success of Hitchcock's more effective surrogate, the insistent vendor. In part, the manipulative power of the vendor reproduces the entrapping effect of *The Secret Agent*'s overbearing narrative voice, which often seems to lock characters into place within an unforgiving economy, but the allusion to the novel also highlights important distinctions between film and fiction. Sitting down with a novel, readers can pause, reread, or skip over the words on the page; in a darkened theater, the aesthetic event materially envelops the seated spectators, who, short of standing up and leaving, are unable to control it. Control over the audience recommends film to the modernist as well as to the propagandist. By embalming and reanimating process in sequential framed images, film

FIGURE 1.1   Losing the audience: Verloc and his wife's empty chair in *Sabotage* (1936).

continuously arrests decay; it aspires, to borrow T. E. Hulme's formula for a new modernist mode, to a "visual concrete" language that "always endeavors to arrest you, to make you continuously see a physical thing."[19]

FROM NOVEL TO THEATER TO FILM TO HOLLYWOOD: IN SEARCH OF AN AUDIENCE

Particular problems of audience inflect Conrad and Hitchcock's efforts "to *make* you see."[20] Hitchcock's genius for exploiting the materiality of film spectatorship was unmatched by his contemporaries. With *Psycho* he would forever alter the film-going experience by coercing theaters into refusing entry to anyone after the movie began, this at a time when viewers were habituated to wandering in and out whenever they pleased; he also requested that the lights be kept off for a bit afterwards. As the ad copy put it, "During these thirty seconds of stygian blackness, the suspense of *Psycho* is indelibly engraved in the mind of the audience, later to be discussed among gaping friends and relations."[21] The film itself begins with a tracking shot through an open window into a darkened room, where the gaze finds an empty chair and then, suddenly embodied, seems to sidle over to it and sit down for a good look at John Gavin and Janet Leigh, partially undressed on the bed. From that moment the viewer's voyeurism is located at once on the screen in the movement of the camera and in the darkened theater in the body of the spectator. Hitchcock's self-reflexive interest in spectatorship testifies to his desire to control his audience by thoroughly understanding its desires, and his huge popular success marks his ability to do just that. Hitchcock did not bother to attend showings of his own films. Asked whether he missed hearing his viewers scream, he offered a cool explanation that contrasts sharply with Conrad's white-knuckled hysteria during rehearsals for his dramatization of *The Secret Agent*: "No. I can hear them when I'm making the picture."[22]

Unlike Hitchcock, who achieved commercial success relatively early in his career, Conrad did not fare well with the public until *Chance* in 1914, his sixteenth published volume in nineteen years. In 1907, during the composition of *The Secret Agent*, Conrad's mind dwelled "very much on popularity" even as he admitted that his characteristically peculiar treatment of the sensational subject matter probably would never captivate the popular imagination.[23] Caught between rapidly diverging markets for popular and elite literature, Conrad hoped that *The Secret Agent* would achieve popularity by treating "a widely discussed subject" from "a modern point of view" (*Letters*, 3:439–40). Yet it was precisely the modernity of Conrad's treatment of espionage, sea adventures, and melodrama that had sustained his critical reputation without providing the means to pay his bills, and *The Secret Agent* was no exception. Moreover, despite his occasional ability to write strategically "magazinish" stories, part of Conrad did not want to write for the emerging mass audience Hitchcock would later master, and *The Secret Agent* repeatedly betrays this ambivalence.

The novel's Assistant Commissioner mirrors Conrad's desire for a large audience when he speaks of the pressing need to secure the attention of "the great mass of the public" through a public prosecution of Verloc (*The Secret Agent*, 227). In a characteristic Conradian irony, however, once the Assistant Commissioner successfully cracks the espionage mechanism, its workings are quickly covered over again by the death of Verloc. The frustration of thwarted ambitions is then located in another authorial surrogate, the Professor—wired as a human bomb—who is explicitly linked with the difficulty of reaching the man on the street.[24] Consumed with resentment toward the indifferent masses and disdainful of the written propaganda produced by Ossipon, the Professor is committed to propaganda by the deed: "Madness and despair! Give me that for a lever, and I'll move the world" (ibid., 309). The Professor's anxiety about the resistant force of "the mass of mankind" is sometimes overwhelming: "What if nothing could move them? Such moments come to all men whose ambition aims at a direct grasp upon humanity—to artists, politicians, thinkers, reformers, or saints" (ibid., 82). (Hitchcock, perhaps sensing Conrad's investment in the Professor's frustration, playfully cast William Dewhurst, a portly man bearing a striking resemblance to Hitchcock himself, as Conrad's small, shrunken anarchist.) Early in the novel Vladimir, the embassy official who orders Verloc to commit a bombing outrage, seems to corroborate the Professor's sense of the artist's lowly status in his dismissal of museums as potential targets for attack: "Artists—art critics and such like—people of no account. Nobody minds what they say" (ibid., 32–33). If literature as an institution still felt secure in its dominance, Conrad clearly felt more embattled.

Anxiety over not being heard runs deep in *The Secret Agent*. Verloc may have a preternaturally powerful voice, but Vladimir dismisses his booming vocal performance during their interview as a parlor trick. The "dismal row of newspaper sellers" the Professor and Ossipon pass by after discussing the likely effects of the botched bombing of Greenwich Observatory get at Conrad's underlying fear: "the grimy sky, the mud of the streets, the rags of the dirty men harmonized excellently with the eruption of the damp, rubbishy sheets of paper soiled with printers' ink. The posters, maculated with filth, garnished like tapestry the sweep of the curbstone. The trade in afternoon papers was brisk, yet, in comparison with the swift, constant march of foot traffic, the effect was of indifference, of a disregarded distribution" (ibid., 79). Conrad's target is as much the disconnection between words and their intended audience as it is journalism. In his essay "Autocracy and War" (1905), he heaps scorn on journalism as an increasingly important rival for readers: "there must be something subtly noxious to the human brain in the composition of newspaper ink; or else it is that the large page, the columns of words, the leaded headings, exalt the mind into a state of feverish credulity. The printed page of the Press makes a sort of still uproar, taking from men both the power to reflect and the faculty of genuine human feeling; leaving them only the artificially created need of having something exciting to talk about."[25] Here Conrad anticipates Ford Madox Ford's concern a few years later that the surfeit of information produced by the new mass press was overwhelming readers' ability to think and feel.[26] But in *The Secret Agent*, the printed word, even when it "erupts" into the streets, scarcely makes its presence felt: the newspapers, even if they sell, go unread, and posters meant to arrest the attention of distracted urbanites are reduced to a trampled, unheeded collage on the sidewalk. Conrad's resentment over the "disregarded distribution" of his own words registers in the novel's patent hostility toward character and reader alike.

Returning to *The Secret Agent* in 1919 in order to write the author's note and to begin the dramatization, Conrad felt the need to reassure his readers that he had no desire to commit "a gratuitous outrage on the feelings of mankind" but acknowledged at the same time that the "bare bones" would make "a grisly skeleton" on the stage (*The Secret Agent*, xv). Perhaps Conrad felt that only a grotesque vision of Stevie's shattered body would be enough to stimulate "the faculty of genuine human feeling" that journalism was numbing. It did not, in any case, stimulate ticket sales.

Conrad's ambivalent attraction to the theater has a long history in his correspondence: the "dread" he mentions in a 1921 letter to John Galsworthy about the dramatization of *The Secret Agent* harks back to a more openly neurotic letter about actors written to R. B. Cunninghame Graham just after publishing *The Nigger of the "Narcissus"* (1897).[27] Struggling to make the transition from master mariner to professional author, Conrad hoped to stake his reputation on *The Nigger*, and years later still regarded it as a turning point: "The finishing of 'The Nigger' brought to my troubled mind the comforting sense of an accomplished task, and the first consciousness of a certain sort of mastery."[28] Yet the first review was quite negative, and his letter bitterly rehashes it before responding to Graham's query about *Admiral Guinea*, a light melodrama by W. E. Henley and Robert Louis Stevenson that was favorably reviewed by George Bernard Shaw three days before. Noting that he had read but not seen *Admiral Guinea*, Conrad dismisses the theater as an "amazing freak of folly," only to confess immediately to a "dark and secret ambition" to try his hand at it. Anticipating Hitchcock's well-known animus toward actors, Conrad soon approaches hysteria:

> The actors appear to me like a lot of *wrongheaded* lunatics pretending to be sane. Their malice is stitched with white threads. . . . To look at them breeds in my melancholy soul thoughts of murder and suicide—such is my anger and my loathing of their transparent pretences. There is a taint of subtle corruption in their blank voices, in their blinking eyes, in the grimacing faces, in the false light in the false passion, in the words that have been learned by heart. But I love a marionette show. Marionettes are beautiful. . . . I never listen to the text mouthed somewhere out of sight by invisible men who are here to day and rotten tomorrow. (*Letters*, 1:418–19)

Although Conrad's fear of losing control carries, as in Hitchcock, a range of erotic implications—the marionettes, for instance, "fall upon one another" and "embrace" in a safely distanced fashion—his anxiety evidently attaches to the body per se.[29] Drama would seem simultaneously to offer the promise of perfect mastery—the audience is right there to be gripped—and its negation: Frankensteinian in their monstrous

inauthenticity ("their malice is stitched with white threads"), actors, unlike the novelistic characters on which they are based, can resist their author's intentions. Imagining the need to make his language perform,
Conrad is consumed by the elusiveness and deception of language, above
all when it is relocated in the wayward bodies of actors.[30] Marionettes,
unlike the "transparent pretences" of "*wrongheaded* lunatics," are char-
acterized by an opacity that conceals nothing and a malleability that off-
sets the untrustworthiness of the living body. Unsurprisingly, Conrad's
nerves kept him from attending any of his play's ten performances.

Of course, the distinction between unmanageable actors and dependable characters is not necessarily so clear. If, as Cynthia Ozick has observed, "characters are often known to mutiny against the writer by taking charge of their books,"[31] Conrad insisted on remaining captain of his
ship. In *The Nigger of the "Narcissus,"* only by throwing overboard
James Wait's potentially mutinous black body can Captain Allistoun restore order and permit the ship to regain its heading. In *The Secret Agent*
the narrator polices characters who threaten to grow into full-blooded
Forsterian roundness by flattening them into satiric reductions. So disci-
plined, characters sometimes resemble the marionettes of Conrad's letter
to Graham. Verloc, for instance, opens a door "woodenly, stony-eyed, like
an automaton whose face had been painted red" (*The Secret Agent*, 197).

After watching rehearsals, Conrad tried to pull strings by writing insistent letters about particular aspects of actors' performances to the
producer, Harry Benrimo. It is hard to blame Benrimo for contriving
ways to avoid him. Conrad's thoughts about the conversations he managed to have with Benrimo expand his anxieties about controlling actors
to encompass the more general problem of filling seats: "An air of unreality, weird unreality, envelops the words, the ideas and the arguments
we exchange, the familiar words of the play, the figures of the people;
clings to the very walls, permeates the darkness of the fantastic cavern
which I can by no means imagine will ever contain anything so real as an
audience of men and women."[32] Conrad's anxiety over the play transcends opening-night jitters to reflect "one of the major anxieties in the
history of modernism": "If the audience is not altogether an absence, it
is by no means a reliable presence."[33]

Hitchcock left no commentary on the play Conrad could not bear to
watch—beyond, that is, *Sabotage* itself. Although allusions and verbal
nuances indicate that Hitchcock and his collaborators returned closely
to the novel, Conrad's dramatization also influenced the film's structure
and thematic emphases.[34] More important, the mediation of the play is
linked to Hitchcock's efforts to establish his cinematic authority as a
form of mastery. William Rothman, observing that a transumption of
theatrical conventions plays a central role in many great films of this era,

argues that Hitchcock's early films establish their authority by announc- ing their independence from the theater, where most film treatments originated.[35] Although Rothman's hyperformalism, reproducing Hitch- cock's obsessiveness in its incisive frame-by-frame analysis, brackets his- torical analysis, his insight into the filmic impulse to outdo drama illumi- nates the cultural dynamics of Hitchcock's early career in England.[36] The camera, with its close-ups, point-of-view, and reaction shots, claims ac- cess to a realm of privacy unplumbed by theatrical role-playing, and the power to invade a character's innermost being gives the camera and the director a "godlike power" (Rothman, *Hitchcock*, 102–3). While Hitch- cock considered some of his adaptations from the stage, such as Galsworthy's *The Skin Game* (film, 1931), as simply photographed the- ater, in *Sabotage* his self-conscious investment in mastery induces him to explore the specifically filmic dimension of his work. From the outset, Hitchcock draws attention to this aspect of a story that will return re- peatedly to scenes emphasizing reactions to film.

With a need for control that may well have exceeded Conrad's, Hitch- cock clearly felt empowered from knowing his audience to a degree Con- rad could only have envied. Already renowned for sticking closely to the shot-by-shot storyboards he sketched out before setting foot in the stu- dio, Hitchcock had particularly strong motivation for redoubling his ef- forts to arrest the audience in *Sabotage*: established as England's premier director and master of the thriller with *The Man Who Knew Too Much* (1934) and *The 39 Steps* (1935), he had begun to think about Holly- wood. World War I had hindered the British film industry, leaving it backward compared with the more professionalized, technically profi- cient world of Hollywood, and an American contract would give Hitch- cock the opportunity to exploit the latest film technology within a pro- duction budget commensurate with his talents. In *Sabotage* he began to focus more intently than ever before on the day-to-day preparation of the treatment and to dominate his partners in collaboration.[37] Around the same time he offered his notorious description of actors as "cattle." Indeed, his "sole purpose" in *Sabotage* may have been to achieve the rep- utation for technical virtuosity necessary to garner a Hollywood contract; some critics have found that the result, however "dazzling" its "virtuos- ity," is "academic, cold, and meretricious."[38] This judgment strikes me as fundamentally wrong, but virtually the same criticisms have been leveled against the "clinical" virtuosity of Conrad's novel.[39] Graham Greene, re- sponding more favorably in the *Spectator* to the same sense of mastery, observed that Hitchcock had achieved a new level of technical proficiency with *Sabotage*, a view shared in America by *Variety*.[40]

Hitchcock's decision to use a cinematic adaptation of *The Secret Agent* as part of an overture to Hollywood was at once logical and per-

verse. When Michael Balcon signed two American stars in 1935, Hitchcock quickly capitalized on their Hollywood cachet. In *Secret Agent*, a
1936 film based on Somerset Maugham's Ashenden stories (and not to
be confused with *Sabotage*), he cast as the surprise villain Robert Young,
a leading man who already radiated the geniality that ultimately landed
him in *Father Knows Best*. In *Sabotage*, retitled *A Woman Alone* for
America, he undertook a yet more aggressive antagonistic seduction:
casting Sylvia Sidney in a story that pivots on the horrible death of her
innocent young brother, he showcased her grief to an American public
whose taste for sentimentalized innocence made Shirley Temple the
number-one box-office attraction from 1935 to 1938.[41] Of course, making another thriller could only consolidate Hitchcock's reputation as the
master of suspense, and adapting a novel whose technical virtuosity
links perfection of style with cruel disregard for the imagined lives of its
characters provided a fitting way to broadcast his mastery.

Hitchcock secured the desired contract, but his need for control
sometimes became too much for those around him. Ivor Montagu, who
worked with Hitchcock in the 1930s, believed that Hitchcock's example
reveals that "a good director must have something of the sadist in him.
I do not necessarily mean to a pathological degree, but that his looking
at things and telling characters to do this, undergo that, is necessarily
akin to dominating them, ordering them about" (quoted in Spoto, *Dark
Side of Genius*, 149). On the first day of shooting *The 39 Steps* Hitchcock told his two stars, Robert Donat and Madeleine Carroll, who had
not previously met, that he wanted to walk them through a sequence in
which they would be handcuffed together while fleeing across the Scottish countryside. At 8:30 a.m., having explained the sequence, Hitchcock snapped on the handcuffs, claimed to have mislaid the key, and
vanished until late afternoon. Donat and Carroll were "tired, angry, di-
sheveled, uncomfortable, and acutely embarrassed. But Hitchcock was
delighted when the rest of the cast and crew found out about his little
trick and were shocked. He wanted to know how many people were
discussing the manner in which the humiliated couple had coped with
details of a decidedly personal nature" (ibid., 148). On the spectrum of
Hitchcock's practical jokes, from the sophomoric to the actionable, this
represents only moderate cruelty: Hitchcock once bet a crew member
who was afraid of the dark an extra week's salary that he could not
spend the night alone in the studio chained (where else?) to a camera.
To fortify the man's spirits, Hitchcock gave him a bottle of brandy laced
with a powerful laxative. The cast and crew returned the next morning
to find the man weeping in a pool of his own waste (ibid., 111). Spoto
savors Hitchcock's "dark side" for its own sake: one anecdote tumbles
out after another. But recognizing Hitchcock as sadistic auteur helps to

draw out the latent cruelty of his icy manipulations of character and viewer in *Sabotage* while casting retrospective illumination on the underlying violence of Conrad's impulse to master his characters and readers in *The Secret Agent*.[42] Just as a will to perfection need not entail violence, mastery need not entail domination; but in Conrad and Hitchcock they do.

KILLING STEVIE: DEATH BY LITERALIZATION/DEATH BY CINEMATOGRAPHY

Repeatedly underscoring his final authority as the (un)maker of his novelistic world, Conrad's open domineering of his characters sheds a different light on his assertion in 1912 that an author "stands confessed in his works," "the only reality in an invented world."[43] If it makes sense to speak of moral relations between authors and their characters, respect for the otherness of characters may require novelists to suspend disbelief in the fictiveness of their own creations. Conrad, in any case, was more likely to treat his characters generously in novels with participant narrators, such as Marlow in *Lord Jim* and *Chance* or the language teacher in *Under Western Eyes*. The omniscient extradiegetical narrator of *The Secret Agent*, in contrast, sometimes seems like the only reality in an invented world in a way Conrad probably did not intend. Very few of the characters are permitted the complexity of consciousness the narrator assumes for himself ("itself"? Certainly not "herself"), which makes the narrator seem flesh among shadows. Hitchcock, who as early as *The Lodger* (1926) literally placed himself on the screen, would have appreciated Conrad's musings on authorial "reality." In *Sabotage* he does not make one of his trademark cameos, but Hitchcock signals his presence clearly in the way he sets up the film's climactic event.

  Jonathan Arac has argued that Conrad uses Stevie's death to reintegrate otherwise meaningless urban shock into "motive and consequence and feeling." By resituating a minimalist anecdote about the historical bombing of Greenwich Observatory in a complicated novelistic network of crossed purposes, Conrad transforms mere information into the significance of lived experience, empty event into Walter Benjamin's "storytelling." Stevie's death is thus an "outrage," but not the "gratuitous" outrage Conrad wants to disavow in his author's note.[44] But this analysis gets at only half the story. As André Gide recognized, Conrad was fascinated by *l'acte gratuit*, and in *The Secret Agent* Arac's deeply ethical Conrad is doubled by the anarchist-novelist eager to produce the very rupture of experience that his narrative works to heal. A demonstration of the power to destroy, after all, is one way to prove one's mastery.

Conrad's representation of Stevie's death embodies the novel's most spectacular instance of what I have discussed elsewhere as the violence of thematization, the sense that characters are endowed with the illusion of autonomous existence only to be violently processed into expressions of theme.[45] Early on the anarchist Karl Yundt describes social relations as a form of cannibalism: the rich are "nourishing their greed on the quivering flesh and the warm blood of the people." Stevie, overhearing him, "swallow[s] the terrifying statement with an audible gulp" (*The Secret Agent*, 51). Later, after Verloc has exploited him as a bomb courier, Stevie is transformed into "an accumulation of raw material for a cannibal feast" (ibid., 86), and the Chief Inspector peers into his remains as if "with a view to an inexpensive Sunday dinner" (ibid., 88). By the time Verloc sits down to a meal of roast beef "laid out in the likeness of funereal baked meats for Stevie's obsequies" (ibid., 253), one allusion to *Hamlet* seems to cover for another, for it is a supper not where Stevie eats but where he is eaten. In an uneasy blurring of literal and figurative, the cannibalism theme culminates in Verloc's symbolic consumption of Stevie, whose swallowing of Yundt's trope initiated the pattern.[46] By literally and figuratively sacrificing corporeal integrity to the demands of verbal and thematic coherence, Conrad implicates himself in the exploitation that the novel's characters routinely impose on each other.

His treatment of the moment of Stevie's death intensifies the sense that Conrad subjects his characters to a gruesome mischief. Stevie tends to respond violently to "tales of injustice and oppression": once he set off some fireworks in a stairwell; another time "a magnanimous indignation" over the inhumane treatment of a horse "swelled his frail chest to bursting" (ibid., 169). When he is blown to pieces, the bursting and fragmentation that otherwise might remain incidental or comfortably metaphorical turn grotesquely literal. In death Stevie becomes his own characteristic response to suffering by exploding "in the manner of a firework": "After a rainlike fall of mangled limbs the decapitated head of Stevie lingered suspended alone [in his sister's imagination] . . . like the last star of a pyrotechnic display" (ibid., 260). Verloc suffers a similar fate when stabbed: in a novel obsessed with time, his blood drips "with a sound of ticking growing fast and furious like the pulse of an insane clock" (ibid., 265). The deaths perfect the intricate verbal and thematic designs imposed by authorial fiat on the imagined lives of the characters. Bursting with indignation, Stevie dies in a moment of literalization.

Hitchcock's Stevie dies a correspondingly cinematographic death. *Sabotage* opens with a self-conscious allusion to the conventions of adaptation, but instead of the trope of a hand turning a novel's title page to initiate a dissolve into the cinematic narrative, Hitchcock substitutes a dictionary page with a definition of "sabotage": "Wilful destruction of buildings or machinery with the object of alarming a group of persons or inspiring public uneasiness." From this point on he repeatedly links the act of sabotage to an investigation of the medium of film. The opening sequence dissolves from a close-up of a faltering lightbulb into a montage that links Verloc's sabotaging of a power station with his ownership of the cinema. A close-up of Oscar Homolka's sinister face as he walks toward the camera through the darkened city gives way to shots of laughing commuters in the Underground apparently enjoying the blackout and then to a more restless crowd gathered outside the Bijou cinema, where Mrs. Verloc, with Ted's unwanted help, is trying to talk her customers out of demanding their money back. (From the perspective of the completed story, the moment reads as Hitchcock's doubly proleptic concession to possible revulsion from Stevie's death.) The conjunction of flickering light, power station, and cinema suggests a metonymic linkage between Verloc's sabotage and a desire to control the very medium of cinematic projection. Yet as surrogate director Verloc falls so short of Hitchcock's example that his controller later mocks him with a newspaper article showing that the West End experienced Verloc's thriller as a comedy: "When one sets out to put the fear of death into people, it's not helpful to make them laugh." Verloc's failure prompts his superior to assign him a more violent task: placing a bomb timed to detonate in Piccadilly Circus during Lord Mayor's Show Day.

The chain of circumstances that culminates in Stevie's death contributes to the foregrounding of cinematic experience. The first link is cast when Ted, posing as a greengrocer bearing a selection of lettuce, barges into the Verlocs' living area, separated by a narrow space from their movie theater. As the detective turns to leave, a small window, or fanlight, suddenly falls open with a screech, prompting him to joke that he thought someone was being killed. "Somebody probably is," Verloc responds, "there on the screen." The consequences for the unfolding plot are profound. Later Ted passes through the cinema and enters the narrow space to spy on Verloc and his conspirators through the fanlight opening. A film is playing: the images are visible on the back of the screen, and the soundtrack, as well as the audience's laughter, is continuously audible as the detective scrambles up to his hidden vantage. Eavesdropping on the "real people" behind the film within a film, Ted hears virtually nothing before his hand, visible in a reverse shot from within the anarchist assembly, betrays his presence and he is pulled into the room through the opening. Because one of the conspirators recognizes him as a policeman, they scatter, and Verloc is left to perform the bombing himself. But when Ted, worried about the mysterious plotting, intensifies surveillance on the theater, Verloc is unable to leave the house and presses Stevie into service in his place.

The self-reflexive moments in these sequences—the repeated play between film and the reality it claims to represent and between the screen and the viewer in danger of being pulled through it—recall a similar scene in the novel in which a player piano occasionally starts up on its own as Ossipon talks with the Professor about the explosion near Greenwich Observatory. The apparently random autonomy of Hitchcock's fanlight and Conrad's piano has a dual effect. It evokes both the uncanny senselessness of the urban scene, where objects have a kind of life and people can be virtually inanimate, and the director's or author's arbitrary manipulations. The conventionally invisible hand of authorial intention, "the only reality in an invented world," fleetingly makes its presence felt in acts of extravagant self-assertion, which in *Sabotage* and *The Secret Agent* alike reaches its most devastating urgency in relation to Stevie.

Knowing that the bomb on his dining-room table is timed to detonate at 1:45, Verloc sends Stevie out to a claim check in Piccadilly Circus to drop off some film tins and a package said to contain a "projector gadget" in need of repair. What's really broken, of course, is his plot. Hitchcock invites his audience to see Verloc's machinations, played out before Stevie with theatrical nonchalance, as akin to the whirring of the machinery not far behind the viewers' backs as it projects images over their heads through a small window similar to the fanlight in Verloc's parlor. Narrative machinery, in other words, is aligned with the cinematic apparatus.

Sabotage's original full treatment, which frequently differs from the shooting script, displays an even more pointed interest in the technology of film. There, as a movie plays, Ted gets Stevie to show him "the projection box" and its "apparatus," as well as the loudspeakers, as a pretext to getting a peek into the parlor through the fanlight.[47] When Ted clambers up by the loudspeakers to spy, "we see that the wire is torn from a terminal and his foot causes an intermittent noise to come from the screen—in fact, the drama of the film is rather wrecked by the queer effect of the voices due to the terminal being short-circuited by Ted's foot" (*Sabotage*, full treatment, 35). Literally drawing Ted's body into the apparatus, the treatment comically articulates Hitchcock's interest in the physicality of spectatorship and highlights the degree to which embodied characters, if not properly subordinated, may interfere with the director's intentions. But whereas in the treatment Ted momentarily sabotages the film, in *Sabotage* Hitchcock characteristically remains in complete control.

The finished film links the materiality of the cinema with its manipulative power in at least two ways: by reminding us (once through Verloc and once through a bus conductor) of the explosiveness of nitrate film and by reserving the movie's most complex treatment for the sequence in which a "projector gadget" and film tins explode in a crowded bus. Calling attention to the calculated artifice of montage, the sequence throws into relief both the narrative and spectacular dimensions of Stevie's death while implicating the viewer in the network of circumstances that make it inevitable.

On his way to the center of the city, Stevie is forced to walk through the busy streets for a time, because film tins are not allowed on public vehicles. After enduring the delay with the vendor discussed earlier, Stevie tries to push his way through a crowd waiting for the Lord Mayor's Show Day parade, but he is stopped by a policeman who makes him wait in the crowd for the procession to pass.[48] At the end of the parade, Stevie realizes that he must talk his way onto a crowded bus if he is to be on time; happily, he finds a seat next to a woman holding a puppy. Stevie thinks he is along just for the ride. But taking a seat in *Sabotage* is never a simple matter, and in this instance remaining seated proves fatal.

Now the already brisk pace of Hitchcock's editing sharply increases: with approximately forty shots in the two minutes between Stevie's entry into the bus and the explosion, the sequence approaches in complexity the famous shower sequence in *Psycho*. Just as Hitchcock would deliberately outrage his audience by killing off Janet Leigh, an established star, so early, his need to shock dictates the circumstances of Stevie's death.[49] In both scenes editing subordinates the actor's body to formal technique until it surrenders its will and inwardness to the logic of the image.[50] In *Sabotage*, rapid intercutting during the mounting crisis of Stevie's bus trip (replaying Conrad's surreal account of the "Cab of Death" that takes Winnie's mother to her final resting place) epitomizes the fragmentation of continuity and the body that underlies the filmic effect. Recalling the stylistic decomposition of Stevie in Conrad, the relationship between editing and acting entails a form of domination through dissection: actor becomes cattle becomes marionette; star becomes body becomes body double becomes body part. Hence Stella's comment in *Rear Window* (1954) (exquisitely delivered by Thelma Ritter) on the possible murder and dismemberment of a neighbor—"I don't want any part of it"—and the prescience of Conrad's describing Stevie's exploded body as "nameless fragments" (*The Secret Agent*, 87).

Hitchcock's cutting between public clocks visible from the bus, the heavy traffic, Stevie's increasing agitation, the traffic lights, and the film tins links the rhythms of the city, the passage of time, and the experience of tension with the medium of film. Just as a traffic light clicks to GO, Stevie begins to pet the puppy, and the intercut clocks culminate in a full-frame, straight-on closeup of a clock face; the time is precisely 1:45. After a tighter closeup of the tip of the minute hand, which suddenly sweeps upward the breadth of the frame from 1:45 to 1:46, the film seems to freeze for a split second in the very act of representing the passage of time—perhaps the miraculous escape one expects is imminent—then a quick cut to the package gives way to two rapid shots of the exploding bus. (Too bad Stevie did not make it into a theater; maybe then one of the special attendants provided by the Cinematograph Act could have protected him.) Then comes the cruelest cut of all: the image of the wrecked bus is instantly displaced by an interior shot of the Verloc home, where Ted has been questioning Verloc in the presence of his wife. All three are laughing. "Well," Verloc comments, "now everything seems to be alright."[51]

By cutting to a scene of laughter precisely at the moment of the explosion, Hitchcock both foregrounds its status as spectacle and implicates his viewers in the horror they have just witnessed. In a film notable for its visual wit, the sharply ironic conjunction holds up an unforgiving mirror to spectators who have paid to be entertained by, it turns out, the death of an innocent child. In effect, Hitchcock punishes the audience for taking the sadistic position he forces on them: objectifying others and consuming them wholly as entertainment. In later years Hitchcock claimed to agree with François Truffaut's critique of Stevie's death as "almost an abuse of directorial power" and confessed to Peter Bogdanovich that he had made "a cardinal error there in terms of suspense."[52] But as Hitchcock himself probably recognized, the scene's unnerving power derives from its giving viewers precisely what they want: closure and release from suspense, even at the expense of a character's life.[53]

The sequence from the moment Stevie leaves the house is a picaresque series of arrested moments haunted by the demands of narrative. Momentarily drawn to the vendor's pitch, Stevie is rendered part of the spectacle when he is forced to sit in the vendor's chair; escaping the chair, he pauses over the wares on display in a stall; hoping to cross the street, he is instead made to watch a parade. All the while, the tick-tock music of the soundtrack—and, once, a fine lap-dissolve, in which a slow zoom on a handwritten note revealing the time of detonation is superimposed on Stevie's striding legs—pressures such moments of arrest back into the flow of the plot. Nonetheless, wandering among spectacles, resisting them, drawn into them, Stevie finally becomes one, "the last star of a pyrotechnic display."

Yet narrative is as implicated in Stevie's death as spectacle is. Hitchcock's complex crosscutting aids suspense so well because, like the vendor, it repeatedly *delays* the climax even as it ensures its explosiveness: manipulating the pace at which reality unfolds, the sequence paradoxically expresses the desire to triumph over time even as it records the impossibility of doing so in the fatal sweep of the minute hand. As Stevie is

FIGURE 1.2   Destructive agents: propaganda by the deed in *Sabotage* (1936).

waylaid by the parade, Hitchcock conflates the film apparatus with two agents of destruction, time and the bomb, by means of a closeup of Stevie's package that dissolves into an overlay of turning gears and a spinning flywheel (figure 1.2). The image simultaneously suggests the bomb mechanism, the workings of an ordinary clock, and the fictitious projector gadget. One thinks of Verloc's death in *The Secret Agent*, in which the clock trope describing his dripping blood evokes the body's subordination to mechanical time, and of a film precisely contemporary with *Sabotage*, Charlie Chaplin's *Modern Times* (1936), in which the little tramp is wound through the massive cogs of an industrial machine that also resembles the film apparatus. Insofar as the cinematic narrative destroys Stevie in its gears, his fate is a tragic version of Chaplin's comic shtick. Hitchcock's manipulation of Stevie parallels his manipulation of film, and his exploration of film's power becomes a form of sabotage: Stevie is the *sabot*, or shoe, thrown into the gears to slow production. The production in question here is the usual production of narrative, or the production of the usual narrative. In a film calculated to appeal to Hollywood producers, Hitchcock demonstrates his mastery of conventions by destroying them. Appropriately, the only clue to Stevie's identity after the blast is a twisted piece of the film canister.

This key sequence exemplifies the entangled impulses of modernism and propaganda. By literalizing the stylistic vivisection peculiar to montage and taking place at the precise juncture where the rhythms of narrative and the shock of spectacle meet, Stevie's journey through the kaleidoscopic street fair becomes a characteristically modernist return to origins. Film found its first cultural foothold as an exhibit in traveling fairs. Prior to 1907, trick films (featuring, for instance, disappearing objects and people), vignettes of actuality (sometimes filmed from moving vehicles), and erotic films, often interspersed with live vaudeville acts, were primarily designed, Tom Gunning has argued, "to solicit the attention of the spectator" coming see a new mechanism on display.[54] Hitchcock invokes the "cinema of attractions" in Stevie's halting progress through Lord Mayor's Show Day, as well as in the trick photography later used to simulate his grief-stricken sister's hallucinations, thus producing an allegory of the social origins of film. Yet even as he returns to the cinema of attractions, Hitchcock indulges his desire for mastery by subordinating his modernist allegory to the rigorous suspense structure that soon endeared him to Hollywood, where classical cinema came to institutionalize the subordination of spectacular display to narrative structure and diegetic absorption.

PICKING UP THE PIECES: MODERNISM, PROPAGANDA, AND FILM

Conrad's Stevie is sacrificed to a fantasy of empowerment. Profoundly moved by every word he reads, Stevie stands in for the readers whose attention Conrad seeks even as he serves to affront the readers Conrad already has. After reading of Winnie's suicide, Ossipon feels his "brain pulsating . . . to the rhythm of journalistic phrases" (*The Secret Agent*, 311), and the Professor is quick to point out that Ossipon's socialist propaganda will never have comparable impact. Not content with overshadowing Ossipon, Conrad's words aspire to go the newspaper's one better: literalizing Stevie, they have to the power to kill. As readers we fare better than Stevie, yet with Conrad's disjunct chronology drawing us into Winnie's gradual recognition that her beloved younger brother died in the bombing, not Verloc, the novel summons considerable power to shock. Blandly named "time shifts" by Ford, Conrad's extravagant manipulations of narrative chronology, like the inscription of his imagined audience in framed narrations, are characteristic of his efforts to master the readers of his fiction.[55]

The death of Hitchcock's Stevie, we have seen, has specifically cinematic resonance. As the major narrative art to emerge from nineteenth-century modernization, film in general is part of a transformation of perception in mass society in which a sense of the personal is produced as already lost. The human body may itself become mechanized, its present moment locked into an imposed narrative; think of Chaplin in *Modern Times*, continuing to tighten bolts after the production line has stopped. Or, reversing the comedy, the body, like Ted's foot, may be drawn *into* the mechanism, only to emerge intact, in Chaplin's case, with a balletic grace unknown to the machine. The little tramp's transformation reads like an appropriation of machine action: he triumphs over machine-like regularity by transmuting the patent brutality of unchecked efficiency into classical dance. Stevie's death, in contrast, represents the sacrifice of the personal to public exigency in a starkly horrifying fashion.

For his dismemberment marks the ambivalent advent of film as the dominant art of modernity: Mrs. Verloc's love for her brother clearly compensates for the inadequate intimacy of her marriage, and the loss of what, she tells Ted, means "everything" to her is turned inside out as a spectacle within a narrative designed for public consumption. Extending the spectacle, Hitchcock makes Mrs. Verloc faint in the crowded street when she reads about the bombing in the newspaper. An earlier scene has anticipated the morbid evacuation of the personal in the film's world: when Hitchcock's Professor, who stores his explosives in the kitchen, opens a cupboard, his granddaughter's doll tumbles out from between deadly jars of tomato sauce and strawberry jam. Partly the doll is a metonym for Stevie, the child reduced to a play thing in a game of terror and an object for the spectator's pleasurable consumption. But through its volatile conflation of domesticity and terrorism the scene also expresses Hitchcock's hostility toward the clumsy actors/marionettes who enact his fable. Film-spectatorship, mediating between public and private spheres during the emergence of mass culture, promised the re-covery of the private within the public conditions of viewing.[56] Pleased with its power to eliminate Stevie, *Sabotage* insists on the persistence of loss within the effort of recovery.

The manipulative shock aesthetic Hitchcock drew out of Conrad con-stitutes a pervasive yet not inevitable consequence of early twentieth-century modernization. As if in reaction to modernist aggression, Jean Renoir used deep-space composition and sustained shots in *Rules of the Game* (1939) to create a sense of openness diametrically opposed to Hitchcock's often claustrophobic mastery. Actors wander in and out of Renoir's frame with a casual freedom that draws viewers into a capa-cious cinematic world. André Bazin contrasts the "reciprocal freedom" between viewer and object in this mode with what he understands as the antidemocratic effect of classical editing, in which "the logic of the shots controlled by the reporting of an action anesthetizes our free-dom."[57] Effects comparable to Renoir's depth of focus survive today, but

Hitchcock's closed aesthetic tends to dominate mainstream Hollywood. Accelerated and amplified by the expansion of consumer culture and the increasingly capital-intensive nature of the film industry, Hitchcock's shrewd attention to viewer response, marketing, and self-promotion has evolved into today's investment in the blockbuster, and efforts to duplicate the success of *Jaws* (1975) or the *Star Wars* trilogy (1977–83) tend not to issue in invitations to linger in a richly ambiguous mise-en-scène. Hitchcock's financially successful inheritors are more likely to use a manipulative ensemble of cuts, angles, and closeups in their efforts to jolt the audience into a predetermined response that is tested in prerelease screenings.

The degree to which focus groups shape Hollywood films before they are released suggests a convergence with propaganda techniques that was foreseen by Aldous Huxley in *Brave New World* (1932). In the future imagined by Huxley, the distinction between art and propaganda has been entirely effaced by the ascendancy of a stimulus-response model of communication. Helmholtz Watson, a lecturer in the College of Emotional Engineering (Department of Writing), gets into some trouble with the authorities when he deviates from his lesson plan during his lecture "On the Use of Rhymes in Moral Propaganda and Advertisement." Instead of using the set text, he recites his own poem in hopes of engineering his students into feeling as he did when he wrote the rhymes. Huxley suggests that Helmholtz's nascent desire to produce art is doomed to fail in a society in which the aesthetic no longer exists as an independent category, and when John the Savage treats Helmholtz to a dramatic reading of *Romeo and Juliet*, Helmholtz is so moved by the poetry of Shakespeare's language that he declares, "That old fellow . . . he makes our best propaganda technicians look absolutely silly."[58] The British MoI expected that Hitchcock would too.

In my account of Hitchcock's closed aesthetic I do not mean to suggest that detailed attention to set-ups and editing produces bad art or that cinema after Hitchcock has steadily declined. Rather, I have tried to map an aesthetic trajectory in which both mainstream film and cinematic propaganda hope to consolidate techniques of manipulation that were emerging in Conrad's modernism and developed by Hitchcock. Within this trajectory, Hitchcock's *Sabotage* looks back to the cultural origins of film even as it intensifies and transforms the modernist impulse toward simultaneous shock and distanciation that was already emerging in *The Secret Agent*. *Sabotage*, in this reading, allegorizes the way in which the technique of shock, enfolded in narrative and put at the service of ideology, begins to render modernist alienation interpellative. In closing I want to suggest that this trajectory also throws into relief a hidden dialectic between propagandistic persuasion and modernist notions of aesthetic autonomy. Detectable across multiple domains, the dialectic comes to the foreground in exemplary fashion in the work of two influential theorists and practitioners of modernism, Walter Benjamin and Sergei Eisenstein.

In "The Work of Art in the Age of Mechanical Reproduction," Benjamin cites Eugene Atget's photographs as representative of the shift from the cult value of the unique piece of art to the exhibition value associated with mass reproduction. Atget's shots of empty Paris streets replace the "remembrance of loved ones" in family photographs, "a last refuge for the cult value of the picture," with a new kind of image that challenges the viewer's "free-floating contemplation" and *demands* a particular kind of attention. Benjamin connects these more "directive" photographs with the simultaneous appearance of captions in picture magazines and argues that captions operate differently than "the title of a painting": "The directives which captions give to those looking at pictures in illustrated magazines soon become even more explicit and imperative in the film where the meaning of each single picture appears to be prescribed by the sequence of all preceding ones."[59] Benjamin's abutment of painting, photography, and film suggests the dialectical interdependence of aesthetic autonomy and persuasion: the "refuge" of autonomous art arises to compensate for the loss of cult value to exhibition value, and as exhibition value grows more dominant, emptying Atget's photographs of human content, the postpainterly work of art asserts more control over the viewer through aesthetic "directives" (designed "to make you see") that culminate in the managed experience of film.

Benjamin's understanding of film as the most prescriptive of arts is consonant with Eisenstein's theory of montage, first articulated in the early twenties and then refined over the next twenty years. More than anyone in film theory, Eisenstein fostered the notion that montage techniques mark what counts as a specifically cinematic practice, and he links such practice both to the art of manipulation and to modernist exemplars such as Joyce. Eisenstein's influential work thus underscores the equivocal status of film in the overlapping terrain of modernism and propaganda. For Eisenstein, montage is at once representative of modernism's several investments in discontinuity, simultaneity and polyphony, and a highly effective tool for influencing audience response. Thus, on one hand, Eisenstein argued in 1928 that Joyce was "very close to contemporary cinema. Certainly more than half way to what lay ahead." In part Eisenstein saw in Joyce a verbal anticipation of filmic " 'de-anecdotalisation' and the direct emergence of the theme through powerfully effective raw material"; he saw in each the "same 'physiologism' of detail."[60] But more fundamentally, he also felt that the aims of interior monologue, one of the hallmarks of narrative modernism, were best realized through the visual resources of montage.[61] On the other hand, Eisenstein also stresses that montage is cinema's chief means of "*influencing* [the] *audi-ence in the desired direction* through a series of calculated pressures on its psyche."[62] In the Soviet Union of the 1920s all artists were highly aware that Leninist ideology determined the appropriateness of "calcu-lated pressures," but Eisenstein, who briefly worked as a poster artist in the Red Army, was particularly attuned to techniques of manipulating public opinion, and in a late essay, "Dickens, Griffith, and Ourselves" (1942), he returns explicitly to propaganda as a key reference point for the evolution of montage techniques.

Eisenstein provides a genealogy of montage, first by showing D. W. Griffith's indebtedness to Dickens and Dickens's indebtedness to earlier forms of melodrama, then by revealing what he considers the impover-ishment of American montage in comparison with Soviet technique, owing to the lamentable failure of Griffith and his successors to cotton onto the truths of dialectical materialism.[63] Eisenstein argues that the dominance in American film of "parallel action" montage—editing de-signed to show the simultaneous unfolding of multiple narrative lines—reproduces the nondialectical character of bourgeois ideology: you've got your rich and you've got your poor, and, like parallel lines, never the twain shall meet. Soviet cinema, in contrast, deploys montage in order to generate metaphor and allegory that coalesce to reveal a coherent ideo-logical concept fused into an organically unified image. Contemporary film theory tends to give Griffith more credit for the complexity of his montage effects, but for Eisenstein, where American montage is con-cerned only to show a key detail and is thus a matter of mere *seeing* or *vision* in the most literal sense, Soviet montage unfolds the contradic-tions intrinsic to the image into a sequence imbued with political signifi-cance.[64]

To clarify the advances made by Soviet cinema, Eisenstein posits an in-termediate kind of film between the old and new, whose use of juxtapo-sition achieves a kind of speculative parallelism of ideas without yet pro-ducing the "emotional fusion" or higher unity characteristic of more recent Soviet films. To locate this intermediate mode more precisely in relation to the Griffith's parallel editing, Eisenstein turns to popular So-viet propaganda of the early 1920s, writing that the transitional moment in film is "exactly in the spirit of the posters of those days, which used a sheet of paper, divided in two, to show a landowner's house *before* (the master, serfdom and floggings) on the left—and on the right *now* (school and nursery, in that same house)" (Eisenstein, *Writings*, 2:235). The du-bious accuracy of Eisenstein's distinction between American and Soviet montage is less important than his turn to propaganda posters as the hinge from one to the other, for the connection not only glosses his praise for Griffith's ability "to subjugate his audience . . . irresistibly" (ibid., 2:221) but also underscores Benjamin's sense that the meaning of each shot is "prescribed by the sequence of all preceding ones." For both Eisenstein and Benjamin, propaganda is a formative element of the modernist moment.

My effort to complicate the binary opposition of modernism and propaganda by situating the medium of film at their boundary turns on the will to mastery that is a legacy of all three. Miriam Hansen has undertaken a complementary project by challenging a related binarism between modernism and classical cinema. Criticizing the long-standing opposition in film studies between modernism as a self-reflexive aesthetic practice that exposes contradictions and Hollywood film as a form of ideological mystification that "sutures the subject in an illusory coherence and identity," Hansen argues that Hollywood film in the interwar years constituted a form of vernacular modernism by providing an alternative public sphere through which the masses became visible to society and themselves by sharing new forms of sensory experience.[65] Engaging "the contradictions of modernity at the level of the senses, the level at which the impact of technology on human experience was most palpable and irreversible," "cinema not only traded in the mass production of the senses but also provided an aesthetic horizon for the experience of industrial mass society" (Hansen, "Mass Production of the Senses," 342). Where my argument turns on manipulation, Hansen's pivots on self-reflexivity. Both are as fundamental to propaganda as they are to modernism: if film helped bring the masses into self-awareness by making them global citizens of modernity, propaganda did so by mobilizing them as members of communities that were sometimes national, sometimes local, sometimes global ("Workers of the world, unite!").

Sabotage occupies a significantly equivocal and therefore illuminating position in the matrix of modernism and propaganda. One surreal, dislocated scene featuring a Disney cartoon recapitulates the film's aggressive stance toward its audience by offering an object lesson in the dangers of absorption, an effect of narrative that propaganda often exploits. Durgnat captures an important dimension of the cartoon sequence, calling it an "extraordinary yet absolutely plausible disjunction of the stream of consciousness," in which "Hitchcock anticipates that sense of city existence—of the mass media's so-called 'global village'—as an onslaught on the integrity of the individual, and on the continuity of emotional consciousness."[66] But more than an historically prescient evocation of trauma, the moment also reads as a self-reflexive instance of extreme manipulation in which Mrs. Verloc becomes, like Stevie with the vendor, Hitchcock's demonstration model or Conrad's marionette—becomes, that is, both the subject of propaganda and the occasion for its formation as cinematic theme. Nearly catatonic after learning of Stevie's death, she wanders away from her husband into the theater, where Walt Disney's *Who Killed Cock Robin?* is playing. Ringing the last changes on the film's bird motif (they're everywhere) and introducing another conspicuously American element, the cartoon shows Cock Robin courting a Mae West bird while the audience laughs appreciatively at his Bing Crosbyesque crooning. Even Mrs. Verloc, momentarily escaping from her grief into the romantic fantasy of the cartoon, begins to smile and laugh, when suddenly a shadowy figure shoots an arrow through Cock Robin's heart. Precisely as her grief is forced back into consciousness, we see a close-up of her sudden frown, and the cook appears to inform Mrs. Verloc that dinner is ready. As if sleepwalking, she returns to the dinner table, where, faced with Stevie's empty chair and a warm joint of meat, she soon stabs her husband to death in a much-discussed montage sequence. In 1941 Preston Sturges used a Disney cartoon at the climax of *Sullivan's Travels* to represent the comic relief that Depression-era audiences were thought to desire. When Mrs. Verloc's cinematic absorption in a quintessentially innocent entertainment explodes in her face, Hitchcock's film remains as true to its modernist antecedents as it is prophetic of propaganda's assimilation of modernist techniques.

Hitchcock's position within the history of modernism is similarly double-edged. I have emphasized Hitchcock's investment in mastery as a constitutive element of his modernism, but an antithetical case can be made for Hitchcock as exemplary of a modernist aesthetics of disruption.[67] In this strand of modernism, emphasis falls on moments in which representational codes unexpectedly shift, identification is solicited only to be broken, and the totalizing aspirations of mastery are denied. Examples range from the elaborately foregrounded narrative architectonics of Conrad's *Under Western Eyes* and *Chance*, which intermittently make readers aware of *how* they see, to the antimimetic experiments of Joyce and Gertrude Stein and the dispersion of individual identity in Virginia Woolf's *The Waves*. Many of Hitchcock's films can be assimilated to this tradition. Ina Rae Hark, for instance, has argued that Hitchcock's political films encourage a form of active spectatorship in order to warn against "the perils for citizens who are content to sit quietly in the audience while the spectacle of world affairs unfolds before them."[68] Rather than remain passive, "citizen-amateurs" in *The Man Who Knew Too Much* (1934) and *The 39 Steps* (1935) choose to intervene in staged spectacles to prevent international crimes from proceeding as planned, and their disruption operates as a model of participatory democracy.

But if Hark's argument works well for many films, including *Foreign Correspondent* (1940), *Saboteur* (1942), and *Torn Curtain* (1966), its failure to account for *Sabotage* is instructive. In all these films the figure of the involved citizen-amateur solves problems that have proved intractable for professional politicians and bureaucrats. But in *Sabotage*, the only candidate for heroic citizen-amateur is Mrs. Verloc, whose murder of her husband is an act of revenge for a crime that has already been committed, not the thwarting of a plot that has baffled professionals. The murder has no significant ramifications beyond the domestic sphere—Verloc never wanted to engage in the violence in the first place and was unlikely ever to make another attempt—and Mrs. Verloc's crime goes unpunished only because she is protected by the one person with knowledge of Verloc's crime and her own, Ted, a professional law enforcement official. Designed to display Hitchcock's professional mastery to Hollywood, *Sabotage* is ultimately less interested in the capacity of amateurs to intervene than in the ability of the professional to control them. Not that Mrs. Verloc is a docile spectator: she watches a comic cartoon and in response plunges a knife into her husband, the man who owns the theater. But Mrs. Verloc's act of rebellious spectatorship occurs within a film that grinds her little brother into nameless fragments while mocking its customers for consuming the tragedy. Hark has to explain away the fact that in the films she discusses Hitchcock "avoids using audiences viewing films" (Hark, "Keeping Your Amateur Standing," 13), but *Sabotage*, as we have seen, places film spectatorship very much in the foreground, and by dramatizing diegetic failures to control its audience, Hitchcock's film underscores its own power to do so.

The magnetic repulsion of *Sabotage* may have earned Hitchcock a Hollywood contract; like Conrad's novel, however, it was not a popular success. In the long run, Hitchcock's superior ability to ironize the conventions of popular entertainment without emptying them of consolation would allow him to straddle more successfully than Conrad an audience that might include Graham Greene and a real-life approximation of Mrs. Verloc in adjacent seats. The story of this success begins in *Sabotage*, where Hitchcock, aligning himself through the vendor with the power of advertising, begins to let the residual ethical coordinates of Conrad fall away to reveal what most concerns him, the empty chair in which he wishes to pin his audience while the bomb continues to tick. At the same time, his modernist play with the film-within-a-film encourages the viewer to keep a skeptical eye on the space behind the screen, where conspirators gather to inspire our uneasiness.

It is easy to see why government conspirators turned to Conrad in World War I and to Hitchcock in World War II. Conrad's experience as a master mariner in the British Merchant Marines made him seem a natural to spin a useful tale of the sea for the Admiralty, just as Hitchcock's mastery of film recommended him to the film division of the MoI. But however appropriate they seemed at the time, their imaginations ultimately proved too mutinous. I will return to Hitchcock's World War II propaganda films in my last chapter. In the meantime, the next chapter returns to the pre–World War I years of Virginia Woolf, and to a medium whose newness is recognizable only through an effort of historical imagination: the picture postcard. Woolf's first novel tells a cautionary tale about a young woman's vulnerability to the wiles of propaganda. Like Mrs. Verloc in *Sabotage*, Rachel Vinrace learns a lesson about the danger of absorption. Unlike Mrs. Verloc, however, Rachel does not survive her education. Rachel, one could say, is Woolf's Stevie.

Chapter Two

THE WOOLFS, PICTURE POSTCARDS, AND
THE PROPAGANDA OF EVERYDAY LIFE

V IRGINIA WOOLF WAS inclined to view modernism as the antithesis of propaganda, in part owing to modernism's rejection
of moralizing narrators, but also because she shared the common view (belied by Ford Madox Ford) that where propaganda depends
on simplicity, art is complex.[1] Hence her reflections in *Three Guineas*
on the potential for staging *Antigone* as propaganda. Although Antigone
could be transformed into suffrage activist Emmeline Pankhurst and
Creon into Hitler or Mussolini, the appropriation is bound to fail because Sophocles' characters "suggest too much": "if we use art to propagate political opinions, we must force the artist to clip and cabin his
gift to do us a cheap and passing service." Propaganda neuters art—
"Literature will suffer the same mutilation that the mule has suffered;
and there will be no more horses"—and art disrupts propaganda by
overcomplicating the message.[2] But like Ford's impressionist propaganda, Woolf's anxiety over the polemical aims of "The Pargiters"—
"this fiction is dangerously near propaganda, I must keep my hands
clear"[3]—underscores why a critical narrative in which the modernist
writer rescues art from the dragon of propaganda is inadequate: modernism and propaganda are too complexly entwined to permit the con-
solations of facile redemption.[4] Unlike Ford, however, Woolf does not
exploit their entanglement but turns their difference toward critique.

Looking only at Woolf's most discussed fiction, one might not guess
that the proximity of modernism and propaganda was a concern. Beginning with her short story "The Mark on the Wall" (1917), Woolf's expressive form openly questions official pieties—or what the story suspi-
ciously terms "those real standard things"—that propaganda aims to
secure, and in later novels the critique becomes sharper yet.[5] In *Mrs.
Dalloway* (1925) and *To the Lighthouse* (1927), for instance, the alienating effects of Woolf's narrative strategies and descriptive style clearly
contest the nationalist fictions disseminated by government propagandists during the World War I. In *Mrs. Dalloway* the would-be poet Septimus Smith, deranged by the trauma of war, is a failed version of Wilfred
Owen or Siegfried Sassoon.[6] All the war poets emphasized the difficulty

of making people at home understand the true horror of their experience at the front. But where Owen's and Sassoon's poems violently attacked consoling fictions about the nobility of sacrifice, Septimus is consumed by the desire to communicate a great truth that he cannot articulate. The novel does what Septimus cannot: in service of his muttered wisdom that "communication is health," it makes us hear the anguish that Septimus lives through in isolation.[7] *Mrs. Dalloway*'s critique of cultural reticence also expands beyond the war by establishing an analogy between Septimus's mute suffering and the loss on which socialite Clarissa Dalloway's marriage is founded. As Septimus's wife, Rezia, puts it, "Every one has friends who were killed in the War. Every one gives up something when they marry" (*Mrs. Dalloway*, 66). Septimus and Clarissa both suffer under the authority of Sir William Bradshaw's twin "goddesses": Proportion, who counsels quiet submission to dominant norms, and her more violent sister, Conversion, who destroys competing beliefs by feasting on "the wills of the weakly" (ibid., 100). Septimus escapes conversion at the hands of Bradshaw's agent Dr. Holmes only through suicide; Clarissa is more fortunate: the mystical connection she feels with Septimus helps her protect her own difference against the pressure of "normality." These are limited victories, of course: Septimus dies, and Clarissa's parties sustain the very society that threatens to erase her difference, the "thing . . . that mattered; a thing, wreathed about with chatter" (ibid., 184).

But as a complex utterance, the novel reaches well beyond Clarissa's moment of vision. It intervenes in postwar English life to ask pointed questions about how societies cope, or do not cope, with trauma. At what price do we look away from the invisible wounds of war or the hidden costs of heteronormativity? Clarissa can do nothing for Septimus, but in *Mrs. Dalloway* Woolf sets her own boldly idiosyncratic vision against the acculturating power of Proportion that impels Septimus out the window. By making his pain and Clarissa's palpable, the novel's attention to otherwise unregistered currents of thought and feeling— "life, with its varieties, its irreticences" (ibid., 51)—disrupts the restrictive affective economy that propaganda aims to enforce. The modernism of *To the Lighthouse* works similarly. The symbolic obliquity of Woolf's rendering of the war in "Time Passes"—"an ashen-coloured ship"; "a purplish stain upon the bland surface of the sea as if something had boiled and bled, invisibly, beneath"—links war propaganda with repressive domestic ideology by filtering the war through imagery associated with "The Fisherman's Wife," a cautionary tale about female appetite that Mrs. Ramsay reads to her son James.[8] At least as effectively as the brutal realism of Henri Barbusse's influential novel *Under Fire* (*Le feu*) (1917),[9] the sixth section of "Time Passes" challenges propaganda by punctuating its radically experimental mode with the shocking death-in-brackets of Andrew and Prue Ramsay.[10] Within Woolf's phantasmagoric evocation of time passing independently of a perceiving subject, the brackets entombing Andrew and Prue suggest the inconsequence of their deaths, Andrew sacrificed to war, Prue on the altar of marriage, both dying in accordance with the strict gender roles propagated by their mother.

Given the power of these novels, it may seem perverse for this chapter to focus (as it ultimately will) on Woolf's first novel, *The Voyage Out* (1915). After all, if Terry Eagleton exaggerates when he criticizes Woolf's decision to kill off the novel's heroine, Rachel Vinrace, as "an extreme enough remedy" for marriage, "rather like cutting off someone's head to stop them squinting," it is the rare reader who finds Woolf's apprentice novel as satisfying as her later works.[11] But *The Voyage Out* can adequately represent Woolf's place in my argument for several reasons. First, it is illuminating as a failed version of what Woolf accomplishes with greater confidence in her later novels. Having served as a catalyst in the representation of Rachel's fatal fever in *The Voyage Out*, propaganda became more manageable for Woolf owing to the rhetorical liberation it precipitated. Second, rather than engage directly with war propaganda, the novel is in dialogue with more diffuse forms of propaganda, especially imperial propaganda, that were later consolidated and professionalized by Wellington House in World War I and by the new MoI in World War II. Early Woolf thus fills out the cultural history *Modernism, Media, and Propaganda* traces. Finally, in its less effective struggle with propaganda, *The Voyage Out* illuminates how the problem of proximity sometimes ended with the triumph of propaganda. The fact that Woolf coped so successfully in her later fiction makes her relative failure in *The Voyage Out* all the more revealing.

Obsessively rewritten and nearly abandoned, *The Voyage Out* records the troubled emergence of Woolf's modernism as an act of defiance against the propaganda of everyday life, or what Jacques Ellul terms "integration propaganda." Integration propaganda, or the "propaganda of conformity," aims for "total adherence to a society's truths and behavioral patterns" by encouraging individuals to participate in their society in every way.[12] Less targeted than government propaganda designed to mobilize citizens in response to a particular policy or cause, such as war, "integration propaganda" is an umbrella term that makes visible the ways in which diffusely constellated organizations and institutions effectively reinforce official political propaganda. A sociological phenomenon intrinsic to modern society, integration propaganda finds expression in a variety of ways, from advertising and public relations to popular movies and education.[13] Confronting this decentered form of propaganda, *The*

Voyage Out struggles with the dominant "pattern" of life and literature—*Mrs. Dalloway* calls it "Proportion"—that constrains both Woolf and her protagonist, Rachel, as they voyage out into the world. Through the dense weave of its allusiveness, *The Voyage Out* comments on the long shadows cast by influential writers, including Jane Austen and Joseph Conrad, but it is also deeply engaged with the influence of two less apparent intertexts: Leonard Woolf's first novel, *The Village in the Jungle* (1913), and colonial postcards.

In *The Voyage Out*'s opening pages, when Helen and Ridley Ambrose jostle their way through London's narrow streets toward the ship that will take them and Rachel to South America, Ridley momentarily becomes "entangled . . . with a man selling picture postcards."[14] When Rachel later attempts to recall London life while strolling through the South American town of Santa Marina, she begins by acknowledging the kind of entanglement Ridley tries to leave behind: "First there are men selling picture postcards" (*The Voyage Out*, 89). It makes sense that Rachel's effort to think her way back into England should begin with the selling of postcards, for by 1915 a craze for picture postcards had made them a prominent feature of everyday life. The first picture postcards were made for the Paris Exhibition of 1889, and many more were produced in England for such large-scale exhibitions as London's Imperial International Exhibition in 1909 and the British Empire Exhibition at Wembley in 1924. Begun as early as 1904 and substantially complete in September of 1913, *The Voyage Out* was composed during the so-called golden age of picture postcards, and when Rachel travels up a great river in search of a place "where none but natives had ever trod" (ibid., 224), what she discovers instead is the difficulty of disentangling herself from a characteristically modern form of cultural expression.[15] Picture postcards, as we shall see, came in many forms. Of particular interest in relation to *The Voyage Out* are colonial postcards representing the indigenous other. Such postcards were part of the wave of modern propaganda that began to crest in World War I.

Modern propaganda is sometimes thought to have developed only with the advent of mass media such as radio or film, but while electric media did indeed extend propaganda's reach, propaganda by saturation began in the late nineteenth century as soon as "printed and visual materials became available at prices so low as to place them in almost every home."[16] The postcard industry benefited both from new printing technologies and from new postal regulations, and Britain's imperial ambition made the inculcation of its ideals by any available means both necessary and profitable. With information from afar speeding across British telegraph lines into newspapers increasingly named for the telegraph, remote skirmishes at the edges of empire became a form of entertainment for the home front.[17] Thus if the Boer War (1899–1902) shook British confidence in its imperial might, the conflict was a boon to the predominantly jingoistic press. Because the press and citizen-based patriotic organizations sang British praises so insistently, the government largely refrained from official propaganda before World War I. But with the expansion of various media industries (printing, photographic, and advertising among others) and the consequent diffusion of pro-imperial messages in picture postcards, advertisements, cigarette cards, newspapers, and posters, along with growing respect for the military and new reverence for royalty promoted by the new imperialism, it became increasingly difficult to draw a line between a "self-generating ethos" that reinforces itself through repetition—think national identity—and "conscious manipulation" of public opinion by those who controlled "powerful religious, commercial, military, and official agencies."[18] *The Voyage Out* testifies to the difficulty of distinguishing between shared ethos and state-sponsored manipulation even before the Wellington House campaign permanently muddied the distinction.

Rachel's story is clearly a surrogate for Woolf's, and Rachel's entanglement with colonial postcards mirrors Woolf's complicated encounter with Leonard's colonial novel. Becoming engaged to Leonard while rewriting her first novel, Virginia was faced with the dual problem of how to establish her authority as novelist and how to maintain her autonomy as a woman. She felt the problem in her bones. Indeed, it is no exaggeration to say that the writing and rewriting of *The Voyage Out* almost ended Woolf's career before it could begin. She may have rewritten the novel as many as twelve times and at one point was developing at least two different versions simultaneously. Whenever she rewrote the scene of Rachel's fatal delirium, she was in danger of lapsing into madness, and in September 1913, several months after she finally finished the manuscript, she became delusional and attempted suicide, delaying publication by several years. Then, just as the book was being released in February 1915, Woolf again became so deranged that she was confined for most of the year and did not see Leonard for eight weeks.

The engagement in May 1912 complicated Woolf's effort to find her voice as a novelist. *The Voyage Out* assumed its final form only after Virginia returned from her honeymoon with Leonard to read *The Village in the Jungle* in manuscript. Literary history alone would not assign much weight to Leonard's novel. Had Virginia not read *The Village in the Jungle* while revising *The Voyage Out*, the novel would be of interest mainly to postcolonial critics and students of colonial Ceylon.[19] But Woolf's engagement and marriage heightened her ambivalence toward male authority, and Leonard's parallel efforts to produce a first novel could not but affect her own story of a young woman who becomes engaged to an aspiring novelist, Terence Hewet. For Virginia *The Village in the Jungle* was particularly powerful because she found in it a disturbing version of the English novel's traditional marriage plot that bore directly on the problems of autonomy she was exploring through Rachel and living out in her relationship with Leonard. How does a young woman establish her own authority in a public sphere dominated by powerful male voices? By reinforcing sexual, political, and aesthetic norms enshrined in the institution of marriage and disseminated by the propaganda of everyday life, *The Village in the Jungle* made an answer to this question all the more difficult, and all the more important.

For Woolf, then, colonial postcards and Leonard's novel were significant elements within the matrix of influences that Ellul analyzes as integration propaganda. Over the course of her career, Woolf steadily sharpened her critique of such propaganda. As a public intellectual in the thirties, for instance, she was ferociously critical of the ideological snares that ultimately defeat Rachel in *The Voyage Out*. But whereas in *Three Guineas* (1938) Woolf imagines an Outsider's Society of women who refuse the ideological hailing of the state, her first novel narrates Rachel's inability to live either outside or inside propaganda.

Although it ultimately falls prey to the fallacy of the excluded middle, *The Voyage Out* is more than a powerful cautionary tale. Beyond highlighting the masculinist bias of Edwardian propaganda, it reveals through its unresolved tensions and structural uncertainty the sharp edges of conflicts rounded off by the more assured formal harmony of Woolf's later style. Even though Rachel ultimately cannot think past the dominant ideologies that fuse to overwhelm heterodox aesthetic and sexual energies, she is nevertheless the locus of modernist sensibility in the novel, and her death suggests that Woolf's modernism should be read as a protest against the propaganda that inscribes Rachel's body into a pattern she is unable, finally, to resist. The key moment occurs upriver in South America, where Rachel comes face to face with a group of indigenous women. Mediated by colonial postcards and Leonard's novel, Virginia's village in the jungle is a complex nodal point in which the pressures of everyday life, literary tradition, and imperial ideology converge. The resulting scene, feverishly rewritten after her honeymoon, gestures beyond the constraints that tighten around Rachel to evoke the dissident character of Woolf's emerging modernism.

Brought into alignment with Woolf's later novels, *The Voyage Out* has been understood as a univocal critique of bourgeois domesticity and empire,[20] but the pivotal scene upriver reveals a more complicated meditation on the potential entanglement of Englishwomen in imperial norms of gender, sex, and race. Woolf would pose the issue more pointedly in *Three Guineas* in connection with new economic opportunities for

women: "how can we enter the professions and yet remain civilized human beings?" Inasmuch as a woman's success in "the patriarchal system" runs the risk that "the words 'For God and the Empire' will . . . be
written, like the address on a dog-collar, round your neck," Woolf worries that Englishwomen already colonized under patriarchy "like slaves
in a harem" may become colonizers in their turn as they follow the procession of educated men into the public sphere.[21] Her critique of war and
empire in *Three Guineas* is more straightforward and forceful than the
implicit critique worked out in Rachel's story, but *The Voyage Out*
probes more deeply into the gap between gendered and racial identities
that the polemical invocation of "slaves in a harem" obscures. Indeed,
much of the interest of the novel lies in just this gap. On one hand,
Woolf's struggle with racial difference in the novel's culminating scene
upriver brings her to the brink of acknowledging the imperial grounding
of her own whiteness, and the depth of her affective engagement makes
race a crucial feature of her work, for the first and last time.[22] On the
other hand, Woolf's complicated positioning of Rachel in relation to
motherhood and domesticity in the native village foreshadows the very
different status the maternal will take on in her later writing. Thus if *The
Voyage Out* marks the limits of Woolf's imagination of race, it also provides insight into the origins of her modernism.[23]

POSTCARDS, EXHIBITIONS, AND EMPIRE

The process of globalization in the early twentieth century was not yet
far enough along to require the late-century coinage "globality" to describe the economic integration of a wholly interconnected world. But
The Voyage Out registers an impression of impending globality by linking the crowded banks of the Thames to the exotic streets of Santa Marina through the ubiquity of the picture postcard: Ridley's literal entanglement with the postcard seller becomes Rachel's imagined one. Far
from mere exotic throwaways, widely collected colonial postcards contributed to imperial stereotyping by disseminating primitivist images of
indigenous peoples during the most jingoistic period of England's global
dominance. Images of the native other were also imprinted onto the English imagination by domestic postcards printed for imperial exhibitions.
Given that Woolf never set foot in South America, it is not surprising
that the mossy path running alongside the river begins to resemble "a
drive in an English forest" (*The Voyage Out*, 256) or that her description of native women upriver is informed by the popular ethnography of
colonial postcards and imperial exhibitions. As if transplanted from the
pitch at Wembley, this scene of ethnographic exhibition reproduces the

complex dynamics of spectatorship that obtains when one's only real knowledge of the other comes from looking at picture postcards or people on display.[24]

Recognizable now as a symptom and bearer of modernity and modernism, at the turn of the twentieth century the picture postcard began as an amusing novelty and soon became an outright craze. Much like the vogue for posters that hit London and Europe around the same time, picture postcards, first used in Great Britain in the 1890s, quickly became highly prized objects for English collectors and the general public.[25] An astonishing range of cards suffused all levels of culture: images of new technology, photos of actresses, Boer War battle commemorations, novelty cards, and popular crazes from ping-pong to roller skating. Political groups of various stripes quickly found a new agent of propaganda, and topical postcards began to enter into debates about suffrage, tariff reform, and imperial policy. C.F.G. Masterman's secret propaganda campaign run out of Wellington House in World War I also recognized the power of the postcard. According to Masterman's *Third Report*, the division in charge of visual media sent 100,000 postcard greetings from British soldiers to Russian soldiers during Russian Easter in 1916, and 20,000 cards showing General Cadorna and Lord Kitchener in medallions surrounded by flags of the Allies to Italy.[26] The advertising industry had already capitalized on the new form so effectively that by 1903 a man sending a South African postcard of an African woman washing a young child with the caption "O dirty boy!" to his sister on the Isle of Wight suggested it would be "a very good adv. for Pears Soap/you ought to send it to the firm"(figure 2.1).[27] This postcard evinces not only the deep link established by the turn of the twentieth century between advertising and postcards but also the degree to which both, spreading along paths cut by empire, were mediating English views of the world.

The picture postcard spread so quickly owing in part to changes in British and international postal regulations. In 1899 British postal regulations permitted the standard-sized card already used in Europe to circulate freely, and a special postal rate of one halfpenny for domestic delivery encouraged Edwardians to send postcards on the slightest pretext: " 'Hope to be in time for tea this afternoon!' " (quoted in Byatt, *Picture Postcards*, 13). Just as journals arose around the poster phenomenon, so monthly publications such as *The Picture Postcard & Collector's Chronicle* (1900–1907) and *The Postcard Connoisseur for Postcard Collectors* (1904) sprang up to serve the needs of avid collectors. "During the quarter of a century that preceded the Great War in 1914," according to one historian of the postcard, "it would have been hard to find anyone who did not buy postcards from genuine pleasure. People preserved them carefully in their albums, or they posted them to their friends or relations, in the expectation of receiving others in return."[28] Royalty was

"O, you dirty boy!"

FIGURE 2.1 Postcards, advertising, empire: "O, you dirty boy!" Black and white postcard, dated by hand "Sunday 13th"; Orange River Colony with partially legible postmark (1903?) on back; second postmark indicates it was received in Southhampton at 9 a.m., January 2. Photographer and printer unknown (same insignia "SECD" as figure 2.8 below). The inscription reads: "A very good adv. for Pears soap you ought to send it to the firm."

more cautious yet not immune: Queen Victoria asked a relative to compile an album for her.

Not everyone was pleased. The picture postcard soon became as inescapable as the cell phone is today, though not quite so annoying. "At the height of the industry's boom, postcards were virtually everywhere in the world"; in 1909 over 800 million were posted in Great Britain alone.[29] As in contemporary fears about the rise of consumer culture, women in particular were figured as both victims and carriers of a new cultural disease.[30] An article in the *Standard* in 1899 observes drily that "the illustrated postcard craze, like the influenza, has spread to these islands from the Continent, where it has been raging with considerable severity. Sporadic cases have occurred in Britain. Young ladies who have escaped the philatelic infection or wearied of collecting Christmas cards, have been known to fill albums with missives of this kind from friends abroad" (quoted in Staff, *Picture Postcard*, 60). Woolf herself evidently caught the bug: "I was much amused by your post card of the two novelists," she wrote to Stephen Spender, "and have stuck it in my album" (*Letters*, 6:74). In 1903 the *Glasgow Evening News* worried that "in ten years Europe will be buried beneath picture postcards" (quoted in Carline, *Pictures in the Post*, xv). Evidently Germany was to blame: "The traveling Teuton seems to regard it as a solemn duty to distribute [picture postcards] from each stage of his journey, as if he were a runner in a paper chase" (Staff, *Picture Postcard*, 60). Pundits were right to single out Germany—a drawing in the *Illustrated London News* in 1909 shows Germans in an open-air restaurant buying cards for immediate posting from a postman with a letterbox on his back—for it was there that new methods for the mass reproduction of color photographic images made the modern picture postcard possible. The end of the craze was a more cosmopolitan affair: the decision of popular newspapers and magazines after 1910 to start publishing photographs gave commercial photographers, who previously relied chiefly on postcards, a new outlet for their work; the spread of the inexpensive Kodak Brownie, first produced in 1900 in America, increasingly made picture postcards less necessary; and World War I made the production of high quality cards unfeasible (Woody, "International Postcards," 14–21).

To a degree the postcard fad merely intensified processes of modernization already put in play by the emergence of print culture and the birth of the British postal system. But three new developments distinguish English epistolary culture at the turn of the twentieth century: the growing dominance of the image, the global circulation of information, and the increasingly formative influence of empire. First, the picture postcard fused word and image, subordinating the former to the latter in such a way that Ezra Pound's contemporaneous definition of the "image"—"an intellectual and emotional complex in an instant of time" that produces a "sense of freedom from time limits and space limits"— could apply just as well to England's newest mass cultural form.[31] Second, picture postcards began to circumnavigate the globe along information routes pioneered by British maritime trade and rendered functional by the widespread adoption of the English postal system. If an increasingly efficient system for mass distribution of mail in the eighteenth century had the effect of "abstracting distance into pure exchange,"[32] the circulation of colonial postcards in the twentieth century began to shrink not just England but the entire world. It is not surprising, then—and this is my third point—that many domestic English postcards disseminated complementary views of empire. Cards showing scenes of cricket, for instance, betokened the expanding sphere of a sport used to train colonials how to be English, and cards featuring Kew Gardens evidenced the gravitational pull of a global collection of plants and seeds gathered from outposts of empire.

The pump driving colonial postcards through the world's far-flung circulatory system was the modern problem of authenticity. In a historical moment increasingly self-conscious about the inescapably mediated nature of reality, the thrill of the postcard, Susan Stewart has argued, derived from a hunger for a sense of authenticity attached to location.[33] An unprecedentedly public form of communication, postcards paradoxically functioned as a guarantor of the authentically personal. "Here I am," the postcard declares to the recipient, thus bringing into being the "I" as both familiar sender and exotic locale, the two temporarily equated through the metaphor of location. Insofar as the postcard's uncanny subject assumes a dual relation to the pictured site, one that restages (in a less threatening register) the precarious dynamics of colonial exchange, the colonial postcard contributes to the formation of imperial subjects: the tourist assumes the subject position of the colonizer by appropriating the exotic site and returning it to the metropole; yet the familiar subject, with its articulation propped on the authenticity of "being there," also appears to have "gone native" by merging with the space of the exotic, a transformation typically triggered within the recipient as well, who gazes at the image as if through the sender's eyes.

Viewed from the twenty-first century, then, the picture postcard begins to look like an emerging modernist form—displacing the formal conventions of epistolary style with now familiar vacation shorthand; subordinating authorship to mechanical reproduction; seeking authenticity beyond the artifice of civilization and eschewing the totalizing expansiveness of Victorian narrative in favor of fragmentary utterances and the primacy of the image. Among contemporary commentators, James Douglas captured the peculiar modernity of postcards best in

1907 when he imagined thirtieth-century archeologists fastening on "the Picture Postcard as the best guide to the spirit of the Edwardian era": "Every pimple on the earth's skin has been photographed, and wherever the human eye roves or roams it detects the self-conscious air of the reproduced" (quoted in Staff, *Picture Postcard*, 79). The "self-conscious air of the reproduced": the phrase nicely evokes a range of experiences of modernity, from Walter Benjamin's ambivalent eulogy for the aura in an age of mechanical reproduction to the growing desire in late-imperial romance for the authentic in the guise of the exotic.

Woolf undoubtedly was attuned to the increasingly inescapable influence of postcards. Like everyone else, she sent picture postcards, requested them from others, and complained about them as well, sometimes because she did not receive enough from friends abroad, sometimes because she did and would have preferred a letter (*Letters*, 2:452, 6:244). Woolf mocked the older generation's belief that postcards were killing the art of letter-writing, believing instead that the penny post was making letter-writing less studied and more sincere—which is to say more modern.[34] In 1930 Woolf even wrote a caption for a National Portrait Gallery postcard of George Eliot.[35] Yet she also saw picture postcards as emblems of transience and diminishment, writing of Ellen Terry that those who saw her only in a recent relatively undistinguished role would remember only "a picture postcard compared with the great Velasquez in the gallery."[36] *The Waves* (1931), published well after the craze for postcards subsided, registers their diminished visibility in Neville's thoughts about Percival: "He will forget me. . . . I shall send him poems and he will perhaps reply with a picture post card."[37] Bittersweet tokens of neglect, postcards here seem to speak of their own evanescence.

However evanescent, postcards nevertheless helped Woolf fill in the blank spots on the map. To a friend in 1925 she wrote: "Send me a picture post-card so that I may imagine your house" (*Letters*, 3:188). Like Rachel when imagining England from abroad, Fanny Elmer in *Jacob's Room* (1922) also turns to postcards to compensate for absence: her stylized "idea of Jacob" while he is abroad for "two months" is "sustained entirely upon picture post cards."[38] But such ephemera are not always sufficient, as Woolf acknowledged while struggling with her biography of Roger Fry: "how can one make a life," she wrote to Vita, "out of Six Cardboard boxes full of tailor's bills love letters and old picture postcards?" (*Letters*, 6:374). How indeed? The problem of making a life out of postcards—of imagining and living a life beyond socially determined frames—is fundamental to the world Woolf imagines in *The Voyage Out*.

Woolf was also well-versed in one of the major sources of picture postcards, the Edwardian culture of exhibition. In 1909, when she was laboriously reworking the manuscript that would become *The Voyage Out*, the Imperial International Exhibition in London brought several native settlements to Shepherd's Bush. Like colonial postcards, imperial exhibitions collapsed the distance between periphery and center by reproducing versions of colonized life on English soil. But where the dynamics of postcard circulation subtly mimed the process of imperial subject-formation, imperial exhibitions materially reproduced the operations of power by bringing actual bodies back to England, where they became human exhibits within reconstructed native villages.

As many have shown, such exhibitions were designed to consolidate belief in imperial superiority, most obviously in the evolutionary vision that emphasized the enlightened progress from benighted colonies into the aptly named White City, the main exhibition center in England from 1907–14.[39] Beginning with the 1878 Paris Exhibition, reconstructed native villages became more prominent than ever before,[40] and many domestic postcards show not only villages but also English spectators lined up for a peek at "real natives." Such postcards "complemented efforts of exposition sponsors in England and France to construct national identities that would embrace specific national colonial projects as a central component of modernity."[41] In this context, postcard collections can be said to epitomize the effort of imperial exhibitions to assemble a complete image of the emerging global system even as individual cards herald the fragmentation of the totality that such exhibitions sought to represent. From the 1890s to 1914 the rising number of simulated native villages created a species of "human showcase": "people from all over the world were brought into sites in order to be seen by others for their gratification and education. . . . [An] audience would pay to come and stare."[42] With the whole world (in the form of the assembled peoples and objects) spread out before their controlling vision, spectators would watch one another watch the spectacle and thereby become part of the human showcase. But the English spectators became part of the display only in a privileged way: by seeing from an empowered position even as they were seen, spectators came to understand themselves as belonging to a particular kind of national community (Bennett, *Rise of the Museum*, 69). At one moment visitors might travel over the grounds by electric railway or enjoy a simulated trip to Paris through the long-planned "chunnel"; the next they might wander into a Mongolian camp where twenty horsemen, "uncouth allies of a civilized power," engage in "a mimic battle" over "the body of a goat."[43] Designed to persuade the metropolitan spectator that the "there" of colonial space had become the "here" of domestic English experience, such villages sharpened the contrast between England's technological modernity and the backwardness of outlying colonies by plunging the spectator into a form of "state-sponsored hallucination."[44] Here's what we are and will be, the Hall of Science might say; here's what we might have been once but are no longer, say the native villages.

Woolf's essay on the 1924 British Empire Exhibition, "Thunder at Wembley," suggests that she had attended imperial exhibitions before, possibly the 1909 London exhibition, and recognized their power to absorb the spectator into an artificially transformed world.[45] The official guide to the Imperial International Exhibition describes what Woolf would have experienced in the hallucinatory space of the Dahomey Village:

> We are at once transported to Western Africa, the land of the Dahomeys and the Amazons. The beating of tom-toms, the panigan clanging, and the grinding roar of the rattle greet us. Only a few years ago these sounds meant the call to human sacrifices, but in this instance they announce that these dark-skinned men and women and children are anxious to entertain us by dance and song. Over 150 Dahomeys have taken up their residence here, and reside in thatched huts just as they did before they left the Dark Continent for the White City. (*Daily Programme*, 49–50)[46]

Magically transported, the spectator is asked to see West Africa as at once out of history and modernized: the thatched huts may be unchanged, but the exhibition transforms barbaric violence into civilized spectacle, bloodthirsty savages into anxious entertainers. The official guide's strolling observer encourages an expansion of the exhibition's sphere of influence: "Purchasing some picture-postcards from one of the many stalls here, we plunge into the Post Office on our right, and despatch them to unfortunate friends who have not seen the exhibition" (ibid., 10).[47] Whether Woolf ever received such a postcard (e.g., figure 2.2) is impossible to say, but "Thunder at Wembley" reveals that she thought deeply about the propagandistic effects of colonial exhibitions.

Woolf and the Culture of Exhibition

Woolf's relation to exhibitionary culture evolved over the years, and her essay on the 1924 British Empire Exhibition at Wembley reads like a halfway house between the later optimism of *The Waves* (1931) and *Between the Acts* (1941) and the early pessimism of *The Voyage Out*. Reading Woolf's career in reverse, one can see that her later belief that spectacles can catalyze change is steadily displaced by worry over the seductive power of state-sponsored spectacles, and her confidence in the power of individuals to deflect or transform ideological conditioning decays.

Bernard's fantasy of Percival in India in *The Waves* produces a sharply

Figure 2.2   A reconstructed native village: "The Fetish Priests, Dahomey Village Imperial International Exhibition, London, 1909." Black and white postcard; photographer and printer unknown.

satiric perspective: " 'I see India,' said Bernard. '. . . I see the gilt and crenellated buildings which have an air of fragility and decay as if they were temporarily run up buildings in some Oriental exhibition.' " Within this imagined scene of exhibition, Percival, wearing his sun helmet, solves "the Oriental problem" of "the uselessness of human exertion" in a trice by "applying the standards of the West" (*The Waves*, 135–36). The "air of fragility and decay" suggests that the power of such displays has passed—they function now only as metaphors—and secures Woolf's ironic distance from the imperial values implicit in "Oriental" exhibitions. A decade later in *Between the Acts* Woolf turns to a pageant play to explore the deploying of spectacles for progressive ends. Miss La Trobe's historical pageant culminates in a late-modernist assertion of fragmentation—not only its inevitability but its potential power—when in its closing moment the players hold up shattered mirrors to the audience. By pushing spectators "between" versions of themselves—or "jerk[ing] the ball out of the cup"—La Trobe produces a moment of radical defamiliarization from which new possibilities or "unacted parts" can emerge. "What a small part I've had to play! But you've made me feel I could have played . . . Cleopatra!" says Lucy Swithin, an elderly woman unlikely to be mistaken for the Queen of the Nile.[48] Feeling neither here nor there, La Trobe's audience begins to reexamine their national past in light of a transformed present, and her play becomes Woolf's trope for the power of spectacle to loosen an audience's otherwise secure ideological moorings.

Woolf's attitude toward ideological spectacles is less assured and more equivocal in "Thunder at Wembley" (1924). E. M. Forster predicted that while millions spend their money on the pitch at Wembley, "a few highbrows will make fun."[49] Woolf does not entirely disappoint. Her only extended description of exhibition-going anticipates the satiric tone of *The Waves* by pitting the ideological hold of empire, located in a display of global commodities, against an apocalyptic vision of nature rising up in the form of a sudden summer thunderstorm; the storm breaks the imperial "spell" and purges the world of the exhibitionary blight. Woolf suggests that "Nature" also asserts herself in the individuality of spectators able to resist the show's blandishments. The failure of the exhibition's ideological project leads to Woolf's dry observation that perhaps the Duke of Devonshire, who praised "the Imperial spirit" of the exhibition in the *Times*, should have denied entrance to all natural forces (*Essays*, 3:414 n3). The essay closes with a mock prophecy: "The Empire is perishing; the bands are playing; the Exhibition is in ruins" (*Essays*, 3:413).

The "dissolving" pagodas and general "decay" of Woolf's Wembley (ibid., 3:413) probably are the originals for "the fragility and decay" of the "temporarily run up buildings" in Bernard's vision of Percival. Yet

Wembley's attractions are not without effect. For if the "dignity" of Woolf's stubbornly independent compatriots makes them "a product to be proud of," they are also "a little languid perhaps, a little attenuated," even docile as they "stand in queues to have their spectacles rectified gratis . . . gaze respectfully into sacks of grain; glance reverently at mowing machines" (ibid., 3:411–12). The idea of having one's vision corrected while studying commodities at an imperial exhibition implies that the "product to be proud of" may actually be precisely what Woolf says it is not: a mass-produced, mesmerized English collectivity "trailing and flowing" between the "coffee-grinder" and the "cream separator" (ibid., 3:412). Woolf's description of previous exhibitions at Earls Court and the White City raises comparable questions about her own immunity. In the earlier exhibitions, "the area was too small; the light was too brilliant. If a single real moth strayed in to dally with the arc lamps, he was at once transformed into a dizzy reveler; if a laburnum tree shook her tassels, spangles of limelight floated in the violet and crimson air. Everything was intoxicated and transformed" (ibid., 3:411). Given Woolf's well-known trope of the moth as the artistic spirit or soul, this example of the exhibition's absolute mastery of nature suggests the danger that state propaganda might be able to intoxicate and transform even her own imagination.

Yet "Thunder at Wembley" also implies that Woolf is protected from dizzy revelers by her class position, for both ends of the class spectrum seem insulated from the ideological hailing of the state, epitomized mockingly by a man banging a "bladder" while imploring spectators "to come and tickle monkeys" (ibid., 3:412). At one end of the spectrum is a lower-middle-class woman "in the row of red-brick villas outside the grounds" who wrings "a dish-cloth in the backyard" (ibid.). Situated beyond the boundaries of the exhibition, this woman remains unswayed by imperial propaganda. At the other end is an obvious surrogate for Woolf, a thrush to which Woolf attributes the "cynical reflection, at once so chill and so superior," that the spectators surely could not be seduced into tickling monkeys or otherwise responding to the siren song of the exhibition. The song of the thrush does for exhibition-goers what Woolf wishes to do for her readers: it undermines the efficacy of the official message by calling attention to the beauty of nature—"a whole chestnut tree with its blossoms standing . . . ordinary grass scattered with petals"—that was transmogrified by earlier exhibitions. Nevertheless, the suspicion underlying "Thunder at Wembley" is that the vast middle class lying between the chill superiority of the thrush and the unwitting washer of dishes may be inclined to settle into the posture refused by the sky: in an otherwise inexplicable negation, the sky, Woolf informs her readers, is *not* found "lying back limp but acquiescent in a green deckchair," and therefore never becomes "part of the Exhibition" (ibid.). Insofar as other spectators, foils for the rebellious sky, presumably do become part of the scenery, the vision of the empire in ruins belongs only to the thrush and Woolf.

Woolf's surrogate in *The Voyage Out* is more vulnerable to the hailing of empire, for the critical distance enjoyed by Woolf and Forster at Wembley is usually unavailable to Rachel. In the novel's opening chapter, London's West End, with "its electric lamps . . . vast plate-glass windows . . . carefully-finished houses, and tiny live figures trotting on the pavement," is described as a "finished work" produced by the "enormous factory" of east London. This is more than a familiar modernist lament over the increasing regimentation of modern life. The plate-glass windows, equally suitable for the display of goods or antiquities, metonymically invoke the convergence of consumerism and exhibitionary culture, and the English urbanites, far from resisting the propagandistic display of consumer goods, themselves become commodities, "tiny live figures" manufactured to populate the streets of the West End showcase. As the Ambroses pass through this scene on their way to the *Euphrosyne*, they can expect "neither help nor attention," we are told, from "a world exclusively occupied in feeding waggons" (*The Voyage Out*, 6). Woolf hints that Rachel is similarly helpless; she may even be part of her father's inventory: when Rachel later sighs over the "poor little goats" (ibid., 16) her father is shipping to South America, Woolf is coyly alluding to her own family nickname, "Goat."[50]

As the ship sets out, England is reduced to a "shrinking island in which people were imprisoned" (ibid., 24). It is in this oppressively commercial prison that Ridley Ambrose momentarily finds himself entangled with a man selling picture postcards. And it is this crowded space that Rachel reinvokes when her imaginative reconstruction of England begins with postcards. South America, always an imaginary realm of the exotic for Woolf, ought to be different,[51] but as Rachel is educated abroad, London's human showcase rematerializes across the ocean and up a great river, transforming native women into ethnographic exhibits and Rachel into an object destined for enjoyment by a young Englishman.

EDUCATION AS PROPAGANDA: *BILDUNGSROMAN*, SEX, AND EMPIRE

Rachel's education is supervised by Helen at the request of Rachel's father, who wants a polished hostess around the house to further his Tory ambitions. Early in the novel Woolf links Rachel's education to colonial exploration by framing Helen's realization that she would like to teach her niece "how to live" with allusions to Helen's embroidery (ibid., 74). As if weaving the river expedition that will shape Rachel's fate, Helen works at "a great design of a tropical river running through a tropical forest, where . . . a troop of naked natives whirled darts into the air" (ibid., 25). The alliterative repetition of "tropical . . . tropical . . . troop" suggests the status of Helen's embroidery as trope, and her "great design" grows more capacious as the novel unfolds. It includes, among other things, her hopes that Rachel will marry as well as her entrusting of Rachel's education to Hirst, Terence's arrogant friend. From this point on *The Voyage Out* combines conventions of the *bildungsroman* with those of late-imperial romance in order to narrate Rachel's painful struggle to disentangle herself from what the novel repeatedly terms "the pattern" of everyday life, a pattern designed to assimilate her to the dominant order.

The line between education and propaganda is sometimes difficult to draw, and when the inculcation of norms takes precedence over incitements to critical thought, the distinction tends to disappear altogether. Both cultural and imperial politics suffuse Rachel's education. Well before Hirst lends her his copy of Gibbon's *Rise and Fall of the Roman Empire*, Rachel learns about empire from the Dalloways, who make their first appearance in *The Voyage Out*. Boarding the *Euphrosyne* in Lisbon, the Dalloways offer formative lessons in culture, empire, and sexuality. Clarissa, who strikes Rachel as a gallery exhibit, seems able to make "the enormous globe [spin] round this way and that beneath her fingers." Richard too seems to Rachel "a fascinating spectacle" with virtually global power. But where Clarissa's lessons are primarily cultural—she chides Rachel for not having read Jane Austen—Richard's are political and sexual. Like a display from the Palace of Industry viewed from a patently erotic perspective, he comes from "the humming oily centre of the machine where the polished rods are sliding, and the pistons thumping" (ibid., 38). His political beliefs, he tells Rachel, can be summed up in "one word—Unity. . . . The dispersion of the best ideas over the greatest area" (ibid., 55). Clarissa is nearby but apparently does not overhear Richard turn the conversation toward the nature of sexual desire. Just as Rachel, increasingly agitated, confesses her ignorance, they are interrupted: "Warships, Dick!" Clarissa calls out. As Rachel watches Richard raise his hat to "two sinister grey vessels," Clarissa squeezes her hand and exclaims: "Aren't you glad to be English!" (ibid., 60). Upset by Richard's probing, Rachel remains quiet, looking "queer" and "flushed." Clarissa's enveloping enthusiasm, however, gathers into Englishness a link between empire and sexuality that receives increasing attention as the narrative unfolds.

Richard later becomes a more hands-on instructor in the pleasures of being English when he drops into Rachel's cabin and impulsively kisses her. "You tempt me," he explains (ibid., 67). Though his kiss produces a passing pleasure, only then does Rachel begin to realize why women cannot walk alone in public. From this moment on she is haunted by a dream in which she walks down a "long tunnel" with "damp bricks on either side" that opens into "a vault," where she is "trapped" with "a little deformed man who squatted on the floor gibbering" (ibid., 68). Trapped at once by her own sexuality inside a damp womb and by an internalized cityscape evocative of an underpass or the Underground, Rachel's sudden sexual awareness seems to put her on the street along with the women she had never before recognized as prostitutes. What Rachel has discovered "hidden in ordinary life" (ibid., 67) are not only desires she cannot trust but unspoken rules of everyday life that Helen later tries to explain. Helen's tutelage affects Rachel in contradictory yet equally profound ways. On one hand, by trying to help Rachel work through her upsetting experience, Helen draws her young charge into a normative vision of heterosexual relations that Rachel finds stifling. When Helen confirms that "those women" in Piccadilly are prostitutes, Rachel suddenly sees "her life for the first time a creeping hedged-in thing, driven cautiously between high walls, here turned aside, there plunged in darkness" (ibid., 72).[52] On the other hand, by demystifying the Dalloways' allure, Helen helps Rachel experience an expansive "vision of her own personality . . . as a real everlasting thing, different from anything else, unmergeable" (ibid., 75). It is characteristic of Woolf's ambivalent presentation of Helen that Helen explicitly rejects the connection between sex and politics that Rachel intuits. Discounting "this confusion between politics and kissing politicians" (ibid., 74), Helen continues to stitch at her embroidery, unaware that her great design helps propagate Dalloway's vision of a unified world.

When the *Euphrosyne* arrives in Santa Marina, Richard's imperial ideals are immediately reinvoked through an allusion to Marlow's map in *Heart of Darkness*. English sailors in "Elizabethan barques," we learn, had established a "great British colony" only to be displaced by Spanish galleons: "All seemed to favour the expansion of the British Empire, and had there been men like Richard Dalloway in the time of Charles the First, the map would undoubtedly be red where it is now an odious green." In the years prior to their arrival a second chance has developed in the form of "a small colony" of English "in search of something new" who found in Santa Marina a place "full of new forms of beauty," including "strangely beautiful" natives and "primitive carvings coloured bright greens and blues" (ibid., 79–81). The desire to find something new ushers the reader into the attenuated exoticism of *The Voyage Out*'s invocation of imperial romance. True to the conventions of late-imperial romance, Woolf emphasizes the difficulty of discovering a space for adventure within a thoroughly domesticated world. But rather than indulge in an imaginative unmapping of the world, as Conrad does, Woolf sharpens the sense of shrinking horizons by organizing Rachel's South American experience around two excursions into the already mapped: the picnic ascent of Monte Rosa and the river expedition to a native village.

The ascent of Monte Rosa locates the story of Rachel's growing intimacy with Terence within a vision of global domestication and elaborates the link between sexuality and politics already implicit in Rachel's ambivalent response to Richard Dalloway. As Evelyn Murgatroyd and Alfred Perrott overlook the South American plains from the summit, Evelyn announces that if she were a man, she would "raise a troop and conquer some great territory": "I'd love to start life from the very beginning as it ought to be" (ibid., 124). Through Evelyn, parodic archetype of woman as colonizer, or Amazonian conqueror of the Amazon, the novel repeatedly links the domestication of women to the domestication of the globe: at one moment Evelyn is turning down yet another marriage proposal; in the next she fantasizes about becoming a second Napoleon. The rest of the chapter sustains the tension between Evelyn's bracing vision of unexplored worlds to conquer and the prospect of a wholly domesticated globe by counterpointing the omnipresence of rituals of social engagement with Rachel's impulse to withdraw. Two moments mark opposite ends of the spectrum: the sudden connection between Helen and Mrs. Thornbury forged by the discovery of a single common acquaintance and the closing words of the previous chapter, in which Terence asks Rachel what she is looking at as she reclines away from the others: "Human beings," she responds. Though Rachel tends to adopt an ethnographic position outside her own culture, the plot soon pulls her into hotel society, where she plays the piano at Susan Warrington's engagement dance and later becomes engaged herself. If Evelyn wants to remake civilization "from the very beginning" (ibid., 124), Rachel evidently has good reason to feel increasingly suffocated by a culture always ready to materialize whenever the English meet up with another. Just as "Mrs. Parry's drawing-room, though thousands of miles away, behind a vast curve of water on a tiny piece of earth, came before their eyes" (ibid., 134), so Englishness envelops Rachel wherever she turns.

Rachel often feels the pressure, most acutely on her body. When Terence sees her as having "a young woman's body not yet developed" and for that reason finds her "interesting and even lovable" (ibid., 195), Woolf betrays Terence's *need* to see Rachel as undeveloped by reminding us a few sentences later that she is twenty-four years old. The pressure on Rachel's body intensifies when she finds herself caught up in a series of obscurely instructive and ambiguously erotic encounters with other women in the hotel. First, Evelyn's aggressive challenge to seize the day—"We don't *do* things. What do you *do*?" (ibid., 235)—takes on an erotic cast when she places her hand on Rachel's knee, which Rachel finds both "exciting" and "disagreeable" (ibid., 236). Escaping Evelyn's clutches, Rachel is soon gathered up by the spinster Miss Allan, who cajoles her into sampling some preserved ginger—"I make it a rule to try everything" (ibid., 240), and offers a taste of her regular traveling companion, a bottle of crème de menthe named Oliver that a female friend bestows on her whenever she travels abroad. Although Rachel quickly spits out the ginger and turns down the offer of Oliver, the tension between a muted eroticism urging untried experiences and the insistent banality of existence intensifies her sense of being trapped in an increasingly familiar pattern. Leaving Miss Allan's room, Rachel finds herself in "a complete block in the passage" when they run into Mrs. Paley. The hallway being lined with shoes set out for cleaning, Miss Allan tries to make conversation with the nearly deaf older woman by repeating three times: "I was just saying that people are so like their boots." She is about to repeat this home truth for a fourth time when Rachel bolts away to a cul-de-sac at the end of the hall, where she is gripped by a vision of the world "in its true proportions": "She disliked the look of it immensely—churches, politicians, misfits, and huge impostures. . . . For the time, her own body was the source of all the life in the world, which tried to burst forth here—there—and was repressed now by Mr. Bax, now by Evelyn, now by the imposition of ponderous stupidity, the weight of the entire world" (ibid., 244). Mr. Bax has earned Rachel's anger with a sermon on the duty the English owe the colonized that translates Dalloway's imperial vision into a Christian imperative. Properly practiced, Christian sympathy, like a drop of water falling into the ocean, "alters the configuration of the globe" (ibid., 219). Once again, Woolf links Rachel's everyday life to a sense of global interrelatedness, weaving Christianity along with English imperialism, marriage, and patriarchy into the great design shaping Rachel's confused maturation.

The "weight of the world," "the configuration of the globe": against pressure of this magnitude Rachel's desire for release grows. It is thus not surprising that Mr. Flushing's exotic picture of what might await them upriver captures Rachel's imagination: "wonderful treasures lay hid in the depths of the land. . . . there might be giant gods hewn out of stone in the mountain-side; and colossal figures standing by themselves in the middle of green pasture lands, where none but natives had ever trod. . . . Nobody had been there; scarcely anything was known" (ibid., 224). Far from entering the "lost world" of Conan Doyle's South America, however, the expedition party will travel into a world to which, as in the vision of India in *The Waves*, "the standards of the West" have already been applied. The native women they meet upriver resemble the post-card images of native woman that flowed into England from South America and Africa, and the circulation of such postcards, as I will show in the following sections, both reinforced and undermined the imperial stereotypes that Rachel must negotiate as she attempts to establish an independent sense of self within what she experiences as an increasingly global culture of Englishness.

SCRIPTING THE BODY: COLONIAL POSTCARDS AND THE JOURNEY UPRIVER

In their insistent framing and arranging of the female body, colonial post-cards propagate a normative vision—Rachel's "ponderous stupidities"—that Richard Dalloway would find congenial. Rachel's struggle with "normalization" continues in her journey upriver, which culminates in three tightly-linked scenes: her engagement, a scene of partially erased sexual dissidence, and her encounter with the native women.

Postcards featuring native women often operate as a form of colonial denigration that reinforces normative values at home.[53] In an early century card from Peru, three bare-breasted women, all of whom are short, heavy, and sullen by prevailing European standards, earn the title "*las tres gracias de las Indias Piros*" (figure 2.3). Circulating with huge numbers of cards displaying English actresses, music hall performers, and famous courtesans, this card hardly bothers to disguise the snicker behind the cross-cultural gesture of its caption. The imposition of a Western frame is often more stark, as in a card bearing the caption "A Zulu Masher" (figure 2.4). Dated by hand February 14, 1905, the card shows a smiling young Zulu woman whose native beads and belt are supplemented with top hat, monocle, jauntily held cigarette, and stylish walking stick. Given the common Western assumption that Africans, particularly women, were oversexed, a male recipient might construe the card as a mocking performance of his masculinity in black face.[54] Yet if cross-dressing often disrupts cultural norms, the cross-racial and cross-gender masquerade in this exchange seems more likely to have reinforced traditional roles. Addressed on Valentine's Day to a "Miss F. Southwell" by "Georgie Southwell" (a playful joke at a sister's expense?), the card implies that a woman's failure to rein in desires may subject her to ridicule.

Less satiric cards sometimes inscribe nonwhite women into English culture as objects of genuine aesthetic and erotic appreciation. In an early-century card collected in Kenya (figure 2.5), a woman from the Boran tribe is posed to display her visual appeal; similar cards sometimes use the caption "A Native Beauty." In other cards a more stylized composition

Las tres gracias de las Indias Piros (Rio Pichis Perú).

FIGURE 2.3   Framing the native: *"las tres gracias de las Indias Piros."* Colorized black and white postcard, circa 1905; photograph by Edward Polack; printer unknown, Lima, Peru.

produces a kind of formal portraiture that further aestheticizes the women, abstracting them from the scene of colonial encounter. In a card from Natal (figure 2.6), for instance, the symmetrical arrangement of trees and women doubly framing a Zulu woman made to stage her toilet for the camera partially transforms the indigenous environment into the artificial space of a studio. The effacing of the indigenous setting is complete in other cards, such as Eduardo Polack's shot of a "Bella India" in Peru (figure 2.7), which whites out any trace of the model's own environ-

A Zulu Masher

From George
Feb 12t 05

Published by Sallo Epstein & Co., Durban

FIGURE 2.4 Colonial denigration and the performance of gender: "A Zulu Masher." Black and white postcard, dated by hand February 14, 1905. Photographer unknown; printed by Sallo Epstein and Co., Durban.

The Boran Tribe

FIGURE 2.5 Capturing a native beauty: "The Boran Tribe." Black and white postcard, circa 1908; photographer unknown; printed by Howse and McGeorge, Ltd., Photographic Chemists, Kenya and Uganda.

Figure 2.6 Framing and its discontents: "The Toilet: Zulu Girls." Black and white postcard, circa 1908; photographer and printer unknown; Natal.

Bella India Campa Rio Pichis (Perú).

Eduardo Polack, Lima (Perú).

FIGURE 2.7 Involuntary acculturation and the returned stare: "Bella India Campa Rio Pichis (Peru)." Colorized black and white card, circa 1910; photograph by Eduardo Pollack; printer unknown; Lima, Peru.

ment. Insofar as these women become interchangeable with images of English actresses and courtesans circulating in England, the photographic abstraction blurring the differences between the English and "the native" begins to resemble a form of symbolic acculturation: in Elizabethan times, Woolf imagines, European women were imported into Santa Marina's first settlement (ibid., 80); these cards complete the exchange by shaping South American women into objects suitable for export.

The sexual and racial meanings disseminated by such cards depend in part on the interplay between production and circulation. In an early-century example from Natal (figure 2.8), three signs plot the card's itinerary: the postmark (July 24, 1904), the address to a "Miss Ashby" in Yorkshire, and the message inscribed on the front: "I am feeling better again. Will write next week." With the angles of her right arm balanced by the angles formed by her left arm and the banjo, the "native musician" is virtually abstracted. The subordination of the body to an angular design is both heightened and complicated by the musical instrument, for the banjo does not simply complete the triangular motif established by the women's right arm: in origin an African instrument, the banjo would have been recognized by European and American audiences as a signifier of race owing to its incorporation into minstrel shows.[55] In fact, this complex articulation of a racialized body within a Western design, in circulation just over a year before Picasso began to "Africanize" *Les Desmoiselles d'Avignon*, constitutes a popular anticipation of the vogue for primitivism that would transform European high art over the next decade. Race is thus inseparable from the abstraction, as is the prurient interest in the woman's nudity, the pose evidently being dictated as much by the desire to have her breast lifted toward the camera as by the formal requirements of symmetry. The suggestiveness that would have been activated by any sexual innuendo in a message sent to a man is mitigated here by the banality of the inscription and the fact that the addressee is an unmarried woman. Instead, consonant with the emergence of museum culture, the image takes on a certain clinical quality, an effect amplified in the ethnographic perspective solicited by the printed caption, "A Native musician." The card's trajectory from Natal to Yorkshire thus partially erases the erotic investment in the exotic other that shaped the production of the card in the first place. In many staged photographs a glimpse of the reality of the models' lives shows through, and I will return to such moments later in the chapter. Here, however, the rescripting through exchange (the inscription and mailing of the card) of a body already scripted within the colonial scene of production (the photographer's arranging of the model) results in an overdetermined cultural coding that obliterates any sense of the historical body prior to its entry into the studio. A token of exchange, the model is transformed into an image of racialized sexuality sanitized for export to England.

"A Native musician"

I am feeling better age Will write / next week

FIGURE 2.8 Eros and abstraction: "A Native Musician." Colorized black and white card, circa 1910; photograph by Eduardo Pollack; printer unknown; Lima, Peru.

Without this coding, the strict norms regulating English sexual expression at home (although under siege from many quarters) never would have permitted the open circulation of bare-breasted women in postcards.[56] (A related domestic postcard strategy covered naked women with white powder and posed them as classical statuary.) These norms find distinct expression in *The Voyage Out* in the banishing of a prostitute seen late at night in the hotel corridors and in the instant decoding of the significance of Susan Warrington and Arthur Venning's first embrace: "Well, we may take it for granted that they're engaged," Terence remarks (ibid., 128). The frank sexuality attributed to nonwhite women under the cover of the ethnographic alibi in postcards provided a form of licensed titillation while also throwing into relief the relative virtue of respectable Englishwomen, whose sexuality remained bound by marriage. Filtering native life through English concerns, other cards reinforced these norms by highlighting images of socially sanctioned sexuality. Card after card evinces a need to identify images of far-flung domesticity. A representative Cape Town card postmarked July 1908 shows a reclining woman breastfeeding a child over the caption "A Native Woman and Child" (figure 2.9); an early-century card from Lagos (figure 2.10) showing a woman holding a small child is labeled "Motherhood." A British East African card showing three adults and seven children grouped casually on the ground before a hut is labeled "A Kikuyu Family" (figure 2.11), but who is to say what brought them together in the frame? Like the nostalgic images of Edwardian idylls in domestic cards and pastoral novels, the fascination with native mothers and families is symptomatic of a cultural need to ease anxieties in a time when falling birthrates were thought to presage the decline of England's imperial power.[57]

Against this backdrop, the potential dissidence of Rachel's desire in the scene of her engagement and its immediate aftermath becomes all the more striking. Over the course of rewriting the novel, Woolf steadily normalized sexual energies that in earlier versions were less bound by heterosexual conventions. Yet the published novel reads like a palimpsest in which traces of each round of revision, however contradictory, are preserved. As a result, the scenes upriver in *The Voyage Out* resonate not only with the normative scripting at work in the postcards but also with discordant postcard elements that disrupt such scripting. This is especially true when Rachel meets the gaze of a group of native women who seem to have stepped out of the kind of postcards discussed above. The ideological hailing of such cards, I have argued, draws on the interpellative designs of the Edwardian culture of exhibition, and in the logic of the novel Rachel's encounter with what might be called "postcard women" changes her life as much as her engagement to Terence does.

But the fact of the change is less interesting than the conditions that

A Native Woman and Child

FIGURE 2.9 Popular ethnography: "A Native Woman and Child." Black and white postcard, stamped and postmarked July 1908; photographer unknown; printed by P.S. and Co. Cape Town.

MOTHERHOOD

FIGURE 2.10 Imperial desire: "Motherhood." Black and white postcard, circa 1908; photographer unknown; printed by C.M.S. Bookshop, Lagos. Handwritten on the reverse: "Dear Kath. Isn't this friccan nice. If they only stayed like this. Love Auntie Bell."

Kikuyu Family.   BRITISH EAST AFRICA.   Photo : Knowles.

FIGURE 2.11   Claiming kin: "A Kikuyu Family." Black and white postcard, circa 1908; photograph by Knowles; printed by the Standard P. and P. Works, Nairobi and Mombasa, British East Africa.

make it possible. The effectiveness of specific propagandistic appeals is always mediated by the life histories and particular circumstances of their recipients: the dystopian fantasies of the Frankfurt School notwithstanding, what works on one person does not always work on another. For this reason, before turning to the self-subverting dimension of postcard images, I want to address the biographical circumstances that made Woolf particularly sensitive, as she was rethinking *The Voyage Out*, to the kind of propaganda spread by colonial postcards: her marriage to Leonard, and her response to Leonard's first novel, *The Village in the Jungle*. Distilled from Leonard's experience in Ceylon, *The Village in the Jungle* is itself a kind of colonial postcard.

Leonard's Jungle, Conrad's Trees

The tortuous composition of *The Voyage Out* has received a lot of attention, thanks in part to Elizabeth Heine's meticulous bibliographic labor and to Louise DeSalvo's publication under the title *Melymbrosia* of a reconstructed version of the novel as it existed prior to the Woolfs' engagement in late May 1912.[58] Leonard and Virginia worked closely together that year as they were becoming engaged and finishing their novels. Leonard remarks in his autobiography that in January and February of 1913, two months after she read the version of *The Village in the Jungle* that he sent to the publisher Edward Arnold, Virginia was "writing every day with a kind of tortured intensity."[59] Rewriting *The Voyage Out* after reading *The Village in the Jungle*, Woolf radically changed three crucial scenes upriver: the moment in which Rachel and Terence declare their love while deep in the jungle; the ensuing moment in which Helen wrestles Rachel to the ground and stuffs grass into her mouth; and the culminating moment of the expedition, the entry into a native village. Most strikingly, the extended tableau of staring native women in *The Voyage Out*—the scene on which, in my view, the entire narrative hinges—is twice as long as the comparable moment in *Melymbrosia*. Oddly, however, when not explicitly rejected, the idea that *The Village in the Jungle* influenced *The Voyage Out* has largely been ignored.[60] Although *Melymbrosia* reveals that many scenes were radically revised after Woolf's honeymoon, even DeSalvo, who maps the relationship between the revision process and the progress of the engagement, never mentions Leonard's novel during her discussion of the many intertexts that haunt *The Voyage Out*.

Any exploration of intertextual relations between *The Voyage Out* and *The Village in the Jungle* must take into account their common debt to Conrad. Virginia Woolf held Conrad in the highest regard, paying her respects to "the spell of Conrad's prose," his "moments of vision," "the astonishing solidity" of his fictional world, and the "lasting importance" that made him a "giant" among living writers.[61] She felt that *Heart of Darkness* in particular revealed "the most complete and perfect expression of one side of his genius—the side that developed first and was most directly connected with his own experience. It has an extraordinary freshness and romance" (*Essays*, 2:159). It had, in other words, precisely what Woolf felt was lacking in Jane Austen, the romantic qualities Woolf appreciated in the gothic fiction of Ann Radcliffe.[62] Conrad's novella haunted *The Voyage Out* from its inception, providing, among other things, a model for the journey upriver that not only initiates but effectively ends Rachel's marriage plot. Leonard was indebted to Conrad too.[63] Not long after finishing *The Village in the Jungle* Leonard gave a public lecture, "Conrad's Vision: The Illumination of Romance," in which he displayed wide-ranging familiarity with Conrad's work as well as a tendency to identify with him as an adventurer-turned-writer.[64] The novel itself echoes Conrad's florid descriptions of the lurking evil of the jungle to such a degree in its opening pages that the narrator's indictment, as one critic points out, "runs counter to the real nature of the jungle" as the characters know it.[65]

This triangular literary historical relationship is complicated further by the likelihood that Virginia would have experienced Leonard as a double for Conrad, who was very much in the news at the time. Returning to London from Ceylon as an accomplished colonial administrator and aspiring novelist, Leonard was the writer-adventurer returning to the metropole after having been, like Conrad, "directly connected" with the exotic periphery. In letters to friends Woolf was inclined to exaggerate her fiancé's doings in Ceylon into heroic proportions by lengthening his tenure and supplying a number of incidents out of Conradian romance (e.g., *Letters*, 1:628). One letters links Leonard's colonial administration to his writing by shifting immediately from the (false) claim that "He has ruled India" to *The Village in the Jungle*: "He has a written a novel; so have I: we both hope to publish them in the autumn" (*Letters*, 1:504). Woolf's hopes for her own book went unfulfilled; the first time Virginia Stephen's married name was attached to a published novel it was appended to her husband's in the form of a dedication to "V. W."

If Woolf did associate Leonard, the "penniless Jew" who seemed so "foreign" to her (*Letters*, 1:500, 496), with Conrad, the Pole (imperfectly) turned Englishman, this association may explain why Conrad becomes an increasingly insistent presence in the massive revisions she undertook after her marriage: as Leonard loomed in her mind, so did Conrad.[66] What is certain, at all events, is that during the transition from

Melymbrosia to *The Voyage Out* Woolf added allusions to Conrad and elaborated others.[67] Most telling is Woolf's revision of a passage in which Rachel responds to the power of Gibbon's prose. For Rachel, "never had any words been so vivid and so beautiful"; they seem "to drive roads back to the very beginning of the world . . . by passing down them all knowledge would be hers, and the book of the world turned back to the very first page" (*The Voyage Out*, 160). For Woolf, the book in question seems to be *Heart of Darkness*, in which Marlow, evoking a return to human origins, tells his audience that "Going up that river was like travelling back to the earliest beginnings of the world, when vegetation rioted on the earth and the big trees were kings" (*Heart of Darkness*, 35).[68] Popping up with surprising frequency in *The Voyage Out*, big trees become a nodal point for Woolf's troubled yet productive relation to masculine power. Repeatedly thrusting their way into Rachel's awareness, they are often associated with a sense of heightened consciousness and with Conrad's conjunction of explosive energy ("vegetation rioted") and constraining male authority ("the big trees were kings"). In one revealing instance, Rachel gazes at a particularly striking tree and experiences a sense of defamiliarization that betrays the intensity of Woolf's ambivalent attraction to Conrad.[69] It happens just before Rachel pauses to read Gibbon. Stopped in her tracks by a tree "so strange that it might have been the only tree in the world," she lingers over its sublime singularity in "one of those unreasonable exultations which generally start from unknown causes" (ibid., 159). Earlier some trees rising "massively in front of her" make her shiver "with anger and excitement" (ibid., 142). More powerful, this one elicits the kind of "moment of vision" that Woolf valued in Conrad and even seems to achieve parity with the novel itself: it is one of "those trees . . . it was worth the voyage out merely to see" (ibid., 159).

And yet the repetition of this moment of exaltation when Rachel sits down to read Gibbon sends her running away, "her body trying to outrun her mind," from "the discovery of a terrible possibility in life" (ibid., 161). On the level of plot Rachel is fleeing from her newly discovered sexual attraction to Terence, perhaps from sexuality altogether. Stepping back, we can also see that Woolf is struggling with a powerful male predecessor, for though she finds quintessentially modernist moments of vision in Conrad, the experience of thinking back through him could not have been entirely congenial to a woman who later advised other women to think back through their mothers.[70] Rachel's flight from Gibbon also draws on Woolf's impulse to withdraw from Leonard's sexual advances. However one assesses the long-term consequences of Woolf's deeply troubled response to sex on her honeymoon, it is clear that Woolf shied away from conventional heterosexual relations and yet found a way to make her marriage with Leonard work.[71] Woolf's response to *The Village in the Jungle* was comparable: however much the book might have troubled her, she was able to engage productively with it. She ultimately had good reason, that is, to return her husband's favor by dedicating her first novel to him, though not because she found it inspiring in any straightforward way.

Critics often have read *The Village in the Jungle* as Leonard's anxious expression of inferiority as a Jew engaged to a woman such as Woolf; he is the black ram tupping the white ewe.[72] Although for readers today the novel may seem comic when viewed as Bloomsbury in black face, if one tries to read it through Virginia Woolf's eyes, its tales of the domestication of wild native women are enough to make one wonder why she did not run screaming into the night. Writing to Leonard after reading his novel in manuscript, she says only that it seems to her "amazingly good"(*Letters*, 2:12). Yet there is reason to suggest that the anguished ambivalence in Woolf's letter "accepting" Leonard's marriage proposal—"I feel angry sometimes at the strength of your desire" (*Letters*, 1:496)—could stand also as her response to the erotic violence of his novel. Whatever Leonard's motives, and there is no need to question them, *The Village in the Jungle* reads as if written to get under his bride's skin.

The Village in the Jungle tells the story of twin sisters, Punchi Menika and Hinnihami, each of whom has a "strangeness and wildness" associated with the jungle (*The Village in the Jungle*, 27). Despite Amazon-like independence, each is brought under the thumb of a dominant man. Imagine Woolf, newly returned from her honeymoon, reading Leonard's description of the near rape through which a young man, Babun, claims Punchi Menika as his mate: "She allowed him to take her into the thick jungle, but she struggled with him, and her whole body shook with fear and desire as she felt his hands upon her breasts. A cry broke from her, in which joy and desire mingled with the fear and the pain" (ibid., 30). However frightening Babun's lust, Punchi Menika's married life may be more chilling, for soon her "wildness" becomes "dimmer and vaguer": "she became the man's woman, the cook of his food, the cleaner of his house, and bearer of his children" (ibid., 40). One waits in vain for an acknowledgment of the loss this domestication entails.

Hinnihami fares worse. A hideously scarred old shaman, Punchirala, begins to hanker for her, and despite elaborate efforts to resist him, Hinnihami finds that the old man's magic is potent enough to endanger her father's life. Reluctantly, Hinnihami agrees to be given to Punchirala, but she defiantly interprets their agreement to mean that she will be his sexual partner for only one night. Nevertheless she becomes pregnant, and soon after giving birth she begins to suckle an orphaned fawn alongside her daughter, Punchi Nona. The girl dies, and Hinnihami comes to think of the deer, which she continues to nurse, as her son. When drought and other ills descend on the village, its superstitious inhabitants, blaming Hinnihami's aberrant behavior, surround the deer to stone it. Hinnihami tries to intervene, but they throw her to the ground, tearing her jacket to shreds, and beat her. The deer dies later that day; Hinnihami is dead by the next morning. The narrative then turns back to Punchi Menika. She is soon pursued by a powerful older man, Fernando, who ultimately gets her husband sent off to prison, where he dies; Fernando himself is shot dead by Punchi Menika's father, who is then imprisoned for life. The novel ends with Punchi Menika alone in the deserted village, waiting for death, which comes in the ambiguously metaphoric form of a wild boar gliding into her hut with gleaming white tusks.

In an imperial romance such as *The Village in the Jungle* or *Heart of Darkness*, one expects to find metropolitan subjects who see, at the boundaries of civilization, their own desires mirrored in the face of the other. Officially committed to duty and discipline, Marlow finds Kurtz, a mass murderer he is willing to see as a visionary, as well as Kurtz's native mistress, "savage and superb, wild-eyed and magnificent" (*Heart of Darkness*, 60), redolent of the sexuality missing in Kurtz's virtually disembodied Intended. Leonard's imperial romance creates an exotic land of violently untrammeled desire in which two superb sisters meet their match in desires even more powerful than their own. Leonard's next novel, *The Wise Virgins* (1914), is transparently a roman à clef in which Virginia and her sister Vanessa appear as Camilla and Katharine Lawrence. Something of the Stephen sisters also entered into the portrayal of Punchi Menika and Hinnihami, and by dressing Virginia and Vanessa in native garb, Leonard recapitulates the common trope of the male colonizer projecting his desire onto the female colonized.

Of course, Leonard would have been shocked at the suggestion that his novel in any way reproduces the uneven flow of power in colonial discourse. He felt that *The Village in the Jungle* was an expression of his growing anti-imperialism after leaving the Civil Service, and the respect he shows the indigenous people of Ceylon in the novel could be construed as a subversion of the Eurocentrism of most colonial literature. Leonard later wrote that he tried "somehow or other vicariously to live their lives" (*Beginning Again*, 47), and the story is related almost entirely through the perspective of indigenous characters. Yet Douglas Kerr's comparison of *The Village in the Jungle* with Leonard's Ceylon diaries and letters suggests that however unusual the novel is in granting its native villagers such autonomy, the narrative reinstates colonial domination at a higher level. The European magistrate, a relatively marginal character, cannot get to the bottom of the cases over which he presides, but the bulk of *The Village in the Jungle* plumbs "the life lived by the native people of Ceylon *when there was no colonial presence to observe them.*" Kerr concludes that the novelistic power to see into the indigenous lives whose opacity frustrated Leonard in his role as colonial administrator appealed to Leonard the novelist as "a sheer compensatory fantasy of omniscience." The novel thus exercises "a more complete discourse authority" over the natives than "the most missionary of colonial powers ever aspired to."[73]

Leonard's anthropological omniscience may lie behind a conversation in *The Voyage Out* in which Rachel recoils from Terence's "determination to know" (*The Voyage Out*, 201). Rachel initially takes pleasure in his interest, but his increasingly ethnographic focus on her as a specimen of womanhood makes her feel "at once singular and under observation" (ibid., 200). Indeed, Terence's desire to find out "what on earth the women [are] doing" inside the houses he passes on the streets (ibid., 200) by talking with Rachel echoes Leonard's attempt to live vicariously through the natives of Ceylon. Closely watched, Rachel might be one of Leonard's characters, always under the author's hidden gaze: "Why did he sit so near and keep his eye on her?" (ibid., 203).

The omniscience of *The Village in the Jungle* also throws into a relief a telling anomaly in the narration of *Melymbrosia* and *The Voyage Out*. Although both versions of Woolf's novel use omniscient narrators, their knowledge is significantly undercut in a pivotal sequence that connects Rachel and Helen to the hotel where the other Europeans are staying. One night Rachel and Helen, who live in a nearby villa, spy on the hotel lounge through a window until Hirst notices them and they scurry away. The narrative perspective soon enters the hotel and begins to survey the people going to bed, pausing over Miss Allan reading Wordsworth and Susan Warrington writing in her diary, before making a curious transition into William Pepper's room: "A glance into the next room revealed little more than a nose, prominent above the sheets. Growing accustomed to the darkness . . . one could distinguish a lean form, terribly like the body of a dead person" (ibid., 95). The suddenly embodied narrator, having cast off omniscience, seems to outdo the eavesdropping women by creeping into the unsuspecting Pepper's room. If Leonard's characters are in effect being watched without their knowing, for a moment Woolf's narrator is in danger, like Rachel and Helen, of being discovered in the act of watching.

This blip in the narrative mode is symptomatic of Woolf's desire to devise an alternative to Leonard's narrative omniscience. Although the narrative mode of *The Voyage Out* remains conventionally omniscient throughout most of the novel, the countercurrent felt in the fleetingly embodied narrator registers also in the flux of irrationality introduced into the narrative by Rachel's fever, and in the way vision presses upon the body in Woolf's rewriting of Leonard's jungle, to which I now turn.

In Virginia's Jungle

For the episodes that lead into her native village, Woolf uses the same narrative sequence in *Melymbrosia* and *The Voyage Out*. On the river expedition, Rachel and Terence declare their love to one another while walking through the jungle; when the newly engaged couple returns, Helen pounces on Rachel; the reassembled group then visits a native village. Yet Woolf altered each scene a great deal in revision.

In the love scene between Rachel and Terence, the romantic cliches of *Melymbrosia* disappear and are replaced by a prolonged moment of surreal dislocation in which Rachel and Terence seem drugged and confused, the landscape uncanny and disorienting. When in *Melymbrosia* Rachel opens her arms in answer to Terence's whispered declaration of love, the embrace could have been lifted from a romance by Ethel Dell, Barbara Cartland's early-century soul-mate: "More as people who grope, who push away a veil between them than as man and woman in midday they sought each other's arms. They embraced passionately" (*Melymbrosia*, 197). In *The Voyage Out* they walk as if "at the bottom of the sea" before pausing to sit down, "unable to frame any thoughts" within a heavy silence (*The Voyage Out*, 256). The acknowledgment of shared feeling (if that is what it is) when Terence declares his love is almost lost in Rachel's benumbed echoing, which seems to drain Terence's words of sense. " 'You like being with me?' Terence asked. 'Yes, with you,' she replied":

> "That is what I have felt ever since I knew you," he replied. "We are happy together." He did not seem to be speaking, or she to be hearing.
> "Very happy," she answered.
> They continued to walk for some time in silence. Their steps unconsciously quickened.
> "We love each other," Terence said.
> "We love each other," she repeated. (ibid., 256–57)

Their first kiss elicits fear: " 'Terrible—terrible,' she murmured after another pause, but in saying this she was thinking as much of the persistent churning of the water as of her own feeling. On and on it went in the distance, the senseless and cruel churning of the water" (ibid., 257). Later Mrs. Flushing's crassly cynical intuition that something has happened between the two comes closest to naming Rachel's inner turbulence as the frightening rush of desire: "One reads a lot about love," Mrs. Flushing observes, "But what happens in real life, eh? It ain't love!" (ibid., 259). The churning of Rachel's desire, moreover, recalls the "river torrent" in Helen's embroidery, thus underscoring the erotic character of their penetration of the jungle.

But the revised scene also feels peculiarly dislocated because their engagement takes place in a jungle landscape that seems at once cleansed
of all meanings and suffused with cultural significance. On one hand, the
alien quality of a world unarticulated by conventional categories makes
them talk like nonhuman life forms encountering the idea of love and
marriage for the first time. On the other hand, their walk through the
jungle is laden with established meanings.[74] The jungle, after all, is
clearly a garden: Hirst cautions them against snakes, and Terence
chooses to break the silence by flinging a "red fruit" into the air and
watching it fall to the ground. Many verbal details in the Fall narrative
resonate with crucial moments in Rachel's life, thus reanchoring in
everyday life a moment of being that would otherwise drift away from
plot. To cite one example among many, a path "hedged in by dense
creepers" that "burst here and there into star-shaped crimson blossoms"
recalls Rachel's anxious vision of her life as "a creeping hedged-in thing"
as well as her angry response to the disciplining of her body, which
"tried to burst forth here—there—and was repressed"; the knottedness
of the creepers also resonates with Rachel's sense that Austen's marriage
plots—urged on her by Clarissa—are too like a "tight plait" (ibid., 256,
72, 244, 49). The deep tension within the scene thus derives not simply
from an unresolved wavering between heterosexual and lesbian desire
but from an encompassing anxiety about *any* fixing of desire.

If the revision of the engagement scene suggests that Woolf was trying
to cope with anxiety stirred up by marrying Leonard, the revision of the
next scene suggests she was struggling to renormalize a narrative that had
become very weird indeed during the young lovers' walk in the jungle. In
both *Melymbrosia* and *The Voyage Out* Helen intuits that Rachel and
Terence are engaged and wrestles Rachel to the ground in a sea of grass,
but the two versions read very differently. In *Melymbrosia* Helen chases
after Rachel until Rachel suddenly stops to open her arms; Helen then
rolls her down to the ground "stuffing grass into her mouth" and orders
Rachel to say "you worship me!" When Rachel exclaims that she loves
Terence better, Helen confesses: "I've never told you, but you know I love
you, my darling." Rachel reminds Helen of Rachel's dead mother
Theresa, whom Helen also loved (*Melymbrosia*, 209). *Melymbrosia*'s in-
tensely realized moment of desire—simultaneously lesbian, sororal, and
maternal—survives in *The Voyage Out* only as a glimpse of potentially
dissident desire in a scene so dislocated that more than one edition of the
novel offers an explanatory footnote.[75] As Rachel and Terence walk
along comparing notes on their experience of happiness, without warning
or explanation "a hand . . . abrupt as iron" knocks Rachel to the ground;
her fragmentary impressions gradually reveal that Helen is "upon her"

rolling her about in tall grasses that whip across Rachel's eyes and fill her mouth and ears: "she was speechless and almost without sense." Recovering her mental equilibrium, Rachel looks up to see, in an almost parodic vision of the cultural hegemony of heterosexuality, "two great heads, the heads of a man and woman, of Terence and Helen": "Broken fragments of speech came down to her on the ground. She thought she heard them speak of love and then of marriage. Raising herself and sitting up, she too realised Helen's soft body, the strong and hospitable arms, and happiness swelling and breaking in one vast wave" (*The Voyage Out*, 268). As in *Melymbrosia*, here too Helen's embrace moves Rachel in a way Terence's kiss does not, but Helen's perspective (and thus her declaration of love) has disappeared altogether, leaving only Rachel's subjectively-rendered experience of confusion, which distorts potentially errant desires almost beyond recognition. As if confirming Rachel's re-entry into the narrative of heterosexual love and marriage that Helen and Terence seem to break over her like an egg, the paragraphs immediately following the engagement show Rachel beginning to follow Terence's lead, "stopping where he stopped, turning where he turned, ignorant of the way, ignorant why he stopped or why he turned" (ibid., 258). The process of normalization is complete by the time they follow Mr. Flushing into the native village, "falling into line" in his wake (ibid., 268).

Undoubtedly the partial erasure of Rachel and Helen's erotic entanglement exemplifies what DeSalvo has described as Woolf's retreat from self-revelation in revision. But it is worth bearing in mind that this awkward rebinding of errant desire was written only after Woolf read Leonard's account of how wild women are tamed in the jungle. Consider again in this context the horrifying scene of Hinnihami's comeuppance, a cautionary tale about the fate of those whose desires deviate from communal norms:

> The sight of the bleeding deer and the woman lying on the ground, naked to the waist, seemed to send a wave of lust and cruelty through the men. They tore Hinnihami's cloth from her, and, taking her by her arms, dragged her naked up to the deer.
> "Bring [her] to her child," they shouted. . . . "Is there no milk in your breasts for him now?"
> They held her that she might see what they did. The deer was moaning in pain. One of the men cut a thick stick and struck him upon the hind legs until they were broken. Hinnihami fought and struggled, but she was powerless in their hands. At length, when they had become tired of torturing them, they threw her down by the deer's side and went away. (*The Village in the Jungle*, 83)

Stripping her naked in a moment of cruel lust, the "jeering knot of men" re-establishes the sexual dominance visited on Hinnihami by Punchirala, the father of her child, and reclaims her body for "normal" motherhood. Though none of the pressures on Rachel's body match the violence of this scene, Woolf's revision of Rachel's encounter with Helen reads as if it were written to pre-empt just such a "correction." In light of these revisions, Rachel's frustration earlier in *The Voyage Out*, when she feels the weight of worldly conventions repressing her body, reads like a complaint against Woolf, who gives Rachel more discernment than power.

In her revisions of the ensuing scene in the village, which the tourists enter right after Helen wrestles Rachel to the ground, Woolf again introduces a sense of the overwhelming power of the normative. In *Melymbrosia* the scene goes by quickly. Barely two pages, the chapter devotes as much attention to Mr. Flushing's negotiations for native goods as it does to Rachel's response to the women who carry the goods back and forth for Flushing's inspection. The opening paragraph sets the scene: "The Indian women were squatting at the doors of their huts making baskets and did not stir from their triangular position when the strangers arrived though their long narrow eyes slid round and fixed upon them. As no one except Mr Flushing could speak to them the silent stare had to be continued" (*Melymbrosia*, 211). As the English move past peering into the natives' huts, "eyes seemed to follow them without hostility but without great interest." Rachel feels that her newfound intimacy with Terence ought to enable her "to understand their faces," but she is forced to own that "she knew nothing about them" and her happiness is "dashed" (ibid., 211, 212). After a paragraph describing Flushing's efforts to buy some artifacts, Terence asks Rachel why she is sad and is told, "Because it makes us seem small." But Rachel immediately retreats from this feeling by adding: "But what I have in my heart is as great as anything in the world" (ibid., 212). The chapter ends with Rachel overwhelmed by the intensity of her love for Terence and they embrace, sobbing.

Unremarkable in *Melymbrosia*, in *The Voyage Out* the scene becomes highly charged and more than doubles in length. Most striking is the intensity newly attributed to the stare of the native women. After the English look "for a moment undiscovered," their bodies fall under the women's unrelenting gaze:

> Their hands paused for a moment and their long narrow eyes slid round and fixed upon them with the motionless inexpressive gaze of those removed from each other far far beyond the plunge of speech. Their hands moved again, but the stare continued. It followed them as they walked, as they peered into huts where they could distinguish guns leaning in the corner, and bowls upon the floor, and stacks of rushes; in the dusk the solemn eyes of babies regarded them,

and old women stared out too. As they sauntered about, the stare followed them, passing over their legs, their bodies, their heads, curiously, not without hostility, like the crawl of a winter fly. As she drew apart her shawl and uncovered her breast to the lips of her baby, the eyes of a woman never left their faces, although they moved uneasily under her stare, and finally turned away, rather than stand there looking at her any longer. (*The Voyage Out*, 269)

The steady stare is commonplace in European accounts of "primitive" peoples. In *Women in Love*, for instance, D. H. Lawrence draws on a common lexicon when the narrator invokes the "unwearying stare of aborigines" to describe the downtrodden wives of miners.[76] But in *The Voyage Out* the trope is unusually charged and unnerving. Regarded "without hostility" in *Melymbrosia*, here the English are watched "*not* without hostility." In response Hirst feels bitter, unhappy, and alone; Helen, perhaps roused into maternal solicitude by the nursing mother, experiences "presentiments of disaster" (ibid., 270). Rachel and Terence, having felt at first that the women were "peaceful, and even beautiful," now feel "very cold and melancholy" (ibid., 269). Woolf's emphasis on staring and the dread of falling under scrutiny, which she greatly amplified in revision, derives in part from her response to Leonard's narrative omniscience in *The Village in the Jungle*. But the vivid intensity of the staring in Virginia's native village also has roots in specific passages.

As she searches for her husband, for example, Punchi Menika suffers under the unsettling stare of villagers:

The stream of passers-by upon the road, the unknown faces and the eyes that always stared strangely, inquiringly at her for a moment, and had then passed on for ever, made her feel vaguely how utterly alone she was in the world. And nowhere was this feeling so strong for her as in the villages where she slunk through like a frightened jackal. Everywhere it was the same; the crowd of villagers and travellers staring at her from in front of the village boutique, the group of women gossiping and laughing round the well in the paddy field— not a known face among them all. (*The Village in the Jungle*, 171)

Here is the link between staring and the intense experience of alienation that the English feel in *The Voyage Out*. The specific form of Rachel's melancholy response to the stare also can be traced to *The Village in the Jungle*. Before Punchi Menika leaves to find her husband, she looks into the face of the woman who raised her, Karlinahami:

The jungle had left its mark on her. Her body was bent and twisted, like the stunted trees, which the south-west wind had tortured into grotesque shapes. The skin, too, on her face and thin limbs reminded one of the bark of the jungle trees; it was shrunken against the bones, and wrinkled, and here and there flaking off into whitish brown scales, as the bark flakes off the kumbuk-trees. . . . And under the lined forehead were the eyes, lifeless and filmy, peering out of innumerable wrinkles. The eyes were not blind, but they seemed to be sightless—the pupil, the iris, and even the white had merged—because the mind was dying. It is what usually happens in the jungle—to women especially—the mind dies before the body. Imperceptibly the power of initiative, of thought, of feeling, dies out before the monotony of life, the monotony of the tearing hot wind, the monotony of endless trees, the monotony of perpetual hardship. (ibid., 166)

This passage, which joins the staring to the tree imagery I have discussed, offers insight into what bothers Rachel so much about the women in *The Voyage Out*: specular doubles for her own future as a wife, they bring home to her the pressures of domestication and normalization against which she has been struggling ever since she left England for South America. The theme of unwanted scrutiny appears in the same context in a long scene, canceled from the later typescript, in which Rachel and Terence, "sounding very much more like Leonard and Virginia," discuss the experience of speaking with Mrs. Thornbury and others about their engagement (Heine, "Virginia Woolf's Revisions," 443). Terence remarks: "Well, Rachel, that wasn't so very dreadful was it?—the eyes of all those women?" (quoted in Heine, "Virginia Woolf's Revisions," 443).

Finally, in response to *The Village in the Jungle* Woolf also alters the words that Rachel and Terence exchange after wilting under the stare of the native women. Where in *Melymbrosia* Rachel comments on how small the women make her feel, in *The Voyage Out* that sentiment is attributed to Terence, and her revised remark to him echoes "the monotony of the tearing hot wind, the monotony of endless trees" in Leonard's jungle: "So it would go on for ever and ever, she said, those women sitting under the trees, the trees and the river" (*The Voyage Out*, 270). In the intertextual logic I have traced, to sit forever under the trees is to risk turning into a tree, as Karlinahami essentially does. No wonder that before leaving the native women far behind Rachel and Terence feel the need "to assure each other once more that they [are] in love, [are] happy, [are] content" (ibid., 270).

Turning into a tree hints at two ultimate fates. One is suggested by Mrs. Thornbury, an emblem of motherhood as loss of self, who reminds Terence of "a large old tree murmuring in the moonlight, or a river going on and on and on" (ibid., 278). Her long life and children seem to Rachel, remembering Terence's words, "to have rubbed away the marks of individuality, and to have left only what was old and maternal" (ibid., 301). The second fate complements the first: in an ironic revision of

Daphne's flight from Apollo, to become a tree is to be absorbed into the phallic power that holds such ambivalent fascination for Rachel.

This ambivalence, sharpened by Woolf's response to Leonard, also enters into her engagement with the Edwardian culture of exhibition. Woolf's decision to stage her encounter with Leonard's jungle as a scene of exhibition adds another layer of complexity to the palimpsest of *The Voyage Out*. For if *The Village in the Jungle* underscores the imbalance of power that underwrites colonial supervision, *The Voyage Out* both reproduces the dynamic and undermines it. In Rachel's response to the native women, issues of gender and sexuality implicit throughout the novel come to the foreground and are mapped onto race. But if Rachel's encounter recalls the Dahomey Village in London's Imperial International Exhibition, the scene both challenges and reinforces the racial hierarchies that such exhibitions were designed to promote.

Destabilizing the Ethnographic Frame and the Returned Stare

In Tony Bennett's account, as exhibition spectators watch one another watch the spectacle, they become a self-regulating crowd that consolidates its national identity through their mutual regard (*Rise of the Museum*, 69). But the extended description of Rachel, Terence, Hirst, Helen, and the Flushings entering the village does not suggest English superiority to the "soft instinctive people" on display but a breakdown of boundaries between English subject and native object. Indeed, far from reinforcing a sense of racial and cultural superiority, Woolf's exhibition unnerves her central characters.

The blurring of boundaries begins with confusing pronoun references that Woolf introduced in revision. In a previously quoted sentence describing the reciprocal staring—"As she drew apart her shawl and uncovered her breast to the lips of her baby, the eyes of a woman never left their faces, although they moved uneasily under her stare, and finally turned away, rather than stand there looking at her any longer" (*The Voyage Out*, 269)—"they" momentarily seems to refer back to "the eyes" of the native woman rather than to the strolling tourists. In the next sentence— "When sweetmeats were offered them, they put out great red hands to take them, and felt themselves treading cumbrously like tight-coated soldiers among these soft instinctive people"—the "great red hands" seem to belong to natives who reach out to accept English confections, but the next clause reverses the relation by identifying those receiving the sweetmeats as the tourists, "treading cumbrously like tight-coated soldiers."[77]

Mr. Flushing literalizes the breakdown of the frame by entering the clearing, where the contrast between his body and the conventional majesty of the noble savage makes the Englishman part of the spectacle. (Soon afterwards Flushing and his wife acknowledge another blurring of boundaries when they question whether the artifacts they bought from the natives do not show "signs here and there of European influence" [ibid., 270].) Eventually the rest of the party joins Flushing within the frame and is "absorbed" into the life of the village (ibid., 269). For all but the Flushings, who remain impervious to introspection, their absorption into the village coupled with the intensity of the returned gaze proves deeply unsettling.

Yet Rachel's positioning within the scene of exhibition complicates Woolf's apparent critique of the imperial hierarchy that normally would preserve European privilege. On one hand, insofar as the narrative equates Rachel and the native women, patriarchal and colonial oppression coincide to produce a feminist critique of colonialism. On the other hand, by transforming the native women into a mere backdrop for Rachel's inner drama, Woolf partially reproduces the imperial hierarchy the novel otherwise attacks. These claims require more detailed attention.

Woolf clearly indicates that the gender politics informing Rachel's life also govern the native village. The women's "plaiting of straw," for instance, both echoes Austen's "tight plait" and anticipates a related image when Terence reads aloud Milton's marriage masque, *Comus*: the water nymph "sitting / Under the glassy cool translucent wave, / in *twisted braids* of lilies knitting / the loose train" of her hair (ibid., 311) gives Rachel the headache that portends her protracted death over the last three chapters of the novel. As water laps at the foot of Rachel's bed during her first day of fever, these lines haunt her, suggesting both the symbolic threat of Milton (author of the first domestic epic) and the more immediate threat of domestic life with Terence. Before the engagement Evelyn says approvingly that there's "something of a woman" in Terence (ibid., 234), but afterwards he tries to silence Rachel's music by suggesting that her playing of a Beethoven sonata resembles "an unfortunate old dog going round on its hind legs in the rain" (ibid., 276). Similar gender politics operate in the native village. In *Melymbrosia* the native women carry goods back and forth to Mr. Flushing; but when Mr. Flushing moves into the clearing to conduct business in *The Voyage Out*, the native women remain literally and figuratively at the periphery. The implied structural parallel between Rachel and the native women suggests an equality in subjection.[78]

But the scene of exhibition also positions Rachel and her fellow travelers as involuntary agents of the dominant powers to which Rachel typically feels subjected. Clearly accustomed to the European stare, the women are just one more stop on a well-trodden path. When Hirst sees deer bounding away from the riverbank as they approach the native village, he laments having left his Kodak behind, even though his camera would simply literalize the framing power the tourists already possess. Even Rachel's identification with the women implies a reassertion of her hierarchical advantage. Intuiting her affinities with them, Rachel begins to see herself as a woman destined to have a child at her breast and a sewing kit on her lap. As her vision of eternal stasis maps her married future onto the colonized—"So it would go on for ever and ever, she said, those women sitting under the trees, the trees and the river" (ibid., 270)—Rachel transforms the women into a colonial-domestic hallucination.

As both resistant bodies and projections, the native women occupy a curiously contradictory place in the logic of the narrative. The unsettling force of their stare renders them semiautonomous beings, subject to but not wholly dominated by the tourists who gaze at the human showcase. But as emblems of female abjection and the normalization of desire, they merge, like Karlinahami, into the cycles of nature. Rachel thus becomes not only the colonized woman subject to the framing power of English patriarchy but also the colonizing woman with a monopoly on the power of articulation: while Rachel formulates them with a phrase, the "motionless inexpressive" women remain "removed from each other far far beyond the plunge of speech." At once the photographer and the photographed, Rachel is implicated, even as she turns away, in a form of power she cannot escape.

Such unresolved tensions in *The Voyage Out* help to make visible comparable moments in colonial postcards. Woolf's interest in the interplay between the represented and the representer and between the representation and the spectator emerges distinctly in an earlier description of a photograph of Rachel's dead mother: "The need of sitting absolutely still before a Cockney photographer had given her lips a queer little pucker, and her eyes for the same reason looked as though she thought the whole situation ridiculous" (ibid., 75–76). The women in colonial postcards can also seem to transgress the boundaries of the frame, particularly when the returned stare, "not without hostility," expresses a distinct sense of the model's dismay over her enforced pose. Consider again some of the postcards discussed earlier. In "The Toilet: Zulu Girls" (figure 2.6) the apprehensive yet sullen stare of the woman made to stage her toilet for the camera radiates resentment toward the viewer peering in over the photographer's shoulder. Faced with such a look, one can understand the discomfort of Helen, who blames the Flushings "for having come on this expedition, for having ventured too far and exposed themselves" (ibid., 270). Although Helen never explains the precise nature of this exposure, she evidently feels they have all become vulnerable simply by opening themselves to the hostile stare of the women. Viewed in this light, the Boran beauty photographed in Kenya (figure 2.5) can be seen to challenge the alibi, at once aesthetic and ethnographic, that would otherwise remove her from the politics inform-ing the shot: her braceleted wrists pressed together and her sad counte-nance begin to suggest a handcuffed captive trapped by the power rela-tions that placed her before the camera. More militant, the "Bella India" of Peru (figure 2.7) defies the scopic regime of colonialism with an accu-satory stare that demands reciprocal exposure.[79]

With the benefit of hindsight, one can read the penetrating gaze re-turned in such cards in complementary ways: as signs of the resistance that would ultimately culminate in rebellious new nationalisms, and as harbingers of a modernism that would return Woolf to the mothers she refuses here. The imperial reading accords with Woolf's fantasy of the end of empire at Wembley as she watches the rain whip through the ex-hibition grounds. In both cases, carefully arranged scenes become self-subverting when elements refuse to remain neatly in the frame: the sky will not lie back "limp" and "acquiescent" at the fair grounds; the flicker of independent subjectivity in the eyes of native women disrupts colonialism's aestheticizing of its own power. The complementary read-ing opens onto the place of the maternal in Woolf's modernism and, ulti-mately, onto the question of "female modernism" more generally. The two remaining sections of this chapter take up these two anticipatory readings in order to locate Woolf's modernism in relation to the struggle with everyday life she dramatizes in Rachel.

EMPIRE, RACE, AND THE EMANCIPATION OF WOMEN

To return to the question with which I began: can an Englishwoman col-onized under patriarchy avoid becoming a colonizer in her turn? The an-swer returned by The Voyage Out, unlike any other in Woolf, turns on the way Rachel's complex positioning within the novel's climactic scene of exhibition illuminates a critical hesitation in Woolf's understanding of race. Insofar as the unstable relation between autonomous beings and hallucinatory projections places Woolf's novel and the postcards in a mutually illuminating relationship, this instability is critically produc-tive: the postcards highlight the pressure of normalization within Woolf's representation of the native women even as their challenging stare breaks through the Orientalism of the postcards, now seen to antic-ipate a postcolonial desire to shatter the frame.

It would be easy to criticize Woolf for a form of "white solipsism" that "passively colludes with a racist culture."[80] Certainly one would be

hard pressed to find in her fiction any of the cross-racial masquerades
that criticism over the last decade has linked to the emergence of Anglo-
American modernism.[81] Indeed, if the dubious image of Woolf in black
face during the Dreadnought hoax is any gauge, racial masquerade for
her was simply a masquerade, a prank rather than a strategic racial
repositioning in relation to dominant society.[82] But the singularity of her
treatment of race in *The Voyage Out*—the way in which it strains
against racial self-enclosure—emerges distinctly against the background
of her later writing. In a 1925 diary entry Woolf describes giving a bis-
cuit to a little girl who reminds her of herself; moments later she looks
down from a bus at "a nigger gentleman, perfectly fitted out in swallow
tail & bowler & gold headed cane." Clearly he is as improbable for
Woolf as the Zulu Masher must have been for its intended audience (figure 2.4). "What were his thoughts?" Woolf wonders. Her speculative response charts a racial gulf. Was he thinking, she muses, of "the degradation stamped on him, every time he raised his hand & saw it black as a
monkeys outside, tinged with flesh colour within?" (*Diary* 3:23).
Woolf's ability to imagine other minds in this entry clearly turns more on
race than on gender, and the stark dichotomy between the opacity of the
black man and the transparency of the white girl throws into relief the
relative complexity of *The Voyage Out*, which remains suspended between imperial objectification and intimations of an equivalent center
of self.[83]

The singularity of *The Voyage Out* can be further clarified in relation
to a little-discussed moment in *A Room of One's Own* (1929). Following
her famous discussion of Shakespeare's martyred sister, Woolf turns to
women's historical need to remain chaste, where chastity refers to the
preservation of anonymity as a defense against a public life dominated by
men. The idea of chastity already looks back to *The Voyage Out*, in
which Rachel's death can be construed as an attempt to remain chaste, a
point underlined by Woolf's use of *Comus*. But a racially grounded connection between *The Voyage Out* and *A Room of One's Own* becomes
more striking when Woolf explains how women differ from men: men
have a need for publicity and ownership—of a passing woman, a dog, "a
piece of land or a man with curly black hair. It is one of the great advantages of being a woman that one can pass even a very fine negress without
wishing to make an Englishwoman of her" (*A Room of One's Own*, 52).

However ironic the tone or humorous the intent (and the word "even"
implies a familiar Bloomsbury archness), this last sentence clearly replays the key scene in Woolf's native village. In both cases, a mobile
white woman passes by a motionless black woman who becomes a passive object of the white woman's purportedly benign gaze, and race provides a way to think gender. In *A Room of One's Own* the silent black

body serves simultaneously to define the relative emancipation of white women while absolving them of the guilt of colonialism: *men* want to own the "negress" by assimilating her, women do not. Woolf returns to this blunt disavowal in *Three Guineas'* vision of an Outsider's Society of women who would shun "all such ceremonies as encourage the desire to impose 'our' civilization or 'our' dominion upon other people" (*Three Guineas*, 109). In *The Voyage Out*, Rachel, like Woolf, discovers her identity as a woman by measuring herself against a racial other. Passing by, she discovers not her freedom but her constraint.

Killing Rachel off, Woolf responds to Rachel's resistance to becoming both subject and object of imperialism by removing her from a dichotomy that is fundamental to all forms of hierarchy. Woolf's later efforts to collapse subject-object relations, most explicitly in *To the Lighthouse* (1927), remain on the plane of philosophy and aesthetic expression, perhaps because her first effort to work through the distinction in the context of race, patriarchy, and empire ends in a dispiriting reassertion of oppressive norms. Ironically, it is Helen, Rachel's would-be mentor, who sees most clearly into the cultural claustrophobia she unwittingly heightens: "It seemed to [Helen] that a moment's respite was allowed . . . and then again the profound and reasonless law asserted itself, moulding them all to its liking" (*The Voyage Out*, 249). In *The Voyage Out* Woolf proposes multiple candidates for the reasonless law: imperialism, patriarchy, capitalism, heteronormativity, and their tendency, within the matrix of integration propaganda, to reinforce one another. When Hirst settles back comfortably to watch "the pattern build itself up" after Rachel's death, "pattern" evokes an almost paranoid vision of cultural and political interconnection (ibid., 352). The circulation of picture postcards, linking the Thames to the waters of the Amazon, operates as a metonymy for this dystopian consolidation, one in which the world is constituted, as Richard Dalloway would have it, as England's object.

It would be easy to dismiss Woolf's analogy between the bodies of European and third world women in *The Voyage Out*, not to mention her suggestion that Helen's "profound and reasonless law" can sum up everything from globalization to the shaping power of sexual norms. Yet it is this vision of overdetermined global domestication that pushes Woolf toward her most provocative encounter with imperial propaganda. For even as the rest of the novel discounts the possibility of stepping beyond one's own culture, Woolf struggles to find a way for Rachel to identify with the native women without finding herself complicit in their subjection. Although Woolf's use of race as a stage on which to understand gender partially reproduces colonial ideology by remaking the natives in Rachel's image, the faint acknowledgment of the native women's perspective in the momentary glimpse of the tourists as "tight-coated soldiers" keeps her from becoming a subtler version of Evelyn, who imagines herself a great captain "sent to colonise the world" (ibid., 250). That trace of autonomous subjectivity also suggests Woolf's desire to grasp what she fails to imagine in her diary entry and her subsequent fiction: an acknowledgment of racial difference that remains untainted by hierarchy.[84] It seems that what Woolf wants to effect in the native village but cannot is a suspension of imperial ideology in the act of representing it, or what Louis Althusser called the "internal distanciation" of ideology. Instead, she ends up creating a world in which only death can release Rachel from the bind of either stepping into a picture postcard or snapping one.

But as many have noted, Rachel's failure betokens Woolf's success. If Rachel's conflicted relation to the native women traps her in a fundamentally imperial epistemology, it also adumbrates the complex place of the maternal in Woolf's career. Indeed, it is this ambivalence that makes *The Voyage Out* a key text for understanding how Woolf's modernism develops in response to the masculine bias of integration propaganda.

FROM MALE PROPAGANDA TO FEMALE MODERNISM

"Female modernism" is a vague term that nevertheless remains indispensable.[85] For some it refers to the recovery of women writers obscured by the canonization of male modernists, Wyndham Lewis's Men of 1914: Joyce, Eliot, Pound, and Lewis himself.[86] Sandra M. Gilbert and Susan Gubar's influential three-volume overview of the woman writer in the twentieth century, *No Man's Land*, falls largely in this category by understanding "male modernism" as a cultural strategy for retarding the social and literary progress of women and by showing how female writers have contested forms of aesthetic containment deployed by male writers.[87] Bonnie Kime Scott's *Refiguring Modernism* contributes to the project of restoring women's place in modernist culture by proposing the (female) trope of the web as a supplement to the (male) master trope of modernist "scaffolding" in order to restore a network of relations that brings to the fore the "Women of 1928": Djuna Barnes, Rebecca West, and Virginia Woolf.[88] Another approach understands female modernism to refer to the notion that some forms of modernist innovation, irrespective of the gender of the writer, may have progressive, antipatriarchal implications. The most radical version of this approach posits a principle of femaleness as fundamental to modernism and argues that modernism's various subversions of received models—for instance, of selfhood, signification, hierarchy, and epistemology—are cognate with what Hélène Cixous and other feminist theorists have called "*écriture féminine.*"[89] This intrinsically feminist model of modernism has been most influentially advanced by Julia

Kristeva, who understands linguistic fragmentation in modernism as a subversion of male mastery.[90]

Marianne Dekoven, who takes the relationship between *Heart of Darkness* and *The Voyage Out* as an exemplary case, bridges the differences among these competing understandings of female modernism by arguing that modernism evolved as it did to offer adequate representations of the "terrifying appeal" of turn-of-the-century feminism and socialism.[91] My understanding of female modernism harmonizes with Dekoven's in that I too attempt to synthesize potentially divergent approaches, but where Dekoven ultimately turns to a poststructuralist model of modernism, I attend more closely to the shaping power of integration propaganda and to the tangle of interpersonal and intertextual relations that informs literary production. According to Dekoven, the reassertion of the repressed maternal in modernist literature contributes to the subversion of prevailing social hierarchies by deconstructing binary oppositions. My interpretation coincides at many points with Dekoven's reading of Conrad and Woolf, particularly with her claim that both *Heart of Darkness* and *The Voyage Out*, despite their provisional deconstructions of patriarchy, ultimately reinstate "the patriarchal maternal" (Dekoven, *Rich and Strange*, 138), a maternal principle not yet strong enough to commit to an expression of its difference. But the recovery of *The Village in the Jungle*'s role in Woolf's revisions reveals three things: the crosscurrents of desire that motivate and shape specific literary debts in *The Voyage Out*; the degree to which violence against the mother is part of the process of undoing subordination to the father; and the importance of the scene upriver in the development of Woolf's modernism.

Rachel's encounter with the women in the native village, which Dekoven reads as a last glimpse of a positive figuration of the maternal (ibid., 125), is better understood as a culminating instance of the kind of disconnected connection Rachel has felt with mother figures throughout the novel. Rachel, whose own mother is dead, sometimes gives in to a furious need to distance herself from her nearest mother surrogate, Helen, and when she sees a photograph of an acquaintance's mother, she remarks: "Well, I don't much believe in her" (*The Voyage Out*, 237).[92] This alienation from a mother she cannot ignore becomes palpable as Rachel stands face to face with the women in the village. Being situated "far far beyond the plunge of speech," as the native women are, might, in the logic of the novel, be a good thing, particularly given the suspicion toward language Rachel voices when discussing the relative virtues of words and music with Terence. Indeed, in psychoanalytic terms the native woman nursing her child to the rhythms of nature suggests the pre-Oedipal bond between mother and child, and the violence implicit in the "plunge of speech" suggests the alienating power of the symbolic order. Yet in *The Voyage Out* the presymbolic bond between mother and child, idealized in psychoanalytic theory as a refuge of wordless connectedness, is tainted. For bonding with Helen would mean joining with a male-identified woman who is revealed as an agent of patriarchy well before she stands with Terence over Rachel's newly betrothed body. Inasmuch as in her later career Woolf would draw on the rhythms of the pre-Oedipal, this highly charged scene holds out the promise of an enabling, rather than a fatal, identification with the mother.[93] But these women, silent as trees, come from Leonard's jungle, and to think through them is not to tap into the flow of female vitality Woolf would posit in *A Room of One's Own* but to enter into the living death of Karlinahami.

Remote from the English tourists and also "removed from each other," these women, then, are not positive representatives of a "pre-oedipal sanctuary of semiotic utterance"[94] but symbols of the mothers that Rachel must reject and Woolf, as she would argue in "Professions for Women," must destroy. Woolf felt that to become a writer she had to dispatch "The Angel in the House," a figure adapted from the Coventry Patmore poem and aptly described in a draft of her 1931 talk as "the woman that men wished women to be": "I turned upon her and caught her by the throat. I did my best to kill her."[95] Woolf pleads self-defense: "Had I not killed her she would have killed me" ("Professions for Women," 238). During Rachel's delirium, the portion of the novel that always threatened to push Woolf over the edge into madness, Rachel too comes face to face with a dangerous older woman. The "old woman with the knife," who surfaces in her fever right after she sees an un-named "they" "rolling off the edge of the hill" (*The Voyage Out*, 314), embodies several figures from earlier in the narrative: an old woman Rachel sees at the hotel cutting off a chicken's head and the sight, upsetting to her, of Arthur Venning and Susan rolling on the ground together during the picnic. The old woman in her dream clearly represents Rachel's anxiety about heterosexuality, domesticity, and marriage. But she also represents more.

When the old woman resurfaces after Terence has kissed Rachel, Rachel does not imagine the woman as a threat to herself: she sees "an old woman slicing a man's head off with a knife" (ibid., 320). Why a man? A psychoanalytic perspective would suggest displaced hostility toward Terence (and Leonard), but this iteration of the old woman also leads back to the woman writer's need to kill the angel in the house. In her 1925 essay on Austen, Woolf comments on the "divine justice" Austen metes out to characters such as Dr. Grant in *Mansfield Park* (1814): "Sometimes it seems as if her creatures were born merely to give Jane Austen the supreme delight of slicing their heads off" ("Jane Austen," *Common*

Reader, 140). Similarly, the old woman at the hotel cuts off the chicken's head "with an expression of vindictive energy and triumph combined" (*The Voyage Out*, 239). The old woman in Rachel's delirium not only expresses a fear of heterosexuality and its social institutions, then, but prefigures the "phantom" in "Professions for Women" who will kill or be killed. In other words, the restoration of the patriarchal maternal that in Dekoven's reading suspends *The Voyage Out* between the old and the new is driven in part by a desire to slay the mother. In *The Voyage Out* Woolf allows Austen to kill Rachel so that she herself can kill Austen.

It is thus fitting that Rachel's delirium produces some of Woolf's most experimental writing in *The Voyage Out*. Lying outside the constraints of plot, linearity, and conscious rationality, the passages evoking her hallucinations and dreams monitor only the flow of Rachel's unconscious; they struggle to articulate her "unknown and uncircumscribed spirit, whatever aberration or complexity it may display" ("Modern Fiction," *Common Reader*, 150). Woolf later recognized that if *The Voyage Out* was "too loose" in form, her next novel, *Night and Day*, was "too tight"—too like the "tight plait" Rachel dislikes in Austen (*Letters*, 2:400). In a 1912 letter about the future of the novel, Woolf tries to explain to a fellow writer what "we, in our generation" must do: "renounce finally the achievement of the greater beauty: the beauty which comes from completeness, in such books as War and Peace, and Stendhal I suppose, and some of Jane Austen" (*Letters*, 2:599). In preparing to "attack the whole," Woolf talks herself into embracing something like the "fragments" and "splinters" she has disparaged in reference to Joyce. What is the generation to do? It must "break its neck in order that the next may have smooth going" (*Letters*, 2:598–600). Any way you slice it, heads must roll before Woolf can arrive at the "orts, scraps and fragments" of her last novel, *Between the Acts* (188).

As she revised *The Voyage Out*, the emotional cost of identifying with the angels in the hut was brought home to Woolf not only by her decision to marry Leonard but by the way the propaganda of everyday life amplified the pressure of Leonard's text on the embattled subjectivity of her own. But however threatening Leonard's tale of the jungle might have been, its influence on *The Voyage Out* was not, ultimately, inhibiting, nor can their interrelation be reduced to Gilbert and Gubar's model of modernism as a battle between the sexes. Rather, the scene in the jungle that registers both the pressure of Leonard's book and the influence of colonial postcards marks a moment of recognition in which Woolf, through Rachel, realizes the possibility of finding her own voice as a modern writer, able to ground her fiction on her "own feeling and not upon convention" ("Modern Fiction," *Common Reader*, 150). In "Professions for Women," Woolf believes that she has not been able to solve the problem of how to tell "the truth about [her] own experiences as a body" (241), but in *The Voyage Out* she begins the process by anatomizing the pressures that place "the weight of the entire world" on Rachel's body. In the specular relation between Rachel and the native women, where a connection with the mother is denied even as it is formed, a fault line opens to reveal a glimpse into an as-yet-unrealized future. Staring back at the women, Virginia Woolf saw not only the monotony of bourgeois domesticity and the normative vision propagated by picture postcards. Looking through Conrad's trees at Leonard's jungle, she also saw the origins of her own modernism.

Chapter Three

IMPRESSIONISM AND PROPAGANDA:
FORD'S WELLINGTON HOUSE BOOKS
AND *THE GOOD SOLDIER*

LIKE VIRGINIA WOOLF, Ford Madox Ford considered the didacticism of Victorian literature a form of propaganda. In this broad sense, most artists who aspired to become modern identified the newness of their enterprise with a release from Victorianism as cultural propaganda. For Ford, the authorial thumb was too often on the scales, shaping our evaluation of characters; for Woolf, comedy, tragedy, and plot itself were too laden with the past and its blinkered modes of thought and being. But once we look past this broadly shared need to stigmatize the immediate past, modernists negotiated the contested terrain between art and propaganda in very different ways. Fundamentally dissident, Woolf's modernism develops as a response to what Jacques Ellul calls "integration propaganda," the loose constellation of forces and institutions that encourage and secure conformity, in part by soliciting active participation in rituals of political cohesion, in part by normalizing forms of cultural and political reticence. Hence Woolf's commitment in her fiction to life's "irreticences," a word that is peculiarly her own.[1] Ford is a different story, and not only because with Ford we turn to the new species of propaganda-as-information-control that Wellington House innovated in World War I. As garrulous as Ford and his narrators typically are, too much irreticence, as we will see, made him nervous. And if Woolf's modernism is defined against propaganda, Ford's modernism is nearly indistinguishable from his propaganda.

When Ford set out to define literary impressionism in 1914, he was quite clear about what the impressionist must not do: "He must not write propaganda."[2] That task was better left to the propagandist—which Ford himself had probably already become by agreeing to join the government's secret campaign run out of Wellington House. It is possible that when Ford proscribed propaganda in "On Impressionism," he was covering for the fact that he was beginning to write *Between St. Dennis and St. George* (1915) and *When Blood Is Their Argument* (1915) for C.F.G. Masterman, who organized the campaign in September 1914.

Ford insisted that he was not writing propaganda but impressionist comparisons of English, Prussian, and French culture, and both books are notable for their deployment of impressionist techniques that Ford had perfected in *The Good Soldier*, published that same year.[3] But impressionism and propaganda are not, as Ford would have it, mutually exclusive. If Ford's ideal impressionist remains scrupulously aloof while "rendering," not "reporting,"[4] Ford's propaganda books marshal impressions in order to suggest that Prussia and its inhabitants ought to be wiped off the face of earth.

One might be tempted to resolve the apparent contradiction by observing that Ford was a "peddler of suspect anecdotes" or, less sympathetically, a notorious liar.[5] The government enlisted in a secret propaganda campaign a writer who had defiantly announced his contempt for facts a few years earlier in *Ancient Lights*,[6] and his natural tendency to fabricate happily coincided with the injunction to cover his tracks: I'm not writing propaganda—that's what Germans do. But two facts remain. In their winding digressions, anecdotal structure, and personal immediacy, *Between St. Dennis and St. George* and *When Blood Is Their Argument*, dictated to Richard Aldington a few months after Ford finished dictating *The Good Soldier* to Aldington's wife, H. D., read very much like Ford's modernist masterpiece. By leaving the reader with a plausible sense of why French culture might be considered superior to Prussian culture, and why the English would do well to save the former from the latter, they also work pretty well as propaganda.[7] The conjunction of propaganda and modernist style is not in itself surprising, but with Ford grounding his theory of impressionism in a refusal to propagandize even as he writes propaganda grounded in impressionist technique, it becomes possible to tease out a fundamental complicity between the two. Indeed, what Ford means by each term is not as different as one might expect. Understood within the information ecology of early-twentieth-century England, Ford's impressionism and propaganda begin to look like two sides of the same coin.

Michael Levenson has described Ford as an "exemplar of the early development of modernism," owing to his attempt to extend the legacy of "the art of the novel" into "the pre-war critical arena" and his "acute susceptibility to the movements of the age."[8] My argument here is that Ford's exemplary responsiveness also makes him a key figure for studying the problematic entangling of British modernism and propaganda during World War I. Impressionism is not intrinsically propagandistic. Rather, it is highly susceptible to mechanisms of propaganda because the impression, as Ford understands it, is a utopian solution to the same problem of information—what might be called the "dehumanization of fact"—to which propaganda responds. Churned out by the newly dominant popular press and by the bewildering proliferation of specialists and experts clamoring for the public's attention, facts, Ford argues, have been split off from the values that make them significant, and the impression repairs the damage by reinvesting facts with feeling. But by humanizing facts in this way, Ford's impression also includes a dehistoricizing and decontextualizing operation that opens the door to the propagandistic manipulation of the historical record, or impressionist history.

Ford's work for Wellington House exemplifies the originality of the British propaganda campaign, which understood propaganda in just this way—not as matter of spreading lies but as a subtle manipulation of facts in a world in which facts were becoming increasingly unmoored. In this context, Ford's doctrine of impressionism offers a pre-theory of what has come to be called "spin," and his most famous novel, *The Good Soldier*, provides commentary on a form of propaganda whose effects it is in danger of replicating.

FORD AND WELLINGTON HOUSE

The British propaganda campaign was designed in response to perceived shortcomings of the German campaign. Masterman thought that "German methods provided an admirable object lesson in how not to do it,"[9] and in consequence decided that instead of flooding neutral countries with official propaganda from state information services, the British would undertake a secret campaign. Officially called the War Propaganda Bureau, Masterman's organization soon came to be known simply as Wellington House, in part because the name would serve to disguise the state's role in Masterman's publishing enterprise. Eventually Wellington House would become the publishing branch of a much more complex, evolving enterprise, which became the Department of Information (DoI) in 1917 and then the Ministry of Information (MoI) in 1918. Ironically, British techniques proved so successful that Adolph Hitler and Joseph Goebbels reportedly based the Nazi propaganda campaign on the British prototype.[10]

Deciding to eschew blatant deception for the controlled dissemination of facts, to a significant extent the British stuck to the high road during World War I. (The Nazis later turned Britain's effective control of media in the other direction by deciding that lies repeated often enough from multiple sources become as effective as truths.) When Germany expected that the war would be over by late fall in 1914, their propagandists had little compunction about spreading false accounts of damages inflicted or territory gained, and as the war dragged on British counterpropaganda could effectively reply with factual proof to the contrary. After the war, one British propagandist went so far as to say that British officials never circulated "a deliberate untruth" and that "infinite pains were taken to sift information."[11] Given today's political climate, in which governments routinely lie to their citizens, one may be inclined to dismiss such claims as the kind of sanctimonious blather expected in a political memoir. But the distinction between deliberate untruths and well-sifted information is not only valid but important. The notorious Bryce Report on atrocities committed by the German Army during the invasion of Belgium undoubtedly contained untruths, but it is far from clear that the investigating commission knew that it was publishing dubiously partial accounts alongside accurate testimonies. Most historians today would say that the information was poorly sifted. The British also did not engage in so-called black propaganda, that is, the dissemination of false information among the enemy that purports to be from enemy sources, nor did they fabricate atrocity stories.

The point, however, is not to exculpate British propagandists but to clarify the nature of their propaganda. Neither black nor white, it explored various shades of grey. For if the British recognized that effective propaganda should be grounded in facts, they also knew that the flow of information required manipulation, that factual accounts had to be tailored to suit different audiences around the world, and that the power of facts to make an impression varied according to the media through which they were disseminated. On one hand, the novelist John Buchan, who became head of the DoI early in 1917, published two propaganda books on the battle of the Somme that are remarkably judicious in their rhetorical restraint and adherence to fact.[12] Masterman, moreover, often refused to countenance unsubstantiated atrocity stories circulated by the press and strenuously avoided outright fabrications. On the other hand, British officials did not keep their hands entirely clean. The Foreign Office Press Bureau chose not to censor atrocity stories, and when questions were asked in Parliament about especially egregious stories, such as the notorious German corpse factory reported in the *Times*, the government declined to refute what it knew to be false. Wellington House, moreover, published and distributed a collection of political cartoons that included allusions to the fictional *Kadaververwertungsanstalt*.[13] Thus if British officials did not make up atrocity stories, the increasing subordination of facts to spin made it easier for officials to declare their fidelity to facts while also allowing the public to believe that Germans at the front were boiling down the corpses of their own dead to extract glycerin.

As I argued in the introduction, Mary Poovey's notion of "the modern fact" helps illuminate the unarticulated epistemological underpinnings of the British campaign.[14] Exploiting the internal bifurcation of modern facts—that is, their tautological relation to theories that both generate and depend on them—propaganda deploys the factual as a form of rhetoric unconstrained by its putative empirical grounding. The Bryce Report provides a perfect instance of how propaganda can exploit the apparent neutrality of facts to bolster a highly partial (in all senses) account of historical truth. The Bryce Report is crucial for three reasons: first, it exemplifies the efficiency of the British media campaign; second, it established one of the dominant propaganda myths of World War I: English civilization was fighting a war against German barbarism; and third, it reveals how factuality was being detached from empirical grounding and transformed into a form of rhetoric. Soon after the German army marched into Belgium on August 4, atrocity stories began to appear in the press. Belgian women were said to have been raped in the streets, children's hands cut off, and citizens massacred, burned, and buried alive. Also reported were stories of atrocities committed by Belgian citizens: German soldiers had their eyes gouged out, German women and children living in Belgium were shot down in cold blood, German patients were turned out of hospitals.[15] Despite the skepticism with which early reports were met, the stories of German atrocities ultimately carried the day because Lord Bryce's *Report of the Committee on Alleged German Outrages*, which Wellington House translated into thirty languages and sent around the world, overwhelmed German publicity. The report also bore all the signs of detached objectivity. Its introduction insists that all the depositions taken from Belgian and English soldiers were "tested" and the dubious ones rejected: "though taken at different places and on different dates, and by different lawyers from different witnesses, they often corroborate each other in a striking manner."[16] Along with depositions, the three-hundred-page appendix includes excerpts from the diaries of German soldiers, together with ten photographs of sample pages. Viscount Bryce himself, recipient of honorary degrees from German universities and popular former ambassador to the United States, was convinced that German soldiers had systematically engaged in war crimes against the Belgian people (Reid, *Atrocity Propaganda*, 203–4).

And yet the Bryce Report is filled with exaggerations, misstatements, and probably some outright fabrications. The depositions corroborate one another because they were taken from Belgian refugees in England who had had plenty of time to trade stories; the committee never went to Belgium and never interviewed *anyone* face to face. The diary entries in the appendix, moreover, do not actually corroborate any of the notorious atrocities, though they do record the usual business of war, including looting and the execution of Belgian citizens. The Germans admitted that their strategy was to shorten the war by advancing through Belgium with extreme ruthlessness, but when a Belgian commission investigated in 1922, none of the gruesome reports of torture or mutilation could be substantiated. Thus if the report often gets the facts right, its apparatus of objectivity frames the facts misleadingly, and insofar as some Belgians deliberately fabricated atrocity stories out of patriotic motives, it lends erroneous tales the authority of fact. Circulating throughout the world, the Bryce Report made mutilated Belgian children as real as the actual brutalities the Germans committed. An official government document, the Bryce Report was advertised as such, but Wellington House's efforts to ensure that other publications, such as Ford's books, bore no trace of their state sponsorship heightened the rhetorical power of their factual underpinnings. Well-known authors writing for Wellington House, including Arthur Conan Doyle, Arnold Toynbee, and Mrs. Humphrey Ward, published their books and pamphlets through commercial and university presses that were subsidized by the government through secret funds, and the publications were sent abroad to influential individuals accompanied by letters of recommendation from well-known British intellectuals, academics, and journalists, as if from one private citizen to another.

Ford was not among those in attendance when Masterman first invited England's most influential men of letters to his Wellington House office on September 2, 1914.[17] Even though a close friend of Masterman, he probably was not invited. Half-German by birth, Ford was already suspect in some circles as not being a true Englishman.[18] A few years earlier he had actually labored to present himself as a German in order to claim citizenship and prepare the ground for a German divorce from his wife, Elsie: "For, after all," Ford wrote in *The Desirable Alien at Home in Germany* (1913), "[Germany] is my beloved country."[19] The attempt backfired, deepening the existing scandal surrounding his affair with Violet Hunt, and later causing M.I.5 to investigate Ford's citizenship.[20] Nor did Ford help himself when, several weeks after the war broke out, he wrote in his weekly column for the current affairs journal *Outlook* that he deplored the violent language of nationalism in the press and hoped that his fellow countrymen might revive the "old-fashioned" and "honourable" phrase "the gallant enemy" to describe Germany. His editor felt obliged to disavow the sentiment in a footnote: "Gallant is as gallant does. The English may be pardoned not appreciating German "gallantry" as displayed in Belgium and in the North Sea" (*Outlook*, August 29, 1914, 270). Ford was also inclined to blame the war on nationalist propaganda from both sides: "the present war . . . is simply a product of the indefinite, mysterious, and subterranean forces of groups of shady and inscrutable financiers working their wills upon the ignorant, the credulous, the easily swayed electorate" (*Outlook*, August 8, 1914, 175). In any event, Masterman did contact Ford later, and Ford duly offered his assistance. Having decried England's penchant for referring to the enemy as "a mad dog" in *Outlook* (August 29, 1914, 270), he strikes a different note in the propaganda books, in which he claims that "the German nation has to all intents and purposes become . . . a nation of madmen": "I wish Germany did not exist and I hope it will not exist much longer."[21]

Thomas Moser, one of Ford's biographers, has argued that the gratuitous vehemence of Ford's turn against Germany was motivated by a need to reject his German heritage in order to establish his credentials as a genuine Englishman. According to this argument, Ford deferred changing his German family name, Hueffer, to Ford until 1919 only out of pride.[22] Clearly this is part of the truth. In *The Good Soldier* John Dowell's sense that personal identity is always propped on identification with a loved one reflects Ford's own shaky sense of self, and during the war there was enormous pressure to present oneself as a solid citizen—this was a time, after all, when dachshunds were reportedly stoned in the streets of London. (As a younger nation, the United States has always had more faith in the Adamic power of naming: well before the transformation of French fries into freedom fries during the Iraq War, dachshunds became liberty pups, and their owners ate Salisbury steak instead of hamburgers.) Add to this Ford's sense that Germany represented the apotheosis of all the worst trends in Britain, from materialism (capitalism) and collectivism (Fabianism) to the growing power of the state over the individual (liberalism), and it becomes clearer still why Ford would take up the pen against Germany.[23] Indeed, so committed was Ford to ending Germany's threat to Europe that in July 1915, having finished his propaganda books, he enlisted in the army at the age of forty-one and served for several months in France, where an exploding shell knocked him through the air, leaving him with a concussion and (like Christopher Tietjens in *Parade's End*) temporary memory loss. Though he returned to France after hospital treatment, he was invalided home in March 1917 and spent the rest of the war in staff positions on the home front.

But biography alone cannot entirely explain the anti-German vehemence of Ford's propaganda. His experience of war at the front would greatly temper his views, opening them to a broader, more complex sense of international relations, and a more inclusive range of sympathy. As Ford biographer Max Saunders points out, in Ford's recollection of a near-miss from a sniper's bullet in his 1916 essay "A Day of Battle," Ford is able to adopt the perspective of the would-be killer.[24] But with England only having crossed the threshold of a four-year war that would accelerate social and cultural changes Ford already deplored, Ford was not yet the writer who would produce *Parade's End*, a tetralogy that criticizes, often brilliantly, the war he championed in 1915. *Parade's End* might seem the logical place to turn to explore the relation between Ford's fiction and his propaganda. After all, Tietjens's dismay over the way his calculations for the Department of Statistics are distorted for political ends may be read as Ford's mea culpa for his spinning of numbers and facts in the Wellington House books. But *Parade's End*, for all its interest as a war novel, merely thematizes issues of information and propaganda that are part of the formal weave of his earlier writing. Along with careful attention to Ford's stylistic and narrative practices, any account of the propaganda books and *The Good Soldier* must address Ford's analysis of the place of the writer within the media environment of early twentieth-century England. For Ford's understanding of both propaganda and the impression were shaped by his evolving sense of the writer's duty to a society newly flooded with information.

Ford's Critical Writings: Propagating the Impression

When Ford proscribes propaganda in his various writings on impressionism, he is beginning the codification of modernism's preference for showing over telling that Percy Lubbock would enshrine in his influential *The Craft of Fiction* (1921). As Ford later put it in *A Personal Remembrance*, "an author-creator, presenting his narration without passion, may not indulge in the expression of any prejudices or like any one of his characters more than any other" (*Critical Writings*, 69). The injunction not to write propaganda in "On Impressionism" thus refers more to the intrusive moralizing of Victorian novelists than to state-sponsored efforts to organize public opinion. As in Woolf's "The Leaning Tower," moreover, impressionism is valued as an antidote to the cultural propaganda of Victorianism.[25] Consistent with this attitude, in his 1914 study *Henry James*, Ford praises James's novels for rarely giving in to the seductions of dogmatism or the impulse to "propagandise in favour of his particular interpretation" of "any of the things that are properly written with capital letters": "Politics, War, the Lower Classes or Religion."[26]

Yet the distinction between cultural and state propaganda becomes tenuous under closer scrutiny, for Ford's point is that the novelist should resist the temptation to indulge his own opinions not in order to shield readers from those opinions but to ensure that readers share them. The novelist, Ford argues, "must not write rolling periods, the production of which gives him a soothing feeling in his digestive organs or wherever it is. He must write always to satisfy that other fellow—that other fellow who has too clear an intelligence to let his attention be captured or his mind deceived by special pleadings in favour of any given dogma. You must not write so as to improve him . . . and you must not write so as to influence him" (ibid., 54). In *The Good Soldier*, Leonora Ashburnham receives similar advice from her priests when she worries over raising her children Catholic with her Protestant husband Edward: "she would just have to make the best of things, to influence the children when they came, not by propaganda, but by personality."[27] In terms of Ford's aesthetic theory, the Catholic Church is advising Leonora to be an impressionist. For in Ford's paradoxical formulation, if "the Impressionist author is sedulous to avoid letting his personality appear in the course of his book," at the same time "his whole book . . . is merely an expression of his personality" (ibid., 43). We will return to the ramifications of Ford's embrace of this paradox, but for now it is enough to resolve it provisionally by saying that the impressionist presents the world as mediated through his own experience. Whereas naturalists such as Zola or newspaper reviewers aim for scientific objectivity by presenting purely factual accounts, "art must be the expression of an ego," and "the Impressionist gives you his own views, expecting you to draw deductions, since presumably you know the sort of chap he is"; the "ideal critic," accordingly, wants to produce "a frank impression of personality" (ibid., 34, 36).

But if the church's advice to Leonora echoes Ford's distinction between propaganda and personality, the lines already are blurring. Kipling, Ford's example of the artist as propagandist, fails to see that "the business of the imaginative writer is to stir up and thus to sweeten and render wholesome the emotions," not to "set out to attack world problems from the point of view of the journalists' club smoking-room and with the ambitions of a sort of cross between the German Emperor of caricature and a fifth-form public school boy."[28] But Kipling's failure must be one of degree, not kind. Where the propagandist hectors the reader, telling her what to think, the impressionist is more sly. The impressionist solicits the reader's identification by offering vicarious experience of the seemingly immediate; drawn into the impressionist's perspective, the reader momentarily shares his views, but remains free "to draw deductions," since the reader knows "the sort of chap" the impressionist is. Of course the more absorbing the vicarious experience, which is to say the more effective the impressionist, the more likely the reader is to draw the same deductions the writer would, even if those deductions go unstated. Clearly that is what Leonora's priests are counting on. In rhetorical terms, this is persuasion by means of ethos, the same kind of appeal Marlow uses in *Heart of Darkness*: "Of course in this you fellows see more than I could then. You see me, whom you know."[29] But how does the impressionist ensure that the reader will be drawn into an intimate relationship with a trustworthy witness? Or to put it another way, how does the impressionist go about "the business of the imaginative writer," which is "to stir up and thus to sweeten and render wholesome the emotions," so as to make the reader not only see Marlow but see through his eyes? "The Impressionist," Ford writes in "On Impressionism," "must always exaggerate" (ibid., 36). If exaggeration is a key impressionist technique, it is easy to see how propagandists might find impressionists useful.

It is worth pointing out, however, that Conrad's impressionism is not Ford's.[30] Even though Ford took great pains in later life to describe his collaboration with Conrad as their working out a shared theory of impressionism, Conrad disdained the term and referred tellingly to Stephen Crane as a *"only* an impressionist."[31] In Conrad's epistemology, as in Woolf's, facts retain some empirical heft independent of their implication in theories and values. Just as Rezia in *Mrs. Dalloway* finds it "comforting" when a child runs "full tilt into her" and jolts her out of the inwardness that encloses her husband, so the drift of Conradian impressions typically runs aground on what Conrad considers the hard rock of factuality.[32] Thus when fog falls like a white shutter in *Heart of Darkness*, Marlow is right to set anchor: anxious about feeling unmoored, he feels profoundly disoriented and confused, but he knows the fog will lift. For Ford's Dowell, in contrast, the fog never really lifts, and he is left with impressions only. As for facts, he's not really interested in those except insofar as they have a bearing on his story. In Ford's epistemology, fiction attuned to the impression is more true, more accurate than are factual accounts, and the gap between fact and impression, so fundamental to Conrad, does not so much close as disappear within the enveloping authority of impressionism.

Differences between Ford and Conrad notwithstanding, the example of *Heart of Darkness* may suggest a simple means of disentangling Ford's impressionism from his propaganda: *Heart of Darkness*, a notoriously interrogative and ambiguous text, tends to raise questions while propaganda tends to answer them. And yet Noam Chomsky defines propaganda in a way that, as it were, re-unsettles the distinction when he suggests that propaganda operates by substituting one set of questions for another. Thus the issue of government war policy gets displaced by the question of whether one supports the troops required to enact the policy.[33] From this perspective, one can imagine Chinua Achebe, who first raised the issue of racism in *Heart of Darkness*, arguing that the novella operates propagandistically by replacing the issue of colonial oppression with the problematic fate of Kurtz's soul. I do not mean to suggest that this is an adequate account of *Heart of Darkness* but rather to point out that Ford's characteristic emphasis on vicarious experience in impressionism tends to convert political issues into moral ones in a way that distances the overt propagandizing of Kipling even as it enables a more subtle form of propaganda by delimiting the kinds of questions that can be asked.

But the deepest connection between Ford's impressionism and propaganda lies in the relationship between his definition of the impression and his role as a civic intellectual. Readers familiar with Ford mainly through *The Good Soldier* may be surprised to understand how deeply committed he was to assuming an active role in the public sphere. Like Ezra Pound, he was a tireless promoter of other writers, even those whose aesthetic and political commitments were very different from his own. As founding editor of the *English Review* (1908–9), Ford described the journal in typically grandiose terms as having "the definite design of giving imaginative literature a chance in England."[34] Fordian bluster to be sure, but given that under his editorship the *English Review* published, among others, Conrad, Henry James, Yeats, and Pound, and introduced Wyndham Lewis and D. H. Lawrence, Ford can be said to have achieved his goal of intervening in public life as a highly influential cultural broker. His commitment to British culture, moreover, was not purely aesthetic. He regularly published articles on current affairs in *Outlook*, and his editorials in the *English Review* focused on the importance of art to the health of the state. Many of these editorials were later revised and published in book form as *The Critical Attitude* (1911).

Ford's open nostalgia for a coherent moral order in *The Critical Attitude* may initially obscure the degree to which his insights into contemporary life anticipate critiques of the mediated nature of existence that would not become widespread for another decade or so, when the publication of Walter Lippmann's *Public Opinion* (1922) inaugurated modern media studies. But *The Critical Attitude* engages with relations among culture, media, and the state in remarkably prescient terms. In "On the Functions of the Arts in the Republic," the book's second chapter, Ford argues that England, "the country of Accepted Ideas," needs art to restore "a sense of what life is really like" (*Critical Attitude* 33, 26). For Ford, this kind of realism derives not only from freshness of perception but from moral values, and when the state promotes only what is acceptable, not what is true or just, it remains for art to provide citizens with the experience of participating in a meaningful world: "the life we live to-day renders us dependent on the arts for our knowledge of life in a degree that probably never before obtained. We have so many more small contacts with our fellow-men; we have so much less knowledge of how men really live. So that almost every man of normal life to-day has the greater part of his view of the world from vicarious experience" (ibid., 27). This is Ford's intimation of what Walter Lippmann described as a "pseudo-environment" of mediated images suffusing the public sphere in the wake of World War I. Formed by the interactions among widely circulated photographs, popular press stereotypes, and cinematic images, the pseudo-environment creates "pictures in the head" to which individuals respond and on which they base their decisions.[35] More recently, John Thompson, writing about the late twentieth century, has underscored "the double-bind of mediated dependency" that is already implicit in Ford's reflections on the increasingly vicarious quality of interpersonal relations: "the more the process of self-formation is enriched by mediated symbolic forms, the more the self becomes dependent on media systems which lie beyond its control."[36] Sharing Thompson's concern over the potential loss of autonomy for selves decentered within the modern pseudo-environment, Ford is less worried about the increasingly mediated nature of existence—he seems to take for granted that modern urban life makes atomization inevitable—than about the quality of that mediation. Thompson is thinking about telephones, television, film, and the Internet; Ford, as yet hardly aware of film and unconcerned by the telephone, is thinking about popular newspapers, which "combine" with increasingly academic works of reference and popular memoirs to act as "mental anodynes with which the English reader of to-day so persistently drugs himself" (ibid., 63).[37]

It is the surfeit of dry facts produced by this mix that motivates Ford's critique of "a world grown very complicated through the limitless freedom of expression for all creeds and all moralities" (ibid., 27). While Ford's view is distinctly illiberal, his allusions to "freedom of expression" betray a concern less with an individual's right to state his views than with the sheer number of public channels through which these views could now be uttered. He was out of sympathy, in other words, with the Woolfian value of irreticence, but the distinction between rights and their effects matters. Ford undoubtedly preferred a feudal vision in which the reasonable voice of the lord would be heard by attentive underlings, and insofar as easily available information is the lifeblood of democracy, his views are clearly antidemocratic. But Ford was less worried about the rabble gaining a voice than about the incoherence he associated with the sharp increase in the number of voices making themselves heard. Hence his linked allusions to Henry James and Matthew Arnold: "so many small things crave for our attention that it has become almost impossible to see any pattern in the carpet. We may contemplate life steadily to-day: it is impossible to see it whole" (ibid., 28). In this Ford resembles the more democratic E. M. Forster—he was able to summon two cheers, anyway—who uses the same line from Arnold's "To a Friend" as a leitmotif in *Howards End* (1910).

For Ford, not only are there too many sources of information and therefore too much to assimilate; these information flows are divorced from any meditation on value and make moral reflection more difficult. The chief culprit in the decay of public discourse is the increasingly dominant popular press.[38] In a later chapter of *The Critical Attitude*, "The Passing of the Great Figure," Ford muses ambivalently over a vacuum of authority in contemporary affairs caused by the decline of public sages such as Carlyle or Ruskin. Although he clearly feels relief from the oppression of the "school-master endowed with great moral prestige" (ibid., 124), in the absence of such figures public discourse is dominated by the press, which tends "to force the relatively unimportant things, in a perpetually flickering cloud of small claims upon the attention, into the foreground" (ibid., 122). Ford sees the Boer War, the first war fought "since the telegraphic Press was really organized," as pivotal because it "made the fortune of the more frivolous Press" (ibid., 123, 124). The popular press began to fill the mind with "the sharp facets of facts hardly at all related" to such an extent that today "the Englishman is overwhelmed every morning with a white spray of facts" (ibid., 125). Most troubling to Ford is that the turn to factual enumeration has undermined the foundations of citizenship: "Practical politics have become so much a matter of sheer figures that the average man, dreading mathematics almost as much as he dreads an open mind, is reduced, nevertheless, to a state of mind so open that he has abandoned thinking—that he has abandoned even feeling about any public matter at all. His vote at a general election will be influenced by some mysterious catchword, by some accidental happening of the moment or by some private scandal or facial characteristic of the upholder of one or other cause" (ibid., 115). Not only is the capacity for critical thought put to sleep, but perhaps more crucially for Ford the capacity *to feel* in response to "any public matter at all" is disappearing.[39] For if the title of Ford's book, *The Critical Attitude*, and the first chapter, "On the Objection to the Critical Attitude," emphasize the dulling of reason's edge in a nation unwilling to challenge received opinion and a consequent lapse into disengaged passivity, his deeper concern lies with the affective dimension of what he understands as a crisis of information. If facts are to become meaningful to minds that are in effect too full of information ever to close around an issue, they must be reinvested with feeling and restored to human proportion through the agency of the impression. The impression permits one to see life steadily, and see it whole.

It is this aspect of the impression that Michael Levenson misses in his otherwise excellent account of the relation between Ford's impressionism and what he calls Ford's "civic realism."[40] For Levenson, what Ford understands as a social problem in *The Critical Attitude*—the collapse of hierarchies within the babble of contemporary voices and the disintegration of coherence caused by the rise of specialization and the expansion of technical knowledge—also becomes a literary opportunity. Part of what is lost with "the passing of great figures" is widespread moral consensus, and the loss of this shared framework permits the artist "a release from extra-artistic responsibilities" (Levenson, *Genealogy of Modernism*, 54). An artist deprived of the moral consensus that Victorian sages consciously upheld can engage in a guilt-free generational revolt by cultivating a characteristically modernist region of willed innocence, for if moral generalizations are no longer possible and politics have become too complex to take on, who can blame contemporary artists for adopting the pose of childish innocence (ibid., 57–58)? This is the logical culmination of a subjectivism, or literary individualism, that can be traced back through Conrad and Henry James to Arnold and J. S. Mill. But as Levenson points out, Ford's commitment to civic realism, the notion that the contemporary artist must assume "the responsibilities of citizenship in the modern world and . . . reflect contemporaneity" (ibid., 108), also aligns him with the objectivist tradition. Hence Pound's repeated acknowledgment of Ford's poetic doctrine as a foundation of imagism. The subjectivist and objectivist extremes meet in civic realism, Levenson argues, owing to the way Ford alternately idealizes objective mimesis and the artist's *perception* of the objective scene. Thus if Ford rejects Yeats's early spiritualism and Arthur Symons's emphasis on transcendence by means of the symbol in favor of direct treatment of the here and now, the ideal of impressionism as realism begins to slide toward impressionism as egoism (or "personality") when "this world," the shared world of modernity, becomes "my world," the world as the artist sees it, and then, in Ford's final gesture of simultaneously extreme subjectivism and objectivism, "my world" dissolves into a "scientific" rendering of the instantaneous registering of impressions (ibid., 118–19), or what Virginia Woolf describes in "Modern Fiction" as "atoms" falling on the brain. Here we have arrived at the peculiarity of Dowell's narration in *The Good Soldier*, his perpetual bewilderment in the face of impressions that seem to compose "a picture without a meaning" (*The Good Soldier*, 161).

Levenson's account has the considerable virtue of recasting what has often been dismissed, even ridiculed, as a typically Fordian contradiction as the product of a "logic of immediacy" (Levenson, *Genealogy of Modernism*, 117) that is fundamental to modernism's self-understanding as a higher form of realism. Flickering perceptions in Ford, Woolf, and Joyce are objective renderings of the immediate experience of reality that Victorian conventions failed to register. But Levenson's emphasis on the impression as the final atomistic stage of ever more immediate renderings of the real fails to square with Ford's belief that it remained for art to supply values no longer available in life: "The artist to-day is the only man who is concerned with the values of life; he is the only man who, in a world grown very complicated through the limitless freedom of expression for all creeds and all moralities, can place before us how those creeds work out when applied to human contacts" (*Critical Attitude*, 27). The goal of Fordian impressionism is not simply to restore the freshness of sensations gone stale or to dramatize David Hume's conception of human identity decomposed by skepticism, "a bundle or collection of different perceptions."[41] It is rather to reinvest dead facts with coherent value. The facts of human existence, endlessly reiterated in the daily press, anatomized by technical specialists, and laid out in reference works and actuarial tables, have been split off from experiential immediacy, and by fusing facts and human feeling in the impression, Ford hopes to restore a lost wholeness.

Jesse Matz has shown that this impossible task constitutes the fundamental goal of literary impressionism.[42] Matz understands the impression as a metaphor for perception that aspires to mediate between the sensuous and the rational, the subjective and the objective, the personal and the universal. Aiming to unite opposites by occupying a space and a moment somewhere between pure sensory input and its transformation into thought, the impression gestures toward the synthesis of subject and object theorized by the philosophical tradition of phenomenology without ever proposing anything so definite. Impressionist mediation also differs from the more assured mediation of the Romantic imagination. With secularization undermining the analogy between divine creation and the integrative power of the Romantic symbol, "the work of the symbol is taken up, far less successfully, by the impression, which corresponds to an imagination which can only repeat mundane acts of secular organization."[43] The impression, in this understanding, could be said to mediate between the Romantic symbol and the modernist image. In Ford's case, the impression is tasked with mediating between fact and experiential value by relocating facts within a particular human sensorium and integrating them into meaningful complexes. Matz suggests that in aiming for such a synthesis, Ford in effect makes the impression the foundation for what Raymond Williams (working from a distinctly different political orientation) calls "structures of feeling," "the conditions of affect," in Matz's paraphrase, "that arbitrate lived social experience."[44]

Rather than naming the transitory data of perception, then, Ford's impression is meant to counter the unmanageable welter of modern facts by transforming them into assimilable information. Whereas the "sound English reviewer," Ford's favorite whipping boy, must "sacrifice his personality" to give readers "as many facts about the book under consideration as his allotted space will hold" (*Critical Writings*, 35), the impressionist eschews received templates of understanding propagated in the press by filtering facts through his sensibility. W. H. Hudson, writing about a subject as mundane as grass, trumps the agricultural correspondent by providing "the pleasure of coming in contact with his temperament" (ibid., 35). Thus if Ford, as Levenson suggests, made the modern information ecology and the disappearance of shared moral norms an excuse for becoming an impressionist rather than an Edwardian sage, it is nevertheless also true that he wanted artists to interpret facts up into a kind of pleasurable coherence, not to analyze them down into their component elements, a task already being performed all too effectively, he felt, by the daily press and specialists of all stripes.

This is where the shared dynamic between impressionism and propaganda becomes most apparent. Each aims to restore wholeness and feeling to information, though for quite different reasons. To return to Jacques Ellul, propaganda is not something imposed on passive individuals by evil manipulators. Ellul posits a symbiotic relation between information and propaganda: "Almost inevitably information turns into propaganda; it makes propaganda possible, feeds it, and renders it necessary. It creates a need for propaganda in man."[45] The logic is powerful: Ellul defines information as pure fact, and facts are useless if not made to seem credible and assimilable; information therefore must be couched in rhetoric, and the introduction of techniques of persuasion begins to turn information into propaganda. The state inevitably spreads propaganda because the need to publicize its accomplishments results in the dissemination of information designed to alter public opinion. The public accelerates the transformation of information into propaganda because public opinion generally prefers the clarity of myth (propaganda's specialty) to a chaotic profusion of facts, and there is simply too much information in circulation for most people to process. Overwhelmed, confused, resentful, and alienated, modern citizens subjected to decontextualized information about issues too complex to be grasped in their entirety are responsive to propaganda because it makes sense of the world while gratifying the propagandee's desire to participate in public life in a way that is meaningful. Propaganda thus transforms ideologies into myths one can live by, and in the figure of the common enemy it offers a safety valve for negative affect that otherwise can find no socially approved mode of expression. Like Ford, then, Ellul sees the increased flow of information undermining democracy by splitting society into those with and without the requisite powers of synthesis and memory to process information effectively. By fusing facts with techniques of psychological persuasion, the most effective propaganda paradoxically uses information to drive information out of circulation: tweaked facts, or spin, triumph over less alluring facts.

The integrative aims of the impression and propaganda are not identical, of course. Whereas propaganda by definition fabricates affective and ideological coherence in order to encourage specific actions, the impression, in Ford's theory, aims to produce individual pleasure in the very experience of coherence. But propaganda too has a stake in pleasure through the reduction of anxiety and the focusing of energies, and the impression, like propaganda, aims to produce coherence where it otherwise would not exist. Indeed, without the fusion of fact and feeling effected by the impression, propaganda could not operate. As Ellul points out, propaganda depends on information—accurate facts, as British propagandists recognized, are more effective than lies—and information paves the way for propaganda, not only by informing but also by confusing, in the manner of Ford's "white spray of facts" (*Critical Attitude*, 125). If propaganda offers explanations that permit individuals to assert themselves within a world that would otherwise seem chaotic and threatening, the impression operates at the microlevel to generate a sense of psychological comfort in living in a world that, even before it is coherent, is at least human. Ford writes in *The Critical Attitude*: "the tendency of humanity is to crowd into the large cities, and within their bounds to live semi-migratory lives. Of the history and of the thought of the great number of men with whom we come into contact we have no knowledge at all. We see them for allotted minutes, for the allotted hours. Of their lives and passions we know nothing. So that unless the imaginative writer help us in this matter we are in great danger of losing alike *human* knowledge and *human* sympathy" (ibid., 67; emphasis added). In the repetition of "human," a qualifier not strictly necessary to the overt meaning of the sentence, Ford registers a prescient resistance to the emergence of what would later be called the "posthuman," the notion that with information outstripping the capacity of consciousness to encompass it, consciousness itself may not be as central to human identity as the Cartesian tradition assumes.[46] The "great danger of losing human knowledge and human sympathy" lies not in the threat to knowledge or sympathy but in the threat to recognizably human versions of them. The impression functions to recontain information in the human, and propaganda steps in to manipulate the unified individual into the greater unity of a collective cause. Viewed in the context of the early twentieth century's interrelated economies of affect and information, then, the impression can be described as a utopian information technology opposed but related to the structure of propaganda. And with this interrelation in mind, we can return to Ford's dual practice as war propagandist and experimental novelist.

IMPRESSING FACTS: *WHEN BLOOD IS THEIR ARGUMENT* AND *BETWEEN ST. DENNIS AND ST. GEORGE*

Ford's propaganda books posed a considerable rhetorical challenge. On one hand, he needed to encourage the English to feel sympathy for their traditional enemy, the French. On the other hand, he had to turn the English against Germany, a country whose ruling family was related to their own. The books' general strategy therefore depends on elaborating anti-German stereotypes that were common in England in the prewar years—Germany is excessively materialistic, nationalistic, and militaristic—while celebrating the French for their altruism, love of learning, and cultural achievements. This produces a happy confluence of Ford's politics and his aesthetics in the closing pages of *Between St. Dennis and St. George*, in which Ford offers a ten-page commentary on the problems inherent in rendering the delicacy of the first sentence of a Flaubert story into English. The blunt instrument of German is not even an option.

At the same time, Ford's German stereotypes are more generous than those found in most propaganda. He had never been hesitant to trot out national generalizations, however odd, when they suited his purposes. Thus the passing remark in "On Impressionism" that "all Germans have a peculiar loathing for the rabbit," a fact the impressionist must have in store if he is to find a suitably indirect means for explaining why a character dislikes rabbit pie (ibid., 45). But in *Between St. Dennis and St. George* Ford is careful to balance the usual attack on German militarism against praise for the culture of Southern Germany, which the evil empire of Prussian *Kultur*, in Ford's view, has all but extinguished. The most sympathetic account of Ford's stated aim in *Between St. Dennis and St. George*—"to reconstruct from my own consciousness the psychologies of the three Western Powers chiefly engaged in the present contest" (*Between St. Dennis and St. George*, 29)—would see it, as Max Saunders does, as anticipating the focus on *mentalités* in the *Annales* school of historiography that emerged in France in the late 1920s.[47] Yet Ford's hostility to rigorous analysis and research—his representative Englishman is, of course, himself—not to mention his rhetorical goal of making the reader take sides, distinguishes his propaganda books from more serious work on the history of mentalities. And yet Saunders is right to suggest that the books are more worthy of close attention than is most of the work sponsored by Wellington House.

When Blood Is Their Argument and *Between St. Dennis and St. George* (both titles are lifted from *Henry V*)[48] stand as perfect examples of the kind of propaganda one would expect in the media environment first mapped by Lippmann and later analyzed by Ellul. Ford overwhelms his reader with a mixture of facts and opinions offered as facts—all disarmingly offered as mere impressions—that accumulate into a plausible picture that may bear little relation to a more systematic account. And if one doubts his claims, Ford also offers appendices and footnotes to back up his anecdotes, though sometimes the footnotes simply offer another anecdote. In this Ford's strategy recalls the apparatus of objectivity in the Bryce Report. Similarly, Ford's sustained indictment of the state's influence on German education in *When Blood Is Their Argument* is grounded in fact, but if Ford's impressionist presentation, filtered through his temperament, invests facts with the authority of the "authentically human," it also strips away the broader European context that makes the German university system seem less exceptional. From the outset Ford makes plain that he will not let mere facts obscure his critique. The preface acknowledges that his articles in *Outlook*, which form the basis of *When Blood Is Their Argument*, were charged with "deliberate unfairness to the traditions of German learning and of German scholarship" (*When Blood Is Their Argument*, vii). His defense amounts to a defense of impressionism: his father and grandfather inculcated in him from his "earliest years a deep hatred of Prussianism, of materialism, of academicism, of pedagogism, and of purely economic views of the values of life"; they also taught him a "deep love and veneration for French learning, arts, habits of mind, lucidity, and for that form of imagination which implies a sympathetic comprehension of the hopes, fears, and ideals of one's fellow-men. So that, since this work is, in essence, a reassertion of the claims of, or of the necessity for, altruism, whether Christian or Hellenic, I may be said to have passed the whole of my life reflecting upon these propagandist lines" (ibid., vii). In other words, Ford's propaganda is not propaganda because he is saying what he is saying only because the situation demands that he repeat what he learned at the feet of his father. Full disclosure of "the sort of chap" he is accounts for the kind of impressions Ford offers and absolves him from the charge of propaganda that he levels against the Germans.

Easily mocked, Ford's strategy is nevertheless effective in its own way. Thus on one hand Ford engages in what might be considered a proleptic parody of New Historicism's propensity for finding History in a grain of sand by telling an anecdote about a dinner party. At this meal he encountered a workman, a Mr. Rangsley, who apparently had been threatening violence to his neighbors for years, but his threats had always been laughed at as empty. Over dinner, Rangsley plunges a carving knife into the eye of the man across from him and breaks the back of the one man who had always warned everyone else that one day Rangsley would snap. "That," Ford concludes, "is pretty much the case of Germany . . . and I do not see that much further comment is called for" (*Between St.*

Dennis and St. George, 154–55). Ford also blames the sinking of the *Lusitania* on the German emperor's having read too much Captain Marryat in the 1880s (ibid., 99). On the other hand, Ford's critique of the Prussian educational system as an instrument of state propaganda is so forcefully put that I momentarily felt inclined to follow Ford's lead by anglicizing my name, perhaps in the same euphonious way, before I learned that Germany was not unique in subjecting its university system to state control.[49] Indeed, insofar as changing my name to Mark A. Mark was bound to undermine my academic authority, I was relieved to discover that all European universities, with the sole exception of England's, were closely regulated by the state.[50]

Thus impressionism not only guarantees the truth of his claims—you see me, whom you know—it also has the specific function here of distinguishing Ford from German scholars, whose empiricism and "impersonalism" are facades designed to mask their true aims. German scholars merely compile "*Quellen*," or sources, and these apparently impersonal compilations disguise the subjective perspective that animates their disquisitions. Thus Professor Hans Delbrueck, who once criticized the naive metaphysics of English constitutionalism, ought to have dispensed with his aloof generalizations and come clean by admitting that

> I, Professor Hans Delbrueck, am a paid official of the Prussian State who was once fined five hundred marks for criticising the action of the Prussian State. By inclination, by self-interest, by national interest, and by conscientious belief I am forced into thinking that the methods of the Prussian State are beneficent and necessary if I and humanity who are of good will are to prosper. I am therefore ransacking history in order to find incidents and precedents that shall make effective propaganda. I am, in fact, a barrister employed by Prussia and I am doing my best for my client. (*When Blood Is Their Argument*, ix)

Alas, Delbrueck, whose objectivity is merely a pose, is no Ford, whose confession of inherited bias absolves him from deceit. Delbrueck does not merely conceal the influence of the state but may also be guilty, Ford suspects, of forging his *Quellen*, like "a police-sergeant . . . distorting facts in order to secure a conviction of an innocent female accused of streetwalking" (ibid., x). Ford, in contrast, is "a special pleader" on behalf of "altruism" and "constitutionalism," and is honest enough to embrace subjectivity in the act of identifying himself with objectivity per se: "I claim in short to be the '*Quellen*' " (ibid., x, xiii). The claim is at once consonant with Ford's impressionism and deeply misleading. If the notion of Ford-as-*Quellen* reasserts the aim of impressionism by giving facts a human face, it also neglects to acknowledge that Ford himself, even more than Delbrueck, is writing at the behest of his client, the British state. Ford's accusation that Delbrueck is manipulating rules of evidence to convict an innocent woman of streetwalking also turns back on the accuser. Elsewhere, when Ford wants to describe techniques the impressionist might use to capture the reader's interest, he concludes that the effective impressionist not only will exaggerate; he will employ "all the devices of the prostitute" (*Critical Writings*, 54). The return of the trope of the writer as prostitute, about which I will have more to say later, suggests that in condemning Delbrueck as a propagandist Ford inevitably imagines Delbrueck accusing him in return. Prostitutes presumably recognize one another on the street.

Ford's seeming impulse to confess that he is a prostitute twice over, selling his services to the state and his impressions to the reader, is held in check by efforts to legitimate his writing as fundamentally true. One strategy of self-legitimation casts Ford as the exemplary historian; in another, entwined with the first, Ford describes himself as an artist whose professional expertise permits him to recognize the truth of impressions in the same way a scientist understands the invariant workings of chemical reactions. Ford argues in *Between St. Dennis and St. George* that in an age of gossip, rumors, and flawed information, it becomes necessary for "the immense bulk of the population . . . [to] cultivate something of the historian's faculty. And the historian's faculty is nothing more or less than a habit of mind . . . which from the uproar of a thousand sentences selects and retains only those things which are first-hand evidence" (*Between St. Dennis and St. George*, 5). The citizen as historian, in other words, must learn to find the trace of the human perceiver from within a welter of impersonal facts. But this sifting of impressions from facts turns out to be merely preliminary to the trickier business of assessing the reliability of the human perspective built into the impression. Ford's case in point here is George Bernard Shaw, whose *Common Sense about the War* is the official target of *Between St. Dennis and St. George*. Shaw's widely distributed pamphlet argues that German and British motives for war are grounded in the same class interests and therefore are fundamentally indistinguishable; compared with their similarities, the differences between the English and German ruling classes seem arbitrary and inconsequential, making a negotiated settlement the only reasonable course. Wellington House acknowledged the power of Shaw's argument by charging Ford to respond. Shaw's shortcomings, Ford argues, are twofold: he is short on *Quellen* and the perspective through which he filters his few sources is flawed. Ford denounces Shaw and his ilk as "intellectual fictionists" who invent characters that resemble historical figures and then make up historical dramas to suit their ideological agendas (*Between St. Dennis and St. George*, 9). But by claiming that Shaw lacks "ground facts," Ford finds himself aligned with German empiricism and is thus quick to acknowledge that imagination too is important when advancing an historical critique. Tolstoy, Ibsen, Galsworthy—these are writers whose imaginations bring history to life. But the methods of Shaw and similar "controversialists" resemble those of "the irresponsible artist" (ibid., 18) whose fiction propagandizes against a particular kind of character by always, for instance, portraying landowners or socialists in a negative light. Bearing in mind Ford's stricture against Victorian novelists' propaganda on behalf of favored characters, his critique of Shaw and fellow "intellectual fictionists" casts them as Victorian dogmatists who fail the test of truth as measured by the impression.

The impressionist's truth is grounded not just in fidelity to immediate experience but in his professionalism. Demonstrating the validity of his approach, Ford observes that he has never met an Englishman who believed that war would better mankind, and he has never met a German who did not believe that "war had very great advantages as a panacea for human and national diseases" (ibid., 32). Could Ford's "very exactly recorded impression of the relative bellicosities of these two peoples" be tainted with bias? Ford has two grounds for replying "*Nein!*" First off, he has always found that "normal Germans," unlike Englishmen, display a "love for literature," so Ford, who has made of literature his "profession in life," clearly is "predisposed . . . to take favourable views of many German manifestations" (ibid., 34). Second, although his impressions admittedly are not the kind of "direct evidence" one might get from an eyewitness at a murder trial, they are "the impressions of a man who has spent the great part of his life in recording impressions with an extreme exactitude" (ibid., 34). Ford's report on the poison of militarism in the body politic of Germany therefore carries as much weight as the testimony of an "analytical chemist who finds traces in the body of a victim of a poison difficult of analysis" (ibid., 34). Through the alchemy of professional expertise—writers *know* impressions, and this writer, moreover, *knows* Germans—Fordian impressions are transmuted into scientific fact. It follows that in order to combat the tendency of "lazy and loose-thinking analogists" to consider Germany and Britain alike in their militarism and devotion to class interests, it is enough for Ford "in writing the pages that follow . . . to reconstruct from my own consciousness the psychologies of the three Western Powers chiefly engaged in the present contest" (ibid., 29).

Ford is highly conscious that his project will be deemed a failure if his reconstructions amount to little more than common stereotypes. In *When Blood Is Their Argument* he explicitly disavows "group condemnations" by revealing his familiarity with them: "To say that every inhabitant of the United States worships nothing but the Almighty Dollar or is a dope-fiend; to say that every Englishman is a hypocrite or is exclusively in love with comfort; to say that every Frenchman is a miser or a fornicator; or to say that every German worships titles or official rank—these things appear to me nauseous, and even when the allegations are more seriously framed, they still appear to me dangerous" (*When Blood Is Their Argument*, 168–69). I have observed, seemingly in the spirit of Ford's disavowal, that his deployment of stereotypes is more generous than in most contemporary propaganda. Yet it is also true that Ford's splitting of Germany into the good Germans of the south and the wicked Prussians of the north, which tempers the group condemnation by subdividing the group, reproduces the fundamental logic of the scapegoat. Scapegoating, as Dominick LaCapra has observed, contributes to the production of pure oppositions, "insofar as internal alterity, perceived as guilty or fallen, is purged, and all 'otherness' is projected onto the discrete other."[51] In line with this logic, Ford often ends up finding in Germany what he likes least about contemporary England. Projected criticism of this sort is a common enough gesture, particularly in war time, but for a useful point of comparison, and one that will lead us into a concluding discussion of *The Good Soldier*, let me turn for a moment to Forster.

In *Howards End*, Forster provides dual German genealogies for the opposed values represented in the Wilcoxes and the Schlegels: old Germany, the Germany of the Romantics, is associated with the idealism of the Schlegel sisters, whereas new Germany, the imperial country devoted to all things big and expensive, is the prototype for the Wilcoxes' purely commercial interests. Published four years before the outbreak of World War I, Forster's novel acknowledges the building pressures exacerbated by "the gutter press" with the casual observation that "England and Germany are bound to fight," but the German nation is never presented as a threatening imperial other whose existence threatens England's. Rather, by using old and new Germany as analogues for the conflicting values of the Schlegels and Wilcoxes, and by attempting to treat even Henry Wilcox sympathetically, Forster implies that the projection of internal battles onto external foes tends to evade underlying questions of value that England must find a way to cope with at home.[52]

In contrast, when Ford splits Germany in two in *When Blood Is Their Argument*, his propagandistic aims render him all too happy to make Germany the scapegoat for what he despises about England without openly acknowledging his fellow citizen's complicity. The "whole programme" of social decorum in *The Good Soldier* (31), for instance, becomes the "immense, sedulous, and never-sleeping system" of the Prussian educational system in *When Blood Is Their Argument* (106). Yet in his fiction Ford's gaze, like Forster's, is turned inward toward the English character, and *The Good Soldier*, written a few months before the propaganda books, is openly, if ambivalently, critical of the English stereotype of "quite good people." Other national stereotypes, while frequently deployed, are also subjected to skeptical inquiry. But *The Good Soldier* does not simply ironize stereotypes that Ford will redeploy with a vengeance in the propaganda books. One way to describe the novel, to which I now turn, is to say that it charts Dowell's anxious exploration of the problematic relationship between the impression, on which he relies, and the stereotype, which he cannot escape.

NAVIGATING THE PSEUDO-ENVIRONMENT IN *THE GOOD SOLDIER*

Much of the brilliance of *The Good Soldier* undoubtedly lies in the psychological complexity of Ford's presentation of Dowell, whose baffled innocence and contradictory evaluations of duplicitous friends and loved ones beckon readers into the obscurity of his motivations. Ford's stylistic virtuosity, beguiling in its own right as a form of writerly *sprezzatura*, deepens the felt reality of Dowell's voice by capturing distinctive movements of mind in vivid turns of phrase. But what to make of this voice— that is the enigma at the heart of the novel. Is Dowell an emotionally crippled eunuch or a portrait of the writer as social critic? Unreliable or trustworthy? Insane or merely peculiar? To highlight the difficulty of reconstructing dependable meanings from Dowell's meandering narration, one critic has floated the suggestion, in serious jest, that Edward Ashburnham, apparently a suicide, might have been murdered by Dowell.[53] If such a claim seems over the top, Dowell's frequent recourse to conjectural narration of events that he did not witness, not to mention his "forgetting" to tell us about Edward's death, licenses skeptical reworkings of the story.

But most critical evaluations of Dowell take one moment in particular as the crux of the matter: Dowell's assertion, late in the novel, that he resembles his good friend Edward.[54] Given that Edward is a philandering English gentleman who was cuckolding Dowell for nine years, and given that Dowell is a seemingly clueless American businessman who never consummated his marriage and presumably remains a virgin, efforts to understand what Dowell means by the claim that "in my fainter sort of way I seem to perceive myself following the lines of Edward Ashburnnam" (*The Good Soldier*, 151) tend to focus on psychology. After all, it is hard not to speculate about the mental machinery of a character who acknowledges that he lacks Edward's "courage," "virility," and "physique" while also asserting that "he was just myself" (ibid., 161). And so the question is posed: is Dowell delusional? Was Ford? The arguments have been enlightening, but missing from the discussion has been an adequately historicized account of Dowell's relation to the world and, implicitly, Ford's. My contention in the remainder of this chapter is that in the context of Ford's propaganda books, Dowell's problematic identification with Edward can be seen to rehearse the ideological conversion Ford underwent when he chose to serve the needs of Wellington House. The key to this conjunction are the ways in which all three books engage with stereotypes.

The proliferating stereotypes that Dowell confronts in *The Good Soldier* and that Ford labors to vivify in the propaganda books are characteristic of the pseudo-environment the war helped to produce. Lippmann, the first to devote serious attention to the study of stereotypes, devotes five chapters of *Public Opinion* to the ways in which stereotypes make an increasingly confusing world familiar by mediating experience and knowledge.[55] Lippmann begins by acknowledging the subjective dimension of what Poovey calls the "modern fact": "A report is the joint product of the knower and known, in which the role of the observer is always selective and usually creative. The facts we see depend on where we are placed, and the habits of our eyes" (*Public Opinion*, 80). Echoing William James's famous description of sensory immediacy, Lippmann argues that in "the great blooming, buzzing confusion of the outer world, we pick out what our culture has already defined for us, and we tend to perceive that which we have picked out in the form stereotyped for us by our culture" (ibid., 81). Though intrinsic to perception, the filtering process becomes increasingly codified in the twentieth century owing to the converging pressures of new media: "the moving picture is steadily building up imagery which is then evoked by the words people read in their newspapers" (ibid., 91).[56] Much of the appeal of the media stereotype derives from its "economy of effort": "Photographs have the kind of authority over imagination to-day, which the printed word had yesterday, and the spoken word before that. They seem utterly real. They come, we imagine, directly to us without human meddling, and they are the most effortless food for the mind conceivable" (ibid., 92). Stereotypes are more than mere cognitive shortcuts, however: "[The stereotype] is the guarantee of our self-respect; it is the projection upon the world of our own sense of our own value, our own position and our own rights. The stereotypes are, therefore, highly charged with the feelings that are attached to them. They are the fortress of our tradition, and behind its defenses we can continue to feel ourselves safe in the position we occupy" (ibid., 96). They provide, in other words, much of what Ford finds in the impression, and to evoke their value Lippmann returns to the same Arnoldian touchstone used by both Forster and Ford: "the stereotype not only saves time in a busy life and is a defense of our position in society, but tends to preserve us from all the bewildering effort of trying to see the world steadily and see it whole" (ibid., 114). Indeed,

Lippmann's stereotypes, fusing fact and feeling, are routinized Fordian impressions that screen out distractions produced by discordant impressions not yet assimilated into familiar patterns.

When *The Good Soldier* is read in relation to Ford's theory of impressionism, as Jesse Matz observes, the novel is typically positioned as a refutation of the theory: Dowell's failure to realize that Edward has been having an affair with his wife for nine years testifies either to his mistaken faith in the impression by indicating that one cannot rely, as Dowell claims one can, on first impressions, or to the fact that Dowell is a solipsist whose unreliable narration betrays his inability to know others.[57] Yet Dowell's problem can be seen as a highly charged version of the predicament faced by every Englishman as he reads the morning papers: how to make sense of "the white spray of facts" that overwhelms his critical faculties without resorting to the blinkers of crude stereotypes. This is not to scant the sexual dimension of the story. As all the biographical treatments make clear, Ford undoubtedly was working through his own tangled sexual affairs by writing *The Good Soldier*. But information and propaganda too, as we have seen, are matters of the heart.

If in *When Blood Is Their Argument* and *Between St. Dennis and St. George* Ford speaks as a propagandist, in *The Good Soldier* Dowell speaks in the voice of someone desperately in need of propaganda. Asking himself what a "proper man" is, Dowell can only answer: "I don't know. And there is nothing to guide us. And if everything is so nebulous about a matter so elementary as the morals of sex, what is there to guide us in the more subtle morality of all other personal contacts, associations, and activities? . . . It is all a darkness" (*The Good Soldier*, 15). One might reasonably question the wisdom of making sexual mores the baseline for certainty, but there is ample reason to believe that Dowell's naivete echoes Ford's here, and however one arrives at this level of skeptical crisis—for Marlow simply gazing at Jim's apparently trustworthy visage in *Lord Jim* is enough to plunge him into an epistemological crisis—the pressing issue is not the crisis itself but how one responds.[58] Traumatized by sexual betrayal, Dowell looks around himself and asserts that where formerly he saw "quite good people," "no smoking-room will ever be other than peopled with incalculable simulacra amidst smoke wreaths" (ibid., 10, 12). This new vista of uncertainty comes as a particular blow to a man who responds to having been "for so long a wanderer upon the face of public resorts" with a maniacal investment in the calculated pleasures of the familiar. For Dowell, the feeling of being at home, where a favorite chair seems "to enfold one in an embrace," is "a very important part of life," and the spa at Nauheim, where Florence is taking a cure for her "heart," gives him "a sense almost of nakedness" (ibid., 21). When Dowell tries to describe the affective state the spa inspires, his sentence, slipping into an anaesthetizing rhythm, reproduces the evasion of "the personal note" that Dowell sees as a defining characteristic of "good people" (ibid., 29): "But the feeling that I had when, whilst poor Florence was taking her morning bath, I stood upon the carefully swept steps of the Englischer Hof, looking at the carefully arranged trees in tubs upon the carefully arranged gravel whilst carefully arranged people walked past in carefully calculated gaiety, at the carefully calculated hour, the tall trees of the public gardens, going up to the right; the reddish stones of the baths—or were they white half-timber châlets?" (ibid., 21–22). The contemplation of "carefully" arranged forms holds so much appeal that Dowell's syntax remains incomplete and the initial telos of the sentence, "feeling," is infinitely deferred. In its place Dowell indulges in the compulsive pleasures of repeated calculation. Dowell makes himself at home in Nauheim, it turns out, by counting his footsteps: "I could find my way blindfolded. I know the exact distances. From the Hotel Regina you took one hundred and eighty-seven paces, then, turning sharp, lefthanded, four hundred and twenty took you straight down to the fountain" (ibid., 22). With "nothing to guide [him]," Dowell lays down tracks that make navigation superfluous.

This is precisely the kind of alienated citizen that propaganda reaches out to embrace. Dowell is, in Ellul's terms, the perfect instance of the kind of modern man who *needs* propaganda. Dowell's marriage and his friendship with the Ashburnhams seem to him (before he learns otherwise) "an extraordinarily safe castle" (ibid., 11), but with the discovery of Florence's infidelity, the refuge of interpersonal relations turns out to be a mirage, his wife as much a simulacrum as the mysterious others in the smoking room. Viewed through loving eyes, Florence resembles "a gay tremulous beam, reflected from water upon a ceiling" (ibid., 17); less sympathetically, she is "a personality of paper" that "represented a real human being . . . only as a bank note represents a certain quantity of gold" (ibid., 83). In a world of "incalculable simulacra," Dowell hungers for the kind of substance he thought he had found in Leonora, who was "so extraordinarily the real thing that she seemed too good to be true," before discovering that she, like everyone else, was only "acting" (ibid., 13). Given that stereotypes, as Lippmann observes, are "the fortress of our tradition, and behind its defenses we can continue to feel ourselves safe in the position we occupy" (*Public Opinion*, 96), how could Dowell not seek shelter in the safe castle of his relationship with Florence, who is the image of a "bright thing," and with the Ashburnhams, "the model couple" (*The Good Soldier*, 17, 13)? The economy of effort Lippmann cites as part of the stereotype's appeal is no doubt attractive to a man who takes as his sole "profession," "career," and "ambition" the shielding of his wife from excitation. When Dowell undertakes some business in America (vaguely Jamesian and therefore vaguely financial), he is satisfied with "first impressions" of those he meets because "automatically docketing and labelling" each person seems to him as reliable a gauge of character as any other (ibid., 102).

Character is fundamentally unknowable for Dowell because it cannot be predicted (it is "incalculable"), and yet throughout his narration he introduces categorical distinctions—political, religious, and national—as if their explanatory power were indisputable. When his favorable impression of "a nice young fellow called Carter" in America is confirmed by Carter's employers but contradicted by Dowell's Republican relatives, who distrust Carter as a Democrat, Dowell professes that such categories are meaningless to him. It is never worth making inquiries to get past one's first impressions, "for who in this world can give anyone a character" (ibid., 104)? Yet Dowell imagines that Florence would be attracted to a marriage without physical passion because "Americans, you know, can envisage such unions without blinking" (ibid., 58), and he believes that "Nancy's love for Leonora was an admiration that is awakened in Catholics by their feeling for the Virgin Mary and for various of the saints" (ibid., 133). Despite their prevalence, these group characterizations tend to dissolve even as they are articulated. Dowell believes that Leonora's silently suspicious scrutiny of Edward at Nauheim is characteristic of a Catholic mindset—"of a people," that is, "that can think thoughts alien to ours and keep them to themselves" (ibid., 89). But if such reticence is Catholic, then surely all the Protestant "good people" of the novel, such as Edward, are also Catholic.

The seeming arbitrariness of such labels is reinforced when Dowell implies that religious and national distinctions mean nothing in comparison with the homogenizing force of class. The "modern English habit of taking everything for granted," which Dowell suspects is at the root of his misery, turns out to be not so much English as "the modern civilised habit":

> And the odd, queer thing is that the whole collection of rules applies to anybody. . . . You meet a man or a woman and, from tiny and intimate sounds, from the slightest of movements, you know at once whether you are concerned with good people or with those who won't do. You know that is to say, whether they will go rigidly through with the whole programme from the underdone beef to the Anglicanism. It won't matter whether they be short or tall; whether the voice squeaks like a marionette or rumble like a town bull's; it won't matter whether they are Germans, Austrians, French, Spanish, or even Brazilians—they will be the Germans or Brazilians who take a cold bath every morning and who move, roughly speaking, in diplomatic circles. (ibid., 31).

This is Dowell's version of Helen Ambrose's passing fear in *The Voyage Out* that everyone is subject to a "profound and reasonless law" that molds individuals "to its liking" (*The Voyage Out*, 249). But what for Woolf is largely a matter of gender inflected by class and race is for Ford more narrowly a matter of class. Nevertheless, Dowell's insight into the increasingly transnational effects of class does not prevent him from continuing to invoke religion and national identity as keys to individual behavior, though by the time Dowell begins to explain Leonora's behavior in terms of *English* Catholicism as opposed to Continental papism— "a dirty, jovial and unscrupulous crew" (*The Good Soldier*, 47)—all such categories have lost their explanatory purchase.

The novel's most celebrated scene underscores the peculiar status of national and religious stereotypes in *The Good Soldier*. The first narrative iteration of the so-called Protest scene, in which Florence seduces Edward Ashburnham under the noses of Leonora and Dowell, is utterly opaque until it is re-narrated later from Leonora's point of view and Dowell's more informed perspective. The first time through it is not at all clear what Florence is up to when she drags everyone on an excursion to a castle (which proves to be extraordinarily unsafe) in order to lecture them on a founding document of Protestantism, signed by Martin Luther, Martin Bucer, and Zwingli. Assembling everyone in "a dim old chamber" that, according to Florence, once was Luther's bedroom, she directs their attention to an old piece of paper in a glass case: "It's because of that piece of paper," Florence says to Edward as she gazes into his eyes, "that you're honest, sober, industrious, provident, and clean-lived. If it weren't for that piece of paper you'd be like the Irish or the Italians or the Poles, but particularly the Irish" (ibid., 37). When Florence lays her finger on Edward's wrist, Leonora flees with the obscurely panicked Dowell in tow. The emotional intensity builds as Leonora denounces *something*, it is not clear what, not only as "the cause of the whole miserable affair" but "of the whole sorrow of the world" (ibid., 38). Dowell, increasingly upset, admits he has no idea what is happening. The chapter ends with Leonora's explanation: " 'Don't you know,' she said in her clear hard voice, 'don't you know that I'm an Irish Catholic?' " (ibid., 38). The first words of the next chapter inform us that this explanation gives Dowell "the greatest relief that I have ever had in my life." For Dowell could not stand the thought that Leonora might be jealous of Florence, but "Florence's mere silly gibes at the Irish and at the Catholics could be apologised out of existence" (ibid., 51).

Ford artfully induces in the reader the same mixture of confusion and intimations of clarity that Dowell experiences. Most readers will initially share Mark Schorer's sense that Leonora's explanation comes as an absurd anticlimax.[59] Only later does one realize that Leonora's Irish Catholicism is absolutely crucial to the plot: Leonora's relatively impoverished upbringing in Ireland induced her father to exempt Edward from the usual Catholic stipulation that the children of a mixed marriage be brought up Catholic; Florence is counting on the fact that Leonora cannot divorce Edward; Catholicism plays into Leonora's effort to persuade Nancy Rufford, the Ashburnhams' protegée, to sacrifice her virginity to Edward in order to save him; and so on. But the fact remains that when Leonora first tells Dowell about her Irish Catholicism, she is deploying the category as a cover for what Dowell feels she ought to have said: "Your wife is a harlot who is going to be my husband's mistress" (ibid., 124). Similarly, what Florence means, as Carol Jacobs points out, "by saying that Edward is clean-lived is that she wishes he weren't."[60] What's more, unbeknownst to Florence, Edward is not "honest, sober, industrious, provident, and clean-lived": he is a lazy spendthrift with a drinking problem on his way to a sixth extramarital affair.

The category of "Irish Catholic" thus comes to exemplify the problematic status of all such categories in the novel: they are at once absolutely determining and absolutely meaningless.[61] In Jacobs's virtuoso reading of the historical subtext for the Protest scene—the debate between Luther and Zwingli over the literal versus metaphoric meaning of "This is my body"—the elusive significance of the moment in which Florence lays a finger on Edward's wrist becomes an allegory for the impossibility of distinguishing between literal and figurative language: Dowell remarks that "[he] can't define it and can't find a simile for it" (ibid., 37). Jacobs links this ambiguity to scenes in which language creates desire instead of channeling it or in which it takes on the literal power to wound. In one instance, Edward discovers his passion for Nancy only as his words generate it; in another, Nancy and Leonora's words flay the flesh from Edward's bones (ibid., 80, 152). Ultimately, Jacobs suggests, *The Good Soldier*, turns the reader into Nancy, who ends up mad, suspended between belief in the stability of God and the arbitrary waywardness of desire. Nancy's apt metaphor, "shuttlecocks," thus applies not only to Nancy herself, bounced back and forth between Edward and Leonora, but also to the reader.

But if Ford's language shuttles the reader between meaning and nonmeaning, so, from a certain perspective, do all texts. What seems crucial in *The Good Soldier* is that Ford's troubled insight into the arbitrariness of the sign, which Ferdinand de Saussure announced as a linguistic principle only a year later, coincides with a profound sense of suffering. In theory, signs may be arbitrary, but the way social and legal conventions in practice bind signifiers to referents may only intensify the pain of imposed meanings for those sensitive to the arbitrariness of the process of binding. That is to say, if Ford is highly conscious that "Irish Catholic" (or "English Catholic") bears no necessary relation to Leonora—when Dowell refers to a photograph of Leonora with her six sisters in Ireland,

Leonora as referent is eclipsed by a "black shadow" that cuts across her face, leaving it "all but invisible" (ibid., 94)—he is equally aware of the designation's social power and the havoc it has caused. If Dowell could depend on transparent relations between signs and referents—if he could answer, that is, in the affirmative to his desperate question, "if for nine years I have possessed a goodly apple that is rotten at the core and discover its rottenness only in nine years and six months less four days, isn't it true to say that for nine years I possessed a goodly apple?" (ibid., 12)—much of the plaintive longing for satisfaction in the book would disappear. But the fall into experience that the book repeatedly stages in Dowell's excruciatingly deferred awakenings to sexual betrayal is also a fall into the snares of signification and its discontents, and the negative affect that gathers around Dowell's frustrated desire for transparency readies him for propaganda, which simplifies problems of reference by positing enemies behind every shadow, truth in every stereotype.

It is Dowell's own problematic relation to truth that has generated critical discussion over the years. Schorer's influential take on Dowell as a narrator unreliable to the point of madness, reprinted as the introduction to two Knopf editions of the novel, singles out Dowell's claim that he loved Edward because "he was just myself" (ibid., 161) as Dowell's "weirdest absurdity, the final, total blindness of infatuation, and self-infatuation."[62] Levenson, in contrast, suggests that Dowell's identification with Edward amounts to "the formation of character," the coming into being of a determinate individual whom Ford had hitherto presented as "a personality virtually without attributes."[63] Deeply embedded in the critical tradition, this split response to Dowell's comments on Edward offers complementary perspectives on what amounts to a conversion narrative. That is, through Dowell's identification with Edward, Ford is dramatizing the moment of ideological interpellation in which the alienated addressee of propaganda enters propaganda's warm embrace. A consideration of how this is so will return us to the question of Ford's own seemingly overcharged investment in writing for Wellington House.

Beyond the consolation of clarity, propaganda offers the gratification of agency, or at least the illusion of agency, the sense that however baffled, thwarted, and mistreated, one still matters as an individual. From the outside, the views of the newly converted may well look like the "weirdest absurdity"; from the inside they confirm one's sense of character, one's newfound grasp of the surrounding world. Far from an effective presence in the world, Dowell is someone to whom things happen, a vehicle for externally provided motivation. His remark about courting Florence is characteristic: "Why does one do things? I just drifted in and wanted Florence" (ibid., 17). Propaganda relieves anxieties about agency not only by encouraging individuals to join together against a common enemy but by soliciting identification with heroic models whose potency in the world is beyond question. On one hand propaganda asks, in a famous poster, "Daddy, What did YOU do in the Great War?" The question is ventriloquized through a young boy, whose father, seated in an armchair, newspaper and pipe in hand, is doing very little. On the other hand, propaganda proffers the positive example of Gary Cooper's Sergeant York, who transforms himself from a turkey hunting conscientious objector in rural Tennessee into a highly successful terminator of gullible German soldiers. Dowell seems to acknowledge that Edward lacks the power of heroic self-fashioning when he observes that Edward is shaped by his profession and his reading. A naive reader who styles his romantic conversation on sentimental novels, Edward, Dowell believes, is, like "all good soldiers," a sentimentalist because "their profession . . . is full of the big words, courage, loyalty, honour, constancy" (ibid., 25). And yet by dwelling on Edward's ability to impose himself on the world Dowell chooses to see Edward as an emblem of potent agency. Others must see Dowell as a nurse or invalid, Dowell suspects, but it is the thought that *Edward* must see him as a woman that immediately triggers his stunning fantasy of the good soldier's sexual potency: "that chap, coming into a room snapped up the gaze of every woman in it, as dextrously as a conjuror pockets billiard balls. It was most amazing. You know the man on the stage who throws up sixteen balls at once and they all drop into pockets all over his person, on his shoulders, on his heels, on the inner side of his sleeves; and he stands perfectly still and does nothing. Well, it was like that" (ibid., 26). Edward functions as the ideal fantasy figure for Dowell precisely because he appears to achieve so much even as "he stands perfectly still and does nothing." Dowell's comparison implies that he suspects that this form of masculinity is merely a party trick, more sleight-of-hand than substance. But his belief in Edward's power only grows stronger as Leonora tries to hold it in check by managing her husband's affairs.

Dowell's refusal to let go of a certain image of Edward, in spite of his insight into Edward's many weaknesses and lack of autonomy, resembles the kind of partisan support one sometimes finds (especially in times of war) for an embattled politician whose leadership virtues are thought to outweigh his shortcomings. Whether these shortcomings consist of sexual foibles or calculated betrayals of the public trust, some supporters will always rally to the side of endangered power, perhaps in hopes of warming themselves in what remains of reflected glory: "It is impossible for me to think of Edward Ashburnham as anything but straight, upright and honourable. . . . I try at times by dwelling on some of the things that he did to push that image of him away, as you might try to push aside a large pendulum. But it always comes back—the memory of his innumerable acts of kindness, of his efficiency, of his unspiteful tongue" (ibid., 78–79). For Dowell, Edward's power does not reside simply in his ability to seduce women; Dowell, after all, claims to have little interest in "the sex-instinct" (ibid., 79). Rather, Leonora's stringent management of Edward's estate, designed to rein in his extravagant generosity, throws into relief Edward's commitment to service. In Dowell's view, when Leonora as modern individualist prevents Edward as Tory collectivist from caring for his tenants in his own way, she transforms him into "a sort of dummy lord, in swaddling clothes" (ibid., 116)—which is to say that she remakes Edward in Dowell's own image. To be a man—a real lord—is to act in the world, preferably in the public interest. For Leonora the pendulum does not swing back, Dowell believes, because she is unable to grasp the value of public service: "It only seemed to her a kind of madness in him that he should try to take upon his own shoulders the burden of his troop, of his regiment, of his estate and of half of his county" (ibid., 100). Dowell even suggests that Edward committed suicide not because he could never have Nancy, but because Leonora would not let him exercise his altruism: "He might have stuck it out otherwise. . . . There was nothing left for him but a dreary, dreary succession of days in which he could be of no public service" (ibid., 127). Looking back at *The Good Soldier* through the lens of Ford's propaganda books, we might say that Dowell in effect casts Edward as France, an embattled paragon of the altruism France exemplifies, and Leonora as Prussia, the calculating tyrant incapable of finer feelings.

By answering the call to write for Wellington House, Ford must have seen himself as taking on, as Edward wished to, "the burden" not only of "his troop," "his regiment," and "his county," but of his country as well. The Ford of *The Critical Attitude*, bewildered by the modern world and in search of guidance within the myriad impressions bidding for his attention, resembles Dowell before he identifies with Edward. To identify with Edward is to decide that there is, after all, a "villain" to a story that seemed to have no shape. Leonora becomes for Dowell what Prussian culture, nearly as rigid in its demands, becomes for Ford, the necessary enemy. Dowell even seems to anticipate his transformation from object to agent of propaganda when he takes the reader by the lapels in order to explain Edward's virtuous daily routine: "I have been *forced* to write very much about his passions but *you have to consider*—I should like to be able *to make* you consider" that Edward is a virtuous man (ibid., 101; emphasis added). This is hailing with a vengeance. Indeed, Dowell's insistent second-person address marks not only his need to connect with his silent listener but a deep need to convince that listener.

The last element of Dowell's lengthy defense of Edward as lord of the manor provides the key to his belief that Edward's passion constitutes only part of the story: Edward, he pleads, was "a hard-working, sentimental and efficient professional man" (ibid., 102). The ideal of the professional is the pivot on which Dowell, Edward, and Ford turn. Momentarily aligning himself with Leonora, Dowell observes that "we were both of the same profession. . . . And the profession was that of keeping heart patients alive" (ibid., 39). Ford's chosen profession, as he notes in *Between St. Dennis and St. George*, is man of letters. Choosing to identify with Edward, Dowell becomes not a man who has "heard" the "saddest story," as he claims in the peculiar first sentence of the novel, but a writer who has lived through it. For Ford, the impressionist is a kind of prostitute, which means that the professional man of letters, as Ford conceives him, resembles Dowell-as-woman. David Trotter has argued that in *The Good Soldier* Ford aimed to assert his status as a highly professionalized novelist by playing out through Dowell his own need to remasculinize himself within a society whose increasing commercialization had marginalized him; he did this, in Ford's own account, by putting into *The Good Soldier* all he knew about writing.[64] To be technically proficient in this context is to be a professional, and Ford wanted to do for the English novel what Flaubert and Maupassant had done for the French, thus enabling him to compete with what he called "the literary Cubists, Vorticists, *Imagistes* and the rest of the *tapageux* and riotous *Jeunes* of that young decade."[65] Of course, coming out as it did in war time with the dubious title *The Good Soldier*, Ford's highly polished experimental novel received powerfully mixed reviews, ranging from Rebecca West's praise (and subsequent homage in the form of her first novel, *The Return of the Soldier*) to the charge that *The Good Soldier* threatened to undermine the national will to wage war.[66] Ford thus found himself uncomfortably in the position of the emasculated Dowell, who longs for a sympathetic ear in which to whisper "the saddest story" but ends up alone in a darkened room with an audience of one, who happens to be quite mad.

Ford's propaganda books promised a different kind of professional role, and a very different relation to his audience. In the Wellington House books, Ford found a new way to fulfill his felt duty as a public intellectual while remaining true to the immediacy of the impression. Like Conrad, he would make you see, but where Conrad was equally concerned to make you see *how* you see, Ford was more concerned to make you see his way, the urgency registering in uncharacteristic redundancy: "I desire that this book," Ford writes in *When Blood Is Their Argument*, "should be read by every person in the habitable globe since the subject is a subject of the greatest importance to every inhabitant of the habitable globe at the present moment" (xix). And while he writes that as "a man of peace . . . [he] cannot entertain with equanimity the idea of every inhabitant of the German Empire with his throat cut, or her brains blown out, contemplating, amidst the smoke of his or her ruined homestead, the pale stars" (*When Blood Is Their Argument*, 293), such are the images of vigorous retribution he chooses to conjure. If in *The Good Soldier*, as Trotter argues, Ford attempted to solidify his professional standing as a master experimentalist through his highly wrought rendering of a powerless narrator recoiling from and then identifying with violent desires, in his propaganda books Ford aimed to gratify his desire for efficacious citizenship by using the secret power of the state to propagate his modernist narratives of cultural value.

And yet, however much the books have in common formally, and however much they are entwined responses to a shared media environment, a critical difference remains. In *The Good Soldier*, Dowell alludes four times to "the saddest story," the referent shifting each time. In my view the single saddest story is the third one Dowell tells, the one about how desire tends to exhaust its objects. Dowell believes that "the real fierceness of desire, the real heat of a passion long continued and withering up the soul of a man is the craving for identity with the woman that he loves" (*The Good Soldier*, 79). From this identification the man receives "the moral support, the encouragement, the relief from the sense of loneliness, the assurance of his own worth": "But these things pass away; inevitably they pass away as the shadows pass across sun-dials. It is sad, but it is so. The pages of the book will become familiar; the beautiful corner of the road will have been turned too many times. Well, this is the saddest story" (ibid., 80). Read reflexively, this points beyond the unhappiness that is in marriage to Ford's challenge as a writer: what kind of text will continually renew the reader's interest, encouraging her to turn the same pages, again and again?[67] Here, then, is the wedge that separates two aspects of Ford. As the writer who projected himself into both Dowell and Edward, Ford remains suspended among multiple possibilities and invites the reader to wander among them. As the man who wrote for Wellington House, Ford responded to the call of ideology with a ferocity that overrode the contradictory desires that animate Dowell's discourse.

Ford's propaganda books, like all propaganda, solve the problem of desire through a strategy of identification that does not outlive the moment of its usefulness. We can all love the French and hate the Germans, until it's time to hate the French again. In *The Good Soldier*, Ford wants to bind desire not in the moment of identification but within "the intricate tangle of references and cross-references" that compose, and discompose, his novel.[68] We may be drawn, inevitably, into Dowell's first-person discourse, and Dowell himself may wish to merge with Edward. But the history of criticism of the novel testifies to its ability to place the reader inside and outside Dowell's perspective at once. The formal proximity and ideological disjunction between *The Good Soldier* and Ford's Wellington House productions can be traced back, I have argued, to their common grounding in the impression, and the impression, I have suggested, is Ford's way of binding together the split identity of the modern fact.

Binding, however, can be a problematic enterprise. Dowell informs us that "I call this the Saddest Story, rather than 'The Ashburnham Tragedy,' just because it is so sad, just because there was no current to draw things along to a swift and inevitable end" (ibid., 109). Grasped together, Ford's modernism and his propaganda serve as a valuable reminder of how wayward currents can be, and how easily their polarity can be reversed. *The Good Soldier*, animating multiple circuits and webbing out into provisional networks of meaning, prevents its pages from becoming too familiar. In the Wellington House books, themselves written with as much art as the novel, the current suddenly coalesces into a single deadly flow, leaving throats cut, brains blown out, and homesteads ruined. Granted, with Edward's throat slashed, Nancy's mind crippled, and the Dowell household wrecked the difference may not seem great. It is, however, critical.

Chapter Four

JOYCE AND THE LIMITS OF
POLITICAL PROPAGANDA

TURNING FROM Ford Madox Ford to James Joyce, we move from an outsider desperate to become an insider to a voluntary exile who needed to feel like an outsider. Joyce was a connoisseur of betrayal, and when he could not find a genuine betrayer, he was always ready to invent one. Of course, Irish history provided plenty of material to work with, most notably for Joyce the story of Charles Stewart Parnell, the Irish parliamentary leader whose career was destroyed when the Catholic Church in Ireland denounced him for adultery and key political allies abandoned him. From an early age Joyce identified with Parnell as a man victimized by his native land, and though he had no objective grounds to fear for his life, he was afraid that a return to Ireland might end in his martyrdom. But as sensitive as Joyce was to Ireland as "the old sow that eats her farrow," he also understood Irish self-destruction as a legacy of British colonial rule.[1] Thus if Stephen Dedalus in *A Portrait of the Artist as a Young Man* bitterly tells his nationalist friend Davin that "the indispensable informer" for "the next rebellion" in Trinity College will easily be found (*Portrait*, 202), *Ulysses* provides an anatomy of the colonial dynamic that made informers, betrayal, and collusion part of the texture of everyday life. It has become relatively commonplace in recent years to dismiss early modernist criticism's image of Joyce as a disengaged aesthete, and for good reason. If debates about Joyce's politics previously could agree on little beyond Joyce's hostility to the apocalyptic nationalism associated with Padraic Pearse, it now seems indisputable that, as Vincent Cheng has put it, "Joyce wrote insistently from the perspective of a colonial subject of an oppressive empire."[2] Over the last decade, criticism has accordingly provided new portraits of Joyce the Irishman, the anarchist, the subaltern, and the postcolonial.[3]

But new waves of criticism always produce an undertow of doubt: was the earlier version of Joyce as a mandarin stylist really so wrong, and if so, how could so many smart people have misread him? And if Joyce was more engaged with his historical moment than earlier criticism acknowledged, how does criticism go about redressing the imbalance without swinging too far to the opposite extreme? This chapter aims to address such questions by situating *Ulysses* within discursive battles over Irish identity that were exacerbated by the British recruiting poster campaign during World War I. Irish recruiting posters, aiming to interpellate a colonial subject tailored to England's international needs, represent a particularly charged contribution to the historical process whereby, as Declan Kiberd has put it, England "invented the idea of Ireland."[4] *Ulysses* is one of the ways in which Ireland returned the favor. Situated within this contested field of mutually constructed national identities, the novel works toward the reversal of the rhetorical project of recruiting posters by re-problematizing the category of Irishness and the very idea of national identity at a time when the majority of Irish colonial subjects were beginning to enter a postcolonial world. Bloom's "final meditations" before retiring habitually turn to the fantasy of creating "one sole unique advertisement to cause passers to stop in wonder, a poster novelty, with all extraneous accretions excluded, reduced to its simplest and most efficient terms not exceeding the span of casual vision and congruous with the velocity of modern life."[5] The aesthetic and political antithesis of Bloom's fantasy, the exuberant stylistic and narratological excesses of *Ulysses* both exploit and counter the arresting effect of the "poster novelty" with a countervailing strategy of disruption and dislocation. Bloom himself momentarily embodies this strategy when handed a flier announcing the arrival of the evangelical preacher Alexander J. Dowie: "Bloo. . . . Me? No. Blood of the Lamb"(8.8–9). Here only a split-second short-circuiting of identification, Bloom's hesitation foreshadows the structural innovations that later in *Ulysses* disrupt the strategic designs of British recruitment.

At one level it is of course unsurprising that an Irish writer would be hostile to a propaganda campaign run out of London. But Irish response to the British cause and to English culture was more mixed than one might expect, and Joyce's fiction honors that complexity. At one extreme, there was the highly critical attitude of the radical weeklies. An editorial in Arthur Griffith's *Scissors and Paste*, a publication Joyce cites in *Ulysses*, seems to intuit Wellington House's clandestine manipulation of Reuters during World War I: "Not one great event but has been seen for the rest of the world through English eyes or told to the rest of the world as England wished to tell it. The traditional racial characteristics of each of us were fitted upon us by England for all the world to learn by heart. And the myth of 'British fair play' stands above all the characteristics we suffer under as the greatest masterpiece of them all" (*Scissors and Paste*, January 2, 1915).[6] At the other extreme is the historical fact that during the Boer War Dublin not only furnished a disproportionate number of Irish recruits, the city enlisted many more soldiers than did Belfast. Moreover, many Dublin theater goers seem to have sat through, unconcerned, as Irish performers sang music hall songs that assumed "a total identification of the Irish actors, singers, and audience with their English government," even songs celebrating Britain's colonial prowess.[7] Joyce's orientation to things British was in most ways much closer to the satiric attitude of *Scissors and Paste*, but *Ulysses*, far from straightforwardly satiric, probes the confused loyalties of the Irish national subject, and it does so in ways that clarify both the effectiveness and the limits of propaganda that was designed to reorganize such confusion.

In all the texts I have discussed so far, identification has been key to the conjunction of modernism and propaganda. Marlow's ambivalent identification with Kurtz in *Heart of Darkness*, like John Dowell's less ambivalent but more strained identification with Edward Ashburnham in *The Good Soldier*, is motivated by the erosion of familiar ethical, epistemological, and political coordinates that made modern propaganda both necessary and effective. When the pressures toward identification prove too much for Virginia Woolf's Rachel Vinrace in *The Voyage Out*, her only refuge is death. In *Ulysses* Joyce's stream-of-consciousness techniques dilate the moment of identification by representing it as a process open to disruption, dissolution, and critique. The novel's detailed representation of consciousness thus traces the process whereby ideological messages disseminated by propaganda do or do not become anchored in the individual. At the same time, by both soliciting and complicating the reader's identification with his characters, Joyce's increasingly experimental narrative modes mimetically reproduce in the reader the contradictory ideological crosscurrents experienced by the Irish colonial subject poised on the verge of a new political reality. By insinuating the reader into the text in this way, *Ulysses* provides not only an anatomy of British attempts to recruit Irish subjects during the war but also comments self-reflexively on the place of novelistic discourse within this highly contested terrain. Ironically, Joyce reported to his brother Stanislaus that *Ulysses* was rumored to be a species of Bolshevik propaganda.[8] But by rooting out what Stephen calls the priest and king within, *Ulysses* may be modernism's most trenchant response to propaganda.

RECRUITMENT AND THE ART OF THE POSTER

Posters, as Claude Gandelman has argued, epitomize the tendency of both modern publicity and modern art to present themselves "as a sort of theater of the enunciative process."[9] Susan Sontag, arguing along similar lines, points out that "posters presuppose the modern concept of the public space—as a theater of persuasion. . . . The poster . . . implies the creation of urban, public space as an arena of signs: the image- and word-choked facades and surfaces of great modern cities."[10] Taking the urban space of colonial Dublin as its subject, *Ulysses* engages modern techniques of ideological consolidation epitomized in the poster while contributing to the invention of a particular form of cosmopolitan subjectivity. Haines, the English ethnographer who wishes to incorporate Stephen's witticisms into a study of Irish folklore, represents (to borrow James Clifford's formulation) a "discrepant cosmopolitanism," one that throws into relief the ways in which the cosmopolitanism of *Ulysses* is able to produce, owing to Ireland's "premature" decolonization, what historical retrospect permits us to recognize as a prototype of postcolonial subjectivity.[11] Distancing himself from violently exclusivist nationalisms and later deeply ambivalent toward what proved a reactionary new state, Joyce nevertheless would have welcomed Frantz Fanon's notion that "it is at the heart of national consciousness that international consciousness lives and grows."[12] For the political project of *Ulysses* is consonant with the declared program of the journal for which Joyce worked as a translator during the war, Zurich's *International Review*: "to oppose to the campaign of lies a war of minds which shall shatter the unholy legends that are forming around us."[13]

In 1916 a writer in the *Spark*, one of Dublin's many radical weeklies, complained: "Someone once said that there were three degrees of false-hoods, namely lies, *damn* lies and—*Statistics*, and now I suggest the fourth degree—*Recruiting posters*" (May 23). Joyce invokes recruiting posters early in *Ulysses* as Bloom, checking for a letter from his pen pal, Martha Clifford, gazes at a poster "with soldiers of all arms on parade" (5.57). Given that this kind of pictorial recruiting poster was not produced before World War I, the poster Bloom studies on June 16, 1904, must be a Joycean invention modeled on posters distributed from 1915–18.[14] Known for his pedantic fidelity to the historically verifiable, here Joyce indulges in an anachronism that distinctly foregrounds the text's complex historical layering, a layering that needs to be acknowledged by situating *Ulysses* more insistently in the period of its composition than is often the case.[15] Expanding in revision the passage in which Bloom "review[s] again the soldiers on parade" (5.66), Joyce highlighted the moment of reading in which an Irish subject internalizes, restages, and revises the ideological messages that were formulated during the war by the British government and obligingly designed and disseminated by Irish advertising agencies, including, as it happens, the agency for which Bloom once worked, Hely's.[16]

Even one of Joyce's most well-known remarks about the universality of *Ulysses* is marked by this context. "I find the subject of Ulysses," Joyce liked to say, "the most human in world literature," for Homer's hero is the only "complete all-round character" ever created.[17] In

Richard Ellmann's influential biography, Joyce's Ulysses, "pacifist, father, wanderer, musician, and artist," comes to seem a portrait of the artist as a complete man, and Leopold Bloom, accordingly, is figured as an avatar of universal humanism, "a humble vessel elected to bear and transmit unimpeached the best qualities of the mind."[18] Yet the two extant accounts of Joyce's remarks register the more immediate historical context. According to Joyce, the one figure able to outwit polytropic man was the "Greek recruiting sergeant" who circumvented Ulysses' feigned madness by placing two-year-old Telemachus in the furrow his father was ploughing. Given that Ulysses was trying to escape from mandatory service, it may seem odd that Joyce casts a scene of conscription as a scene of recruitment. Yet Joyce made these remarks during World War I, as the British government was subjecting Ireland to an intensive recruiting campaign featuring public speakers, parades, and, quite prominently, posters.[19] Frank Budgen was the first to supply the appropriate visual context for Joyce's comments, noting that Ulysses "found his Ajax at the War Office in the shape of Lord Kitchener," an allusion to the poster image on which James Flagg modeled his more famous American poster, "I Want You for the U.S. Army."[20] Having designed his own posters for Dublin's Volta cinema several years earlier, and having understood the Trojan Horse as the first tank, Joyce may well have relished the notion that the story of Ulysses' failed draft evasion could have functioned in its own day as a kind of recruiting poster. The ancient recruiter's filial tactics, after all, can be read as a precursor to one of the most famous recruiting posters of World War I: the comfortable postwar father seated in an easy chair being asked by his children, "Daddy, what did YOU do in the Great War?" When Joyce himself was asked the same question, the story goes, he responded, "I wrote *Ulysses*."[21]

England had been recruiting the Irish since the turn of the century. During the Boer War British recruiting in Ireland elicited fierce anti-British sentiment from some segments of Irish society and strongly sympathetic support for South African resistance to imperial domination. Yet even with various anti-imperialist factions, from radical republicans to moderate nationalists, uniting under the banner of the Irish Transvaal Committee and devoting a good deal of their energy to an intensive antirecruiting campaign, Dublin furnished a disproportionate number of Irish recruits. In "Eumaeus" Bloom is "only too conscious of the casualties invariably resulting from propaganda . . . and the misery and suffering it entailed . . . chiefly, destruction of the fittest" (16.1599–1602). Although radical writers tried to explain away the enlistment on ideological grounds, Joseph O'Brien has probably hit closer to home: "Idle hands and empty stomachs are a powerful antidote to patriotic idealism . . .

and there were more of these in Dublin than in any other part of the country."[22] The years following the Boer War saw the gradual consolidation, accelerated by World War I, of a resistant national consciousness that expanded what had been the relatively restricted influence of various nationalist factions. Despite the existence in 1903 of such nationalist cultural formations as the Gaelic League and the Irish Literary Revival, most of Dublin lined the streets to cheer Edward VII's visit even as the Dublin Corporation refused to honor him with a municipal address. From 1914 to 1918, some 150,000 Irishmen enlisted, yet British recruiting also evoked a variety of antirecruiting responses, including pungent satires in the radical weeklies, one of which cast Irish Parliamentary Party leader John Redmond, whose face had appeared on recruiting posters, as the betraying priest—now a khaki-clad recruiting officer—in the rebel ballad "The Croppy Boy."[23]

Long before World War I, when poster art first became a key agent of state propaganda, the increasingly obtrusive presence of posters in England had already begun to generate controversy.[24] As early as the seventeenth century, bills publicizing theatrical events and other announcements were stuck to posts marking pedestrian paths through the London streets. From the "posting of bills" came the word "billposting," carried out by "billstickers" or "billposters"; hence "poster," the first *OED* reference coming in *Nicholas Nickleby* in 1838, though doubtless the word was current much earlier. In 1895 Alexandre Arsène, writing of French posters, notes that "the poster-mania is a comparatively new disease" and then exemplifies the malady by discussing the difficulty of peeling especially fine specimens off the wall.[25] The phrase the "horrors of the hoardings" became a cliche, and in England the National Vigilance Society worried over the threat to public decency and the dangers of miseducation posed by outdoor advertisements.[26] The poster of Marie Kendall, "charming soubrette" (and like Bloom's recruiting poster, another Joycean invention), typifies the kind of siren that drew the Vigilance Society's anxious gaze. (In "Sirens" Joyce inscribes the classical prototype into a poster for cigarettes: "a swaying mermaid smoking mid nice waves" [11.300].) With billposting completely unregulated, posters and notices were plastered anywhere they would stick, and the public began to complain about their unsightliness. As billsticking evolved from small-scale enterprises into capital-intensive operations, newspapers felt threatened by potential revenue losses and, joining forces with those who opposed posters on ethical and aesthetic grounds, pressed for regulation. In response, rival organizations—each with its own monthly journal, *The Billposter and Advertising Agent* (1886–89) and *The Billposters' Journal and Lessee and Entertainers' Advertiser* (1887–89)—merged in the United Billposters' Association, with a new trade journal called simply

The Billposter (1889–1920). Despite such heroic commercial solidarity, the government began to regulate the new industry in 1889 with the Advertising Stations Rating Bill, which empowered local authorities to tax advertisers for the use of buildings, vacant land, and areas near public roadways.[27] By 1904 regulatory agencies had arisen to ensure that few cities were as thoroughly papered over as they had been in Victorian times. Leopold Bloom, in consequence, wandering the streets of Dublin, has good reason to admire the ingenious circumvention of state regulations by the advertiser of Kino's trousers, whose rowboat on the Liffey rocks "lazily its plastered board": "Good idea that. Wonder if he pays rent to the corporation. How can you own water really?" (8.89, 93–94).[28]

Concomitant with its commercial ascendancy, by the late nineteenth century the pictorial poster, borne up by artists such as Jules Chéret in the 1860s and later Toulouse-Lautrec, was also coming to be recognized as a relatively autonomous form of artistic expression (distinct, that is, from its function as advertisement), and the poster's new authority intensified the effect of its ubiquity. In England Fred Walker's famous design for Wilkie Collins's *The Woman in White* (1860), later used in a poster for the stage adaptation (1871), is often credited with having stimulated the increasingly "aesthetic" advertisements that culminated in Aubrey Beardsley's designs for *The Yellow Book*. By the turn of the century the poster had arrived, within the rapidly shifting coordinates of popular, mass, and elite art, at an ambiguous status—as both objet d'art and utilitarian throwaway—an ambiguity that would soon be exploited in the leveling of artistic hierarchies in modern art more generally.[29] In 1895 the *Chap-Book*, an American avant-garde literary magazine modeled on *The Yellow Book*, notes of a particular item that "for the benefit of Poster Collectors a special edition of fifty copies has been printed on Japan paper," and the *Pall Mall Gazette* takes notice of "an exquisitely clever and amusing design, that would take the blue ribbon, judged by the points of artistic poster-making." A year later the *Daily News* announces an exhibition of "portraits of some of the leading poster artists, with selections from their works." Ten years later, with the poster *artistes* themselves having been deemed as worthy of exhibition as their work, the growing influence of poster art registers in the *Athenaeum*, which complains that some of "our own painters" seem "somewhat abrupt and posterlike."[30] The convergence of poster art's commercial and cultural authority is epitomized in Ivor Montagu's decision in 1926 to save Alfred Hitchcock's first important film, *The Lodger*, by bringing in E. McKnight Kauffer, an American poster artist whose cubist and futurist images helped revolutionize British design (and who later illustrated some poems by T. S. Eliot).[31] It should not be surprising, then, to discover that in 1920, only five years before directing *The Battleship Potemkin*, Sergei Eisenstein, pioneer in the theory and practice of cinematic montage, was a poster artist for the Red Army.[32]

The increasingly insistent force of the poster image early in the century was not lost on novelists. "A poster of a woman in tights herald[ing] the Christmas pantomime" induces Margaret Schlegel to wonder in *Howards End* (1910), "How many of these vacillating shoppers and tired shop-assistants realized that it was a divine event that drew them together?" Resisting the urban scene Joyce takes as his subject, Forster constructs an idealized pastoral retreat into which Margaret and her fellow shopper Mrs. Wilcox, pursued by a vision of a "torrent of coins and toys" issuing "from a forgotten manger," try to escape. More welcoming, the vorticist typography of Wyndham Lewis's *Blast* (1914) suggests a poster influence, as does the typographic play of Italian futurism. By 1918 in Lewis's *Tarr*, Kreisler could loom in Bertha's eyes as "a great terrifying poster."[33] That Bertha has just been raped by Kreisler, a painter, anticipates in Lewis's characteristically violent fashion Sontag's insight into the "visually aggressive" nature of the poster image: "a poster reaches out to grab those who might otherwise pass it by."[34] Rebecca West's *The Return of the Soldier* (1918) even appears to narratize a famous English recruiting poster in which a little boy and two women, one fair (Kitty), the other dark (Jenny), watch from the threshold of a comfortable house (Baldry Court) as soldiers (joined by Chris Baldry) march off to war: "Women of Britain Say 'GO!'"

Beyond instances of self-conscious appropriation, the poster-novel conjuncture can also be referred to the material conditions of cultural production. Writing in 1925, E. M. Forster located the novel along a verbal continuum reaching from the informative (a "tramway notice") to the "useless" (lyric poetry) when he observed (with the melancholy of a man who had written his last) that "the novel, whatever else it may be, is partly a notice board. And that is why men who do not care for poetry or even for the drama enjoy novels and are well qualified to criticize them."[35] Forster's observation gets at the residually equivocal status of the novel as "art" even after the aestheticizing efforts of Flaubert, James, and Conrad. Like the poster, many modern novels addressed information about contemporary life to a mass audience even as they aspired to an aesthetic autonomy, or "uselessness," modeled on the detachment often attributed to lyric poetry. Produced and distributed within the modern urban spaces they increasingly came to represent, modern novels also resemble the poster in their tendency to prefer images to narrative and scenes to summary. The very existence of public spaces through which crowds pass quickly, presupposed by posters and modern fiction alike, no doubt contributed to the appeal of the immediately arresting image. Thus Sontag's insight into the "visually aggressive" nature of the poster image also resonates with the urgency in Conrad's previously quoted remarks about his goals as a self-consciously modern novelist: "My task . . . is, by the power of the written word, to *make* you hear, to *make* you feel—it is, before all, to *make* you see."[36] It is no accident, clearly, that the first novel to feature an advertising canvasser who dreams of a "poster novelty . . . congruous with the velocity of modern life" (*Ulysses*, 17.1771–73) is set in the first European capital to have an electric tramway system, presumably complete (as the Forster quotation requires I mention) with tramway notices.[37] Thus, though in some sense obviously incommensurate (an issue to which I shall return), *Ulysses* and posters can be considered homologous cultural objects.

The power of the poster image was not lost on the Recruiting Subdivision of the British War Office either, whose campaign turned increasingly to pictorial posters.[38] During the Boer War recruiting and antirecruiting materials consisted mainly of small typeset exhortations. The Irish recruiting poster might read, "Your king and Country need another 100,000 men," and an antirecruiting counterpart might call for citizens to "Remember Ninety-Eight" (referring to the failed rebellion of 1798 and the martyrdom of Wolfe Tone). With the onset of World War I, England continued to use purely verbal posters, primarily to hammer away at the supposed economic benefits of joining the army, but early in 1915 the government campaign began to exploit the pictorial strategies that had been developed for commercial purposes by Ireland's leading advertising firms: M'Caw, Stevenson, and Orr, Ltd.; James Walker; David Allen and Sons, Ltd.; Hely's Ltd.; and Alexander Thom. Initially the same images, such as a dramatic rendering of the sinking *Lusitania*, were used in England and Ireland, with only the captions altered; other posters could be used without changes of any kind. Yet in the most intensive recruiting years, 1915 and 1918, posters in Ireland exploited a variety of techniques and images targeted at specific segments of the Irish population. Propagandists realized that in a country whose citizens might react skeptically to patriotic appeals—witness Bloom in response to sentimental nationalist rhetoric in "Aeolus": "Whose land?" (7.273)—recruiting efforts would have to aim at the widest possible range of motivations for enlistment. Not surprisingly, virtually all Irish poster artists, unlike some quite well-known English painters who contributed to the war effort, chose to remain anonymous. With economic and symbolic appeals largely divided between typeset and pictorial posters, respectively, specifically Irish pictorial posters became the locus of contested representations of Irishness, a discursive field in which *Ulysses* also participated.

The turn toward pictorial posters at this historical juncture also throws into relief the increasingly recognized effectiveness of the mass-produced image (propaganda films also came into use at this time) in mobilizing an ideological consensus. The *Billposter* claimed in celebration of the recruiting campaign that "such an illustration of poster power has been given as no country and no age ever saw before": "the poster held before the whole nation a conception of duty, a vision of Britannia in her might . . . a living omnipresent sense of the price of citizenship and of the right and justice and liberty for which the nation is struggling."[39] When sufficient resources were available, antirecruiting forces also exploited the "living omnipresent sense" of visual images: during the Boer War, the nationalist newspaper the *Nation* "erected an outdoor projection screen in College Green on which was flashed nightly the news of the Boer successes, giving the assembled crowd the opportunity to cheer Boer generals and groan at British politicians when their likenesses appeared on the screen."[40] Wellington House recruit Sir Arthur Conan Doyle, writing in support of "a poster campaign to whip up hate against Germany," would underscore the shifting priorities of mass communication by commending the poster's power to hold up visions even before the reluctant eye: "I do not believe in pamphlets, because the prejudiced man never even opens them. I do believe in placards because one cannot help seeing them."[41] Molly Bloom seems to have come to a similar conclusion when she complains, after remembering a time she was so bored that she mailed letters to herself, that men are so "thick" they "never understand what you say even youd want to print it up on a big poster for them" (18.707–8). Posters themselves sometimes include a fantasy of their own efficacy. In one instance, a German soldier on the front is literally run off his feet by a placard announcing the imminent arrival of thousands of fighting Irishmen. Although the placard represented within the poster is nonpictorial, the poster links the placard's red lettering with an explosion in the red sky over the battlefield as if to suggest that the power of the inscribed word were being translated into the force of the encompassing image.

Though not a visual writer in the painterly sense of Conrad, D. H. Lawrence, or Woolf, Joyce builds the material force of poster images into his textual practice. Even beyond the clatter of the printing press in "Aeolus," the sensuous impact of mass-produced signs is pervasive, and visual images in particular typically conjure a scene of reading in—and as—response: "Where was the chap I saw in that picture somewhere?," Bloom wonders. "Ah yes, in the dead sea floating on his back, reading a book with a parasol open" (5.37–38). Earlier, as if acknowledging the aggressiveness of mechanically reproduced images, Bloom sees "parlour windows plastered with bills": "Plasters on a sore eye" (4.237). Such somatic links are insistent: gazing at the recruiting poster in "Lotus Eaters" while holding a copy of the *Freeman's Journal*, Bloom inhales the smell of "freshprinted rag paper" (5.58); Molly, reconjuring the pleasures of Boylan, whom she thinks of as a billsticker, lingers over the smell of "the sweety kind of paste they stick their bills up with" (18.126–27); reading a flier for a Zionist settlement in Palestine, all the while kindling an erotic reverie about the woman ahead of him in line, Bloom holds "the page aslant patiently, bending his senses and his will, his soft subject gaze at rest" (4.162–63). If the collapsing distinction between public and private in such moments gestures toward a brave new world of administered stimulation, it is important to note that even in Bloom's characteristic yielding to sensuality Joyce preserves the possibility of agency within subjected vision by differentiating between sensory reflex and volition. Almost closed here, the space between seeming immediacy and considered response, the space, that is, in which images are read and interpreted, is increasingly dilated as the narrative unfolds. Thus the apparitions of Major Tweedy and Edward VII in "Circe" during Stephen's encounter with the British soldiers derive from Bloom's extended response to the recruiting poster he studies in "Lotus Eaters." The complexity of that initial moment of reading requires some additional unfolding here.

Having just collected his letter from Martha Clifford, Bloom looks back to the post office wall:

> He slipped card and letter into his sidepocket, reviewing again the soldiers on parade. Where's old Tweedy's regiment? Castoff soldier. There: bearskin cap and hackle plume. No, he's a grenadier. Pointed cuffs. There he is: royal Dublin fusiliers. Redcoats. Too showy. That must be why the women go after them. Uniform. Easier to enlist and drill. Maud Gonne's letter about taking them off O'Connell street at night: disgrace to our Irish capital. Griffith's paper is on the same tack now: an army rotten with venereal disease: overseas or halfseasover empire. Half baked they look: hypnotised like. Eyes front. Mark time. Table: able. Bed: ed. The King's own. Never see him dressed up as a fireman or a bobby. A mason, yes. (5.65–75)

Triggering a flood of associations about his father-in-law, the amatory advantage of uniformed soldiers, and the political authority behind them, the poster elicits a flicker of anticolonial sentiment in Bloom's allusion to a leaflet attributed to Maud Gonne. Aiming to promote enlistment late in the Boer War, the British Army had begun to allow soldiers to leave their barracks at night to roam the streets, and Gonne's Daughters of Ireland, a Gaelicist cultural organization, tried to discourage Irish women from "consorting with the soldiers of the enemy of their country"; Arthur Griffith's pacifist paper, the *United Irishman*, was among those that revived the issue in the spring of 1904 when the army refused the Dublin Corporation's demand that the soldiers be restricted.[42]

Yet Bloom's full response to the poster complicates any simple axiology of engagement versus disengagement or resistance versus compliance. The poster clearly exercises a hold on him—he looks at it twice—and his memory of the recruiting controversy sets the stage for the climactic encounter in Nighttown between Stephen and Privates Carr and Compton. Moreover, Bloom's response to the poster anticipates his capacity to act decisively on Stephen's behalf in that scene. For despite his absorption, a critical distance on the poster's propaganda is established in the contrast between the relative incisiveness of Bloom's thoughts and the "hypnotised" gaze of the soldiers, who are cast as drunken ("half-seasover") agents of a sickly yet contagious empire ("rotten with venereal disease")—English "syphilisation" the Citizen will later call it (12.1197).

Still, Bloom's comparatively critical response to the poster can be neither fully assimilated to the cause of active resistance to recruitment nor dismissed as a form of skeptical detachment. Though the insight into uniforms as a technique of recruitment and social control—"Easier to enlist and drill"—is Bloom's, the most critical elements in his interior monologue are held in suspension as fragments from other printed sources: to register the invisible quotation marks around such phrases as "disgrace to our Irish capital" or "an army rotten with venereal disease" is to transform the represented flow of Bloom's consciousness into a series of textual notations, a verbal montage in which the possibility of a more engaged political response can be said to exist, though only in potential, in the unarticulated relationship among the elements of the collage.[43]

In Stephen too the potential for active engagement is articulated only to be suspended. Wandering on the strand in "Proteus," for instance, Stephen is linked, in shifting moments of self-division and identification, to a range of socialist, nationalist, and anarchist stances, none of which is privileged, endorsed, or repudiated. Consonant with the confusions between fathers and sons throughout *Ulysses*, Stephen's meditations in "Proteus" touch on both Patrick Egan and his father, Kevin, the former a self-declared (if timid) socialist, the latter a Fenian in exile linked to nationalist bombings and police attacks. As one might expect, Stephen's recollections of father and son in Paris seem to refuse, through their lightly mocking tone, the communal ties of fellow countrymen abroad. But another memory, interrupting even as it links memories of Patrick and Kevin, suggests an undercurrent of connection. Having approached the post office late in the day with a money order from his mother, Stephen recalls having the door slammed in his face by a postal clerk: "Hunger toothache. *Encore deux minutes.* Look clock. Must get. *Fermé.* Hired Dog! Shoot him to bloody bits with a bang shotgun, bits man spattered walls all brass buttons. Bits all khrrrrklak in place clack back.

Not hurt? O, that's all right. Shake hands. See what I meant, see? O, that's all right. Shake a shake. O, that's all only all right" (3.186–91). Although the cartoon-like comedy and context of Stephen's rage (his mother packed his bags in *Portrait* and now sends a little of the ready) palliate the violence of his imagination, they do so without canceling the suggestion of anarchism uncovered within a wounded sense of entitlement. The "hired dog" is destroyed, after all, for his loyalty to the same government institution, the post office, in which Bloom encounters imperial authority in the form of a recruiting poster while awaiting Martha Clifford's letter—a repetition that gestures toward Dublin's General Post Office, headquarters for the 1916 rising. Just before and after this passage, the multitudes Stephen contains in "Proteus" are momentarily polarized around the issue of violence—the very issue that historically split anarchism off from socialism—and then recast, first as a question of self-division, then as a guilty alliance between self and other. In the first instance, imagining himself identified by two eyewitnesses as a murderer in Paris, Stephen offers an alibi: "Other fellow did it: other me"; in the second, assessing the rhetorical design of Kevin Egan's conspiratorial ramblings, Stephen thinks: "To yoke me as his yokefellow, our crimes our common cause" (3.182, 228–29). Less sure that he is his father's son than Kevin Egan, who hears Simon Dedalus in Stephen's voice, Stephen is nevertheless yoked to multiple identities, including a range of socialist and anarchist stances: "Their blood is in me," Stephen thinks, "their lusts my waves" (3.306–7). But like Bloom, whose thoughts also assume brief residence in a variety of political identities, Stephen never settles into a politically engaged relation to the world.

Apart from Joyce's own early interest in socialism and anarchism, documented and discussed by Dominic Manganiello in *Joyce's Politics*, such instances of politically volatile subjectivity indicate the limitations of pegging the politics of *Ulysses* to any simple form of engaged radical critique or bourgeois detachment. A reciprocal articulation of the staging of ideological appeals in *Ulysses* and Irish recruiting posters, to which I now turn, will suggest an alternative understanding of the political work performed by *Ulysses*.

READING POSTERS/READING *ULYSSES*

Like Ford trying to persuade the English to side with their traditional enemy France, British recruiters clearly faced some significant challenges when commissioning posters for Ireland. The most fundamental problem was how to induce Irish Catholics, some of whom were already responding warmly to Germany's promise of Irish independence, to take up arms alongside its long-standing Protestant oppressors. One poster's silly literal-mindedness underscores the issue of national identity at the heart of recruiting posters' rhetorical project without really offering much of a solution. It shows a saluting soldier standing under an array of British flags, including a centrally located Irish harp on a green background, flanked by large text that reads: "If you are an Irishman, your place is with your chums under the flags." Standing under a flag is one thing, fighting for it another. Cleverer approaches employed specifically Irish materials to counter the problem that the flag poster merely recapitulates.

The peasant woman was one such Irish cultural resource. Recruiting posters throughout Europe deployed strategic images of masculinity and femininity, casting them in such emblematic roles as *La Liberté*, Britannia, Motherhood, and Frailty. Modern publicity often operates nostalgically by selling a version of the past to the future, and the peasant woman in one Hely's poster (figure 4.1) exploits a specifically Irish myth of originary rural purity invented around the turn of the twentieth century. As David Cairns and Shaun Richards have shown, the figure of the peasant woman was not a univocal symbol but was invoked by different segments of Irish society toward contradictory ends.[44] Joyce taps into the myth of purity early in *Portrait* in Stephen's glimpses of mysterious peasant women standing at the halfdoors of cottages and later eroticizes it in Davin's story of a pregnant woman who invited him into her cottage as he walked home one night from a hurling match. As deployed here by British recruiters, the peasant woman is part of a when-are-you-going-to-stop-beating-your-wife? gambit designed to answer the question of why Catholics should join forces with Protestants against Germany. Encouraging national identification with another small Catholic country, this one already overrun, the poster is meant to evoke the alleged German atrocities committed against Belgian women that were widely publicized in Lord Bryce's propaganda report of 1915. That the figure of the peasant woman was constituted within a violently contested cultural field can be gauged by the *Playboy* riots of 1907, triggered in part by the perceived threat to a powerfully invested emblem of national purity, an emblem whose implication in a discourse of Celtic authenticity Joyce would ironize in the old milkwoman of "Telemachus." Highlighting the inventedness and potential paternalism of the Gaelic revival (as well as its debt to Ascendancy figures such as W. B. Yeats), Joyce brings his peasant woman face to face with Haines, who addresses her in a language she cannot even recognize as Irish.

Another Hely's poster (figure 4.2) invokes traditional Irish gender roles more pointedly by transforming the vulnerable Colleen Bawn into a militant figure reminiscent of Cathleen Ni Houlihan, legendary unifier

FIGURE 4.1 "Have You Any Women Worth Defending?" An appeal to Catholicism and masculine honor using the contested figure of the Irish peasant: "arent
they thick they never understand what you say even youd want to print it up on
a big poster for them" (18.706–7). Lithograph; artist unknown; printed by
Hely's Ltd; circulated in March 1915.

FIGURE 4.2   Enlisting gender: "For the Glory of Ireland." Lithograph; artist unknown; printed by Hely's Ltd; circulated in June 1915.

of Ireland's four green fields. Playing on the incongruity of active female and passive male, the image preys on male fears of female empowerment during the war. With her rifle dwarfing his ashplant and her flame-like strands of hair echoing the frightening destruction on the horizon, the woman's eager militancy overshadows the more traditional image of feminine mourning in the background. The female viewer is thus offered split roles that imply a narrative connection: urge your man to do his duty or mourn the losses caused by his cowardice. (Of course that narrative is vulnerable to recasting: urge your man to do his duty and then mourn *his* loss.) In the distant grouping of father and son—or perhaps, more pointedly, grandfather and grandson—we also catch a glimpse of the filial theme emphasized in other widely distributed posters. Impossibly visible on the horizon, a ruined cathedral reinvokes the cautionary tale of Belgium in order, quite literally this time, to bring the war closer to home.

Further collapsing the space between battle front and home front, another Hely's poster (figure 4.3) dramatizes the war as a more direct threat to bourgeois comfort by using a highly theatrical space to break down the boundaries between the private sphere of domesticity and the international theater of world war. Here, as in *Ulysses*, the idea of "home rule" takes on pointedly multiple meanings. (The poster's challenge—"Is *your* home worth fighting for?"—would have found a particularly vulnerable target in Leopold Bloom.) The poker lying at the father's feet in the foreground does not merely suggest that this man is poorly equipped to resist the Prussian bayonet threatening to pierce his wife; it also indicates that we view the seeming rape from the vantage of the hearth, a proverbially secure location violated here by the second soldier's direct gaze. The child in the foreground—whose christological pose invokes the slaughter of the innocents—focuses the fear of helplessness that also attaches to the wife and grandfather; her line of sight, moreover, seems to confirm the dropping of the poker as a symbolic unmanning. Reinforcing fears of invasion were claims, advanced by John Redmond at a Dublin Mansion House recruiting conference, that detailed maps of Ireland had been found on the corpses of Prussian officers at the front.[45]

If such posters carry a certain power in their targeting of Irish hopes and fears, others seem more vulnerable to satire. One poster (figure 4.4) shows a happy soldier with shamrocks in his cap who has stepped out from under the flag and onto the parade grounds. The implication here is that if you are an Irishman, you must look like a model for cigarette ads or shaving kits as you march off to war to the sing-song rhythms of an advertising slogan: "Enlist To-Day, and Have it to Say, You Helped to Beat the Germans." In the nineteenth century, Irish political cartoonists

FIGURE 4.3 "Is *Your* Home Worth Fighting For?" "There's a man of brawn in possession there" (15.1336–37): the melodrama of invasion imperils home rule. Lithograph; artist unknown; printed by Hely's Ltd; circulated in July 1915.

FIGURE 4.4 Marketing war: "Enlist To-Day and have it to say You Helped to Beat the Germans." Ape becomes angel via the commodified attractiveness of the Irish poster mannequin. Lithograph; artist unknown; 7,500 printed by M'Caw, Stevenson, and Orr Ltd; circulated in Dublin and Belfast by the Central Council for the Organisation of Recruiting in Ireland (CCORI) in May 1915.

responded to English caricatures of the Irish as apes and the English as angels by reversing the contrast.[46] As part of the continuing history of mutual misrepresentation, in World War I the English reappropriated the Irish angels and transformed them into commodified images of the handsome hero-shill, as much ventriloquist dummies as the Irish advertising agencies hired by the British War Office.[47] Going to battle with shamrocks in your hat, you hope to come back looking like Michael O'Leary, a frequent speaker at recruiting rallies and subject of a James Walker poster that present him as matinee idol gazing directly at the viewer from within a Victoria Cross (figure 4.5). You too, the poster declares, can take on Germans ten at a time (eight, actually, according to other sources), become a hero, and have your face plastered about town. Collapsing a narrative of achievement into a moment of identification, the poster aims for a process of compression that Joyce reverses in "Circe" by dilating moments of conflicted identification into expanded narratives of empowerment and martyrdom.

Like posters featuring parades, the O'Leary poster is designed to extend the effective range of staged recruiting spectacles by operating as "a kind of instant visual theater in the street."[48] Yet contemporary accounts indicate that the crowds at actual recruiting events were sometimes as fractious and volatile as the audience for Bloom's "stump speech" in "Circe," though no one, apparently, ever met Bloom's fate, having been set afire in a pillory until "mute, shrunken, carbonised" (15.1956). Unsympathetic observers were, however, inclined to view public recruiting oratory as a form of low farce or political pantomime. Commenting on a Dublin recruiter, an anonymous writer in the *Spark* (September 5, 1915) reviews a rally:

He . . . had spoken in Belfast to Nationalists and Unionists on the same platform—an Ireland united for the first time—all together like a bundle of sticks. No one seemed to be quite clear why these people were like a bundle of sticks, but apparently those referred to were tied up. Bundles of sticks are used for starting a fire, and possibly the Belfast folk are to be used to draw fire later on; hence the necessity for tying them up.

At this point a Crimean veteran did a turn which fell very flat, and then the meeting concluded, the band skulking behind the bank and playing "A Nation Once Again" in a furtive, shame-faced way, much to the amusement of the bystanders. Among the bandsmen, I noticed a well-known three card trick man which shows all sections of society have been moved by the great appeals.

It is to be regretted that the listeners seemed to think the whole affair had been arranged for their delectation, and, undoubtedly, if this perverted notion grows among the public, the picture houses and theatres will suffer considerably.

AN IRISH HERO!

1 IRISHMAN DEFEATS 10 GERMANS.

FOR VALOUR

SERGEANT

MICHAEL O'LEARY, V.C.

· IRISH GUARDS ·

HAVE YOU NO WISH TO EMULATE THE SPLENDID BRAVERY OF YOUR FELLOW COUNTRYMAN

JOIN AN IRISH REGIMENT TO-DAY

FIGURE 4.5 Identification and its discontents: "An Irish Hero!" Although some 150,000 Irishmen ultimately enlisted (compare the claim in figure 4.4), newspapers also record arrests for the tearing down of recruiting posters and the disruption of recruiting rallies. Lithograph; artist unknown; 5000 printed by James Walker and Co. in April 1915.

Clearly, if recruiting meetings and parades were often staged before large audiences, not everyone was inclined to accept them as welcome entertainment: the *Spark* mocks failed "turns"—the officer's self-defeating trope, the Crimean vet's flat performance—with the mordant irony that Joyce, hostile to propaganda per se, would direct toward the nationalist martyrdom of Robert Emmett, whose hanging is described in "Cyclops" as an event in the society pages.

One David Allen poster (figure 4.6) encodes an attitude toward Irishness that can be understood as a motivating context for Joyce's satire in the divided narration of "Cyclops," an episode whose expansive interpolations, interrupting the continuity of Joyce's only first-person retrospective narrator, mimics the inflating effects of propaganda. The poster features a paragon of Irish manhood, complete with bagpipes and wolfhound. In "Cyclops" Joyce addresses the manipulation of such national metonyms through epic catalogues and mock heroic descriptions that transform his Citizen, modeled on the founder of the Gaelic Athletic Association, Michael Cusack, into a gigantic caricature of artificial Irish authenticity. Wearing seastones "graven with rude yet striking art tribal images of many Irish heroes and heroines of antiquity," he is accompanied by "the famous old Irish red setter wolfdog" Garryowen, a.k.a. Owen Garry, who composes verses that bear "a *striking* resemblance (the italics are ours) to the ranns of ancient Celtic bards" (12.173–76, 712–23). The Citizen is seated "at the foot of a round tower" (an emblem frequently picked up in recruiting posters) and the list of ancient Irish heroes graven on his seastones takes up nearly an entire page. As if plastered over the mimetic realism of the anonymous narrator's voice, the accumulated excess betokening the Citizen's Irishness ironically reveals the deployment of such symbols as a cover for British interests. Joyce's Citizen, like the poster, is best seen as the ventriloquizer of a polemicized Irishness: the Irish poster boy recruits the Irish to the British cause; Joyce's new stage Irishman, according to the unnamed narrator, has grabbed "the holding of an evicted tenant" (12.1315–16). "Cyclops" epitomizes *Ulysses'* structural modulation from the microparataxis of the first nine episodes—primarily the associational discontinuities within interior monologue—into the macroparataxis of colliding forms.[49] No longer naturalized as the flow of Bloom's memory, what was once a tissue of quotations or allusions begins to fragment into autonomous set pieces in such a way that the very page, as in the simulation of newspaper format in "Aeolus," becomes "posterized"—transformed, that is, into a kind of textual hoarding in which disparate images are linked by the syntactical approximation of collage techniques.

It is worth pausing for a moment over the origins of Joyce's collage aesthetic. Although collages by Picasso and Braque in 1912 are generally

FIGURE 4.6 Artificial Irish authenticity: "The Call to Arms." The Citizen and Garryowen meet the Great War. Lithograph; artist unknown; printed by David Allen and Sons; circulated by His Majesty's Stationery Office in July 1916.

credited with influencing the development of verbal cognates, Joyce may also have been influenced by *Scissors and Paste*, which contested what it considered biased British editing of world news while circumventing censorship by subversively arranging clippings from other publications.[50] An English account of military valor might be juxtaposed with accounts of German victories or, more puckishly, an Englishman's letter to the editor complaining about his verbal passport description might be supplied with the headline, "An Englishman's Face: Oval or Intelligent?" (February 24, 1915). The aesthetic relevance of these political assemblages to *Ulysses* is perhaps clearest in "Aeolus," and in fact it was during the thorough rewriting of that episode in 1921 that Joyce inserted, along with the bold print "headlines" or "captions," an allusion that for a long time was read only as a snippet of Bloom's unspoken commentary on the clipping of an ad out of the newspaper: "Scissors and paste" (7.32).[51] Later, in "Sirens," the first episode to foreground the recycling of earlier narrative materials ("As said before he ate with relish. . . ."), abruptly clipped sentences and even words ("He saved the situa. Tight trou. Brilliant ide") also produce a cutting-and-pasting effect, though in "Sirens" the scissors, as in Dada productions, are handled with less concern for satiric political coherence than they were in *Scissors and Paste* (11.519–20, 483–84).[52]

For the political legacy of *Scissors and Paste*, we must turn back to the colliding forms of "Cyclops." Cutting across the dispersed heterogeneity of the interpolations, the episode's underlying concern with political violence tends to forge associations even across narrative modes: an exchange about national identity (in which the Citizen consolidates his sense of Irishness by excluding Bloom as a Jew) is framed on one side by a newspaper photograph of a black man in the American South, described by the narrator as "strung up in a tree with his tongue out and a bonfire under him," and on the other by a long paragraph detailing a "muchtreasured and intricately embroidered ancient Irish facecloth," whose "emunctory field, showing our ancient duns and raths and cromlechs," idealizes the "dirty crumpled handkerchief" Stephen lends to Buck: "A new art colour for our Irish poets," says Buck: "snotgreen" (12.1325–26, 1438–39, 1447–48, 1.71,73). Regrounding, as usual, idealization in the realism of the body—hallowed Irish traditions become the handkerchief's "incrustations of time"—Joyce juxtaposes jingoist fervor with the recurrent image of the hanged man, prominent in his Cyclopean montage, to suggest the violence inherent in the official British versions of racial, ethnic, and national identity that *Scissors and Paste* came into existence to disrupt.

The "more Irish than the Irish" bagpipe player in the David Allen poster may present an easy target for burlesque, but more complex posters raise difficult questions about design and reception. If potential recruits have trouble hearing "the call to arms" (or if they just can't stand the sound of even an imaginary bagpipe), a James Walker poster (figure 4.7) offers some help, so long as they can read music. If true Irish art, emblematized by the harp and sanctified by a cross between the Virgin Mary and Queen Hibernia, calls one into the army, here truly is Stephen's "cracked lookingglass of a servant" (1.146). As if uttered by the allegorical figure, the question "WILL YOU ANSWER THE CALL?" fuses the theological resonance of "call" as vocation with the patriotic call to arms scripted in the musical notes. The image partakes of a certain brilliant absurdity. With the bugle's clarion call channeled through the harp, the poster translates the duet into a political collage, battle scene overlaying the Irish landscape, Irish art, by implication, resonating to England's tune. The harp seems to effect both a spatial and temporal displacement: the battle scene is at once superimposed over the bucolic background as if transported from Europe, yet the repetition of the lake visible both through the harp and to its side suggests that the musical instrument, like prewar English invasion novels, foretells the time when those Prussian maps of Ireland will be put to use.[53]

The sheer naivete of the harp-bugle image points up the question here. One has to suspect that any Irishman with the slightest nationalist inclination or even a moderately developed sense of irony would laugh Queen Mary (or the Virgin Hibernia) off the wall. Sometimes seeming ineptitude can be written off as simple shortsightedness. Such is the case with an Alexander Thom poster (figure 4.8), in which civilians, marked as shirkers by the casual hats modeled on their heads, watch soldiers parade in front of Trinity College and the Bank of Ireland. It is perhaps inevitable that Joyce and British recruiters, as if trapped in the same labyrinth, should converge on similar materials, sometimes even on the same Dublin street corner. In *Portrait* Simon Dedalus escorts Stephen into the Bank of Ireland to collect Stephen's essay prize: "Mr Dedalus lingered in the hall gazing about him and up at the roof and telling Stephen, who urged him to come out, that they were standing in the house of commons of the old Irish parliament" (*Portrait*, 96). Simon is lost in a moment of nostalgia for the days before the Act of Union, when the Irish Parliament voted itself out of existence and let the building become a bank catering to English needs. As if to underscore the contemporary consequences of the history Simon invokes, Joyce also shows father and son walking up "the steps and along the colonnade where the highland sentry was parading" (ibid., 96). *Ulysses* offers a similar scene, though through "paleface" (Irish slang for English) eyes: "Two carfuls of tourists passed slowly, their women sitting fore, gripping the handrests. Palefaces. Men's arms frankly round their stunted forms. They looked

FIGURE 4.7   Colonial ventriloquy: "Will *You* Answer the Call?" "The cracked looking-glass of a servant": appropriating a traditional symbol of Ireland. Lithograph; artist unknown; 7,500 printed by James Walker and Co.; circulated in June 1915.

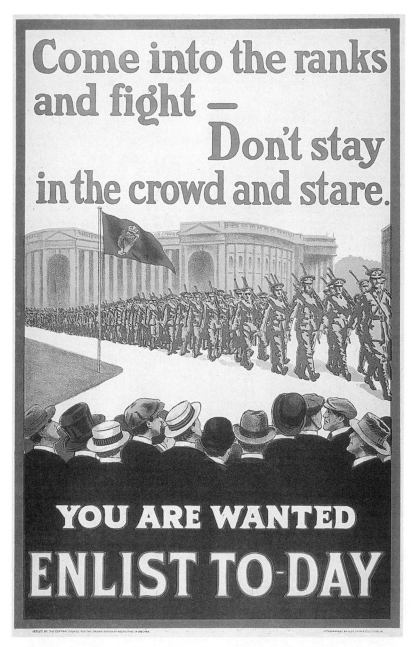

FIGURE 4.8 Recruitment and the historical palimpsest of the city: "Come into the Ranks and Fight." Soldiers parade through College Green, Dublin, past a building that formerly housed, until the Act of Union in 1800, the Irish Parliament. Lithograph; artist unknown; printed by Alexander Thom and Co.; circulated by CCORI in 1915.

from Trinity to the blind columned porch of the Bank of Ireland" (10.340–43). The use of this site in the parade poster (figure 4.8) suggests that "blind" must be a transferred epithet, for only a certain kind of historical myopia could account for the poster's peculiarly self-defeating image. Presumably the poster's imagined spectators are meant to disengage themselves from the passivity of the inscribed onlookers— "Don't stay in the crowd and stare"—yet any such spur to active engagement might just as well stimulate the ironic awareness of historical change that Simon ponders in *Portrait*. By 1915, moreover, many Irish subjects, particularly those in Dublin, where the great majority of these posters were distributed, would prefer not to have the royal crown on the flag.[54] British recruiters, it seems, could not keep their thumbs out of the frame.

The poster showing Hibernia-Virgin Mary with a harp is less easily assimilated to the kind of cultural clumsiness in which military planners seem to specialize. The ventriloquized harp, de-iconized even more than most poster images, foregrounds the appeal structure of recruitment to such extent that one wonders if it could retain any perlocutionary power. Perhaps this poster is better interpreted as an instance of unconscious confession, a baring of the device whereby British propagandists systematically appropriated symbols of Irishness for ends potentially hostile to Irish interests. Certainly there is no warrant, other than the conspiratorial pleasure the scenario affords, to believe that Irish advertisers were gulling their English clients by producing images they knew would be ineffective. (In fact, if most advertising firms were, as David Allen was, owned by Protestants, it may be that representations of Catholicism in these posters encode a form of class condescension.) Elusive intentions aside, it is likely that the political mobilization of national emblems in the context of Anglo-Irish relations at this time necessarily involved such a degree of bad faith that no particular assemblage could have neutralized the contradictions inherent in the project. The volatility of historical contestation inevitably short-circuits, in Slavoj Žižek's terms, the process through which an ideological field is stabilized around an empty or "pure" signifier, in this instance the overcharged sense of "Irish duty" set in place to superordinate national, political, and theological imperatives.[55]

Available evidence verifies the suspicion that some posters simply could not have worked very well. It was illegal to tear down a recruiting poster, and newspapers record various arrests for having done so. Ironically, perhaps the single most significant political poster in Irish history was itself torn down by a member of the Royal Army Yeomanry. In 1916, the one posted copy of the Proclamation of the Irish Republic was plastered over a British recruiting poster on the General Post Office.[56] I have been unable to discover, alas, which poster was effaced; I have, however, turned up one particularly evocative poster and a response to its call.

MAEVE, BLOOM, AND THE LIMITS OF PROPAGANDA

A column in the *Gael*, another radical weekly, lists several items under the heading, "We Want to Find." One item reads: "The equal in audacity to the chap who designed the war poster—'Island of Saints and Soldiers'" (February 5, 1916) (figure 4.9). If sophisticated ideology critique sometimes seems a privilege afforded the present over the past, the following critical narrative in the *Gael*, written three weeks after the brief notice, serves as a reminder that cultural critique does not have to invent contestation so much as recover it for its own purposes.

Having stopped to gaze at the poster, the writer, identifying herself only as Maeve, recalls being accosted by a policeman, who warns her not to touch it and then follows her for a bit down a side street. " 'My good man,' " [Maeve] replied, 'I would not touch it with a ten-foot pole.' " Describing the poster image for her readers, Maeve observes that "the simple and tense legend underneath . . . evidently needs no explanation beyond the picture." Yet precisely by playing the words off against the image Maeve patiently unravels the poster's ideological seams.

> When I was quite a little girl, I learned a good many things about Ireland, one of them being that Ireland was at one time known as the Isle of Saints and Scholars. Scholars, mind you. My memory does not play me false on this point. I was also told that England tried to wipe holiness and religion from the valleys and hills of Ireland; told the meaning of the Mass rock; told of the Penal Laws against religion; told also of ruined churches, of holy women and priests outraged. . . . Later on I read of the Penal Laws against education. Then I knew why so many Irishmen kiss the hand which scourges them—lack of education. . . . I cursed England and began to hate with a bitter hate. By this time I also knew that Ireland had, and has, great soldiers as well as saints and scholars. I learned, too, that the reason they became soldiers was the English occupation of Ireland. Now, is it not strange an English recruiting poster should proclaim Ireland to be an Island of Saints and Soldiers?

In Maeve's reading, the verbal displacement of "scholars" by "soldiers" essentially recapitulates the historical process whereby Ireland's English educational system transforms Irish scholars into "loyal British subjects." Turning back to the remembered image, she continues to unfold its ironies: "The young man in the poster is ploughing, so the farmers are especially appealed to. They got their land so cheaply and easily, and were let keep it so long unmolested for such a long time that they should

FIGURE 4.9 Destruction of the fittest: "The Isle of Saints & Soldiers." Saint Patrick calls a modern Odysseus from the plough to defend Catholicism and the Irish way of life. Lithograph; artist unknown; 7,500 printed by M'Caw, Stevenson, and Orr, Ltd; circulated in Dublin and Belfast by the Department of Recruiting for Ireland (DRI) in May 1915.

be only too glad to run away from it, and extend their operations by manuring the fields of Europe with their own blood and bones, instead of manuring their own land with somebody else's blood and bone mixture." Rising to her concluding paragraph, Maeve completes her "musings" by imagining the insurrection that was just over a year in coming: "Perhaps England may 'get' the soldiers of Ireland in a way she does not anticipate. She may find them lined up not to fight for her, but against her, and she may find them rather good at driving her from the land, as her German cousins are rather good at driving her from the sea."

Although Maeve represents her spectatorship as beginning within a doubly constricted space—in Althusser's terms, an Ideological State Apparatus, the poster, is reinforced by a Repressive State Apparatus, the police—her critical narrative traces several kinds of resistance.[57] If the police patrol the main street, the individual can take to the side streets, bearing with her an afterimage of the offending poster; the internalized gaze of surveillance does not, like some state-sponsored computer virus, exhaust all available memory. The poster trace, like the image of Tweedy that returns to Bloom in "Circe," assumes a place within the individual subject's other memories, which include narratives of Catholic resistance to English attempts to impose Protestant hegemony. Contesting the official indoctrination of the educational system, whose goal, according to another article in the *Gael* (October 17, 1915), is to teach Irish youth that "Cromwell was broadminded in religious matters, and that Irish liberties are perpetually safeguarded by the provisions of Magna Charta, and the Habeas Corpus Act," Maeve offers resistance in an act of critical response that draws on communal memories of subjection to reassert an alternative history occluded by, yet suggested in, the poster.

Maeve's canny reading of the visual image and its verbal supplement re-opens a space of rational, deliberative agency within the individual subject. Even as Stephen's skeptical response to political oratory, "Gone with the wind" (7.880), counsels a more sober assessment, Maeve's stirring rhetoric fosters the sentimental temptation to ignore the institutional forces within which individual agency is constituted. Bound not only by the various historical forces converging to make a wartime rebellion possible, Maeve's self-assertion is both enabled and limited by the particular constellation of subject-positions available to her as an Irish colonial woman: if she could draw on the empowering legacy of the Ladies Land League, suffrage was still several years ahead, and, writing for the *Gael*, she no doubt spoke from within a restricted range of oppositional stances. Nevertheless, without simply dismissing the Foucauldian model of totalized containment, one can say that Maeve's article, neither a ruse of power nor a voice of transcendent critique, serves as a valuable reminder (if modern history is not enough) that reactions to specific hegemonies may result in genuinely effective acts of transgression even within the very real constrictions of modern disciplinary society. The very existence of recruiting posters and other forms of propaganda testifies to England's awareness of the contingency and potential instability of the existing field of Anglo-Irish relations, even as the effort to stabilize and secure such key terms as "Irishness" and "national duty" inevitably encodes the very contradictions meant to be concealed.

The openly violent transgression Maeve advocates is inseparable from such contests over meaning, a point chillingly illustrated in a photograph of Dublin's Four Courts taken just after Easter 1916 (figure 4.10), when British shelling pounded the city into submission. Barely visible in the lower left, just to the right of the gentleman stroller, on the wall papered over with various recruiting advertisements, is a damaged poster showing three jovial soldiers playing bridge. A surviving copy (figure 4.11) makes legible the legend partially torn off in the photo: "WILL YOU MAKE A FOURTH?" The seemingly dapper insouciance of the inscribed spectator, his back to the poster, his gaze meeting our own, challenges the apparent detachment of an observer free to relish the ironic echo of the building's name in the poster's caption, as if the words inscribed on the poster were, like the card game, only a shuffling of signs.

Itself often treated as a semiotic puzzle, *Ulysses* models and enacts multiple instances of resistant reading that resonate with Maeve's. As an advertising canvasser, Bloom is more likely than some to preserve a critical perspective on the public text of the city. In "Wandering Rocks," for instance, Miss Dunne ponders "the large poster of Marie Kendall, charming soubrette": "She's not nicelooking, is she? The way she's holding up her bit of a skirt. Wonder will that fellow be at the band tonight. If I could get that dressmaker to make a concertina skirt like Susy Nagle's. They kick out grand. Shannon and all the boatclub swells never took his eyes off her" (10.380–86). The ease with which Miss Dunne is interpellated as a consuming subject underscores Cheryl Herr's observation that the Kendall publicity poster, which smiles down on the viceregal cavalcade, provides an immanent critique of the English culture industry by exaggerating "the natives' friendly reception of the viceroy, a reception enhanced by attitude-shaping entertainment imported into Ireland."[58] Perhaps Buck Mulligan is thinking of Miss Dunne when, echoing nineteenth-century attacks on outdoor advertising, he facetiously attributes "every fallingoff in the calibre of the race" to the malign effect of "hideous publicity posters" (14.1246–50). Bloom, in contrast, is a tougher mark: "Damn bad ad," he thinks in response to a "horseshoe poster over the gate of college park": "Now if they had made it round like a wheel. Then the spokes: sports, sports, sports: and the hub big: college. Something to catch the eye" (5.551–54).

FIGURE 4.10   Material contradictions in the urban text: bombed-out Dublin, Easter, 1916. After the British bombed Dublin during the 1916 Easter rising, tattered recruiting posters remained on the outer wall of Four Courts, a judicial and administrative building near the center of the city. Photograph; photographer unknown; ca. April 1916.

FIGURE 4.11   War games: "Will You Make a Fourth?" This poster was first circulated by DRI in May 1915; a later edition is visible on the wall in figure 4.10. Lithograph; artist unknown; printed by Alexander Thom and Co.

If the recruiting poster in "Lotus Eaters" elicits a faint anticolonial echo, Bloom's revisionary eye is typically more pragmatic than explicitly political; the racing poster, he feels, simply will not work. Yet Bloom's casual responses to mass cultural forms, sharpened by his professional expertise, suggest ways in which transgression depends on the prior existence of the law without necessarily being contained by it. Wandering through the streets (and side streets) of Dublin, Bloom takes note of the cleverly placed Kino's ad floating on the Liffey before recalling illegally posted ads for a "quack doctor for the clap" in all the public urinals: "Got fellows to stick them up or stick them up himself for that matter on the q.t. running in to loosen a button. Flybynight. Just the place too. POST NO BILLS. POST 110 PILLS. Probably some chap with a dose burning in him." (8.96–101). Bloom is probably remembering the literal subversion of the letter of the law by means of strategic erasures (someone turned the "N" into an "11" and the "B" into a "P"); he may be imagining it. Either way, Bloom offers a model of reading as transgressive response that extends beyond this example of a legal prohibition turned inside out.[59] Indeed, the resistant force of Bloom's poster critique offers two lessons for contemporary cultural criticism, one about the place of the aesthetic, another about the role of the reader.

First, Bloom's pragmatic assessment raises questions about the relationship between aesthetic discrimination and political effects. Without the capacity to impress itself on the reluctant eye, a poster will have no effect whatsoever, political or otherwise. After all, the rhetorical power of the Seymour Bushe oratory delivered by O'Molloy, a polished period too easily assimilated to the supposed emptiness of all rhetoric in "Aeolus," registers in the blushing response of Stephen, "his blood wooed by grace of language and gesture" (7.776). My research in the radical weeklies turned up only one detailed, passionate response to Irish recruiting posters, Maeve's critique of the Isle of Saints and Soldiers. It is of course possible that other responses have been lost over the years, but I believe that Maeve's skeptical analysis was elicited by the superior design of the targeted poster. At once more subtle and powerful than, say, Hibernia with a harp, The Isle of Saints and Soldiers sets up a dynamic relation between foreground and background within a carefully balanced hierarchical arrangement of apparition, cathedral, and farmer; the sweep of the plough handle draws the eye up to the farmer's expression of stunned piety, and the ploughed earth, which comes to resemble the scene of battle by picking up the crumbling form of the cathedral, poses the question of the proper field for male labor in wartime. More than any other, this poster represents a target whose aesthetic power makes it worthy of Maeve's critical intelligence.

Relations between aesthetic and ideological effects have been notoriously troublesome for oppositional theorizations of culture. An absolute distinction between the two, long a central tenet of humanism and often a disguised assumption of materialist criticism, threatens to produce an untenably essentialist notion of the literary as that which disrupts ideology and a reductive notion of ideology as otherwise free of the internal contradictions and contestations brought into focus by the aesthetic.[60] Yet without the distinction aesthetic hierarchies collapse. If some criticism welcomes such a collapse as a form of radical egalitarianism, the potential social value of actively contesting specific cultural hierarchies is thereby lost as well. Here I accept Martin Jay's argument that "the attempt to break down a hierarchical cultural relationship [in various cultural criticisms] may unintentionally have contributed to the maintenance of a still hierarchical social one"—the demystification of "high" art having given us avant-garde lobbies in architecturally postmodern banks and surrealist dislocations in consumer advertising—and that "the process of establishing new hierarchical evaluations itself remains, at least for the foreseeable future, inescapable and indeed worthy of our approbation."[61] If art's critical capacity depends on its estrangement from society in general, then criticism must continue to evaluate (and possibly alter) the relationship to the social established by particular aesthetic objects. To credit the notion of aesthetic value, therefore, even while acknowledging that one's sense of the aesthetic is historically produced and subject to change, makes sense as a strategy of cultural criticism if the aims of such criticism include the preservation or renewal of possibilities for cultural and political change. It follows that if *Ulysses*, as many have argued, levels cultural distinctions, criticism may perform a service by refusing to reproduce that antihierarchical operation—an operation that would include, for instance, the conflation of modern fiction and posters, a move whose heuristic value I have nearly, but not quite, exhausted.

Second, Bloom's professional poster critique momentarily transforms the reader who sees through his eyes into the producer as well as the consumer of poster images. Insofar as the conflation of production with reception carries with it, as Peter Bürger has argued, the avant-garde promise of reception as active restructuring, *Ulysses* strikes an effectively critical relation towards the national culture it explores.[62] POST NO BILLS; POST 110 PILLS: only scratch the surface to uncover English "syphilisation." Through Bloom's role as advertising canvasser, then, Joyce introduces an attitude toward everyday life that reproduces his own relationship to the evolving text of his novel: *Ulysses* having grown by one third in proof, Richard Ellmann points out that for Joyce "the reading of proof was a creative act."[63]

Of course, Bloom remains one character constituted within a larger structure, and Joyce does not aim to sustain, over the course of the narrative, a continuous novelistic identification between the reader and any character. Instead, the novel's increasingly complicated relations between narrative event and narrative discourse intervene in the process of identification in order to lay bare the mechanisms on which propaganda depends. This strategy reaches an apotheosis of sorts in the phantasmagoria of Nighttown, but the ground for Joyce's political anatomy of consciousness in "Circe" is laid in the narrative innovations that precede it.

IDENTIFICATION, CULTURAL PREDICATION, AND NARRATIVE STRUCTURE

Consonant with the Joyce constructed by Richard Ellmann's biography, the widening gap between narrative discourse and narrative event in *Ulysses* could be understood, taking up the model provided by Pierre Bourdieu, to indicate the increasing detachment from social and economic exigencies characteristic of bourgeois aestheticism: a disengaged, ludic space in which form and style function to refine worldly necessity out of existence.[64] Certainly one recognizes a version of Joyce in this characterization, the one who, nearing the completion of *Finnegans Wake* and the onset of World War II, rebuffed his brother Stanislaus's attempt to talk politics with the claim that his only interest lay in "style."[65] And yet to understand the "allincluding most farraginous" literariness of *Ulysses* (14.1412) solely as a sign of its aspiration to bourgeois autonomy is to privilege and generalize versions of Bloom as petit bourgeois functionary and Stephen as escapist aesthete that the text's mechanics of meaning substantially complicates.

That Joyce subjects Stephen's rapturous discovery of his artistic calling and his scholastic theory of art in *Portrait* to a complicated array of ironic qualifications and sentimental investments has been understood for some time.[66] According to Stephen's theory, the detached artist-god who pares his fingernails "within or behind or beyond or above his handiwork" (*Portrait*, 215) produces essentially static, self-contained art objects. But Stephen delivers his aesthetic credo within a text that emphasizes flux and a represented world that, like Stephen's irreverent interlocutor Lynch, repeatedly brings him back to earth. In *Ulysses* Joyce runs through a yet more extended range of attitudes toward Stephen's revised understanding of art, which assumes its most dramatic expression in his theory of Shakespeare, unfolded before a skeptical audience in the National Library in "Scylla and Charybdis." Silently counseling himself to imitate the bard, Stephen tells himself to "Act. Be acted on"; the transcendent artist, apparently having tired of his manicure, has entered the world as both cuckold and sexual adventurer (9.979). Autonomy, however, remains paramount, for the goal of the betrayed artist is to overcome his victimization by reinventing himself and his forebears in an act of self-authorship. When Shakespeare wrote *Hamlet*, Stephen argues, "he was not the father of his own son merely but, being no more a son, he was and felt himself the father of all his race" (9.867–69). But Stephen's departure from the library at the end of the episode delivers him into a world that refuses to respect his fantasies: his former voice instructor, Almidano Artifoni, encourages him to make money off his singing voice, thus invoking all the material compromises associated with the idea of a career; his sister Dilly reminds him of the continuing claims of family and the pressures of financial need; and a pair of British soldiers remind him of the costs of free speech.

In the manuscript of *Ulysses* Joyce wrote "end of part 1" after "Scylla and Charybdis," and in the next nine episodes, which depart from what Joyce called the "initial style," increasingly experimental narrative forms raise the critique of Stephen's fantasies of autonomy to a principle of structure. Comprising interior monologue, naturalistic dialogue, and subtle shifts of focalization, in the first nine episodes the initial style grants an originating centrality to the subjectivities of Bloom and Stephen.[67] In recent years it has become a critical commonplace to demystify this effect as an illusion. Yet however much interior monologue comes to seem a kind of bricolage when passing allusions are traced and their cultural contexts invoked, its immediate effect gives the impression that characters think themselves into existence, or author themselves, under the reader's eye. Thus while there is analytic truth to Franco Moretti's claim (since echoed by many others) that in Joyce's interior monologue distinctions between inside and outside tend to collapse, Umberto Eco (selectively invoked by Moretti) makes the more important point *that for the reader* these distinctions typically remain operative: "Not only do we individuate Bloom, Molly and Stephen, but we also manage to characterize and judge them. . . . Each personage is constituted by the same undifferentiated field of physical and mental events, yet each is united by a personal style of discourse."[68] The fundamentally realist experience of identifying with Bloom and Stephen in order to leap the gaps in the represented flow of their thoughts thus produces a powerful illusion of moving in and out of intimate relation with autonomous subjects.

After the library episode, however, characters increasingly come to seem, in what can be called a process of cultural predication, more objects of discourse than sources of language. Starting with "Wandering Rocks," the trajectory of narrative modes begins to explore the possibility that private experience and individual agency may disappear within increasingly powerful and invasive public discourses. In "Sirens," Bloom becomes absorbed into the songs sung around him, his character seemingly dispersed and overwhelmed by the musical transformations that equally inflect narrative voice, interior monologue, and dialogue. Although he is able to pull himself back together by the end of the episode—"Cowley, he stuns himself with it: kind of drunkenness. . . . Thinking strictly prohibited" (11.1191, 1194)—in the meantime Bloom loses himself in "Siopold," a verbal chord uniting Simon (singing), Lionel (operatic character), and Leopold (listening). Vulnerable to dissolution, Bloom also suffers a grammatical objectification under the gaze of a siren-barmaid: "Winsomely she on Bloohimwhom smiled" (11.309). The cultural and political resonance of this linguistic transformation becomes more explicit in "Circe," when Bloom, accosted by the night watch, is "declined" case by case ("Bloom. Of Bloom. For Bloom. Bloom.") until he reaches the accusative, and his trial, appropriately enough, begins (15.677). Episode by episode the autonomy of characters is diminished (though not extinguished) by the pressure of public discourses. From the seductive influence of song in "Sirens" the reader moves to the vicious imposition of cultural stereotypes in the nationalism, masculinism, and anti-Semitism of "Cyclops," and then in "Nausicaa" to Bloom and Gerty's complex dialectic—mediated by pulp romance, fashion advertising, and pornographic peepshows—of mutual objectification. In "Oxen of the Sun," the history of literary English nearly obscures crucial narrative developments, and in "Circe" music hall pantomime and German expressionism (among other things) distort, dissolve, and sometimes displace character and action alike. Tired journalese comes between Bloom and Stephen in "Eumaeus"; catechistic forms of theology and popular science in "Ithaca" distance us from the possibility of interpersonal intimacy—until the reader is finally returned to what has often been understood as the unmediated flow of Molly's mind in "Penelope."

Yet even in "Penelope" the readerly effort to grasp syntactical relations from the unpunctuated verbal sequence complicates the experience of identification by creating a heightened dialectical shuttling between the writtenness of the text and the illusion of pure voice.[69] That is, the brilliant mimetic effect of the episode as read aloud by, say, Siobhan McKenna, elides the very different experience of hesitation, conjecture, and backtracking as the reader tries to *produce* the fluidity made available by a practiced dramatic voicing. Soliciting intense identification as the only means of navigating the apparent discontinuities within interior monologue in the first nine episodes, in the second nine Joyce increasingly foregrounds the process whereby the seeming privacy of individual subjectivity is not simply imprinted with, but produced by, the operations of culture. That culture, Joyce shows, is thoroughly permeated by the ideological hailings of the British Empire, yet the suggestion that Irish subjects might be utterly subordinated by British propaganda and disciplinary power is exploded in the dramatic climax of the narrative, Bloom's rescue of Stephen in Nighttown.

CARNIVALIZING PROPAGANDA: BLOOM
AND STEPHEN IN NIGHTTOWN

Just before he is decked (or "crowned") by a belligerent British soldier in "Circe," Stephen Dedalus unwisely characterizes his desired relation to Ireland's reigning institutional authorities with a Blakean aphorism: "in here it is," he says, tapping his brow, "I must kill the priest and the king" (15.4436–37). The self-confessed "servant of two masters," Stephen wishes to undo the internalization of authority that renders him, as he dourly observes in "Telemachus," the political subject of "the imperial British state" and the religious subject of "the holy Roman catholic and apostolic church" (1.643–44). Stephen's early-morning complaint is framed, courtesy of Haines, by a stark dichotomy. "I should think you are able to free yourself," says the genially obtuse Englishman. "You are your own master." Retreating before Stephen's cynicism, however, Haines quickly reconsiders: "An Irishman must think like that, I dare say. . . . It seems history is to blame" (1.636–37, 647–49). Pivoting on the relation between individual and nation, Haines's binary opposition between absolute autonomy and utter subjection skirts precisely what Stephen's desire to negate priest and king invokes: the liminal space in which propaganda tries to work its effects.

Given that Stephen's aphoristic attack on the English sovereign conjures, on the next page, Edward VII himself, dressed as a Freemason, wearing "an image of the Sacred Heart," and carrying "a bucket on which is printed *Défense d'uriner*" (15.4450, 4457), it is tempting to say that if king and priest cannot be killed, they can at least, in the manner of pantomime, be re-dressed. Carnivalized as the goofy custodian of Leopold Bloom's emergency bladder movement, Edward steps into "Circe" only to have his sovereignty derided as the war-mongering hypocrisy of an impostor. Yet the idea of carnival has already been complicated in "Circe" by an earlier appearance of Bloom, whose crowning is more dignified than Stephen's: Leopold the First, ruler of the New Bloomusalem, promises "General amnesty, weekly carnival with masked license, bonuses for all" (15.1690). Bloom's carnival may gesture toward the liberating effects of Joyce's comic exuberance. Or, administered by a king, it may suggest that the promise of release is simply another of power's many ruses.

This issue has driven a good deal of ideology critique in literary criticism. The notion that ruses of power inevitably defeat forces of resistance derives from Foucault's influential account of the pervasive regulatory effects of social institutions in *Discipline and Punish*. In like-minded accounts of reading, novel-readers are as regulated as the anxious citizens of modern disciplinary society: citizen-readers enter into socially determined forms of subjectivity not so much against their will as apart from any sense of volition, desire, or resistance. The subjected novel-reader has been most prevalent in Victorian studies, where the action of what is taken to be the typical Victorian plot—the socialization of the protagonist—is said to be replicated in the normalization of the reader; but the modern novel has also been theorized as an agent of social discipline, even though the fragmentation of subjectivity in modernists such as Joyce or Woolf does not seem conducive to the contagious internalization of authority often attributed to earlier fiction. The notion of carnival challenges dystopian models of reading and society, and the king of carnival has been Mikhail Bakhtin, whose work on heteroglossia and the discourse of the novel, like Kristevan semiotic disruptions of the symbolic, invests fiction with the capacity to subvert the disciplinary effects of power.

These polarized and polarizing approaches clearly oversimplify relations between ideology and literary texts. As Patrick Brantlinger has remarked, definitions of the novel as generically dominative or subversive need not be mutually exclusive: "the novel unifies as it pluralizes, or imperializes at it democratizes."[70] The more interesting question is therefore not what the novel *is*, with respect to ideology, but what particular novels *do*. In the case of *Ulysses*, which is devoted to mocking authority, carnivalesque subversion has obvious relevance; it is the limitations of the disciplinary approach when applied to Joyce that reveal most about what can be called the novel's ideological mode of being. Take the question of the novel and the police first articulated in D. A. Miller's readings of Victorian fiction. In Miller's account, the police function as an alibi for other controlling social institutions.[71] Yet if the Irish police are brought forward not as the novel's most visible synecdoche for the circulation of disciplinary power but as indices of the historical particularities of the colonial situation, the complexity of *Ulysses'* positioning within the specifically Irish scene of social discipline becomes more legible.

Joyce's Dublin was the most heavily policed city in the United Kingdom, and both the Dublin Metropolitan Police (DMP) and the Royal Irish Constabulary (RIC), who patrolled the rest of Ireland, were administered from the central site of Dublin Castle.[72] Lord Morely called Dublin Castle "the best machine that has ever been invented for governing a country against its will," and in 1937 Dorothy Macardle looked back on "the Dublin Castle system of espionage" as "the most dangerous of all the instruments of England's policy in Ireland":

The enemy's resources in this respect were boundless. The R.I.C., with their intimate knowledge of the inhabitants, reported to the Castle from the most remote villages in the country; in Dublin a body of plainclothes detectives, the G Division of the Metropolitan Police, watched all places supposed to be visited by prominent Republicans, shadowed the leaders, identified political prisoners, and guided the military in searches, raids, and arrests. Into the Republican organisation were sent spies, paid informers, and *agents provocateurs*.[73]

The influence of the Castle as the United Kingdom's most extensive anti-subversion mechanism registers throughout Joyce's texts. Bloom, having watched a "squad of constables . . . split up in groups" and scatter "towards their beats" (8.406–10), notes that Jack Power's father was a "G man," and the aptly named Power, the Good Samaritan of "Grace" who tries to recruit the Protestant Kernan to Catholicism, is employed in Dublin Castle's RIC Office. Bloom's train of thought also returns to an earlier suspicion that Corny Kelleher is a police "tout" or informer: "Never know who you're talking to. Corny Kelleher he has the Harvey Duff in his eye. Like that Peter or Denis or James Carey that blew the gaff on the invincibles. Member of the corporation too. Egging raw youths on to get in the know all the time drawing secret service pay from the Castle" (8.441–44). Bloom's suggestion that James Carey was from the start employed by the Castle is erroneous, but the tenor of his suspicion is, historically, fair enough. In "Ivy Day in the Committee Room," Mr. Henchy may be guilty of little more than exaggeration when he claims to know for a fact that half the radical nationalists in Dublin are in "the pay of the Castle" (*Dubliners*, 125). Bloom's suspicions that Kelleher is a police informer are confirmed later in "Wandering Rocks" by Kelleher's conversation with a passing constable, and Kelleher's cozy relations with the authorities in "Circe" will figure prominently in the aftermath of Stephen's confrontation with Privates Carr and Compton.

Dystopically inclined readers might take such details, as well as the more general sense of watching and being watched in *Ulysses*, as indicative of the way the British administration of Ireland circumscribes Joyce's characters: like the trams paralyzed at the foot of Nelson's pillar in "Aeolus" or like Gabriel Conroy enacting a horse's orbit around the statue of William III, Joyce's characters seem wholly subordinated to the circulation of imperial power. External evidence can also be assimilated into this logic: "To see Joyce at work on the Wandering Rocks," in Frank Budgen's words, "was to see an engineer at work with compass and slide-rule, a surveyor with theodolite and measuring chain. . . . [Joyce wrote the episode] with a map of Dublin before him on which were traced in red ink the paths of the Earl of Dudley and Father Conmee. He calculated to a minute the time necessary for his characters to cover a given distance of the city."[74] Consonant with this image of Joyce is Richard Ellmann's report that the sculptor August Sutler became "rather irritated to see how Joyce seemed to stage-manage conversations as if to use his friends as subjects for experiment."[75] If, as Budgen claims, "Dublin itself," not Stephen or Bloom, becomes "the principal personage" in "Wandering Rocks," that's because Joyce himself has become the arch bureaucrat supervising the peregrinations of characters whose subjectivities—however minutely detailed by stream-of-consciousness techniques—are transformed into effects of structure within Dublin's urban labyrinth. In this reading, *Ulysses* extends technologies of surveillance to an unprecedented extent by recording in the public space of the page what had previously been shielded in the domain of the private. The novelist who represents police touts himself becomes an informer: we read Bloom as Bloom, in the outhouse, reads *Titbits*. Many of Joyce's critics, turning to computer-generated word counts, maps and photographs of 1904 Dublin, and diagrams of Odysseus's supposed wanderings, may be equally disabled within a wholly administered society by becoming, in effect, census takers, surveyors, and assessors. Even bits of critical vocabulary specific to Joyce may register the paranoid implications of a fictional world behind which the author-god is not paring his fingernails but checking his stopwatch: David Hayman's concept of "the arranger," after all, is cited more frequently than Gerard Genette's more clinical "extradiegetic narrator."[76]

But several problems with this approach require attention. One wants to know, for starters, how the policing effect of a novel changes when the police form part of a colonial occupation whose individual members are recruited almost exclusively from the ranks of the occupied. To elide this context is to posit the kind of abstract, unified subject presupposed by Haines, one that is unproblematically its own master or absolutely determined by history, and this is precisely the model of subjectivity that offers up readers as easy dupes. Although Foucault claims in "The Subject and Power" that power cannot be properly theorized apart from resistance, he never establishes how resistance could even exist within the "new economy of power relations" the essay envisions.[77] As Andreas Huyssen writes of Adorno and Horkheimer's culture industry, "emptied subject and totality immobilize each other. The world appears frozen into nightmare."[78]

Historical records suggest a different picture. When ordered to take what amounted to military action against their fellow citizens, for instance, some members of the RIC refused to do so.[79] In such a case, the British subject within an individual policeman is at war with the Irish one. Such divided loyalties complicate relations among empire, their agents in Ireland, and their Irish subjects. Even the simplest police pro-

cedures were always more difficult in Ireland than in England, sometimes comically so, and by 1901, when an inquiry was conducted into
the DMP, Home Rule agitation had turned even "the more respectable
element" against the police. In the plaintive words of one Inspector
Hourahan,

> "It is very hard to manage traffic in Dublin; the people here are not at all so
> pliable as those in London. . . . In London, as I have myself seen . . . a police-
> man has only to put up his hand, and it is sufficient. It is not so in Dublin."
> "The Irish carman rather likes driving on the wrong side?" inquired a member
> of the commission. "Yes sir," rejoined the Inspector, "he is inclined to be con-
> trary. Even the upper classes frequently offend against regulations; and if you
> speak to a gentleman for doing it, many of them will tell you that you are a
> 'cad of a policeman' or use some other offensive expression."[80]

Bloom learns this lesson in "Circe" when, having raised "a policeman's
whitegloved hand" to stop an oncoming sandstrewer, he must leap to the
curb to escape an abusive motorman (15.190–91). Police efforts were
also hampered on the level of organization. Dublin Castle intelligence reports first published in 1966 reveal that even though the central offices
of the RIC and the DMP were located in the Castle itself, the country-
wide network of surveillance described by Macardle as "the most dangerous of all the instruments of England's policy in Ireland" was undermined by a failure to share information. Questions have also arisen
about the very existence of the network. A 1911 article in the *Irish Freedom* entitled "The Police Game" claims that the " 'Dublin-Castle-
knows-all-about-it' phrase" is part of a police strategy to promote the
fear that anyone might be a traitor. Whatever the merits of this claim, in
1916 the Castle evidently had no informers among the small number of
people who knew of the intention to rise on Easter.[81]

   The generalized concept of policing thus founders on both theoretical
and empirical grounds: Irish circumstances throw into relief the way in
which the multiple subject-positions that constitute subjectivity may disrupt the internalization of discipline, and histories of the pertinent institutions reveal that discipline to have been poorly enforced.

   This is not to say that radical nationalists did not have good reason to
share Bloom's suspicion that you "never know who you're talking to";
plenty of activists were sent to their death by informers "drawing secret
service pay from the castle." Nor is there reason to doubt that fear of betrayal from within was widespread; to this day the FBI (whose "G men"
probably got their name from the DMP's G Division), acting in concert
with the Royal Ulster Constabulary, is reputed to approach Irish immi-
grants asking them to inform on members of the Irish community.[82]
Rather, my point is that if we take seriously the importance of analyzing

concrete individuals and specific institutions, it becomes clear that when a given ideological appeal is directed toward individual subjects with divergent personal histories, that appeal will have variable effects.

Bloom's installation as Lord Mayor of Dublin and Stephen's encounter with the military provide an especially suggestive focus in this context. With the imperial administration of Dublin Castle the true seat of political power, the municipal politics of Dublin were always ambiguously contingent, and Bloom's fantasy of political empowerment reflects that ambiguity by transforming the installation of Dublin's Lord Mayor into a ceremony modeled on the coronation of Edward VII.[83] Stephen's confrontation is staged in the international context of England's attempt to recruit Irish soldiers to the cause of empire. These attempts at ideological consolidation provide points of reference for gauging the place of the novel within discourses more pointedly devised to lock the individual agent into a particular form of subjectivity. Joyce does not suggest that the Irish individual is immune to the hailings of British ceremony, nor does he respond with idealized counterimages, like Synge's noble peasant or Yeats's Cathleen Ni Houlihan, from Ireland's own storehouse of newly invented traditions. Rather, acknowledging the powerful influence of the Imperial Crown and the Roman Catholic Church, Joyce shows how specific ideological appeals may inflect, though not necessarily determine, the operations of desire at their very inception.

Bloom's coronation is attuned to the historical fact that the purportedly timeless traditions of the British coronation were invented in the late nineteenth century as part of a large-scale strategy to identify an increasingly urban and centralized nation-state with the royal and imperial centrality of London. The ideology of the "British" nation-state, a reaction in part to the French Revolution, had been promulgated throughout the nineteenth century, but only at the time of Edward's coronation in 1902, when the nation-state had begun to compete in the international market of imperialism, did national allegiance actually begin to take precedence over local loyalties. In an era of "change, crisis and dislocation," according to David Cannadine, "the deliberate, ceremonial presentation of an impotent but venerated monarch as a unifying symbol of permanence and national community became both possible and necessary." Thanks to the rise of national daily newspapers and the yellow press late in the nineteenth century, the imperial spectacle of Edward's coronation was delivered "with unprecedented immediacy and vividness" to "a broader cross section of the public than ever before." Thus while Victoria was named Empress of India in 1877, it was of Edward's coronation that one appreciative observer wrote: "For the first time in the history of our land, did the Imperial idea blaze forth into prominence, as the sons and daughters of the Empire gathered together from the ends of the earth to take their part." As it happened, the postponing of Edward's coronation owing to the king's poor health heightened the imperial aspect of the event because only the delegates who had traveled furthest remained in England to await the indefinitely delayed ceremony. Ultimately, with colonial delegates from around the world ritually pledging their fealty alongside English peers, and the monarch increasingly identified with imperial ambition, Edward's 1902 ceremony reached beyond national subjects by means of a spectacle designed also for the colonized. Popular royal biographies also date from this time, as does "the massive proliferation [of] popular works explaining, describing and commemorating great royal occasions."[84] The interpellative design of such texts is particularly well illustrated in Sir John Bodley's official account of Edward's coronation.

Well into Bodley's 1903 tome, the royal historian claims that "[i]t has been shown in these pages that the conservation and consolidation of the British Empire has been chiefly due to the influence of the Crown on the imagination of the British race." The crown itself, he asserts, is emblematic of "tradition," which has given the British Empire undisputed "supremacy in the world."[85] If royal ceremony solicits the imagination to participate in the construction and consolidation of imperial traditions, Joyce's intervention in the discourse of ceremonial interpellation reveals those traditions to be vulnerable ideological inventions.

Bloom's coronation articulates Dublin politics as a drama of confused desires. Having donned the purple dalmatic mantle of the English sovereign, Bloom is drenched in hair oil by the Archbishop of Armagh, who, borrowing the formula used to announce the election of a new pope, proclaims: "*Gaudium magnum annuntio vobis. Habemus carneficem*" ("I have a great joy to announce to you. We have an executioner" [15.1487–88]).[86] The intrusion of the formula announcing a new pope into Bloom's installation both associates Bloom with Pope Leopold XII, who happened to die the day after Edward's royal visit, and registers as parody the increasingly religious character of the king's coronation ceremony. Earlier in the century the Anglican Church had not wanted to participate in the celebration of royal power, but by Edward's accession the church enthusiastically took up its role, and the ceremony's origins in the consecration of a Bishop came lavishly to the foreground. Bodley, in a passage that could pass for a parody in "Cyclops," shamelessly invokes Catholic iconography, the mater dolorosa, in his description of King, Queen, and Prince during the ceremony:

With a gesture of infinite tenderness, which needs the heart of a father to command, the royal sire drew to his arms his only remaining son and, in sight of his people, embraced him; while, in the majesty of motherhood, the Queen looked on with eyes which bore the divine trace of sorrows as well as of the joys of maternity and before which, perhaps, passed a vision, unperceived in the jubilant throng, save by the father upon the throne and the brother who knelt before him. The scene lasted only for an instant; yet in a certain sense it had a profound significance. The secret of England's imperial greatness was bound up in it.[87]

Anglicanism, here as a state religion, takes over Catholicism just as Catholicism had once absorbed paganism. Given that Edward's was the last English coronation to disparage Catholicism as a departure from the true faith, the image of the Holy Family as the linchpin of empire carries a nice irony here. In *Ulysses*, Joyce subverts the appropriation of religious symbolism for political ends in his ironic invocation of Bloom, Molly, and Stephen as the Holy Family, a profanation that represents only one facet of his more general interest in the way ideological appeals issued by church and state may become mutually supportive. In "Circe," locating the complicity of secular and ecclesiastical authority in the installation/coronation of Dublin's chief administrative official, Joyce shows Bloom's fantasy of empowerment to be inflected by the hailing of an imperial message that has already appropriated the religious iconography of the colonized subject. Bloom's authority, like that of the Dublin Corporation itself, is marked by the institutional power of the British crown and the Catholic Church.

The declaration of Bloom as executioner rather than as pope following his coronation oath echoes an extended set piece in "Cyclops" featuring Rumbold the executioner and anticipates the horrific execution of the Croppy Boy dramatized in the midst of Stephen's encounter with Privates Carr and Compton. Throughout *Ulysses*, the recurring ballad of the Croppy Boy, a young enthusiast on his way to fight in the Rebellion of '98, operates as an emblem of naive nationalism betrayed not simply by the church but by the implicit collusion between church and state, by the king disguised, like the ballad's British soldier, within the priest. The "Circe" execution, during which Edward contentedly sings a popular song celebrating his own coronation while Rumbold hangs and disembowels the Croppy Boy, reinterprets the identity of civic and religious duty encoded in the coronation ceremony by suggesting that to be a loyal Catholic and a committed nationalist in Ireland may constitute overlapping yet violently contradictory subject-positions. Presiding over this potentially disabling contradiction is the true image of British authority: the executioner.[88]

Stephen's confrontation with the soldiers brings such contradictions to a head. We enter the scene along with Bloom, who, after paying for the lamp Stephen damaged in Bella Cohen's whorehouse, is drawn to a "noisy quarrelling knot" of people on the street. Privates Carr and Compton suspect that Stephen has insulted Cissey Caffrey, and despite Bloom's gentle but persistent efforts to intervene, Stephen, drunk, exhausted, and comically clueless, manages to fan the flames with inappropriate responses to rhetorical questions. "Say," Carr demands, "how would it be, governor, if I was to bash in your jaw?" "How? Very unpleasant," Stephen responds (15.4410–11, 4413). As tensions heighten, the drunken confrontation between citizen and soldier—no doubt a common occurrence in 1904 Dublin—is almost overwhelmed by a growing babble of voices and stage directions that compete for the reader's attention. Joyce wrote to Valery Larbaud that Stephen's "mind is full like everyone else's of borrowed words,"[89] and in this scene borrowed words become the fleetingly embodied voices of contradictory ideological appeals: Edward VII quoting Mulligan's "The Ballad of Joking Jesus," Kevin Egan quoting a French journalist mocking Queen Victoria, the Citizen calling out for vengeance against the British, Old Gummy Granny plumping for Stephen's martyrdom.

The effect of this confusing chorus of jostling appeals is to instill in the reader a sense of the international and factional pressures that animate what otherwise might seem a local dispute. The coronation ditty sung by Edward—"On coronation day, on coronation day, / O, won't we have a merry time, / Drinking whisky, beer and wine!"—was sung earlier in the day by Buck Mulligan, who plays on "coronation day" as slang for payday in anticipation of sharing in the "crowns" or "sovereigns" Stephen will receive from the Anglo-Irish Deasy as payment for teaching school (15.4562–64; 1.300–305). The repetition suggests that Edward is as much a pretender or usurper as Mulligan, and both, Stephen knows, want his money, whether to underwrite "some brutish empire" or to buy drinks for Haines (15.4569–70). The overlapping voices of Mulligan, Edward, and Deasy thus relocate the politics of empire in the transactions of everyday social existence. The church adds its voice to the babble surrounding the Croppy Boy's martyrdom through a Fenian ballad recited by the Citizen that recalls the fall of Parnell: "May the God above / Send down a dove / With teeth as sharp as razors / To slit the throats / Of the English dogs / That hanged our Irish leaders" (15.4525–30). In a travesty of Mary Magdalene's ministrations to Jesus at the Crucifixion, the Croppy Boy's death by hanging then conjures a gaggle of society women who sop up his dying ejaculation with their handkerchiefs. As these women coalesce into Joyce's version of Cathleen Ni Houlihan—Old Gummy Granny—the collusion of religious and political narratives is seen to converge in the meaningless sacrifice of a "hero martyr" (12.609). Having witnessed the execution of the Croppy Boy, the old woman of Ireland tempts Stephen with martyrdom—"At 8.30 a.m. you will be in heaven and Ireland will be free" (15.4737–38)—and so represents Joyce's grim counterpart to Bodley's mater dolorosa.

The soldiers force the international context for Ireland's domestic conflicts into the foreground. When Compton accuses Stephen of being pro-Boer, as many Dubliners were, Bloom attempts to placate him: "We fought for you in South Africa. . . . Isn't that history? Royal Dublin Fusiliers. Honoured by our monarch" (15.4606–7). Indeed it is history, as is the fact that, recruiting drives notwithstanding, Irish troops also sided with the Boers against the British; Bloom himself recalls having been caught up in a pro-Boer demonstration during Chamberlain's 1899 visit to Dublin. Bloom's allusion to the Royal Dublin Fusiliers immediately conjures his father-in-law, Major Tweedy, who emanates, as does Edward's Masonic apron, from the trace left in his mind by the recruiting poster he examined in "Lotus Eaters": Tweedy is dressed as the grenadier Bloom first mistook for a fusilier on the poster. The divided loyalties peculiar to Ireland's colonial history, and in particular, the clash between recruiting forces, is played out in "Circe" in the confrontation between Major Tweedy, sprung from a poster, and the Citizen, whose pro-Irish battle cries join with Tweedy's anti-Boer slogans in the cacophony surrounding Stephen's confrontation with Carr.

Desperate to avert the impending violence, Bloom, reinvoking Bodley's Queen, hopes that "woman, sacred lifegiver," can end the dispute, but Cissy Caffrey, unable to pull Carr away, can only call for the police, a call that quickly becomes a general alarm. Given Carr's increasingly violent if self-defeating desire to protect the name of his "bleeding fucking king," and given the imperial status of the DMP, it is only fitting that following the alarm the violence impending against Stephen is displaced onto the city itself in the ensuing stage directions, an apocalyptic paragraph that mixes bits of Revelation and a black mass with details from the Rebellion of '98 and the British shelling of Dublin in 1916. The DMP were never armed (and thus were conspicuously absent during the Easter Rising), but as reminders that Dublin was a garrison town occupied by a foreign power, they conjure a vision of the urban destruction that was very much on Joyce's mind as he wrote *Ulysses*.[90] Bloom himself momentarily becomes a policeman in the first of his Circean costume changes, but when he tries to stop the real thing from arresting Stephen, he is powerless—until he enlists the aid of someone closer to Castle authority than are the police, Corny Kelleher.

It is crucial to recognize that Bloom's rescue of Stephen constitutes a triumphant exploitation of Kelleher's role as a cog in Ireland's antisubversion system. If "in Ireland, just at the right moment," as Joyce wrote in 1907, "an informer always appears," *Ulysses* transforms that dystopic observation.[91] Long recognized as an Odyssean strategist,

Bloom, to use Michel de Certeau's distinction, is both a strategist and a tactician.[92] Always on the watch to "work a . . . pass" or some favor from the powers that be (4.453), Bloom demonstrates that even powerful institutions may be worked from the inside out and that the conjunction of multiple institutions may offer respite from the totalizing power of a single system. "His fingers at his lips in the attitude of secret master" (15.4956–57), Bloom may owe his success to one gap in particular: the policeman's oath, according to Dublin's 1908 *Policeman's Manual*, ends with a promise not to join any secret society—except the Society of Freemasons.[93]

Rather than the unconscious of characters or the collective unconsciousness of the city, what we see with particular vividness in "Circe" is the way Joyce's theater dramatizes the overdetermined space, at once psychic, cultural, and political, in which ideological appeals are negotiated. Reflex theories of ideology assume that we are all naive readers; like Don Quixote sitting down to read chivalric romances, to be exposed is to be converted. But *Ulysses* aims to produce better readers, particularly in the crucible of "Circe." By projecting as dramatic spectacle the partially introjected appeals that converge in the individual subject, the episode advances the notion that those who wish to may indeed be able to kill the priest and king within. For in Joyce's theater, efforts to interpellate the individual as a particular kind of subject—ads, the coronation ceremony, recruiting posters—are staged in the liminal space where an individual's experience of the world confronts institutional attempts to shape that experience. Before being rescued by Bloom, Stephen, on the verge of being knocked down, is permitted to ask, "Will someone tell me where I am least likely to meet these necessary evils?" (15.4575–76). The reader, like Stephen, meets them in the pages of "Circe," where Joyce, registering the degrees of likelihood that govern collisions between individuals and the forces that would subject them, makes that subjection less likely.

Reinventing Ireland: *Ulysses* and the Art of Dislocation

I have argued that Joyce effectively turns inside out Dowell's identification with Edward in *The Good Soldier*. Identifying with Edward, Dowell clothes himself in the attributes of the Edwardian era, just as Ford, responding to Masterman's call, tried to make himself more British than the British. The manipulation of identification in *Ulysses*—the specific sense in which the logic of the narrative both depends on identification and eschews it—speaks to the relationship between its modernism and its oppositional politics. It is no accident, in other words, that the first structural departure from the realism of Joyce's initial style comes in "Wandering Rocks," where, the pretense of simultaneity notwithstanding, a discontinuous and fragmented narrative mode subverts the idealized colonial harmony solicited by the vice-regal cavalcade. Of the major figures in the episode, only Bloom, Stephen, and Molly, tucked away in the side streets, fail to acknowledge the political procession. Rather than interrupt the display of imperial power with distinctly anticolonial countergestures, *Ulysses* heightens the experience of disruption as such. The "Poddle river," which hangs out "in fealty a tongue of liquid sewage" (10.1196–97), may disturb the dignity of the cavalcade, but not with the political force of, say, Bloom's fart in "Sirens," which sullies the epitaph of nationalist martyr. More often the disruption has no clear political resonance. When Cashel Boyle O'Connor Fitzmaurice Tisdall Farrell walks past "Mr Bloom's dental windows" (10. 1115), the double-take caused by the unexplained insertion of a new Bloom, unrelated to the one readers have come to know, is merely a stone to trip over, a message with no positive content.

Yet such interruptions are designed to provoke, in the words of "Ithaca," an "oscillation between events of imperial and of local interest" (17.428). This oscillation, we are told, was partly responsible for preventing Bloom from "completing a topical song . . . entitled *If Brian Boru could but come back and see old Dublin now* . . . for the grand annual Christmas pantomime." Inhibiting also was "apprehension of opposition from extreme circles on the questions of the respective visits of Their Royal Highnesses the duke and duchess of York (real) and of His Majesty King Brian Boru (imaginary)" (17.417–23, 431–33). Brian Boru, King of Ireland and victorious defender against invading Danes at Clontarf in 1014, represents the pure Irish sovereignty called for by Maeve, herself named for a mythical queen of Ireland; the English royals, cheered on their entry into Dublin, represent the power of total subjection. Eschewing such ideological polarities, *Ulysses* enabled its first readers (as it still does today) to "come back and see old Dublin now"—the now of its publication coinciding with Ireland's troubled decolonization—by establishing an oscillating perspective from which national consciousness could be grasped as a function of (post)colonial global interrelation.

Beginning with Valery Larbaud, who declared that with *Ulysses* "Ireland is making a sensational re-entrance into high European literature," the completed novel's early reception registers a somewhat confused yet revealing response to the cosmopolitan dynamic Joyce set up.[94] What links many of the early reviews of *Ulysses* (apart from complaints about its obscenity, obscurity, and resemblance to a telephone directory) is a shuttling between issues of local knowledge and speculations about how the text might be received elsewhere, that is, from an alternative national perspective. Many reviewers felt that *Ulysses* was a hoax to which some critics in Paris and London had fallen prey, and a London reviewer, well-known for having initiated the emetic tradition by remarking that "the main contents of the book are enough to make a Hottentot sick," was confident that readers in Dublin, London, Glasgow, and Cardiff would be united in a disgust evidently coextensive with the United Kingdom. For Shane Leslie, having lived the life of an Ascendancy baronet before converting to Roman Catholicism and Irish nationalism while at Cambridge University, entry into Joyce's meticulously rendered yet extravagantly reworked local knowledge presupposed the path of colonial power. He presents this power as the very precondition of *Ulysses'* intelligibility: "And all this effort has been made, not to make any profound revelation or to deliver a literary message, but to bless the wondering world with an accurate account of one day and one night passed by the author in Dublin's fair City, Lord Dudley being Viceroy (the account of his driving through the streets of Dublin is probably one of the few passages intelligible to the ordinary English reader)." George Bernard Shaw, in contrast, was disturbed by the novel's overwhelming local realism. On one hand he distinctly resents that his fellow Irish émigré has *forced* him to feel (his letter to Sylvia Beach is filled with the rhetoric of coercion) that he still belongs to Ireland, even at a distance; on the other hand, he wants "to put a cordon round Dublin; round up every male person in it between the ages of 15 and 30; force them to read it." Agitated by the intense inside/outside perspective brought on by *Ulysses*, Shaw evidently experienced his own sense of being an Irish European or European Irishman in terms not easily reconciled with Joyce's: the book reminds him of his motivations for emigration even as it conjures, in the manner of *Dubliners*, a fantasy of enforced internal exile. Mary Colum, writing from within Ireland about Stephen's early exchange with Haines, may have pinpointed the source of Shaw's discomfort: "where has the peculiar spiritual humiliation that the English occupation of Ireland inflicted on sensitive and brilliant Irishmen ever been expressed as in this book?"

In the recruiting posters—English appropriations of the locally Irish—intrinsic contradictions remain latent. In *Ulysses*, as one exasperated reviewer observed, one is made to see through its "distorted" lenses "what essentially was never consciously known."[95] Even temporality, theorized by Benedict Anderson as a privileged mode of propagation for a national imaginary,[96] is revealed in *Ulysses* as a discrepant cultural construct when Bloom, raising his eyes to the time ball on the Ballast Office, stumbles over the relation between Irish time (Dunsink) and English time (Greenwich): off by as much as twenty-five minutes, Bloom's miscalculation is strikingly out of key in a text otherwise obsessed with temporal precision. With the contrast between latent and manifest contradictions, I do not mean to reclaim a power of subversion intrinsic to modernist irony, as if the experimental features of *Ulysses* simply supplied the ironic perspective missing in the posters. Rather, the increasingly dilated space between narrative event and narrative discourse in which interruptions, dislocations, and disruptions are staged promotes a critical estrangement from the social and cultural norms set in play by the realistic ground that Joyce persistently solicits the reader to reconstruct even in the text's most extravagantly nonmimetic moments. That critical estrangement is not the work of a transcendent formalism, nor does it imply a disengagement from history. It is rather the aesthetic realization of an historically specific form of cosmopolitan subjectivity that is inseparable from the history of Ireland's economic, political, and cultural interaction with England.[97]

If Joyce himself had ever leaned toward a form of nationalism (and there is no evidence he did), the cultural repressiveness of the Irish Free State quickly would have ended that flirtation. Even in his essay "A Portrait of the Artist," written in 1904, when Joyce was most interested in radical political theorists, his eventual shift away from a sharply defined ideological position of any kind toward an interest in the propagation of ideological messages across national boundaries is discernible in Stephen's eager awareness that "Already the messages of citizens were flashed along the wires of the world" (*Portrait*, 265). A few months before Easter 1916, a writer in the *Spark*, underscoring, in effect, the need for *Scissors and Paste*, declared: "The time is ripe for an authoritative statement of Ireland's position under England being sent broadcast throughout the world. It should be sent to all the Chancellories of Europe, to the United States, to the British Colonies, to every self-governing country in the world, showing the actual position of affairs here, and the means, the cowardly, immoral but truly English means, by which Irish recruits are obtained to fight England's battles, north, south, east and west, from the Seine to the Ganges" (February 2, 1916). *Ulysses*, written in Trieste-Zurich-Paris and finding its way, eventually, around the world, would answer the call, but with a species of address the *Spark*'s rabid nationalists could neither have foreseen nor accepted.

Chapter Five

FROM THE THIRTIES TO WORLD WAR II:

NEGOTIATING MODERNISM AND

PROPAGANDA IN HITCHCOCK AND WELLES

IF BLOOM HAS HIS eye on posters in *Ulysses*, Joyce, like most moderns, was watching film. Joyce had invested in the movies years earlier, founding Dublin's first dedicated cinema, the Volta, in December 1909. Although the Volta failed seven months later—Joyce was never the canny businessman Bloom was—Joyce's instincts had been correct. A 1922 document from the Irish Department of Justice lists thirty-seven Dublin cinemas that were cited for exhibiting movies relating to military operations in Ireland without passing them by the censor.[1] Though England had been slow off the mark in 1914, by this time government officials across Europe were highly conscious of film's power to move an audience, and its cultural prominence would increase rapidly in the interwar years.

Rebecca West's *The Return of the Soldier* (1918), written during World War I, is prophetic of the influence that film and cinematic propaganda would assert in the coming decades. By insinuating cinematic images into the narrator's nightmares, the novel anticipates what Walter Lippmann analyzed as the formation of a pseudo-environment of mediated images. The narrator, Jenny, and her friend Kitty live in a sheltered world that screens out war, poverty, and other forms of ugliness while Kitty's husband Chris fights in France. Jenny suffers from a kind of secondary shell shock. Her dreams are filled with images from "war-films" in which men tread on severed hands and heads and then "slip down" to their deaths "from the trench parapet," an image that corresponds closely to a famous sequence in Wellington House's *The Battle of the Somme*.[2] Their estate heightens the sense of mediated unreality. Leaning her forehead against the window and looking out onto the view, Jenny remarks: "You probably know the beauty of that view; for when Chris rebuilt Baldry Court after his marriage, he handed it over to architects who had not so much the wild eye of the artist as the knowing wink of the manicurist, and between them they massaged the dear old place into matter for innumerable photographs in the illustrated papers" (*The Return of the Soldier*, 4). The massage of modernity turns the home inside out by transforming its private views—Jenny assumes that the reader has already looked *out* her window—into images for public consumption in the mass press. When Chris, suffering from amnesia caused by shell shock, returns to Baldry Court, Jenny begs him to tell her "what seems real" (ibid., 32). For Chris, the only real thing is the life he once led with Margaret, a woman he loved before meeting Kitty. But if Kitty's memory is real, it can only be a fragment of the real. *The Return of the Soldier* suggests that public memory, suffused with selective images from the front, is likely to be as partial, in every sense of the word, as Chris's.

Like *The Return of the Soldier*, D. H. Lawrence's greatest novel, *Women in Love* (1920), was composed during the war, and Lawrence's loathing for what he felt England was becoming during its long composition fed on his contempt for the paranoia and false consciousness of war time. And like West's, Lawrence's vision of a corrupted public sphere is remarkably similar to Lippmann's. A utopian critic of the pseudo-environment that propaganda helped to create, Lawrence believed in the power of the artist as shaman to conjure a counter-environment in fiction: an apocalyptic vision of an alternative way of being that would negate "counterfeit emotion" and the circulation of mechanically reproduced images.[3] *Women in Love* can thus be considered a war novel in a very particular way. If "the bitterness of the war may be taken for granted in the characters," as Lawrence wrote in his 1920 foreword, the novel also recoils from war's culture of lies and simulacra.[4]

One wonders, then, what Lawrence, who died in France in 1930, would have made of Leni Riefenstahl's masterpiece of cinematic propaganda, *Triumph of the Will* (1934). Notoriously, Lawrence's so-called leadership novels glorify charismatic male authority and an organic model of social organization in ways that anticipate Fascist ideology. *The Plumed Serpent* (1926) even invents a quasi-Nazi salute well before real Nazis were clicking their heels and thrusting up their arms before the Führer. It is conceivable, then, that Lawrence might have experienced a visceral thrill in response to Hitler's stirring oration at Nuremberg and the film's powerful evocation of the pleasure and satisfaction individuals find in joining something larger than themselves. But even though he was sympathetic as early as *Women in Love* to the ideal of blood brotherhood, Lawrence ultimately would have recoiled from the fact that his emotions, skillfully manipulated by Riefenstahl's brilliant cinematography, were elicited by "shadows on a screen."[5] For the same reason, he would have been equally disgusted by the proliferation of democratic propaganda films later produced in England, such as Sidney Gilliant and Frank Launder's *Millions Like Us* (1943) or Humphrey Jennings's *A Diary for Timothy* (1945).

In this last chapter I return to the conjunction of modernism and cine-matic propaganda by returning to Alfred Hitchcock, who made two short films for Britian's new Ministry of Information (MoI) in World War II. In chapter 1 I discussed how Hitchcock parlayed *Sabotage* (1936) into a Hollywood contract by translating Conrad's disciplining of the reader in *The Secret Agent* into an analogous form of cinematic mas-tery. This chapter sets Hitchcock's early Hollywood career against the early career of his American counterpart, Orson Welles. If Hitchcock was the first British auteur, Welles quickly became Hollywood's preemi-nent master-stylist, and their career paths trace the afterlife of issues I have pursued in earlier chapters: the connection between the rise of propaganda and modernism's self-conscious exploration of competing media; artists' ambivalent attraction to the power and efficacy of prop-aganda at a time when an increasingly fragmented audience was becom-ing more difficult to reach; the social function of formal innovation; and the challenge of articulating a space for art within the pseudo-environment fostered by propaganda.

The problem of the pseudo-environment came to dominate increas-ingly charged debates about art and propaganda in the 1930s. For the *engagé*, modernist aestheticism (which persisted under the aegis of "technique") amounted to little more than a retreat into the pseudo-environment, or perhaps an intensification of its cocooning effects through the fantasy of artistic autonomy—a bubble within a bubble. For many devotees of the aesthetic, however, the felt necessity of social en-gagement threatened to exile modernist experimentation to the periph-ery of society by making propaganda the duty of all responsible artists. Rising into prominence, cinema was soon embroiled in the debate. On one hand, film's constitutive interplay between continuity and disconti-nuity and its foregrounding of sensory (especially visual) impressions ar-guably made it an intrinsically modernist medium.[6] Early responses to film, moreover, often associated the flow of its images with the inward-ness of thought. When Henri Bergson wanted to describe the fundamen-tal operations of the mind, he decided that film offered the best approxi-mation of the way human beings grasp becoming. "*The mechanism of our ordinary understanding is of a cinematographical kind,*" he wrote in *Creative Evolution* (1907): "Whether we would think becoming, or ex-press it, or even perceive it, we hardly do anything else than set going a kind of cinematograph inside us."[7] Intuiting the same connection, early reviews of stream-of-consciousness fiction often describe the books as cinematic.[8] On the other hand, film was also welcomed by educators as a potent new pedagogical tool owing to the mnemonic force of the cine-matic impression, and political figures as diverse as Vladimir Lenin, Joseph Goebbels, and Nelson Rockefeller came to recognize its power to manipulate public opinion. Over the first four decades of the twentieth century, film's capacity—or at least its *supposed* capacity—to shape the spectator transformed it into a dominant medium for propaganda across the globe.[9]

Conflicting accounts of the ideology of classical Hollywood cinema in contemporary film studies brings film's Janus face into sharp focus. One school of thought (associated with the psychoanalytic semiotics of Jacques Lacan) understands classical cinema as the antithesis of modernism: an agent of ideological reproduction owing to the very nature of the cinematic apparatus, classical cinema generates meaning and the illusion of a unified subject by suppressing difference, discontinuity, and the process of production.[10] From this perspective, all Hollywood cinema is intrinsically propaganda, regardless of content, because it is necessarily a potent bearer of dominant ideologies, or, in Althusser's terms, an irresistible agent of interpellation. Only self-reflexive films, such as Dziga Vertov's city symphony, *Man with a Movie Camera* (1929), short-circuit the ideological effects that inhere in the cinematic apparatus. And yet it is characteristic of the problematic entangling of modernism and propaganda in the interwar years that Vertov's film, cited by Jean-Louis Baudry as subversive of "specular tranquility" and "identity" in its "revealing of the mechanism,"[11] was produced as a Leninist propaganda film under the sponsorship of the Soviet government. Miriam Hansen has complicated matters further by challenging the definition of modernism in film studies. Discounting the determinism of the apparatus argument, Hansen argues that mainstream Hollywood cinema should be considered a form of vernacular modernism because it created an alternative public sphere through which the masses became visible to society and themselves by sharing new forms of sensory experience.[12] Hansen rejects the binarism in which modernist reflexivity exposes contradictions while the mesmeric effects of Hollywood cinema bind the subject into an illusory identity. Rather, engaging "the contradictions of modernity at the level of the senses," "cinema not only traded in the mass production of the senses but also provided an aesthetic horizon for the experience of industrial mass society"; its newly forged idioms traveling around the world and "mediating competing cultural discourses on modernity and modernization," Hollywood cinema was able to function as "a powerful matrix for modernity's liberatory impulses—its moments of abundance, play, and radical possibility, its glimpses of collectivity and gender equality" ("Mass Production of the Senses," 342, 341). High modernism, in other words, did not have a monopoly on the cultural work performed by aesthetic self-reflexivity.

Drawing on opposing insights from either side of the divide, my approach aims to recast the dispute by understanding modernism, propaganda, and classical cinema as interrelated developments with an evolving media environment. Family resemblances thus coexist alongside significant differences. Hansen is right to emphasize that Hollywood cinema took up and extended modernism's aspirations to universality as well as its attempt to grasp new forms of experience under modernity. But the presumed opposition between Hollywood and modernism can be rethought along different lines as well. As I argued in chapter 1, the modernist will to mastery and the desire to manage reception aligned some strands of modernism with propaganda's techniques of manipulation, and Hollywood undoubtedly refined many of the techniques pioneered by propagandists. At the same time, there is good reason to hang on to distinctions between propaganda and classical cinema, on one hand, and between classical cinema and modernism, on the other. For the conflation of Hollywood cinema and propaganda is tenable only at a level of generality that makes the equation useless as a critical tool, and the distinction between Hollywood cinema and experimental or avant-garde film, which tends to recede within the generalizing force of Hansen's unified field theory of modernism/film/modernity, is necessary to the mapping of film's place within the overlapping terrain of modernism and propaganda.

In the following discussion, therefore, I treat Hitchcock and Welles as both modernists and propagandists. As modernists, both men struggled against the constraints of the studio system in order to broaden the scope of Hollywood realism; but where Hitchcock was a vernacular modernist drawn to more openly experimental modes, Welles was an experimental modernist ultimately unable to secure a place within a system hostile to his deepest impulses. And if Hitchcock can be considered modernist by virtue of his medium-specific self-reflexivity (that is, modernist in the sense championed by Clement Greenberg in response to modern painting), Welles has more affinities with the self-consciousness produced by modernism's mixing of media. As propagandists, both men took time off from their mainstream careers to work under the aegis of their respective governments and made films whose restless experimentalism undermined their value as propaganda. Hitchcock's *Aventure Malgache* (1944) and *Bon Voyage* (1944) were sponsored by the British MoI; Welles's unfinished *It's All True* began filming in Rio de Janeiro under the umbrella of Roosevelt's Good Neighbor Policy. As unusual as these films are in themselves—and the nature of their peculiarity is one of my concerns here—these experiments in modernist propaganda must be seen against the background of the charged relations between art and propaganda that developed in the thirties. For the thirties, which saw the waning of modernism in Britain, also witnessed the institutionalization and extension of propaganda throughout the world.

War, Propaganda, and Film: Pairing Hitchcock and Welles

Although in World War I Wellington House came to recognize that propaganda had to be distributed through every available medium, from postcards and leaflets to academic books and newsreels, with the outbreak of World War II British officials had to relearn the lesson that film could be one of the state's most effective weapons in the battle for hearts and minds at home and abroad.[13] Cinema was at the height of its popularity as a social institution in England, and World War II is often considered a golden age for British film. But the new MoI was slow to exploit film for a number of reasons, the most important being that Wellington House left behind few easily accessible records, and England turned away from propaganda in disgust after World War I. The MoI, along with the War Office Cinematograph Committee, was dissolved on December 31, 1918, and when it was reformed in 1939 the new ministry had to contend with resistance from other segments of the government and from the English people. The public justifiably felt that the press had sacrificed its independence by cooperating so closely with the government, and Arthur Ponsonby's scathing *Falsehood in Wartime* (1927), which, true to its subtitle, detailed "an assortment of lies circulated throughout the nations during the Great War," persuaded many that the British campaign, though officially dedicated to facts, had too often countenanced distortions of the truth. Novelists who worked for Wellington House, including Ford Madox Ford, Arnold Bennett (who actually ran the propaganda campaign for a time), John Galsworthy, and Rudyard Kipling, eventually looked back bitterly on their Wellington House work. Ford's tetralogy *Parade's End* (1924–28) can be read as an extended renunciation of his propaganda books; Bennett criticizes the MoI in *Lord Raingo* (1926), a roman à clef based on his experiences there; Galsworthy published a fierce satire on the propaganda campaign, *The Burning Spear*, under a pseudonym in 1919 and then openly in 1925. Perhaps most bitter was Kipling, whose son was killed in France. The man who earlier wrote "Mary Postgate," a story in which an Englishwoman's decision to deny aid to a dying German paratrooper gives her nearly orgasmic pleasure, later wrote a pseudo-epitaph for soldiers: "If any question why we died / Tell them, because our fathers lied."[14] Revulsion on the part of propagandists and propagandees was reinforced by official disavowal. Speaking for the Foreign Office in

1935, Sir Samuel Hoare declared that government propaganda was "one of the most pernicious features of modern life"; and with England hoping to avoid conflict with Hitler, "the repudiation of propaganda," according to Michael Stenton, became "part of the moral armor of appeasement."[15]

Resistance to propaganda also drew strength from the American response to the British campaign in World War I. British officials knew that Americans strongly objected to foreign interference in domestic affairs, especially from the British, and for that very reason Wellington House departed from the German model by undertaking its clandestine campaign. But the effectiveness of British propaganda later proved its undoing. In the twenties and thirties, American analysts of the war focused on British success in influencing American opinion makers, and most American scholars considered the British campaign to have been a significant influence on the United States's decision to enter the war.[16] Indeed, it was popularly believed on both sides of the Atlantic that the British had duped the United States into a war that most Americans regretted. The unverified information in the Bryce Report on German atrocities in Belgium, which swept America on its release in 1915, came to be viewed with particular repugnance. Propaganda backlash thus fed American isolationism, and in the thirties the U.S. Neutrality Acts were designed in part to counterbalance the power of foreign propaganda by outlawing support for countries at war. For these reasons, the British, mindful of American distrust but needing to renew the alliance, declared the United States off-limits under a policy disingenuously known as "no propaganda."[17]

What this meant in practice was a reinvention of the techniques of information manipulation pioneered in World War I, though now they were deployed under a self-righteous catchphrase, "the strategy of truth."[18] And the British were not completely unprepared: Wellington House might not have left behind an archive of best practices, but propaganda had never ceased entirely. Despite the demise of the MoI, in the 1920s the News Department of the Foreign Office continued to try to push the British point of view on international relations, though its powers were increasingly scaled back by government forces resistant to the idea that modern diplomacy requires publicity, and imperial commercial propaganda began in 1926 with the founding of the Empire Marketing Board.[19] The film industry, moreover, was recognized as an important part of what was known as "the projection of Britain." Named after the title of a 1932 pamphlet by Stephen Tallents, such propaganda aimed, in Tallents's cinematic phrasing, to "project upon the screen of world opinion such a picture of [Britain] as will create a belief in her ability to serve the world under the new order as she had served it under the old."[20] The cinematic projection of Britain had been threatened in the

1920s by Hollywood films, which almost put the British industry out of business, but in 1927 Parliament passed protectionist legislation that imposed quotas. Even the prime minister recognized film's importance, emphasizing in a 1925 debate on unemployment "the enormous power which the film is developing for propaganda purposes, and the dangers to which we in this country and our Empire subject ourselves if we allow that method of propaganda to be entirely in the hands of foreign countries."[21] One obvious place to turn when the renewal of large-scale propaganda became inescapable was documentary film. Ironically, the distinguished British documentary film movement of the thirties had emerged in part as a response to propaganda. Walter Lippmann's influential critique of the public's ability to understand current events derived from his work as a propagandist for the CPI in World War I, and the founding figure of British documentary film, John Grierson, "much influenced by Walter Lippmann's claim that ordinary people lacked the knowledge with which to exercise their proper democratic role, . . . was convinced that appropriate factual films could remedy this situation, giving back to the people just that knowledge and understanding that would enable them to fulfill their democratic responsibilities."[22] By the late thirties, British critics considered documentary films to be the most highly developed genre in England—indeed, they were the only films not dismissed by intellectuals as mere entertainment—and the MoI's Films Division eventually made extensive use of them.

Perhaps the final irony of British cinematic propaganda in World War II is that the British approach ultimately followed the model used for film by Goebbels, whose propaganda campaign for Nazi Germany drew inspiration from the British approach in World War I. Coming full circle, the British in World War II eventually used government-sponsored movies to shape the representation of the nation with greater success than the Germans did.[23] It became the official policy of the Films Division to draw on different kinds of films for different purposes, including studio features, newsreels, and documentaries (despite the clear leftist orientation of documentarists as a group). Occasionally, the government lent support to complex hybrids of heritage, spectacle, and propaganda, the most notable example being Laurence Olivier's production of *Henry V* (1944), which was dedicated to the British troops. But for the most part the blending of studio and documentary styles resulted in a predominantly realist aesthetic for propaganda films, such as Jennings's *Listen to Britain* (1941), Noel Coward and David Lean's *In Which We Serve* (1942), and Charles Frend's *San Demetrio, London* (1943). As in the previous war, the British got off to a slow start, but once again they proved adept at turning modern media to their advantage.

Thus it was that in 1940, Alfred Hitchcock met in London with his old friend Sidney Bernstein, a film producer who had taken an advisory position with the MoI, and agreed to make some French-language propaganda shorts on behalf of the Resistance. A year later, the United States followed suit by calling on Orson Welles, suddenly the most famous filmmaker in Hollywood, who was commissioned by Nelson Rockefeller, a major RKO stockholder and coordinator of the Committee on Inter-American Affairs (CIAA), to make a film that would promote intercultural understanding throughout the Americas. Hitchcock was charged with bolstering French spirits; Welles was to discourage South American flirtation with Nazism. Hitchcock's two propaganda films have never been considered an important part of his oeuvre. Shelved by the MoI on their completion in 1943, they typically figure as footnotes in studies of Hitchcock, in part because they did not become available to the general public until their release in 1994, in part because they are slight in comparison not only with Hitchcock's feature films but with the outstanding propaganda films made by his contemporaries. In contrast, though Welles was never able to finish *It's All True*, the film proved pivotal in his career, and some critics believe it might have become one of the greatest feature-length documentaries ever made. Although most footage remains lost, in 1985 a cache of reels was found in a vault at Paramount, and some of the material has been edited, following Welles's memos, into an approximation of one of the film's three major sequences.[24] Coincidently, Paramount released its hybrid documentary on/reconstruction of *It's All True* the same year Hitchcock's lost propaganda films were released.

Film criticism rarely compares Hitchcock and Welles, perhaps because they seem to come from separate universes, both professionally and aesthetically. Yet there are many reasons to consider them together, and one of them is government support for their propaganda films. In 1943 George Orwell, recognizing that modern governments would always need propaganda, grasped at consolation by suggesting that if "the tendency of the modern state is to wipe out the freedom of the intellect . . . every state, especially under the pressure of war, finds itself more and more in need of an intelligentsia to do its publicity for it."[25] So long as the government needs "pamphlet-writers, poster artists . . . illustrators, painters and sculptors, not to mention psychologists, sociologists, biochemists, mathematicians and what not," it will be "forced to maintain an intelligentsia, [and] the intelligentsia will have a certain amount of autonomy" (Orwell, *Collected Essays*, 2:335–36).[26] Orwell cherished the long-term hope that radio might prove a medium for returning poetry to the common people instead of a conduit for "faked" discussions and the voice of Goebbels. This may sound hopelessly naive coming from the author of *1984*, and it may be that the subsequent history of intellectuals and the state, not to mention the history of radio, has proven Orwell wrong. But just as Orwell was predicting that the state's need to employ skilled filmmakers would mean that "films that are all wrong from the bureaucratic point of view will always have a tendency to appear" (ibid., 2:336), Sidney Bernstein was negotiating with David O. Selznick for the rights to Hitchcock's services and Rockefeller was tapping on Welles's shoulder. Working within government annexes set apart from the studio system, both men arguably made films that were indeed all wrong as propaganda.

Beyond the institutional connection, there are also finer-grained cinematographic affiliations between Hitchcock and Welles.[27] When RKO delayed release of Citizen Kane for fear William Randolph Hearst would sue, Hitchcock was among the many prominent directors, producers, and technicians invited to a series of private screenings.[28] Unlike many of his peers, Hitchcock left no public record of his response—beyond the films he made in its wake. Surely Hitchcock would have noticed that the famous opening and closing sequences of Citizen Kane draw on parallel sequences in Rebecca (1940).[29] A year later, at all events, he nodded back by giving the name Barry Kane to the Robert Cummings character in Saboteur.[30] Many years later Hitchcock borrowed from Welles's A Touch of Evil (1958), taking not only the opening hotel room scene for Psycho (1960) but Janet Leigh as well.[31] But Citizen Kane, as one might expect, played the biggest role in Hitchcock's imagination. Judging from Aventure Malgache and Bon Voyage, Hitchcock seems to have been impressed not only by Citizen Kane's technical virtuosity and complex narrative structure but also by its self-reflexive fascination with the shaping of public opinion. Hitchcock's and Welles's parallel meditations on the political efficacy of their films will therefore be a central concern in what follows. But before turning to the propaganda connection, I want to excavate an overlooked moment in their cinematic dialogue that bears on their dual roles as modernists and propagandists. It is a moment in which Hitchcock's investment in Citizen Kane as a groundbreaking exploration of cinematic interiority briefly comes into view.

When Hitchcock finished Bon Voyage and Aventure Malgache, he returned to the United States to make Spellbound (1945). Angus MacPhail had begun a treatment in London after completing the propaganda scripts, but Hitchcock rewrote it on his return and later spent more than a month with Salvador Dalí designing a dream sequence. Although the plan all along was to subordinate Dalí's surreal imagery to the surrounding psychoanalytic narrative, rendering it in effect transparent to rational analysis, Hitchcock was clearly interested in using Dalí's art to expand the range of Hollywood representation.[32] Dalí's opening sequence of a man with giant scissors cutting through a curtain covered with eyes alludes to the more outrageous sequence at the beginning of his avant-garde collaboration with Luis Buñuel, *Un Chien Andalou*, in which a straight razor is drawn across the eye of a woman. Less shocking but comparably surreal, Dalí's interlude at one time included a ballroom scene in which pianos and a turbaned orchestra were suspended over the heads of oblivious waltzers, and a transformation scene in which Ingrid Bergman breaks out of a plaster statue.[33] Owing to various production problems, including Selznick's dissatisfaction with the dream footage, Hitchcock ultimately had very little to do with the final sequence, and the fundamental irony of the Dalí collaboration is that it finally feels less surreal than many of the "realistic" scenes in earlier Hitchcock, such as the nun in high heels in *The Lady Vanishes* (1938) or the lone phone ringing in the middle of a Western ghost town in *Saboteur*.

In fact, the real dreamwork in *Spellbound* takes place within the psychoanalytic frame, and it is here that the influence of *Citizen Kane* is felt. Gregory Peck plays John Ballantine, a man suffering from amnesia who comes to believe he is Dr. Anthony Edwardes, a psychiatrist in charge of a mental hospital. Wrongly accused of having murdered the real Dr. Edwardes, he is treated while on the run from the law by Bergman, who plays Dr. Constance Peterson, a psychoanalyst. As Peck (who still does not know his name) recounts his dream to Dr. Peterson and her mentor, Dr. Brulov, the film shifts to a flashback structure, alternating between the frame and the dream, until Peck suddenly blanches and turns away from the newly opened windows. Throughout the film Peck has become visibly disturbed whenever he sees a pattern of dark parallel lines against a light background, and the recurrence of the phobia gives Peterson the clue she needs to unravel the mystery of Peck's identity. Flanked by Peterson, who is seated by Peck's side on one side of the frame, and by Brulov, who stands on the other side, we see out the window along Peck's eye-line, and the camera tracks out through the window to reveal a boy playing in the snow—on a sled. The framing precisely recapitulates the scene in *Citizen Kane* in which young Charlie Kane's mother signs him over to the guardian Thatcher, and out the window we see Charlie playing in the snow with his sled. In *Citizen Kane*, the camera tracks back in through the window to reveal his mother watching him; in *Spellbound*, the motion is reversed as the camera follows Peterson's eye-line out the window. Each scene is part of a self-consciously psychoanalytic narrative, *Citizen Kane* returning us to the loss of the mother, *Spellbound* to the death of a brother.

But Hitchcock borrows more than the sled. As *Citizen Kane* continues, Thatcher heads cheerily out into the snow to meet his young charge, but Charlie knocks him off his feet with Rosebud. When the commotion dies down and Charlie's fate is sealed, we cut to a lovely image of the

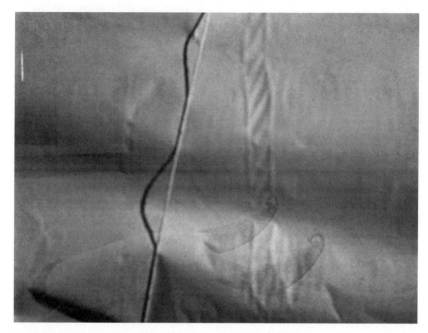

FIGURE 5.1   A broken bridge between identities: unwrapping one sled, covering over another. The image in *Citizen Kane* (1941) resurfaces in *Spellbound* (1944).

work of repression, the abandoned sled slowly being covered over by falling snow. This image then dissolves into several frames of whiteness bisected diagonally by a dark line descending from the midpoint of the top of the frame down to the left; the line is shadowed by two gentle curves, giving the surface an undulating quality; another fainter pattern divides the image vertically on the right, two parallel lines joined by diagonal crosshatching (figure 5.1). For a split second the image is abstract, a pattern of dark lines on white, and then the white is torn away to reveal young Charlie, formally dressed, holding a new sled. The interior setting solicits a rapid naturalizing of the puzzling image that intervenes, and the viewer recognizes that the pattern came from wrapping paper and string covering the sled, a present from Thatcher. In *Spellbound* the image reappears in its more abstract form as a kind of visual stutter that repeatedly threatens to release Peck's repressed memories until, writ large in the snow by the sleds glimpsed out the window, it leads back to the ski slopes, where the murder of the real Dr. Edwardes had awakened Peck's guilt over the accidental death of his brother in childhood, causing his amnesia. In a final tribute, Hitchcock echoes Welles's image of snow slowly burying Rosebud by cutting from Peterson's insight into the cause of Peck's disorder to an outdoor shot in which falling snow slowly covers the sled tracks. Hitchcock's tracks are not so easily covered. In both films the pattern of dark lines on white, irresistibly suggestive of a handwritten text, signifies a broken bridge between identities, the suture between two moments that is not legible as a sign of ineffaceable discontinuity until the completion of the psychoanalytic narrative that gives it meaning. Welles had become, in Bergson's resonant phrase, part of Hitchcock's inner cinematograph.

In the following sections I aim to rebuild bridges between Hitchcock and Welles by showing how each negotiated his conflicting roles as modernist and propagandist. In chapter 1, I followed Hitchcock's career through *Sabotage* in 1936, which left him on the brink of Hollywood. Here I begin by picking up Welles's pre-Hollywood story in the 1930s, a period in which his avant garde theater work benefited from the kind of government patronage he would enjoy again in South America. Doing major work in radio and theater while contemplating the possibilities of film, Welles was both highly attuned to the competing claims of rival media and steeped in the propaganda wars of the thirties. His groundbreaking broadcast of *War of the Worlds* (1938) simultaneously exploited and debunked what he called radio's "voice of authority," which the Nazi party had been using for propaganda purposes since 1934.[34] At a time when so many Americans were listening to the radio for news of unnerving developments abroad—the Munich crisis unfolded in the month before Welles's broadcast—the havoc caused by *War of the Worlds* underscored the point that listeners should be wary of the information brought into their homes on the airwaves. But it was in Welles's theater work that propaganda became an inescapable issue, and when he began to think about leaving New York for Hollywood, his complex attitude toward what he called "the propaganda play" helped shape his understanding of film.

ORSON WELLES: THEATER, FILM, AND THE ART OF PROPAGANDA

In 1938 Welles wrote extensive notes for an essay on the state of the American theater in which he struggled to untangle the relative virtues of art and propaganda. He never finished the essay, perhaps because he could not work out a definitive answer. The notes include multiple drafts of key passages and reveal two wavering lines of inquiry, one into the "propaganda play" in relation to Broadway and the Little Theatre, a second into theater and film.[35] A year later Welles signed a contract to direct two films in Hollywood with RKO, but in these notes he still identifies with the theater. Holding out hope for a revival of its flagging fortunes in

New York, Welles argues (though not without a good deal of equivocation) for theater's superiority to film as an artistic medium. But theater's superiority is grounded problematically in its relation to propaganda. On one hand, Welles feels that the most vital theater has been what he calls the Theatre of Propaganda. On the other, he posits a pure theater—a theatre doing what only theater can do—as a mode of resistance to propaganda.

Before the notoriety surrounding his broadcast of *War of the Worlds*, Welles was already famous as the boy genius who in 1936, at the age of twenty-one, staged a hugely popular all-black *Macbeth* set in Haiti. The play was produced under the umbrella of the Federal Theatre Project (FTP), a New Deal program established in 1935 to provide work for unemployed actors and designers. Under the direction of Hallie Flanagan, the FTP aimed to create a progressive theater for the people, with each regional company free to create its own kind of indigenous dramatic expression. New York City, employing over four thousand theater people, had five units: "The Living Newspaper, which introduced the new concept of documentary plays to Broadway, tackling such popular themes of the thirties as power trusts, monopolies, and the rise of socialism; the Popular Price Theatre, which succeeded in presenting new works by new playwrights; the Experimental Group, which mounted surrealistic and other avant-garde dramas; the Try-out Theatre, a farm team for budding professionals; and the Negro Theatre Project."[36] John Houseman, who ran the Negro Theatre Project, hired Welles to produce classical works, and their first production was *Macbeth*. Welles would not have considered his so-called voodoo *Macbeth* a propaganda play. Though it carried political overtones, its politics were largely social and racial: never before in the history of American theater had whites lined up to see a black production. On the strength of their huge popular success, Welles and Houseman, arguing that the Negro Theatre Project should find black directors and producers, were permitted to set up a new wing of the FTP specifically for the revival of dramatic classics. Their new theater came to be known by its bureaucratic number, Project 891, and under its auspices, Welles directed three more plays: a farce entitled *Horse Eats Hat* (1936); a stunning version of *Faustus* (1937); and a workers' opera, Marc Blitzstein's *The Cradle Will Rock* (1937). Of these productions, Blitzstein's opera is closest to what Welles means by the propaganda play.

When he invokes the vitality of the propaganda play, Welles is thinking not only about the populist message plays sponsored by the FTP, such as Sinclair Lewis's *It Can't Happen Here* (1935), Clifford Odets's *Waiting for Lefty* (1935), and Elmer Rice's *The Living Newspaper* (1936), but about more radical agitprop plays staged by the Workers'

Theatre Movement earlier in the thirties in Britain and the United States. In England the Workers' Theatre Movement was associated with professionals, such as W. H. Auden, but in the United States it was a genuine working-class phenomenon that in turn influenced professional theatrical organizations such as Group Theatre:[37]

> It was the only grass-roots amateur movement in U.S. History in which workers created theatre for their fellow laborers. At its height, the movement involved hundreds of troupes and tens of thousands of workers who wrote, directed, performed and attended their own theatrical pieces. They did so with the deliberate intent of helping to create a distinct working-class culture which they hoped would reflect and inspire their fellow workers in their economic and political struggles. In the course of this activity, they adapted and developed a particular performance style and aesthetic attitude.[38]

The Worker's Theatre largely adopted the agitprop style that developed in Soviet amateur theater in the 1920s and gradually spread worldwide in tandem with the Communist movement: "simplicity and mobility of set, costume, and makeup; the integration of dialogue with chanting, choral reading, singing, music, dance, and circus techniques; the consequent use of an extremely physical, presentational acting style; the use of archetypal characters and symbolic dramatic imagery, which, tied together by political association in the form of montage, became the basic dramatic structure (as opposed to linear plot based on consistency of character, time, and action)."[39] American troupes emphasized mass recitations in which a chorus of workers confronts an archetypal representative of capitalism, but they also used "cabaret-style revues, vaudevillelike comedy routines, political circuses, mass pageants (usually at mass rallies and demonstrations), [and] pantomimes."[40] The Workers' Theatre Movement was thus avant-garde in form and intent: its theatrical styles were designed to break down boundaries between the actors and the audience, and its goal was to integrate theater with real-life struggles of the workers.

Welles's production of *The Cradle Will Rock* came closest to this ideal. Just as the opera was ready to open, the FTP cut off funding for Project 891, ostensibly for budgetary reasons, but undoubtedly in order to censor the production's anticapitalist message. Hampered by lack of government funding, on one side, and by union regulations for commercial enterprises, on the other, Welles was forced to open a stripped-down show with actors distributed among the audience, speaking their lines and singing their songs from wherever they happened to find a seat. By all accounts the performance effectively embodied the collectivist ethos of the opera. Other FTP productions came even closer to the Workers' Theatre ideal. Odets's *Waiting for Lefty*, for instance, took a taxi driver's strike as inspiration for a play so successful as agitprop that by the end the audience was on its feet chanting "Strike, Strike!" along with the actors on stage. It is this sort of phenomenon Welles has in mind in his notes on American theater when he writes, "we may like the vitality of the Theatre of Propaganda and believe even in its cause without liking the propaganda." Though deeply committed to the prolabor message of *The Cradle Will Rock* and a life-long progressive, Welles nevertheless struggles in these notes to distance himself from propaganda—"at best a half truth and it's usually bunk"—by formulating distinctions between propaganda and art. These distinctions, however, prove difficult to sustain.

For one thing, Welles finds himself forced to concede that the vitality of the Theatre of Propaganda derives as much from superior talent and technique as from a more profound commitment to engage with reality. It is easy enough to argue that whereas Broadway has declined into mere diversion and prostitution—"we are a lot of pimps and prostitutes certainly wiggling our wares before the buyer"—the Theatre of Propaganda recognizes "the one screaming reality . . . that the world must be reordered." Admitting the propagandist's superior aesthetic is harder. Welles laments: "We may say their actors are the mannequins of an opinion, that their plays are medicine shows and that they've turned the Theatre into a soap box, but the worse we can honestly say of them is that they're the fever of a sickness, we must admit that theirs is a nice majority of the best talent, and theirs the only valid or significant Theatre in this country." The structure of the utterance is revealing. One expects the string of pejoratives to turn at the halfway point with "but"; but Welles can not bring himself to make the turn. Instead, he sails on, reducing the Theatre of Propaganda to a symptom of a broader malady, presumably the poverty and desperation of the Depression, before concluding with a compensatory overcorrection: "theirs is the only valid or significant Theatre in this country." If so, however, Welles can not decide whether the value of the Theatre of Propaganda is grounded in art or propaganda.

Welles's difficulties are compounded by his attraction to the efficacy of propaganda. In his first attempt to assess the vitality of the Theatre of Propaganda in relation to its aesthetic value, Welles qualifies his admiration by asserting that "a good propaganda play is just exactly as effective and second-rate as a good poster." The equivocation here is evasive, something like telling a poet that her poems are as interesting as they are original. But in a later draft Welles's emphasis shifts: "if a play has something to denounce, deny or demonstrate we may want its terms to be expressed in better perspective than a cartoon. But we must remember that the art of the propaganda play is not only as second rate but as effective as a poster." Here Welles suggests that while the artistry of a propaganda play may be dubious, its power to affect its audience is enviable. A poster may only be a poster, but it works.

But if Welles admires the propaganda play's vital engagement with its audience and its ambition to reorder the world, he also asserts that it is too removed from reality to qualify as art. Fending off the potential contradiction, he tries to clarify the "unreal" dimension of the propaganda play by arguing that art must interpret the real, and the propaganda play does not interpret an existing problem, such as class struggle, but attempts to "impose" a certain kind of self-consciousness in order to make something happen: "It must pose its problem before it can knock it down, plant its plot, raise its Question, exactly what the Theatre of Propaganda is now brilliantly and honestly attempting, exactly why it can lay little claim to reality and exactly the difference between propaganda and Art or propaganda and Theatre." Welles is clearly arguing himself into a corner. He never would have accepted the logical extension of his argument, Soviet-style social realism, and his own avant-garde practice in the theater was certainly closer to Theatre of Propaganda than to Broadway. The innovative lighting and radio-like sound effects of Welles's *Faustus*, for instance, caused a sensation, as did his use of dramatic columns of light in *Julius Caesar* (1936) to recall the lighting of Hitler's infamous rally at Nuremberg. It is also hard to see how plays designed to cultivate class consciousness in the thirties were not responding to a real problem. The claim that Americans lacked radical class consciousness (perhaps less true at this time than at any other in American history) does not necessarily mean that plays attempting to instill such self-consciousness were out of touch with reality.

To some degree Welles may have been attuned to the declining potency of the Workers' Theatre Movement. With the triumph of Fascism abroad and the FTP's sapping of talent away from amateur groups, the Workers' Theatre Movement was in decline by 1938, and Welles may have sensed its diminished relevance. But underlying Welles's train of thought is the problem of how to tap into the vitality, energy, and innovation of the Theatre of Propaganda without himself becoming a propagandist, which by this time was a pejorative term inevitably associated with Nazi Germany's comprehensive campaign and the Soviet domestic policy of conflating propaganda and education. It was not that Welles shied away from topical concerns. On the contrary, his *Julius Caesar*, subtitled "The Death of a Dictator," was designed to evoke the threat of fascism in Europe, and he was thrown out of the FTP when he refused to cave in to government pressure to shut down *The Cradle Will Rock*. Rather, Welles seems to have been split between the desire to have either the power of the propagandist or the aura of the experimental artist dedicated to art for its own sake. Project 891 briefly provided a protected space in which Welles could try to have it both ways, but the vigor of his politico-aesthetic experiments virtually ensured that government support would be withdrawn. As Welles's notes continue, his conflicted investments in art and propaganda motivate the shift in focus from relations between theater and propaganda to relations between theater and film.

Welles's official argument is that theater must do all it can to compete more successfully with film, but his attraction to the medium elicits a paean to filmic power that he subsequently must find a way to counter. In a frank admission that would have horrified D. H. Lawrence, Welles observes that "we must believe our eyes and the movie camera takes over our eyes": "What can't the camera do? At this minute, at the local movie palace, it can put a thousand people in the middle of a clothes closet, shoot them all through the key-hole and up to the chandelier if the view is good from there, and down a staircase just near enough a descending figure, if the figure is good enough to follow, into the street, at kissing distance from a winking eye and from thence into a test tube, the stratosphere or wherever the plot is thickest." If Welles seems to be rehearsing the encyclopedia of techniques he would use in *Citizen Kane* three years later—he was the first, for instance, to put a camera in a phone booth, a relatively minor stunt that Hitchcock would develop into a major scene in *The Birds* (1963)—he soon turns to a very specific anticipation of the film project he undertook before *Citizen Kane*, an adaptation of *Heart of Darkness*:

> I have an idea that we shall soon see the movies taking us still further than out of ourselves. I mean into somebody else. The camera has yet to be proven too impersonal for characterization and it would be interesting to see a picture made in the first person singular. The movies have conclusively demonstrated their ability to identify a character with its audiences, is it impossible for them to identify their audiences with a character, and so completely that the audiences assume it?
>
> This is only a hunch and a hint.

Welles's hunch was borne out, though despite his considerable efforts, he would not be the first director to make the kind of film he gestures toward here. Welles's attempt to film *Heart of Darkness* for RKO with a subjective camera in the role of Marlow retrospectively illuminates what he is trying to describe in this convoluted passage. Much of the difficulty in parsing the sentences derives from the seductive rhythms of Welles's misleading chiasmus: films have identified a character with the audience but not an audience with the character. But at issue is not so much a reversal but a distinction between two kinds of identification, the first being the model at work in most Hollywood films, the second as yet untried over the length of a feature film. In the first model, which depends on what film theory has described as techniques of suture, spectators are encouraged to align their vision with the characters on the screen, who function as their mirrors or representatives. The identification produced by suturing techniques is notional and mobile: looking over characters' shoulders, the audience might shift its point of view from moment to moment, as in a shot–reverse shot sequence, and the seamlessness of the shifting identifications is designed to make spectators forget that the camera is manipulating their vision. In contrast, Welles's first-person experiment aspires to identification as fusion, a closing of the gap between audience and character, and an elimination of the play among perspectives encouraged by more mobile forms of identification.[41] Welles never got to test his technique—budget problems shelved *Heart of Darkness*, making *Citizen Kane* his first film—but if the only attempt to sustain the experiment over the length of an entire feature film, Robert Montgomery's *Lady in the Lake* (1946), is any indication, the technique is as likely to produce alienation as absorption. The gap between audience and character, it turns out, is necessary to the identificatory process: rather than lose themselves in the character-as-camera, spectators find it difficult not to think about the limitations on vision imposed by the first-person camera.

But the importance here lies in Welles's intentions. His aspiration to make viewers identify "so completely" with the character-as-camera that they "assume" the position of the character on the screen cuts two ways. On one hand, it is consonant with an avant-garde effort to break down boundaries between art and life; on the other, it sounds like a fantasy of perfect propaganda: the ability not just to transport the audience but to transform it by literally replacing the audience's point of view with the camera's. In line with this will to mastery, Welles's plan to introduce *Heart of Darkness* with a prefatory sequence "intended to instruct and acquaint the audience as amusingly as possible" with the film's "special technique"—its equation, as Welles put it, of "the eye" with the "I"—emphasizes coercion.[42] In fact, in his planned preface, which was never filmed, Welles makes himself into a comic version of the kind of brutal dictator he planned to criticize in Kurtz.

The sequence would have begun with a dark screen and Welles's familiar voice introducing himself; the voiceover then asks viewers to open their eyes, at which point the opening iris of the camera "places" the viewer inside a bird cage looking out through the bars at a gigantic Welles. Welles's voice informs the audience that it is playing the part of a canary that is asked to sing and refuses: "That's the plot." Welles's gargantuan fingers offer an olive, but "you don't want an olive. This

enrages me" (1). Then, in an anticipation of Hitchcock's famous subjective shot of Leo G. Carroll shooting himself in *Spellbound*, "the
muzzle of a pistol is stuck between the bars of the cage" as Welles's
voice explains: "That's the way a gun looks to a canary" (2). (In a
glancing allusion to the rise of a truly dangerous dictator, the gun is described as a Big Bertha, a well-known German pistol in World War I.)
Welles counts down from three, and when the audience still will not
sing, "the gun goes off with a cloud of smoke and a shower of brightly
colored sparks." Fade to black as Welles comments: "That's the end of
this picture." Then, in case anyone has failed to grasp the full extent of
Welles's directorial power, a second sequence—nominally a "screen
test" for his viewers, who are "part of the story"—turns the "bird's-eye
view" into a *"convict's-eye view"* by placing the audience behind
prison bars (3). Welles as warden unlocks the cell door, leads the
camera-audience down a corridor and into the electric chair, where it is
strapped in and electrocuted: "Sound of current being turned on.
Screen goes into blinding red stain. CAMERA BLURRING ITS FOCUS at the
same time, moves quickly to an electrician whose outline distorts terribly, melts into dirty violet, and sound of current magnified into terrific
metallic ring which completes sound, dies as we FADE OUT" (7). A third
and final sequence points the moral: *"You're not going to see this
picture—this picture is going to happen to you"* (8). Lightening the
mood, a brief golf scene ensues in which Welles enjoins the audience to
keep its eye on the ball before he steps in to fill the frame in medium
closeup: "Now, if you're doing this right, this is what you ought to
look like to me," and his image dissolves into a shot of a cinema interior as it would look from the center of the screen: *"The audience is entirely made up of motion picture cameras"* (9). A last comment from
Welles's voice as the image fades out: "I hope you get the idea" (9).

In Welles's notes on theater these fantasies of cinematic control are not
given full rein, but the felt pressure of such possibilities motivates the essay's turn back toward theater. Having confessed that he now prefers
film to theater owing to film's power to transport him into a casino with
Jean Harlow, and having concluded that "visual theatre is outmoded,"
Welles is compelled by the ostensible aim of his essay to explain what
"we who love the Theatre," "fighting the full fierce force and flow of our
own element," can to do to survive in the swift currents of modernity.
Welles's answer is vague but suggestive: "The movies can make you look
at anything, but the theatre can make you see." Welles had already
adapted *Heart of Darkness* for radio broadcast, making the echo of
Conrad's famous declaration of his artistic aim—"to *make* you see"—
unmistakable. Unlike modern criticism, which has called attention to the
urgent willfulness of Conrad's aims ("to *make* you hear, to *make* you

see . . . to *make* you see"), Welles means to invoke the combination of literal and figurative meanings Conrad originally intended: a commitment to accurate representation of the visible world and to the communication of truth. But in what sense can theater transcend the literal seeing of film to produce the "glimpse of truth" prized by Conrad?[43]

Welles's answer at first sounds a lot like his preface to *Heart of Darkness*: a play happens not "to the actors but to the audience." The difference, however, lies in the nature of theatrical performance, which Welles exalts as a defining virtue: "A movie is yours and mine but never ours. A play is ours and nobody else's. Each performance is an event. You can't open it again like a book, or put it away again like a record, it has gone the way of last night's sunset." But the value lies not so much in ephemerality per se as in the special quality of the moment: theater is not "witnessed": "it's partaken of by a conscious congregation." The phrase "conscious congregation" would not be out of place in a manifesto from the Workers' Theatre: in a moment of near-religious intensity, the audience becomes a community of thinkers united in an instant of understanding. And yet just as Welles is trying to fend off film, on one hand, he needs to distance himself from the Theatre of Propaganda, on the other: "In the movies there are money and fans and even the wonderful responsibility of posterity, but in the theatre we leave behind us but a sentimental memory. . . . Ours is no gain beyond the priceless minute." A cynical reader might hear this as an attempt to reconcile stage actors to low wages, but as Welles continues, it becomes clear that he is trying to evoke a sense of theater as art: "The great moment. Something too shining to see that sings too high to hear." Traditionally aestheticians have turned to music for a symbol of pure art, but Welles subordinates the sounds and sights of theater to a conception of the theatrical sublime that makes theatricality itself the art of arts.

Welles writes here in the voice of a director and actor deeply in love with the moment in which a performance jells, becomes reality, and transcends itself. But with film emerging as the dominant art form of modernity, he is caught in a bind. On one side is the vitality of the Theatre of Propaganda, whose ambition to reorder the world leads directly into the filmic mastery Welles explores in his preface to *Heart of Darkness*. On the other is the ideal of an art that catalyzes thought in order to create a community united not by a shared ideological project but by a common aesthetic experience, one with "no gain beyond the priceless minute." Conrad thus serves Welles both politically and aesthetically. In Welles's Revised Estimating Script for *Heart of Darkness*, Conrad's critique of empire is disambiguated and redirected toward fascist Germany. But Welles's Conrad is also the exquisite formalist of Henry James, who praised his "extraordinary exhibition of method" in *Chance*

(1914) and described Conrad as "absolutely alone as a votary of the way to do a thing that shall make it undergo most doing." To James, Conrad's devotion to style and technique indicated that "the whole undertaking was committed by its first step either to be 'art' exclusively or to be nothing."[44]

Formalism and politics need not be considered antithetical, of course; indeed, the best work of the Workers' Theatre Movement always indicated as much. But Welles was emerging from a decade in which the global economic depression and the pervasiveness and increasing sophistication of propaganda had contributed to a polarization of views on relations between art and politics. At one extreme was the engaged left, whose credo was summed up by the British engraver, sculptor, and writer Eric Gill in the title of his 1935 essay, "All Art is Propaganda": "It is in fact impossible to do anything, to make anything which is not expressive of 'value'. . . . directly [the artist] shows his work to anyone . . . he becomes a responsible propagandist for the 'values,' the ethos expressed in his work and therefore promoted by it."[45] Here propaganda becomes such a capacious term that any expression of belief is necessarily propagandistic, and Gill wants artists to seize on the inevitability of propaganda in order to make theirs count. From this perspective the formal experimentation of high modernism is condemned as a bourgeois evasion of life's pressing political exigencies. At the other extreme, art is defined as the antithesis of propaganda. Thus when in *Principles of Art* (1938) R. G. Collingwood, trying to preserve what he finds valuable in Oscar Wilde's dictum that all art is useless, wants to differentiate between art and that which stimulates a practical or expedient activity, he associates art with self-sufficiency and non-art with advertisement and propaganda.[46] In this polarized climate, the serial publication of *Finnegans Wake* was typically met with either derision or praise. The doctrinaire Marxist view saw Joyce's verbal intricacies as a reactionary elision of "the objective material essence of the external world," while formalists accepted his multilingual, multilevel punning as a subordination of the "message" to the process of decoding that makes messages possible.[47]

Hollywood had an answer for this cultural impasse: make movies that do not call attention to themselves as movies, and stay away from political issues likely to generate controversy. The Hollywood Production Code, popularly known as the Hays Office Code, began to be rigorously enforced in 1934 in response to the perceived moral and political deviance of movies produced in the opening years of decade, the nadir of the Depression. Highly sensitive to the mass appeal of film, the authors of the code felt responsible for the moral effects of movies on the audience and laid out both general principles and examples of what could not be represented. Movie producers, according to the code, "though regarding motion pictures primarily as entertainment without any explicit purpose of teaching or propaganda," nevertheless "know that the motion picture within its own field of entertainment may be directly responsible for spiritual or moral progress, for higher types of social life, and for much correct thinking."[48] Motivated by the desire for moral uplift, the felt necessity of closure, and the need to recoup rising production costs, happy endings were virtually mandated, and political conflicts, no matter how profound or intractable, were converted into interpersonal dilemmas capable of resolution. If the production code carefully policed morality in the name of social regulation, Hollywood also developed a normative visual style whose conventions were rarely breached. Known in retrospect as "classical Hollywood style," the narrative and filmic conventions governing studio production reinforced the illusion of transparent realism. In such films, the story generally unfolds chronologically, editing emphasizes continuity, and causality is grounded in coherent psychological motivation. Governed by strict ethical and formal norms, and designed to appeal to as many people as possible, Hollywood movies were therefore unlikely to express controversial political sentiments or to indulge in sustained formal experimentation.

The next section explores how both Hitchcock and Welles chafed against this system. Each desired, and sometimes enjoyed, greater autonomy. Before arriving in Hollywood, Hitchcock was inclined to push against the limits of the classical style by flaunting his cinematic self-consciousness and directorial control over the unfolding narrative.[49] If *Sabotage*, for instance, had been filmed in strict adherence with classical conventions, its self-reflexive dimension would have been more rigorously subordinated to the demands of transparency: Verloc would have run a shady bookstore, just as he does in Conrad's original, not a popular cinema, and his brother-in-law Stevie would not have been killed by exploding film canisters. In theater and radio Welles had frequently enjoyed far more latitude to experiment than most Hollywood directors would ever know, and Project 891 had underwritten that freedom with government funds. His nearly unprecedented and highly publicized contract in Hollywood granted him comparable artistic license (though not as much as most people thought), but only, it turned out, for one film. The story of how Hitchcock and Welles negotiated Hollywood bears directly on the waywardness of the propaganda they directed during the war.

Autonomy and Innovation: From the Studio to the MoI and CIAA

When Welles signed with RKO in July 1939 to make two features, Hitchcock had been under contract to Selznick since April. Welles's contract was widely reported at the time as offering him absolute freedom from supervision in the making of his first two films as well as a great deal of money. Although the actual terms of the contract did not give Welles the total artistic freedom reported in the press, it was nonetheless highly unusual in the independence it granted him on the set, and the myth was in any case more influential than its reality.[50] When *Citizen Kane* came out in 1941, Welles's first film confirmed many directors' belief that the only thing keeping them from making great movies in Hollywood was Hollywood. Hitchcock had particularly good reasons for feeling this way. The crucial figure in the story of Hitchcock's transition from England to Hollywood is David O. Selznick, whose tight control over Hitchcock's professional life cast a shadow over his early years in the United States.

Michael Balcon, who produced the best of Hitchcock's films at Gaumont, was in many ways the antithesis of Selznick. As I describe in chapter 1, Hitchcock became renowned at this time for mastery, owing in part to the control he exerted over his artistic materials, in part to his control over the audience, which would earn him the title of Master of Suspense. Two things militated against Hitchcock's having similar latitude and control in Hollywood. First, unlike Balcon, who gave Hitchcock considerable freedom, Selznick kept close tabs on his directors and was intimately involved in all aspects of his productions. Master Producer thus faced off against Master Director. Second, Hitchcock loved experimental cinema. Working in Germany in the early twenties he absorbed the lessons of German expressionism at Ufa (Universum Film Aktiengesellschaft, Germany's largest studio, whose name became synonymous with expressionist style), and in the late twenties, thanks to the new Film Society of London, he studied the theories of Vertov, Eisenstein, and Pudovkin.[51] But like every other studio head, Selznick adhered to classical Hollywood style. Hitchcock was not one to suppress his cinematic instincts simply to please a new master, and director and producer clashed repeatedly during their first collaboration, *Rebecca*.

Throughout their relationship, financial arrangements exacerbated their artistic differences. Hitchcock's contract paid him considerably less than was earned by his American peers and offered no participation in profits. Selznick also remained in complete control of Hitchcock's professional life, loaning him out to other studios for huge profits and determining the projects he could undertake. Later, even as Hitchcock's fame began to match that of Frank Capra and Welles, his contract prevented him from achieving comparable independence or financial rewards. Understandably, Hitchcock came to regard this first contract "as a collar that rubbed and choked."[52]

He also had reason to choke on Welles as a counterexample. RKO had made Welles the most envied man in Hollywood, but when the company came knocking on Selznick's door in hopes of borrowing Hitchcock, Selznick held out for so much money that RKO walked away. The adaptation of *Rebecca* eventually came back to Welles also. Hitchcock had wanted to buy the rights to the novel for years but could not afford it. When Selznick stepped in to buy it in 1938, he licensed the radio rights to Orson Welles, who had just broadcast *War of the Worlds*, in order to generate buzz for the planned film. A few years later Selznick sat down with Hitchcock to explain what he wanted in the film treatment, but when Hitchcock proceeded to adapt the novel in his usual freewheeling way, Selznick unleashed one of the long memos for which he was famous in Hollywood—this one some twelve pages—detailing all the ways in which Hitchcock's treatment was an abomination that would cheat filmgoers of their right to see a faithful adaptation on the big screen. His memo culminated in a pointed counterexample:

> The medium of radio is certainly no closer to the novel form than is the motion picture. And yet Orson Welles, throwing together a radio script of *Rebecca* in less than a week's time, had one of the greatest dramatic successes the radio has ever known by simply assembling ten or fifteen scenes from the book word for word—thereby proving that Du Maurier's *Rebecca* in any form has the identical appeal that it had in book form. A clever showman, he didn't waste time and effort creating anything new but simply gave them the original. I hope we will be equally astute.[53]

Don't waste time creating anything new; be more like Welles. Even before *Citizen Kane* rendered Selznick's advice deeply ironic, the comparison could not have sat well with Hitchcock, nor could he have been pleased a few years later when a review of *Shadow of a Doubt* suggested that unlike Welles, Hitchcock had "conspicuously failed" whenever he attempted to move beyond familiar cinematic ground.[54] Later in his career, when Hitchcock finally gained something like the autonomy Welles was given with *Citizen Kane*, he took the opportunity in *Rear Window* (1954) and *Vertigo* (1958) to push his experiments in cinematic self-consciousness much further, often making style, spectatorship, and directorial control as much the focus of his films as the narrative itself. In the meantime, he had to settle for adding to *Rebecca* a scene in which Laurence Olivier and Joan Fontaine watch home movies of their honeymoon until projector problems cut short their celluloid memories of happier times.

Sidney Bernstein's invitation to do some work for the MoI therefore came at a time when Hitchcock's trying professional situation must have made London in war time sound like a working vacation. Hitchcock already had personal and political reasons for returning to England that had been pressed to the foreground a few years earlier. Though too old and overweight to enlist, Hitchcock had always been willing to do his part as a filmmaker. The U.S. Neutrality Act, first passed in 1935 and amended three times over the next four years, made it illegal to raise funds for belligerent foreign nations in war time, but when war broke out a group of expatriate Hollywood film people met regularly at Cecil B. De Mille's office to plot ways to encourage the United States to take sides. Hitchcock sometimes attended and in 1940 agreed to contribute to an anthology picture, *Forever and a Day*, that would raise funds for war-related activities.[55] He also had maintained his British citizenship, and when his old friend Michael Balcon questioned his patriotism, he angrily responded that "the British government has only to call upon me for my services."[56] So Bernstein's request solved two problems at once: Hitchcock could prove his patriotism while also escaping from Selznick's oppressive oversight. Bernstein admired the director "for bringing the art of German expressionism and Soviet montage to the commercial cinema," and unlike Selznick, he would leave Hitchcock alone.[57] With the characteristic generosity of a Hollywood mogul, Selznick immediately suspected that Bernstein's MoI films were a ruse for stealing Hitchcock's services after the war, but after some lengthy telegrams, he eventually let his cash cow head back to his homeland.[58]

The narratives of autonomy in the careers of Hitchcock and Welles thus run in reverse. Hitchcock thrived so well in Hollywood that he was able to outlast the studio system, which collapsed in the 1950s with the passing of vertically integrated production companies. With critical and box office success Hitchcock gradually became able to fund his own pictures without sacrificing the integrity of his vision or the level of technical support provided by Hollywood. In the meantime, his propaganda work at Welwyn Studios, where he made *Aventure Malgache* and *Bon Voyage*, provided a temporary respite from the constraints of the studio system. Serving as a kind of professional annex set apart from Hollywood, Welwyn permitted Hitchcock to indulge in restless experimental impulses without the distraction of Selznick's countermoves and without the censorship of the production code. Welles, sadly, began at the top and steadily lost the autonomy granted by his first Hollywood contract. The loss of that privilege is closely connected with the propaganda film he tried to make for Rockefeller's CIAA.

Citizen Kane and *It's All True*: Documentary and Propaganda

When Nelson Rockefeller asked RKO about bringing Welles into Roosevelt's Good Neighbor Policy, the studio was happy to oblige. Welles had already begun working on a vaguely conceived documentary anthology that would include four linked stories; one segment, "My Friend Bonito," based a short story by documentary filmmaker Robert Flaherty, was already being shot in Mexico. By collaborating with the CIAA motion picture division, RKO in effect received a $300,000 insurance policy against a possible box office loss, and Welles felt buffered from the budget problems that plagued *The Magnificent Ambersons* (1942), his hugely anticipated followup to *Citizen Kane*. What's more, the CIAA's backing of *It's All True* promised to restore the relative freedom from financial constraint Welles experienced during Project 891, which once funded the acquisition of twelve sacrificial goats as part of the preparation for his voodoo *Macbeth*.[59] But it did not work out that way.

Agreeing to the deal with CIAA, Welles and RKO in effect shifted *It's All True* from the realm of straight documentary into the ambiguous border region between documentary and propaganda.[60] The terrain was not entirely unfamiliar to Welles. Welles's New York theater work, as we have seen, provoked reflections on art and propaganda, and *Citizen Kane* offered practice in the strategic blurring of boundaries between history and fiction. In fact, the making of *Citizen Kane* drew Welles into the logic of propaganda on multiple levels. Often cited as an icon of cinematic modernism, *Citizen Kane* is equally a masterpiece of self-reflexive propaganda—that is, a meditation on propaganda that also functioned as propaganda. One of the greatest films ever made, then, offers a good way into one of the greatest never made.

Jorge Luis Borges's well-known description of *Citizen Kane* as a "centreless labyrinth" highlights the film's formalism: it is a structure that invites endless wandering through its carefully contrived corridors.[61] Borges did not intend a compliment. Although his review initially seems to value *Citizen Kane*'s formalist complexity, particularly when he compares it with Conrad's multiple narrators and dislocated chronology in *Chance*, Borges ultimately rejects the film as empty. His labyrinth trope notwithstanding, Borges's review has not stood up well over time. He wrongly predicts that no one will ever want to see *Citizen Kane* a second time, and few spectators have found it dull and pedantic. Borges's critique of the film's empty formalism is anticipated by the film itself in the disparaging description of Xanadu offered by Jedediah Leland, Charles Foster Kane's one-time friend and colleague, who speculates that Kane was "disappointed in this world, so he built one of his own, an absolute monarchy." Leland's commentary thus goes Borges one better by linking Kane's retreat to his desire for mastery.

Unlike Xanadu, however, *Citizen Kane* is far from a solipsistic escape. Welles liked to emphasize the film's foregrounding of the process of decipherment: "the point of the picture," he said in an interview, "is not so much the solution of the problem as its presentation."[62] True enough, but *Citizen Kane*'s polemical edge cuts sharply. Hearst papers worked overtime in the thirties to keep the United States out of the impending war, and by attacking the publisher through Kane, a tired old man secluded in Xanadu, *Citizen Kane* makes a case for resisting the isolationism preached by the Hearst chain.[63] Welles also set out to paint a damning portrait of Hearst's mistress, Marion Davies, as the hapless, sometimes vulgar, and finally boozy Susan Alexander. It may well have been Welles's cruelly distorting portrait of Davies, a woman generally beloved by the many Hollywood moguls and stars who frequented San Simeon, that drove Hearst to attack *Citizen Kane* with such unrelenting ferocity. Hearst was thus not entirely wrong to think of Welles's film as propaganda; Welles himself later confessed that the portrait of Davies was "a dirty trick." Unfortunately for Hearst, his failed attempt to suppress *Citizen Kane* through red-baiting counter-propaganda only highlighted the film's emphasis on the manipulation of public opinion.[64]

Citizen Kane in fact charts the media's role in the shaping of public opinion over the first four decades of the twentieth century. Early on, the unexpected intrusion of the newsreel "News on the March" immediately after Kane's death underscores film's growing prominence as a recorder and interpreter of public events. When the narrative loops back to the story of Kane's rise into power, it returns to the historical moment in which the rapid growth of the popular press invested newspaper magnates, such as Hearst and Joseph Pulitzer in the United States and Alfred Harmsworth (later Lord Northcliffe) in Britain, with unprecedented political power. It was the success of these men in shaping public opinion at the turn of the twentieth century that encouraged the British government to turn increasingly to newspapermen to manage the propaganda campaign in World War I. *Citizen Kane* makes much of the yellow press's most notorious abuse of influence: Hearst's efforts to provoke the Spanish-American War. Already the most powerful media mogul in the world, Hearst also wanted to run for political office, so when war with Spain over the Cuban insurrection began to seem possible, he invented jingoistic stories designed to incite a war that would boost circulation and further his political ambitions. Hence the famous (and probably apocryphal) story, recirculated by *Citizen Kane*, of Hearst's telegram in reply to Frederic Remington, who had been dispatched to Cuba to make sketches: "You supply the drawings, I'll furnish the war." Although British propagandists discovered in World War I that they could be more effective by remaining closer to facts than Hearst often did, Hearst's fabrications were massively influential at the turn of the century, in part because as the first national chain, Hearst papers could dominate the flow of information reaching the public as never before. As Kane says of his readers, "they'll think what I tell them to think."

Kane, of course, discovers that media power has limits: Kane papers cannot save his nascent political career when his opponent Gettys reveals Kane's affair with Susan, nor can puff pieces sustain Susan's career as an opera diva. The film's visual style also ironizes Kane's ambition to mold the public. Consider, for instance, how Welles transforms the common use of newspaper headlines to mark major plot steps. When Kane marries Susan after his divorce, we see the newly married couple descending the courthouse steps through the scrim of a headline, "Kane Marries 'Singer.' " As if literalizing Kane's axiom that headlines do not reflect the magnitude of the news but create it, the lap dissolve remains in place far longer than was customary, and as it lingers over the scene, the viewer is reminded of an earlier headline, "Candidate Kane Found in Love Nest with 'Singer.' " Years later this headline prompts Leland to suggest that Kane married Susan and pushed her into the opera simply to remove the quotation marks from around "singer." Kane may make headlines, in other words, but the headlines also make him.

Welles's sophisticated awareness of both the power and limitation of modern media's influence informs *Citizen Kane* from its opening moments. Among the first words out of Kane's mouth (apart from "Rosebud") is the admonition "not to believe everything you hear on the radio," but this warning is offered within the compass of the newsreel, which is itself criticized by Rawlston, the newsreel editor, for failing to get at the truth of Kane's life. "News on the March" also includes a sequence that is pointedly fabricated: as if reversing the Soviet-style elimination of disgraced figures from historical photographs, Kane is inserted on a balcony with Hitler. When the newsreel breaks off, we find ourselves in the darkened screening room, where we eavesdrop on editors and reporters as they plot ways to make the newsreel more gripping. Suddenly reminding us of our own vulnerability as consumers of cinematic images, the scene recalls Hitchcock's focus on the conspirators gathered behind the screen in *Sabotage*. For contemporary viewers the moment would have been yet more pointed owing to the barrage of criticism in the late thirties that was directed at newsreels for staging events, faking images, and manipulating soundtracks.[65] If *Citizen Kane* itself implicitly lays claim to greater insight and veracity by revealing the identity of Rosebud, a scoop the newsreels will never get, it was part of Welles's genius to make a case against the media for abusing its power to shape public opinion without exempting himself. When Welles turned to *It's All True*, however, his own implication in the problem became more difficult to negotiate.

David Bordwell's account of *Citizen Kane* as "at once a triumph of social comment and a landmark in cinematic surrealism" underscores the continuity of concerns that Welles brought to his South American documentary. Fusing "the two main strands of the cinematic tradition,"

Citizen Kane draws on the tradition of "objective realism" descending from the Lumière brothers through documentary and on the "subjective vision" descending from Georges Méliès through the European avant-garde.[66] The making of *It's All True* saw the development of a similar tension between objective and subjective vision. Welles began "My Friend Bonito" largely to create a part for the current love of his life, the Mexican beauty Dolores Del Rio, but as he warmed to the later Brazilian stories, the desultory documentary became infused with an increasingly subjective vision that was at odds with the official purpose of the film—or so the CIAA thought.

The project began innocently enough, with the director heading down to Rio to film Carnaval, but early on Welles began to depart radically from the usual Hollywood approach. He was determined not to offer up the kind of South American film to which viewers were accustomed, such as *Flying Down to Rio* (1933), which introduced Fred Astaire and Ginger Rogers as a samba-dancing screen couple, or *That Night in Rio* (1941), a garish Fox musical featuring Carmen Miranda and Don Ameche. Welles aimed instead to get beyond stereotypes by commissioning local writers to conduct research into Brazilian customs and by immersing himself as much as possible in the culture. Of course, effective propaganda tends to rely on the deployment of stereotypes, not on their overturning, and Welles's devotion to inquiry and analysis created problems down the line. At first Welles was absorbed by the technical challenge of shooting Carnaval, but as he became increasingly interested in Brazilian popular culture, he decided that the Carnaval sequence should tell the story of samba, the distinctive dance music indigenous to Afro-Brazilian culture. The topic was particularly appealing to Welles, whose musical heroes included Louis Armstrong and Duke Ellington, because his earliest plans for the anthology had included a history of jazz. So where Astaire and Rogers began the popularization of samba in the United States, Welles plunged into the tangled story of its origins, a complex question that has not been resolved to this day. The more Welles looked into samba, the more he was drawn to a political vision the Brazilian and U.S. officials found offensive.

The investigation led Welles to the *favelas*, the poor shanty towns in the mountains encircling the outskirts of Rio, which were inhabited by blacks and *mestizos*. As he shot the samba material, the last piece of the anthology fell into place when Welles heard a story famous throughout Brazil of four poor fisherman, or *jangadeiros*, who a year earlier had sailed to Rio in their primitive fishing boat, a *jangada*, over sixteen hundred miles in sixty-one days, in order to petition the president of Brazil, Getulio Vargas, for social reform and material improvements in Fortaleza, their remote fishing village. Vargas granted their request, and the four men became national folk heroes. Welles flew to Fortaleza, became good friends with one of the men, Jacaré, and immediately wrote a treatment that described how the "Four Men on a Raft" sequence would fit with the Carnaval story. The sketchy project was finally taking shape, but Welles never had a chance to finish it.

Accounts unsympathetic to Welles ascribe his failure to finish *It's All True* to personal weakness: a deep-seated inability to finish projects, his carousing with South American women, and his squandering of RKO's money. But Robert Stam has argued persuasively that such accounts often betray a racial subtext in which anxiety regarding Afro-Brazilian culture is displaced onto Welles's carnivalesque behavior while filming in Rio.[67] A dull-witted RKO unit producer periodically sent damning letters from Rio to the studio, including one that wondered why anyone would want to film "carnival nigger singing and dancing" in "some very dirty and disreputable nigger neighborhoods"; the producer objected in particular to "the continued exploitation of the negro and low class element in and around Rio."[68] The Brazilian Department of Press and Propaganda was not happy to discover that Welles was filming in the *favelas*, and CIAA soon feared that "other Latin American countries such as Argentina would react even more vigorously [than Brazil] in opposition to any film that gave an accurate and sympathetic rendering of blacks in Latin America."[69] The plan for "Four Men on a Raft" added to Welles's political woes. Welles understood the episode "as part of an ongoing tradition of popular Brazilian resistance to oppression, since the *jangadeiros* in the past had been instrumental in the struggle against slavery."[70] But this was precisely the problem. Given that President Vargas had reneged on his promises to Jacaré and his fellow fishermen, the sequence could be taken as an attempt to prod the Brazilian president into living up to the agreement. With Welles's subjective grasp of his documentary materials becoming increasingly political, it became correspondingly unlikely that the film would ever be finished.

As expenses mounted, RKO threatened to pull the plug, but Welles continued to film—until Jacaré drowned in a boating accident during the filming of the *jangadeiros'* triumphant arrival in Rio. Welles had been enormously popular with the Brazilian press and people by virtue of his considerable personal charisma, his genuine curiosity about all things Brazilian, and his commitment to highlighting Brazilian talent. But with the death of a national hero the press turned on him. The new RKO head then decided to part ways with Welles as soon as possible in order to return to more lucrative projects. He permitted Welles to travel to Fortaleza to film in Jacaré's village, but only with a skeleton crew and minimal equipment. Soon after, when Welles submitted what the studio considered an outrageous budget request for a nightclub shoot in Rio, his contract was terminated. When Welles returned to Hollywood, RKO could not find a distributor for his unedited film, and as Welles and RKO negotiated various ways to salvage the project, Rockefeller delivered the news that CIAA was no longer willing to underwrite a project that was unlikely to be released as a major feature.

But Welles felt committed to the documentary and would not let it go. After four years of trying to interest distributors and raise money on his own, Welles made the disastrous decision to sign a promissary note for $197,000 and took over the film. In May 1946 he defaulted and was sued by RKO, which repossessed the footage, some of which was apparently destroyed. Welles was forced to take more acting jobs to repay the studio, which further limited his dwindling opportunities to direct. What drove him on this ultimately ruinous course? Welles's obsession with finishing the film derived in part from a desire to do justice to Jacaré's memory and in part from his commitment to the film's antiracist, democratic message. But he also believed in *It's All True* as a work of art.

The sequences released in Paramount's 1994 documentary/reconstruction justify Welles's belief in the artistic merit of *It's All True* and the large claims many critics have made on its behalf.[71] Particularly compelling is the twenty-two-minute "Four Men on a Raft" sequence, most of which Welles filmed after Jacaré's death. Welles worked in Fortaleza with a single stationary camera, black and white stock, and a seven-person crew. In order to address the production's tragic turn of events, he found someone to play Jacaré and devised a subplot about the drowning death of a newly married fisherman. The opening two minutes of the village scenes detail the building of *jangadas*. Working with first-time actors and inventing a new improvisational style, Welles crafted a beautiful sequence of images in which villagers chop, saw, hew, plane, and drag wood into place. They join carefully crafted pieces, weave ropes, nets, and baskets (figure 5.2), pound dowels into place, sand rough edges, tie off lines, and paint the name St. Pedro on the sail that will take the *jangadeiros* to Rio. Even without sound (which modern post-production has added), the sequence vividly evokes the physical act of creation as a process of communal making. If, as the Paramount documentary indicates, Welles was intent on exploring the feudal system that kept the fisherman poor, he also saw in their labors a mirror of his own. In the previous year he had shuttled between sets night and day while simultaneously directing *The Magnificent Ambersons* and acting in *Journey into Fear* (1943), and in Rio he had done radio shows while working on the Carnaval segment. Created in an isolated village with minimal technical support or distractions, the sequence in Fortaleza reads as an allegory of Welles's return to a nearly artisanal mode of production. The lovingly documented process is imbued with Welles's affec-

FIGURE 5.2   A modernist return to the artisanal: waterfront production and death in *It's All True* (1942).

tion not only for the villagers (seen in the way he lingers over their faces) but also for the rudiments of filmmaking, the cutting, shaping, and splicing that transforms raw materials into a mode of transport.

The love story Welles added to give shape to the Fortaleza materials sounds blandly melodramatic on paper, but the footage he shot is as effective as the boat-building sequence. By telling the story of a young woman's loss of her husband, the segment works beautifully as a moving tribute to Jacaré and the village life he championed. We see the young lovers' marriage, the capsizing of the boat, and many rescuers diving into the sea in vain. Later, a young girl wading among the rocks comes across the fisherman's body and runs back to the village in tears through a tangle of fishing nets (figure 5.3). At once abstract and deeply social, the visual prominence of the nets crisscrossing the frame throughout the sequence suggests both the profound interconnectedness of village life and the actual death woven into the fabric of the story. Scores of villagers wade into the water together to reclaim the body and later form a long, single-file funeral procession that snakes across undulating dunes up to a grave site overlooking the sea. The ethnographic depth of Welles's treatment invests the villagers with great dignity, and the care he

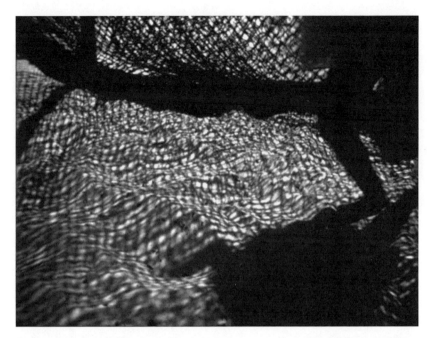

FIGURE 5.3   Social abstraction: recovering community in *It's All True* (1942).

took with his remarkable setups carries over into story of the *jan-gadeiros*' long journey to Rio.[72] In some ways, CIAA's goal of intercultural understanding could not have been fulfilled any better; but the Good Neighbor Policy was looking for the kind of understanding promoted by tourist brochures, not a vision inflected by Welles's interest in cultural heterogeneity and his sense of social injustice and personal loss, not to mention one shaped by a director less interested in sunbathers on the beach than in patterns of shadow on sand. Too tendentious politically and too visually self-conscious, *It's All True* remained on the shelf for forty years.

Welles's inability to finish the film materially damaged his career. Having gone to Rio, Welles lost control of the final cut of *The Magnificent Ambersons* while struggling to make the documentary. RKO butchered the film, cutting some forty-five minutes and adding a happy ending. Released to a war-time audience hungry for something more uplifting than the story of a great family's eclipse, *The Magnificent Ambersons* lost even more money than *Citizen Kane* (whose distribution was impeded by Hearst) and solidified Welles's reputation as box office poison. The production stories of *The Magnificent Ambersons* and *It's All True* forever tagged him as a director prone to extravagance and unable to complete his projects. His opportunities in Hollywood were never the same.

Welles tried to repair the damage caused by his highly publicized disaster in South America by making *The Stranger* (1946), a spy film unrelated to the Camus novel. He came in under budget and a day early, but critics disliked the final product and criticized him for copying Hitchcock's *Shadow of a Doubt* (1943). Welles received the bad reviews around the same time that RKO repossessed *It's All True*, and his subsequent statement to the *New York Times* seems to reflect on both disappointments: "I think pictures are in a bad way. They need revitalizing. . . . We should have theaters financed by the Government for private film experimentation and a chain of adult theaters free from Hays Office code censorship. Films dealing with serious and important subjects should be produced, even if the big boys have to be taxed for them."[73] In Fortaleza several years earlier, Welles thought that his experimentation was being underwritten by the government, but his politically charged exploration of a serious and important subject effectively ended the freedom he had experienced under the FTP's umbrella in the thirties.

Hitchcock's adventure in government financed film met a similar fate. Like Welles, Hitchcock was granted a kind of professional annex set apart from the studio system and the Hays Office, and he too drifted off task. But freed from the Hollywood constraints personified by Selznick, Hitchcock did not chase down stories that proved unpalatable to the powers in charge. He did, however, present his materials in an expected way. His politics, that is, were (largely) unobjectionable, but to the one audience that mattered, the Office Français d'Information Cinematographique (OFIC), the extrapropagandistic elements of his films obscured the points his propaganda was supposed to drive home.

BON VOYAGE, AVENTURE MALGACHE, AND THE MATERIALITY OF COMMUNICATION

When the MoI sent *Bon Voyage* and *Aventure Malgache* to the OFIC in 1944, Sidney Bernstein received a polite yet unambiguous letter from Director Habib that declined to release the films in France. Hitchcock's films also prompted Habib to renew an earlier request to vet "the scripts of all films intended for distribution in our country."[74] How could Hitchcock, a director so keenly attuned to audience response, have gone so wrong? Or since the films were never released in war-time France, perhaps the question should be, did he go that wrong?

As frank as Habib was, the internal screening report he read was blunter. Of *Aventure Malgache*, which focuses on the Resistance movement in Madagascar, a Monsieur Halpert comments: "Dialogue is flat and the propaganda value of the film is nil. Its artistic value is non-existent. In general, there is nothing really pernicious in this film, but neither is there anything to be recommended. It would be preferable not to show it in France." Of *Bon Voyage*, the story of how the Resistance smuggled an escaped RAF sergeant back into England, Halpert observes that "the most capable of the characters is the Gestapo agent who, if the story were to follow its logical course, would come out on top." The plot, moreover, is "clumsy," "improbable," and "overloaded with intricacy." In both films the treatment of the Resistance, in Habib's words, amounts to a "grave political miscalculation." Bernstein continued to push for their release, but the French held firm.[75] Neither film was released until 1994, when a reviewer for *Los Angeles Magazine* dismissed them as "incomprehensibly meandering."[76]

Although both shorts were produced very quickly on a limited budget, there is no reason to think that Hitchcock put forth less than his best effort. He had experienced help from J.O.C. Orton and Angus MacPhail for the screenplays and from Charles Gilbert for art direction. The idea for *Bon Voyage* was provided by Arthur Calder-Marshall, and V. S. Pritchett earned £25 for the treatment.[77] Production records at the MoI also show that Hitchcock was closely involved all the way through post-production, paying particularly close attention to sound editing. For a cinematographer, moreover, he had Günther Krampf, who had photographed at least fifty films, including *Nosferatu* in 1922. Nor was Hitchcock entirely incapable of producing propaganda. He had already directed several antifascist films for commercial release—*Foreign Correspondent* (1940), *Saboteur* (1942), and *Lifeboat* (1944)—re-edited MoI films for release in the United States, and worked with Ben Hecht on a film extolling U.S. foreign policy and the virtues of the United Nations, *Watchtower Over Tomorrow*.[78] After the war, moreover, he edited raw footage of Nazi concentration camps for an atrocity film intended for distribution in Germany.[79]

Admittedly, propaganda did not come easily to Hitchcock. *Lifeboat* was attacked by U.S. reviewers for precisely the same reason that Halpert objects to *Bon Voyage*: Willy, the German U-boat captain, was thought to be so effective and imposing as a Nazi superman that the film could have been used (it was said) as Nazi propaganda.[80] Hitchcock's equivocal treatment of the central Nazis in *Bon Voyage* and *Lifeboat* may reflect the pleasure he enjoyed early in his career working in Berlin and Munich. Ina Rae Hark, however, argues for a more fundamental conflict. Hark argues persuasively that in his antifascist films Hitchcock evaluates the free press as a bulwark against fascism and finds it wanting, particularly in comparison with the greater efficiency and forcefulness of the enemy. Yet however much he wanted his films to take up the role bungled by the democratic press, "his divided sensibilities," she suggests, "kept sabotaging the results."[81]

But Hitchcock's complex attitude toward Germany and divided sensibility do not entirely account for the ways in which *Bon Voyage* and *Aventure Malgache* miss their marks. Though Halpert asserts that they are totally without aesthetic value, the real problem is that they seem to have little merit as *propaganda* films. In fact, they resemble Conrad's ill-fated attempt to write propaganda thirty years earlier in "The Unlighted Coast": instead of concentrating their energies on propaganda, the films become caught up in the idea of propaganda and the media that make modern propaganda possible.

Bon Voyage and *Aventure Malgache* do not follow the usual formula for World War II propaganda films. Departing from the dominant realist aesthetic, they are complexly structured retrospective narrations teeming with confusing detail and obscurely motivated plot devices. Both are marked by a puzzling sense of excess, a surplus of meanings that remains out of key with their overt aims, and much of this extrapropagandistic element falls under the rubric of the materiality of communication. Not only do media figure prominently—telephones, telegrams, radio, letters, newspapers, even smoke signals—but the activity of communicating and interpreting signs becomes a central focus. As we have seen, Hitchcock had good reason to be thinking about Welles and *Citizen Kane* when he returned to London, and the propaganda films' flashback structure and set toward the message (to borrow Roman Jakobson's definition of poetic language) betray the influence of *Citizen Kane*.[82] *Aventure Malgache* attempts to explain a man's character through a series of flashbacks, and its emphasis on coding and deciphering echoes the hermeneutic structure of Welles's film. *Bon Voyage* mimics the competing perspectives of *Citizen Kane*, again in a series of flashbacks designed to unriddle a man's character. Before these films, Hitchcock had never used a sustained retrospective narration.

Nor do Hitchcock's films before *Citizen Kane* (with the notable exception of *Foreign Correspondent*, which is explicitly about the media's role in war time) place media technologies in the foreground as *Bon Voyage* and *Aventure Malgache* do.[83] In contrast, *Saboteur* (the film in which Hitchcock names his hero Barry Kane) builds toward a climactic sequence that enacts a symbolic history of evolving forms of communication: a call for help is scrawled with lipstick on a scrap of paper; the paper is thrown out a window from a skyscraper, and it flutters down along the side of the building, momentarily alighting on a windowsill, which allows us, as if eavesdropping on the room, to hear a radio broadcast of a ship launch, the site where sabotage is expected to occur; the note then resumes its journey, wafting down to some cabdrivers on the street who are listening to the same broadcast on their car radios; their reception of the message triggers a sequence of events that culminates in a chase through a cinema where a film is showing. Tracing the movement from handwritten text to film, *Saboteur* asks what it takes to persuade an audience to take action against an imminent threat.

Because Hitchcock's MoI films are not well known and the nature of their complexity is my central concern, I will offer more detailed descriptions than would otherwise be necessary. *Bon Voyage* begins with a Free French Deuxième Bureau officer in London interviewing a Scottish RAF pilot, John Dougall, who escaped from Germany with the help of the Resistance. Two flashbacks then narrate from Dougall's point of view his odyssey through occupied France with a fellow escapee, Stefan Godowski, a Pole who never made it back to London. After listening to Dougall, the intelligence officer reveals that he knows Godowski gave Dougall a letter to deliver to a London address, but Dougall, who has already delivered the message, refuses to reveal the address as a point of honor. The story suddenly turns at this juncture: the officer tells Dougall that Godowski, a dead ringer for an actual Polish POW, was a Gestapo agent who used our hero as an unwitting tool to carry a letter and to roll up the Resistance network. When Dougall refuses to believe it, the officer retells his story in four additional flashbacks. Nothing was as it seemed. For instance, instead of slipping off alone to the Café du Commerce to rendezvous with the Resistance, Godowski met up with an accomplice, Oskar Enberg, who concocted a plan for use in a different café, the Café du Marronnier. Godowski, it turns out, also killed a French woman whom Dougall hoped to see again after the war. The hapless pilot, persuaded of his gullibility, ends the film staring into space, disconsolate.

Reasonably lucid at this level of summary, the film is also riddled with improbabilities and clouded by unnecessary details. Various plot points depend on Godowski's belief that the smell of an English cigarette in the Café du Marronnier will lure a Vichy spy to a place where he can be killed, thereby proving his bona fides to members of the Resistance (who could also be counted on, evidently, to follow the smell of English smoke); on our not pausing to ask how a train conductor working for the Resistance would know to stop his train at a particular place when he could not know whether a newspaper signal had been sent and received in a compartment several cars back; on our not asking why the Gestapo would send fake police to a French hotel to check the papers of travelers—Godowski's role makes them unnecessary—and why it was necessary that the Pole be a physical double for an actual Polish POW who never left the camp; and so on. Godowski's ability to manage the byzantine plot might have been enough to convince the OFIC that he was "the most capable of the characters"; Dougall is slow to grasp it even with the intelligence officer's help. The OFIC probably was not expecting *Triumph of the Will*, but who would have anticipated a *Rashomon*-like drama of incommensurate points of view about an RAF pilot tricked into becoming a mailman for the Nazis?

Bon Voyage makes the point (hardly worth making, admittedly) that you can't be too careful in war time. And yet Hitchcock's genius for evoking paranoia is not as well controlled as it might be, particularly in comparison with an effective "photo-drama" he directed the year before for *Life* magazine. An eighteen-photograph sequence entitled "Have You Heard?," the photo essay dramatizes the slogan "loose lips sink ships": a false rumor about the destination and departure time of a troop ship is passed along a chain, from church to bus to steamroom to restaurant to gas station, and so on, until by chance the false information is unwittingly corrected in a casual conversation. The accurate information is then overhead in a café by an Axis agent (as Hitchcock, serving drinks behind the bar, looks on) who meets up in a dark cove with a U-boat officer; the troop ship is torpedoed that night. The sequence may sound silly in summary, but it is plausible enough to instill fear. The narrative chain in *Bon Voyage*, in contrast, loops back on itself so often, with multiple links branching off to no clear end, that it cannot generate anything as pointed as the simple moral of "Have You Heard?"[84] Instead, the paranoia instilled in Dougall could just as well spill over into spectators who identify with his disorientation. From this newly skeptical perspective, the French officer's narration of the "real" story, positioned as the full truth against Dougall's blinkered vision, begins to look just as subjective and partial. After all, the presumed source of the officer's information—the captured Polish agent and surviving members of the Resistance—indicates that the flow of images during his voiceover can only be a subjective reconstruction grounded in hearsay.

Aventure Malgache is even more complicated. It too is a framed narration, but where *Bon Voyage* has six flashbacks, *Aventure Malgache* uses fourteen. A title card relates that the French military has organized an acting troupe to present plays for "soldiers, civilians, and the many Britons who love France." The frame setting then shows the Molière Players putting on makeup in the dressing room in preparation for their propaganda play, and when one of the actors complains that he cannot understand his role, explanatory flashbacks ensue from the point of view of a second actor, Clarousse, formerly a lawyer leading the Madagascar Resistance, who knew a police chief in Madagascar whose character might serve as inspiration for his befuddled colleague. Clarousse's intricate story focuses on the complicity of the police chief with the Vichy government and Clarousse's efforts to smuggle soldiers off the island to join the Allies. Successful for a time, Clarousse is later imprisoned when an operative is betrayed by his fiancée.

Even more than in *Bon Voyage*, tangled issues of transmission, reception, and communication distract from the film's simple point that the Resistance is at work even in the far reaches of empire. When a fellow actor asks Clarousse how he managed to stay in touch with the Resistance while in prison, we flashback to his cell in Madagascar, where Clarousse is listening to Morse code through his clock radio. Soon after, when the police chief demands to know the location of the Resistance's transmitter, one can not help thinking that if he does not even know that Clarousse is listening to radio transmissions in his cell, his chances of locating a remote transmitter elsewhere in Madagascar are not very good. A related plot point is so tangled that several critics cannot even agree what happens. As Clarousse awaits trial, a lawyer asks whether he has any incriminating documents, such as telegrams. One critic assumes that the lawyer is genuinely working on Clarousse's behalf; another understands that the lawyer is trying to dupe Clarousse into incriminating himself but mistakenly believes that Clarousse tries to flummox the investigation by fabricating nonsensical telegrams.[85] The mistake is understandable. One telegram reads "Get stuffed, where's the butter?" to which the police chief responds, "*Ça c'est clair.*" Another reads "The chestnuts will be ripe on April 35th," to which the chief, evidently unperturbed by the date, replies, "There *are* no chestnuts in Madagascar." (Here Hitchcock indulges in some intertextual play between the two films: *Bon Voyage*'s Café du Marronniers translates into the Chestnut Tree Café.) Yet Clarousse's telegrams are genuine. They are read aloud to the police chief by a Parisian expert who has de-encrypted them but lacks the secondary code to decipher their meaning. They improbably discover the key in LaFontaine's *Fables*, and Clarousse is sentenced to death, prompting the wonderful interjection from an actor in the frame setting, "So, they killed you?" (It turns out that Clarousse's sentence was commuted to five years' hard labor and Clarousse was later freed from a penal colony by the British.) The next flashback—number thirteen— shows Clarousse broadcasting anti-Vichy propaganda, the British having permitted him to set up Radio Free Madagascar. Then we cut back to Madagascar to the police chief, who is insulted as a "Vichyite lackey" over the radio by Clarousse. Back at the point of transmission, Clarousse finishes his broadcast and immediately tunes his receiver to a different channel, just in time to hear an announcement that the Madagascar authorities have again sentenced him to death, this time for seditious radio propaganda.

Just as in *Bon Voyage*, where crucial information wafts visibly through the air in the form of smoke signals and the elaborate plot transforms Dougall into a living embodiment of the letter, so too media and mediation come to the foreground in *Aventure Malgache*. Early on, Petain's proclamation of the Vichy government is heard as a crackling radio address, a telephone looms in the foreground as the conspirator's fiancée decides to betray him to the police, then come the encrypted telegrams and the improbable clock-radio. Clarousse's radio broadcasts, moreover, are notable not so much as propaganda as for their play with the notion of a singular versus a mass addressee. Like Orwell's Big Brother, Clarousse almost seems to be looking through the radio when he tweaks the police chief by name. The film's only message, beyond the obvious point that Vichy collaborators are corrupt and the Resistance virtuous, seems to be that the underground should avoid entrusting sensitive information to their loved ones—and once again, Hitchcock's photo-essay in *Life* makes the point far more effectively and with greater economy of means.

Hitchcock's account of *Aventure Malgache*'s production suggests that, like the Welles of *It's All True*, he followed his instincts as a filmmaker to the detriment of his role as propagandist.[86] Both directors thus confirm Orwell's expectation that government sponsorship of the arts might bear unexpected fruit. And yet in contrast to the promise of *It's All True*, *Aventure Malgache* and *Bon Voyage* together contain only two powerfully Hitchcockian moments. These moments are telling because they suggest why Hitchcock, unlike Welles, was able to outlast the studio system, and how Hitchcock might well have produced better propaganda than the OFIC knew.

Aventure Malgache's most effective scene comes at the end, right after a newsreel clip (another trace of *Citizen Kane*?) showing the British liberating Madagascar. The narrative then returns to the frame setting, where Clarousse and the actor who was unable to understand his role have been putting on their makeup. Suddenly, the actor turns toward Clarousse, and we see that he has become an exact likeness of the Madagascar police chief. He is, of course, the same actor we have seen throughout the flashbacks, though one would not have realized it before. The "police chief" begins to denounce Clarousse in the angry manner of his Madagascar original, calling him *"cochon"* and spitting on his shoes. The transformation is startling, and Clarousse, like the viewer, is momentarily shaken. But at that moment they are called to the stage, and the new police chief has the last line: "End of drama: let's go." What is the relationship between this moment, easily the most viscerally shocking in the film, and the aims of propaganda?

The stunning transformation might suggest the need to remain vigilant: Nazi collaborators can spring up anywhere. But the moment also seems to work in the opposite direction by dissolving political identity within the fluidity of role playing. That is, the transformation also encodes a fantasy of the film's own persuasive power by testifying to the effectiveness of Clarousse's narration: the actor becomes the police chief through the agency of Clarousse's story. But the film's persuasive power is abstracted from any specific politics—wouldn't it make more sense as propaganda to transform the actor into a member of the Resistance? Political affiliation comes to seem less a significant act of conscious affiliation than an instance of ungrounded role playing.

The distinctively Hitchcockian moment in *Bon Voyage* makes much more sense as propaganda. In the sixth flashback, Jeanne, a beautiful young woman who shelters Godowski and Dougall in her farmhouse, becomes suspicious of Godowski just as Dougall, with whom she has shared some flirtatious moments, is leaving by car on the next leg of his escape. She lifts the telephone to call the Café du Commerce but before she is connected a hand enters to cover the mouthpiece and Godowski slides into the frame next to her; the sequence cuts to a gun held to her ribs, then to a full-frame closeup of her face while we hear Dougall's car pull away; Jeanne suddenly flinches as a shot rings out; her stricken face drops from the frame as the camera pulls back to reveal the gun cocked upright in Godowski's hand. Impassive, he calmly dials a new number, and bends down to steal the dead woman's watch. At the other end of the line we see that Enberg, his accomplice, is surrounded by the Resistance. Enberg's capture suggests that Godowski will be next, though with at least four members of the Resistance exposed and presumably dead, one can see why the OFIC resented Godowski's ability to get things done.

At this juncture, however, I must uncover some information that I buried in an earlier endnote. Documents in the Sidney Bernstein collection at the Imperial War Museum reveal that in October 1944 *Bon Voyage* was given a surprise sneak preview at a cinema in France. According to the screening report, the Scottish dupe Dougall received "*la sympathie immediate,*" but audience identification was shaped less by the formal structure of the film, which positions Dougall as the spectator's surrogate, than by national affiliation, which is always stronger in war time. When the French intelligence officer explained the Gestapo's methods to Dougall, the audience became impatient to see how the story would play out: "*il est outré et ne ménage pas ses impressions*" (they become indignant and do not hide their feelings). And when Godowski's accomplice, Enberg, was shown captured at the other end of the phone line, the audience burst into applause.[87] The response of ordinary French filmgoers, in other words, was at odds with the common response of three seemingly diverse audiences: the OFIC screener, who found the stories overly intricate; the popular reviewer for *Los Angeles Magazine*, who found both films incomprehensible; and the modernist reader (me) trained to read for complexity. Director Habib, it turns out, was being overly protective when he argued that the French were not ready to see on the screen "a grim reality with which they are only too familiar, and which they want to forget quickly."[88] On the contrary, the French audience, highly sensitized to the horrors of the Gestapo, was evidently pulled along by the film's emotional current to such an extent that its potentially distracting superfluities passed by unnoticed. Accordingly, the most Hitchcockian scene in the film, Godowksi's cold-blooded murder of Jeanne, was also its most effective piece of propaganda.

These moments thus work in opposite ways: whereas Jeanne's death in *Bon Voyage* invests the propaganda with affective force, the shock in *Aventure Malgache* provokes ripples of extraneous reflection. Accordingly, the films also gravitate toward opposite ends of the polarity between art and propaganda that Welles maps in his notes on the theater: the transient coherence provided by shared aesthetic experience versus total identification with a single point of view. In this context, *Bon Voyage* begins to look like an effort to exploit subjective vision for propagandistic ends, while *Aventure Malgache*, which culminates in a moment of markedly gratuitous theatricality, is more interested in its own status as fiction.

So in *Bon Voyage*, at least, Hitchcock knew his target audience, the French people, pretty well, but he neglected to take into account the bureaucrats he thought he had left behind in Hollywood. The miscalculation inverts the problem he had with *Sabotage*. There he lost the mass audience, which did not appreciate seeing an innocent young boy blown to bits by a bomb, but he captured the attention of a more sophisticated audience of Hollywood film people, an audience that focused more on the way Hitchcock achieved his effects than on the effects themselves. In *Bon Voyage* his narrative experiments distracted the attention of the analytical spectators at the OFIC, who failed to see that a mass audience burdened by war would respond quite differently. Whether or not the same audience would have filtered out the noisy narrative machinery of *Aventure Malgache* remains a matter for speculation.

It seems clear that if Hitchcock had been given some guidelines by the OFIC, his work in the annex provided by the MoI would have evolved into an effective compromise between formal experimentation and the demands of propaganda. But if the Brazilian Department of Press and Propaganda and the CIAA had drawn up guiding principles for Welles, he very likely would have ended up fired anyway, and his film on the shelf. Partly this is a question of class and temperament. Born into a family of shopkeepers, Hitchcock was always trying to make do. Born into comfort and indulged as a prodigy from an early age, Welles felt the world was his for the asking. But the divergent fortunes of Welles and Hitchcock also testify to the nature of the media ecology that evolved around them. By the end of World War II, with government propaganda booming internationally, public relations firms growing in the United States and Britain, radio transforming the public sphere into an extension of corporate America,[89] and advertising executives gearing up for television, a dominant aesthetic of manipulation and managed response was necessarily entrenched in the capital-intensive film industry. Momentarily sheltered from this world in war-time London, Hitchcock's modernism surfaces as a self-conscious interest in the media that make the shaping of public opinion an increasingly inescapable feature of modern life. Back in Hollywood, he carved out space in commercial film for innovative productions by providing consumers with thrilling cinematic experiences while also pleasing critics with self-reflexive commentary on cinematic technique. His vernacular modernism, in other words, appealed to two very different audiences. Welles, in contrast, ended up obsessed with completing an experiment that neither government nor industry had any interest in sponsoring. Unable or unwilling to accommodate conflicting demands, he found himself in the archetypal position of the modernist exile, an outsider looking in.

CODA

H ISTORY ALWAYS affords analogies, but current events during the composition of this book so often seemed torn from the tangle of my drafts that a more superstitious person might have been tempted to stop writing. Who knew that the "special relationship" between the United States and Britain in the twenty-first century would include resurrecting the play book devised by C.F.G. Masterman for Wellington House's clandestine propaganda program during World War I?

Masterman let the genie out of the bottle in 1914 with the undeniably brilliant idea of combating overt German propaganda with British propaganda covertly funded by the government. Highly respected historians, including Arnold Toynbee and Lewis Namier, published books secretly subsidized through Wellington House, as did Ford Madox Ford, Émile Durkheim, and Pierre Loti. In the United States, the use of government funds for propaganda within the United States has been prohibited since 1951, but in May 2005, President George Bush signed into law a new bill, drafted by Senators Frank Lautenberg and Edward Kennedy, with the refreshingly blunt title "Stop Government Propaganda Now." The law had become necessary because the Bush Administration had ignored a finding by the Government Accountability Office (GAO), an independent nonpartisan arm of Congress, that the Bush administration had repeatedly violated federal law by disseminating "covert propaganda" in the United States. A conservative news analyst had been secretly paid to promote the President's education policies, two columnists were paid for favorable news coverage of his marriage initiatives, and a public relations firm was hired to fabricate fake television news stories praising a new Medicare law. The videos appeared on forty local news broadcasts across the country and featured a public relations consultant posing as a reporter.

The "Stop Government Propaganda Now" Bill tackles the problem head on by giving definitions of "publicity" and "propaganda": a news release, audio or visual presentation, Internet message, or other publication that does not clearly (and in the case of audio or video, continuously) "identify the Government agency directly or indirectly (through a contractor) financially responsible for the message." "Any attempt to manipulate the news media by payment to any journalist, reporter, columnist, commentator, editor, or news organization" was made illegal, and specific punishments and remedies specified. That would seem to close the door that Masterman opened in England some ninety years earlier. If only it were so easy. The bill emphasizes payment, but true believers work for free. Masterman did not pay his writers; he subsidized the presses that published their books; the publication of essays and op-ed pieces required no disbursement of funds. The bill's further efforts to define propaganda underscore the problem: "any message with the purpose of self-aggrandizement or puffery of the Administration, agency, Executive branch programs or policies, or pending congressional legislation"; "a message of a nature tending to emphasize the importance of the agency or its activities"; "a message that is so misleading or inaccurate that it constitutes propaganda." Just how such fine discriminations are to be made the bill does not say. Instead, following a time-honored tradition of disavowal, the legislation displaces the problem by attaching it to foreign evil-doers: "Propaganda had its place in Saddam's Iraq. Propaganda was a staple of the old Soviet Union. But covert propaganda has no place in the United States Government."[1] Yet state propaganda, as Orwell recognized, is inevitable.

Here we return to the deeper problem of the information-propaganda matrix described by Jacques Ellul in 1957. Unless information is made to seem credible and assimilable, it can have no public function; information is therefore couched in rhetoric, and the introduction of techniques of persuasion begins to turn information into propaganda. Governments inevitably spread propaganda because the need to publicize their accomplishments leads to the dissemination of information designed to sway public opinion, and the public accelerates the transformation of information into propaganda because public opinion generally prefers the clarity of myth (propaganda's specialty) to a chaos of facts. Hence the Department of Education's reply to the GAO's charge of having illegally purchased favorable news coverage for the President's "No Child Left Behind" initiative: the covert hiring of a journalist amounted to nothing more than "the legitimate dissemination of information to the public."[2] This is Ellul's point: one person's information is another's propaganda, and while it is easy to argue the difference in the case of the Department of Education, the surplus of information in modern life typically renders the distinction much more elusive. Depending on who's watching, CNN or FOX News provides information or propaganda, and the "Stop Government Propaganda Now" Bill cannot say which is which (even if many readers of these pages can, or think they can anyway). For a time the Internet held out the hope of an antidote by providing easy access to multiple sources of news from around the globe. But critical perspectivism becomes more difficult (though not impossible, thanks in part to blogs) when search engines make deals with governments to censor politically sensitive searches and corporate capital accelerates its colonization of the Web.

The starkness of the way techniques of information manipulation dating from World War I have been redeployed, not to mention the cruder Nazi refinements of repeating lies until they become more effective than truths, may distract from a deeper historical logic. After all, when quoting Ford's concern in 1911 that the vote of citizens overloaded with unassimilable information will be "influenced by some mysterious catchword, by some accidental happening of the moment or by some private scandal or facial characteristic of the upholder of one or other cause,"[3] it is impossible not be struck by the depth of the continuing problem. Given recent blowback from the second Iraq War, Joyce's attitude toward historical repetition, the same anew, also seems appropriate to the angry post–World War I response to the faulty intelligence in the Bryce Report, which swept the globe in 1915. By the twenties, it was popularly believed on both sides of the Atlantic that the British had duped the United States into a war most Americans regretted. As Joyce's favorite historian Giambattista Vico might say, what goes around comes around.

But more linear histories are relevant here as well. With the steady expansion of increasingly efficient global media systems, it is easy to see how the British model of information manipulation spread. Hoping for an ally in World War I, Wellington House naturally focused most attention on the United States, flooding it with books and pamphlets, films, picture postcards, and photo magazines. When President Wilson, elected on a pacifist platform, recognized the need to mobilize support for joining the war, he formed the Committee on Public Information (CPI) and intensified the campaign already being waged by Wellington House. CPI alumnus Edward Bernays went on to found public relations as a profession; Military Intelligence alumnus Walter Lippmann inaugurated modern media studies. Written in response to Lipmmann's cautionary *Public Opinion* (1922), Bernays's influential how-to books were read avidly by Joseph Goebbels, a great admirer of the British propaganda campaign in World War I. The British, meanwhile, having turned against propaganda with disgust after the war, found that their orphaned child, raised into adolescence under a new name (public relations) by the United States before growing up in Germany, had returned to haunt them, and when war erupted again in 1939, it became necessary for both England and the United States to play catch up. Neither government has ever looked back.[4]

Which returns me to the question that the increasing topicality of my topic pushed to the foreground in the preface: What does modernism have to say to us in a cultural moment when the notion of a pre-Orwellian world of lucid information has come to seem a pipe dream? Something more, one hopes, than the Viconian cycles of history that fascinated Joyce.

Clearly aesthetic modernism can do little to restore a world of un-mediated access to facts-as-truth that never existed in the first place. More modest goals are possible, of course, but in the United States effec-tive intervention in discourses of propaganda now seems the province of satiric television news. The *Daily Show*'s finely honed "fake news" on Comedy Central does more to combat government-sponsored fake news or spun facts than any other medium in the United States. Comparable efforts, such as the *Onion*, are available on the Web, but with so many young people increasingly relying on the *Daily Show* for their news, the show's host, Jon Stewart, gets more leverage with his media critiques than his competitors do.[5] Particularly powerful is the *Daily Show*'s de-bunking of government talking points through a rapid-fire montage of diverse talking heads all repeating precisely the same catch phrases. The Goebbels strategy of laying lie upon lie until truth suffocates stops work-ing when culled clips reveal spokespersons as ventriloquist dummies. It helps too when Stewart interrupts footage of a lying politician with a counter-clip of a reputable authority—perhaps one hired by that very politician—providing facts that point up the lie. Comedy Central, more-over, provides a commercial version of the government annexes tem-porarily enjoyed by Alfred Hitchcock and Orson Welles in the forties. Corporate pressure, in other words, is unlikely to silence the *Daily Show*'s cutting irreverence because, as Stewart likes to say, "We're only on basic cable."

But the subtle distortion of facts is harder to contest than lies, which is why the British invented new techniques in the first place. Here's where a particular understanding of modernism and the modes of attention it so-licits become useful.

The ability to distinguish between information and propaganda is fun-damental to good citizenship under democracy, but easy distinctions are unlikely to become plentiful in the foreseeable future. Ford understood the decline of critical thinking and the rise of quantitative analysis—he felt most people could not get their heads around numbers—as serious obstacles to an informed and engaged public. He also lamented that the resulting confusion made it difficult to *feel* the importance of issues, and that without affective engagement citizens could not be expected even to try to think about difficult issues. The study of modernism cannot help with the continuing problem of innumeracy, but it can with crises of af-fect and critical thought. Modernist narrative makes reading difficult; it requires that we slow the process down, become more conscious of the choices we make as we establish provisional networks of meaning. In texts that matter to me, it also embeds these choices in imagined worlds in which choices matter, in which their consequences can be felt on the pulse. Roland Barthes long ago offered the still-useful distinction between writerly and readerly texts. The writerly text is designed to so-licit the self-conscious engagement of readers in the production of mean-ing; the readerly text is a product to be consumed.[6] Barthes acknowl-edged that there are no actual texts that correspond precisely to the distinction, but clearly some works of literature encourage a more writerly response than others, and modernist texts do more than most.

So my contention is this: in a world in which dependable facts in pub-lic discourse have become elusive, in which language is carefully engi-neered by public relations experts and market researchers to trigger spe-cific emotional responses, critical reading attentive to history and to nuances of language is a precondition for good citizenship. To be sure, a great deal of literature provides a valuable experience of difficulty, but modernism—with its self-conscious exploration of multiple mediations of mass experience; its detailed examination of the interpenetration of public and private; its glimpses into deep structures subtending the apparent randomness of daily life; its strategically uncanny departures from still-current idioms; and its defamiliarization of cause and effect through chronological disjunctions—solicits the kind of rhetorical liter-acy appropriate to the discursive dilemmas that have evolved out of the media environment Ford began to recognize almost a century ago. Whereas the *Daily Show* depends on clear satiric cues, modernism had not yet reconciled itself to a mode of exhaustion, a sense that perhaps the most one can do is laugh at the absurdity of forms of arrogance that beggar shame. When Joyce took on recruitment or Woolf the Spanish Civil War, the possibility of wresting readers into a permanently engaged critical perspective on propaganda, not through satire but through a less generically specific mode of estrangement, must have seemed less quixotic than it likely does today.[7] For reasons dating back to the early twentieth century, then, modernist difficulty can be conducive to good citizenship in the twenty-first.

In making such a bald statement, I am reminded of one of my forma-tive undergraduate experiences with modernism. Richard Ellmann had just published the first revisionary account of Joyce's politics, and my professor discounted Ellmann's attribution of an engaged politics to the mandarin God of Modernism on the grounds that modernist literature is like a student smirking in the back of the classroom; it may mock au-thority, but only within a circumscribed space in which politics amount to little more than attitude. It would be easy to dismiss these remarks as the voice of an older generation, or bury them in counterexamples, or question the assumption that modernism really is so opposed to author-ity (Conrad, not to mention Pound and Eliot?); but one knows what he meant. Little read outside the classroom, modernism, unlike the *Daily Show*, is unlikely to intervene effectively in mainstream political life.

But in another way, the classroom is precisely the point. Smirking or not, students leave the classroom with a particular version of modernism, one that may or may not serve as something more than a dose of cultural literacy. I came to *Modernism, Media, and Propaganda* through *Heart of Darkness*, the book I was scheduled to teach the morning after the opening salvoes of the 1991 Gulf War, the bombing of Baghdad narrated on CNN by a terrified Bernard Shaw. That night I watched the greenish streaks of tracer fire crisscross the dark screen for a while until I felt compelled to turn from the television to the computer screen to think about what I would say the next morning. According to the scribblings in the margins of my typed lecture notes, I took some time that day to discuss the political abuse of language, and *Heart of Darkness* proved even more effective in this context than Orwell. I reminded them of Marlow's skeptical response to the French gunboat, "incomprehensible, firing into a continent" at a camp of unseen natives referred to as "enemies" and later his disgust on seeing a string of chained Africans: "They were called criminals," Marlow says, "and the outraged law, like the bursting shells, had come to them, an insoluble mystery from the sea." This yoking of idealizing abstractions to an alien particularity, I suggested, should make them suspicious of the duplicity of state-sponsored rhetoric, such as the technological wonder of "Patriot" missiles, a military invasion called "Operation Just Cause," or foreign leaders stigmatized as madmen. I could have gone on more polemically to suggest analogies between ivory and oil and the language deployed to secure them, but instead I moved into my planned discussion of the difficulties of distinguishing truth from untruth in modernity and Conrad's investment in the idea of necessary fictions, a topic that seemed to take on greater pointedness than it had when I first delivered the lecture a year earlier, and one that subsequent wars have made sharper yet. What I was almost discovering in Conrad then is my topic now, the complex entwining of modernism and propaganda in the early twentieth century.

Ten years later, when the United States attacked the Taliban in Afghanistan, Conrad began popping up regularly in op-ed pieces. A *New York Times* article cited the very lines from *Heart of Darkness* I had cited in my lecture; others cited the novella as a touchstone for the proverbial thin line between civilization and savagery; others, referring not only to the war but to the 9/11 attack that precipitated it, invoked *The Secret Agent* on the futility of political violence. It was gratifying to see Conrad in the papers, but what was important was less his being there—that's a matter of cultural literacy—than the uses to which he was put. Ideally, I would have liked to find Conrad invoked less as an icon of despair and more as an agent of critique, a writer whose oddly textured prose, disjointed narratives, and elusive tonal complexity demand the kind of rhetorical literacy necessary for navigating the deceptive terrain of public discourse.[8]

Critical reading skills do not, of course, live or die with literary modernism, or with a particular intellectual discipline. Given the cultural dominance of Hollywood film, it is more important than ever that we learn how to process vernacular forms of modernism. And if there is anything a liberal arts education should do, it should equip students to work toward distinctions that may require constant revision—between information and propaganda, impressions and knowledge, propaganda and education. But because modernism and propaganda have common roots in a media ecology still recognizable today, I want to conclude by saying: Modernism in the classroom? What starts there does not have to end there.

NOTES

1. George Orwell, *The Collected Essays, Journalism and Letters of George Orwell*, ed. Sonia Orwell and Ian Angus, 4 vols. (New York: Harcourt, Brace, and World, 1968), 2:126.

2. See Eric Gill, "All Art is Propaganda," in *Modernism: An Anthology of Sources and Documents*, ed. Vassiliki Kolocotroni, Jane Goldman, and Olga Taxidou (Chicago: University of Chicago Press, 1998), 530; originally published in *5 on Revolutionary Art* (1935), edited by Herbert Read. For the opposite view, see R. G. Collingwood, who associates art with self-sufficiency and non-art with advertisement and propaganda; *The Principles of Art* (Oxford: Clarendon Press, 1938), 32.

3. Here I adapt Jonathan Dollimore's resonant formulation in his *Sexual Dissidence* (New York: Oxford University Press, 1991), 16. For a valuable discussion of the proximate more attuned to Dollimore's focus on erotic economies, see Joseph Valente, "Thrilled by His Touch: The Aestheticizing of Homosexual Panic in *A Portrait of the Artist as a Young Man*," in *James Joyce's "A Portrait of the Artist as a Young Man*," ed. Mark A. Wollaeger (New York: Oxford University Press, 2003), 246–48.

4. Jacques Ellul, *Propaganda: The Formation of Men's Attitudes*, trans. Konrad Kellen (New York: Vintage, 1973), 118–60.

5. Michael North, *Reading 1922: A Return to the Scene of the Modern* (New York: Oxford University Press, 1999). My argument for the importance of propaganda finds a sympathetic context in North's discussion of "the social fact that literary modernism and modern public relations emerge before the public at precisely the same time and in close association with one another" (79). But if modernism and public relations, as North argues, should be read against one another within what Jürgen Habermas has described as the collapse of the public sphere at the turn of the twentieth century, it is important to acknowledge that public relations is the commercial offspring of modern propaganda. The founding fathers of public relations and media studies, Edward Bernays and Walter Lippmann, respectively, both worked for the U.S. government as propagandists during World War I, and their most influential work is deeply indebted to their experience as propagandists. For North's discussion of Bernays and Lippman in relation to Habermas, see *Reading 1922*, 68–76. For Habermas's influential discussion of the disintegration of the eighteenth-century ideal of public reason as a "rationalizing [of] politics in the name of morality," see his *Structural Transformation of the Public Sphere*, trans. Thomas Burger and Frederick Lawrence (Cambridge, Mass.: MIT Press, 1991), 141–235, 102 (quotation).

6. See, for instance, Jennifer Wicke, *Advertising Fictions: Literature, Advertising, and Social Reading* (New York: Columbia University Press, 1988); *Marketing Modernism: Self-Promotion, Canonization, Rereading*, ed. Kevin Dettmar and Stephen Watt (Ann Arbor: University of Michigan Press, 1996); Lawrence S. Rainey, *Institutions of Modernism: Elites and Public Culture* (New Haven: Yale University Press, 1998); Ann L. Ardis, *Modernism and Cultural Conflict, 1880–1922* (Cambridge: Cambridge University Press, 2002); David Chinitz, *T. S. Eliot and the Cultural Divide* (Chicago: University of Chicago Press, 2003); Melba Cuddy-Keane, *Virginia Woolf, the Intellectual, and the Public Sphere* (Cambridge: Cambridge University Press, 2003).

7. One exception is William Allan Hepburn, "Politics, Propaganda, and the Modern Novel" (Ph.D. diss., Princeton University, 1990), who argues that "the modern novel is a species of propaganda" because narrative is "politically motivated and is directed towards an audience" (1). This argument inverts the more common assumption that modernism and propaganda are antithetical without grasping the dynamic relation between them.

8. As James Duane Squires observes, two developments made modern propaganda techniques possible: universal education, which led to the creation of a mass audience, and the development of new communications technologies; Squires, *British Propaganda at Home and in The United States, from 1914 to 1917* (Cambridge, Mass.: Harvard University Press; London: Humphrey Milford [Oxford University Press], 1935), 13.

9. Ford Madox Ford, *The Critical Attitude* (London: Duckworth, 1911), 125.

10. For both the modernist writer and the propagandist, professionalism was grounded in technical expertise. For the transition from the Victorian entrepreneurial ideal to the professional ideal, see Harold Perkin, *The Rise of Professional Society: England since 1880* (London and New York: Routledge, 1989), 1–26.

11. T. S. Eliot, "*Ulysses*, Order, and Myth" (1923), in *Selected Prose of T. S. Eliot*, ed. Frank Kermode (New York: Harcourt, Brace, Jovanovich, 1975), 177.

12. According to Bell, everyday emotions, such as those in "descriptive" art, "may move us . . . in a hundred different ways, but they do not move us aesthetically." In Bell's view, true art does not convey information, ideas, or emotions, it is rather the object of emotion. That is, like T. S. Eliot's "objective correlative," true art neutralizes the suasive effects of emotion by fusing it with the object of representation. See Clive Bell, *Art* (New York: Frederick A. Stokes, 1914), 3–17. For Eliot, see his "*Hamlet*" (1919) in Kermode, *Selected Prose of T. S. Eliot*, 45–49.

13. Many invasion novels advanced precisely the first argument; William Le Queux's *The Invasion of 1910* (1906), endorsed in a preface by a government official, helped fuel the first modern arms race. The warning advice about the devil was offered in Marie Corelli's bestselling *The Sorrows of Satan* (1896). I do not mean to equate popular fiction with propaganda but simply to acknowledge that popular fiction is more likely than modernist fiction to assert clear stands on contemporary issues.

14. Virginia Woolf, *Diary of Virginia Woolf*, ed. Anne Olivier Bell and Andrew McNeillie, 5 vols. (San Diego: Harcourt, Brace, Jovanovich, 1982), 4:300.

15. Virginia Woolf, *The Moment and Other Essays* (San Diego: Harcourt, Brace, 1976), 151.

16. Ford Madox Ford, *The Critical Writings of Ford Madox Ford*, ed. Frank MacShane (Lincoln: University of Nebraska Press, 1964), 69.

17. Virginia Woolf, *The Letters of Virginia Woolf*, ed. Nigel Nicolson and Joanne Trautmann, 6 vols. (New York: Harcourt, Brace, Jovanovich, 1975–80), 5:249.

18. A representative list of works on modernism and media includes Marshall McLuhan, "Joyce, Mallarmé, and the Press," *Sewanee Review* 62, no. 1 (Winter 1954): 38–55; Hugh Kenner, *The Mechanic Muse* (New York: Oxford University Press, 1987); Leslie Kathleen Hankins, " 'Across the Screen of My Brain': Virginia Woolf's "The Cinema" and Film Forums of the Twenties," in *The Multiple Muses of Virginia Woolf*, ed. Diane F. Gillespie (Columbia: University of Missouri Press, 1993), 148–79; Ivan Kreilkamp, "A Voice without a Body: the Phonographic Logic of *Heart of Darkness*," *Victorian Studies* 40:2 (Winter 1997): 211–43; Garrett Stewart, *Between Film and Screen: Modernism's Photo Synthesis* (Chicago: University of Chicago Press, 1999); *Virginia Woolf in the Age of Mechanical Reproduction*, ed. Pamela L. Caughie (New York: Garland, 2000); and Juan A. Suarez, "T. S. Eliot's *The Waste Land*, the Gramophone and the Modernist Discourse Network," *New Literary History* 32 (Summer 2001): 747–68. For a good introduction to relations between propaganda and literature, see A. P. Foulkes, *Literature and Propaganda* (London and New York: Methuen, 1983).

19. Raymond Williams, *The Politics of Modernism* (London and New York: Verso, 1989), 33. Williams see modernist movements and their attendant manifestos as "defensive cultural groupings" that entered the rapidly diversifying fray of new media in order to declare their "passionate and scornful vision of the new" (33). Part of the thrust of my argument bears on the inadequacy of the word "defensive" in this context, for modernist responses to new media varied greatly among modernists, across movements, and over time.

20. Adolf Hitler, *Mein Kampf*, editorial sponsors John Chamberlain, Sidney B. Fay et al. (New York: Reynal and Hitchcock, 1939), 227–42. For the German debt to the British institutionalization of propaganda, see Phillip Knightley, *The First Casualty: From Crimea to Vietnam: The War Correspondent as Hero, Propagandist, and Myth Maker* (New York: Harcourt, Brace, Jovanovich, 1975), 79–112, 217–41.

21. For the locus classicus of discussions of World War I and modernism, see Paul Fussell, *The Great War and Modern Memory* (London and New York: Oxford University Press, 1975). More recent treatment include Modris Eksteins, *Rites of Spring: The Great War and the Birth of the Modern Age* (Toronto: Dennys, 1989); Allyson Booth, *Postcards from the Trenches: Negotiating the Space between Modernism and the First World War* (New York: Oxford University Press, 1996); Trudi Tate, *Modernism, History and the First World War* (Manchester: Manchester University Press, 1998); Margot Norris, *Writing War in the Twentieth Century* (Charlottesville: University of Virginia Press, 2000); Sarah

Cole, *Modernism, Male Friendship, and the First World War* (Cambridge: Cambridge University Press, 2003); and Vincent Sherry, *The Great War and the Language of Modernism* (New York: Oxford University Press, 2003).

22. Peter Buitenhuis, *The Great War of Words: British, American, and Canadian Propaganda and Fiction, 1914–1933* (Vancouver: University of British Columbia Press, 1987), xviii.

23. Walter Lippmann, *Public Opinion* (New York: Harcourt, Brace, 1922), 15.

24. In essence, Buitenhuis's account cleaves too closely to what Samuel Hynes has called the Myth of the Great War, in particular the notion that the war constituted a fundamental break with all preceding historical experience. See Samuel Hynes, *A War Imagined: The First World War and English Culture* (New York: Atheneum, 1991), xi–xiv.

25. Acknowledging the war as having accelerated changes already underway, Squires notes that one of the defining differences between earlier propaganda and the new propaganda was that from "a useful side-line in the conduct of warfare, managed almost exclusively by civilian volunteers, propaganda came to be so important during the World War that it was adopted officially as an indispensable adjunct of the war-government staff" (*British Propaganda*, 12).

26. In *The Great War and the Language of Modernism*, Sherry provides a compelling new version of the argument that World War I in effect caused modernism. Sherry argues that even though World War I gave the lie to the power of rationality enshrined in the philosophy and language of Liberalism, Liberals tried to justify the war on rational grounds and thereby delegitimated Liberal rhetoric and all it stood for; in response, modernists targeted newly bankrupted Liberal rhetoric and the destruction of public reason through parody and critical mimicry. Though we present different historical narratives, in other ways Sherry and I offer complementary approaches to the relationship between war and modernism. We both aim to reconnect British modernism with historical forces that have been hiding in plain view, and, like North (see note 5, above), we both explore the ways in which an irrational conception of public opinion begins to eclipse established norms of civic rationality. Sherry's argument focuses mainly on poetry, mine on narrative; Sherry explores "the verbal culture of a war" (14), whereas my analysis, taking up film, radio, posters and postcards, underscores the ways in which modernism was always an intermedial phenomenon.

27. Friedrich Kittler, *Gramophone, Film, Typewriter*, trans. Geoffrey Winthrop-Young and Michael Wutz (Stanford: Stanford University Press, 1999).

28. For a critique of military determinism in Kittler, see Geoffrey Winthrop-Young, "Drill and Distraction in the Yellow Submarine: On the Dominance of War in Friedrich Kittler's Media Theory," *Critical Inquiry* 28 (Summer 2002): 825–54.

29. James R. Beniger, *The Control Revolution: Technological and Economic Origins of the Information Society* (Cambridge, Mass.: Harvard University Press, 1986), 1–27.

30. Alexander Welsh, *George Eliot and Blackmail* (Cambridge, Mass.: Harvard University Press, 1985), 33–109.

31. By arguing that the rigorous formal complexity and totalizing impulse of some modernist texts generate a form of critical autonomy, Adorno in effect

posits an intrinsic politics of form. But if the autonomous work of art refuses to resolve "objective contradictions into a spurious harmony" and instead "expresses the idea of harmony negatively by embodying the contradictions, pure and uncompromised, in its innermost structure," I would argue that the negative expression of harmony can, but need not, generate a critical perspective: the experience of contradiction may be empowering or disabling. See Theodor Adorno, "Cultural Criticism and Society," in *Prisms*, trans. Samuel and Sherry Weber (Cambridge, Mass.: MIT Press, 1982), 32.

32. See James Joll, *The Anarchists* (Cambridge, Mass.: Harvard University Press, 1980), 99–129.

33. Dominick LaCapra, *Rethinking Intellectual History: Texts, Context, Language* (Ithaca: Cornell University Press, 1983), 16.

INTRODUCTION
MODERNISM AND THE INFORMATION-PROPAGANDA MATRIX

1. Ford, "On Impressions" (1914), in *The Critical Writings of Ford Madox Ford*, ed. Frank MacShane (Lincoln: University of Nebraska Press, 1964), 54. For a detailed consideration of what Ford means by propaganda in this context, see chapter 3.

2. For the arbitrary relation between form and politics in the visual arts, see Toby Clark, *Art and Propaganda in the Twentieth Century: The Political Image in the Age of Mass Culture* (New York: Harry N. Abrams, 1977): "propaganda in art is not always inherent in the image itself, and may not stem from the artist's intentions. Rather, art can become propaganda through its function and site, its framing within public or private spaces and its relationship with a network of other kinds of objects and actions" (13).

3. Ezra Pound, "Henry James," in *Literary Essays of Ezra Pound*, ed. T. S. Eliot (New York: New Directions, 1968), 297. First published in the *Little Review* in August 1918, the essay suggests that by analyzing culture, poets detect the future and rebroadcast their insights just as antennae receive and transmit radio waves. Pound was also highly attuned to the tendentious side of literary modernism: "It's all rubbish to pretend that art isn't didactic," he wrote to Felix Schelling in 1922: "A revelation is always didactic. Only the aesthetes since 1880 have pretended the contrary, and they aren't a very sturdy lot" (*The Selected Letters of Ezra Pound*, ed. D. D. Paige [New York: New Directions, 1971], 180).

4. See Mark Kinkead-Weekes, *D. H. Lawrence: Triumph to Exile, 1912–1922* (Cambridge: Cambridge University Press, 1996), 293–94.

5. D. H. Lawrence, *The Letters of D. H. Lawrence*, ed. James T. Boulton, 8 vols. (Cambridge: Cambridge University Press, 1979), 2:474.

6. George Orwell, *The Collected Essays, Journalism and Letters of George Orwell*, ed. Sonia Orwell and Ian Angus (New York: Harcourt, Brace, & World, 1968), 4 vols. The quotations come from 2:125, 126. Hereafter cited in the text.

7. Orwell scripted and broadcast commentaries from December 1941 to February 1943. See W. J. West, ed., *Orwell: The War Commentaries* (London: Duckworth, 1985).

8. For a fair-minded account of the controversy surrounding Orwell's list, which is now available in the Public Record Office at Kew, England, see Timothy Garton Ash, "Orwell's List," *New York Review of Books* 1, no. 14 (September 25, 2003): 6–12.

9. For a critique of Orwell's claim that the plain style is nonideological, see Carl Freedman, "Writing, Ideology, and Politics: Orwell's 'Politics and the English Language' and English Composition," *College English* 43 (1981): 327–40.

10. Virginia Woolf, *Diary of Virginia Woolf*, ed. Anne Olivier Bell and Andrew McNeillie, 5 vols. (San Diego: Harcourt, Brace, Jovanovich, 1982), 4:300. Hereafter cited in the text.

11. Woolf is commenting on Ethel Smyth's revisions of her *Female Pipings in Eden*: "I should still like it condensed, pressed, hammered hard; but thats [*sic*] doubtless incompatible with propaganda," which requires repetition and redundancy. Unlike the chapters that "preach," Woolf believes that in the better parts of the book Smyth dips her pen into "a deeper, richer pot: no vinegar, no sand." See Virginia Woolf, *The Letters of Virginia Woolf*, ed. Nigel Nicolson and Joanne Trautmann, 6 vols. (New York: Harcourt, Brace, Jovanovich, 1975–80), 5:249.

12. For discussion of *Three Guineas* in the context of Spanish Civil War propaganda, see Elena Gualtieri, "*Three Guineas* and the Photograph: The Art of Propaganda," in *Women Writers of the Thirties*, ed. Maroula Joannou (Edinburgh: Edinburgh University Press, 1999), 165–78.

13. Susan A. Brewer, *To Win the Peace: British Propaganda in the United States During World War II* (Ithaca and London: Cornell University Press, 1997), 5.

14. See A. J. MacKenzie, *The Propaganda Boom* (London: John Gifford, 1938). MacKenzie is representative in observing that Germany's Ministry of Propaganda and Italy's Ministry of Popular Culture were largely responsible for the sharp increase in propaganda and the consequent concern in many countries about excessive interference in their internal affairs (23).

15. Frederick E. Lumley, *The Propaganda Menace* (New York and London: Century, 1933), 44, 21. Lumley's second chapter, "Conceptions of Propaganda," offers a useful overview and bibliography of postwar thinking about propaganda.

16. For Bernays's own account of his work at the CPI, see his *Biography of an Idea: Memoirs of Public Relations Counsel Edward L. Bernays* (New York: Simon and Schuster, 1965), 155–78. For an account of the cultural significance of Bernays's career, see Stuart Ewen, *PR!: A Social History of Spin* (New York: Basic Books, 1996), 146–73. For a complementary treatment of Bernays and Walter Lippmann, whom I discuss later in this chapter, see Michael North, *Reading 1922: A Return to the Scene of the Modern* (New York: Oxford University Press, 1999), 65–97. North takes the two as exemplary figures for gauging what Jürgen Habermas has analyzed as the late nineteenth-century split into two kinds of publicity: advertising and opinion management. See Habermas, *The Structural Transformation of the Public Sphere*, trans. Thomas Burger and Frederick Lawrence (Cambridge, Mass.: MIT Press, 1991), 193–94.

17. Edward L. Bernays, *Crystallizing Public Opinion* (New York: Boni and Liveright, 1923), 11. Hereafter cited in the text.

18. Edward L. Bernays, *Propaganda* (New York: Liveright, 1928), 20. Hereafter cited in the text. Bernays welcomed as a "fact" that "in almost every act of our daily lives, whether in the sphere of politics or business, in our social conduct or our ethical thinking, we are dominated by the relatively small number of persons—a trifling fraction of our hundred and twenty million—who understand the mental processes and social patterns of the masses. It is they who pull wires which control the public mind, who harness old social forces and contrive new ways to bind and guide the world" (9–10).

19. Jacques Ellul, *Propaganda: The Formation of Men's Attitudes*, trans. Konrad Kellen (New York: Vintage, 1973), 63. Hereafter cited in the text. Bernays, *Propaganda*, 28.

20. For a critique of Ellul's enabling definition of propaganda and his antiempirical bias, see Thomas M. Steinfatt, "Evaluating Approaches to Propaganda Analysis," *Etc.: A Review of General Semantics* 36 (Summer 1979): 157–80. The entire number of *Etc.* is devoted to propaganda and includes valuable articles by Neil Postman, Bernays, and Ellul. For a defense of the breadth of Ellul's definition of propaganda, see Randall L. Bytwerk, "Western and Totalitarian Views of Propaganda," in *Propaganda: A Pluralistic Perspective*, ed. Ted J. Smith III (New York: Praeger, 1989), 37–48.

21. Max Horkheimer and Theodor W. Adorno, *Dialectic of Enlightenment*, ed. Gunzelin Schmid Noerr; trans. Edmund Jephcott (Stanford: Stanford University Press, 2002), xiv, xvi–xvii.

22. Jacques Ellul, *The Technological Society*, trans. John Wilkinson (New York: Vintage, 1964), 4. Hereafter cited in the text. Ellul is highly critical of Lewis Mumford's *Technics and Civilization* (1934), which in Ellul's view (e.g., p. 42) equates technique with the machine. For problems of translation as well as a general introduction to Ellul's work, see Darrel J. Fasching, *The Thought of Jacques Ellul* (New York and Toronto: Edwin Mellen, 1981), esp. 15–32.

23. Horkheimer and Adorno, *Dialectic of Enlightenment*, 107, 109, 103–4.

24. Ibid., 129.

25. Stanley B. Cunningham, "Smoke and Mirrors: A Confirmation of Jacques Ellul's Theory of Information Use in Propaganda," in *Propaganda*, ed. Smith, 153.

26. See Vance Packard, *The Hidden Persuaders* (New York: D. McKay, 1957).

27. Granted, Horkheimer and Adorno do not literally describe a conspiracy run by individual agents of capitalism—this would be to replicate one of the bourgeois fantasies of agency they debunk—but their rhetoric does tend to evoke precisely the forms of paranoia that their dialectical analysis of the operations of enlightenment is supposed to demystify. The 1947 revision of the 1944 version of "The Culture Industry: Enlightenment as Mass Deception" tends to amplify this rhetorical effect, for in an attempt to distance themselves from purely economic forms of determinism, Horkheimer and Adorno removed much of the Marxist terminology of the earlier version in order to throw more emphasis on the controlling agency of the culture industry and politics. Thus where the writ-

ers referred to "monopoly ... entrenching itself in advertising" in 1944, the 1947 text reads: "those in control of the system are entrenching themselves in advertising" (271, 131). See Willem van Reijen and Jan Bransen, "The Disappearance of Class History in 'Dialectic of Enlightenment,'" in Horkheimer and Adorno, *Dialectic of Enlightenment*, 248–52.

28. Jacques Ellul, "Information and Propaganda," *Diogenes* 18 (Summer 1957):64.

29. I thank Ellen Levy for pointing out the relevance of the 1956 Congress.

30. See, for instance, Jane Marcus, "Britannia Rules the Waves," in *Decolonizing Tradition*, ed. Karen R. Lawrence (Urbana and Chicago: University of Illinois Press, 1992), 136–62.

31. E. M. Forster, *A Passage to India* (San Diego: Harcourt, Brace, Jovanovich, 1984), 38; James Joyce, *Ulysses: The Corrected Text* (New York: Random House, 1986), 7:882–83. Later in Forster's novel, the hapless colonial administrator, Ronny Heaslop, optimistic that the incoherence of Adela Quested's memory of the echoing Marabar Caves can be cleared up, opines that "Great is information, and she shall prevail" (211). Forster, clearly, is less sanguine.

32. Sir George Acton, *Secret Service* (London, 1930), 281. In his autobiography Mark Twain attributes the attack on statistics to Benjamin Disraeli, but no version of it has ever been found in Disraeli's papers. The earliest reference, to my knowledge, is in a speech by Leonard H. Courtney in New York in 1895. See *The Phrase Finder* http://www.phrases.org.uk/meanings/375700.html. (viewed February 24, 2006).

33. For the saying, attributed to U.S. Senator Hiram Johnson in 1917, see the epigraph to Phillip Knightley, *The First Casualty: From Crimea to Vietnam: The War Correspondent as Hero, Propagandist, and Myth Maker* (New York: Harcourt, Brace, Jovanovich, 1975).

34. All histories of the campaign's early organization rely on a single account from the inside, the biography of Masterman written by his wife, Lucy Masterman, *C.F.G. Masterman* (New York: August M. Kelley, 1968), 272–308. She is the only authority for the list of invitees and participants, which appears in all subsequent accounts. See also D. G. Wright, "The Great War, Government Propaganda and English 'Men of Letters' 1914–16," *Literature and History* 7 (1978): 70–100.

35. Historical treatments of Wellington House were censored as late as 1932, when Compton McKenzie was fined £100 for revealing war-time secrets in *Greek Memories* (1932). See James Duane Squires, *British Propaganda at Home and in The United States, from 1914 to 1917* (Cambridge, Mass.: Harvard University Press; London: Humphrey Milford [Oxford University Press], 1935), 79. Although Peter Buitenhuis claims that the news broke only with the publication of Squires's book in 1935, Squires cites at least two publications from 1931 (Squires, *British Propaganda*, 27, 30–31). See Buitenhuis, *The Great War of Words: British, American, and Canadian Propaganda and Fiction, 1914–1933* (Vancouver: University of British Columbia Press, 1987), 15. Buitenhuis offers an otherwise reliable and detailed overview of writers' work in the British propaganda campaign. Also see Samuel Hynes, *A War Imagined: The First World War and English Culture* (New York: Atheneum, 1991), 26–29.

36. Gary S. Messinger, *British Propaganda and the State in the First World War* (Manchester and New York: Manchester University Press, 1992), 35.

37. Walter Lippmann, *Public Opinion* (New York: Harcourt, Brace, 1922), 15.

38. Lord Robert Cecil, "British Propaganda in Allied and Neutral Countries." Public Record Office, Kew, England; INF 4/1B.

39. Ivor Nicholson, "An Aspect of British Official Wartime Propaganda," *Cornhill Magazine*, series 3, vol. 70, no. 419 (May 1931): 606.

40. C.F.G. Masterman, *Report of the Work of the Bureau established for the purpose of laying before Neutral Nations and the Dominions the case of Great Britain and her Allies* (June 7, 1915), 2. Public Record Office, Kew, England; INF 4/5. Hereafter cited in the text.

41. The intrinsic difficulties of assessing the effectiveness of propaganda are magnified in the case of World War I because no official history of the British campaign was ever commissioned or written. For persuasive attempts, see George G. Bruntz, *Allied Propaganda and the Collapse of the German Empire in 1918* (Stanford: Stanford University Press, 1938), 188–221, and M. L. Sanders and Philip M. Taylor, *British Propaganda during the First World War, 1914–1918* (London: Macmillan, 1982), 251–65. Also of interest, though limited by lack of historical distance, is Harold D. Lasswell's foundational *Propaganda Technique in the World War* (New York: Knopf, 1927), 216–22. For a critical overview of historical studies, see the preface to Sanders and Taylor, *British Propaganda*, vii–x.

42. Hynes, *A War Imagined*, 26.

43. Thomas Hardy, *The Life and Work of Thomas Hardy, 1840–1928*, ed. Michael Millgate (Athens: University of Georgia Press, 1985), 395–96.

44. See G. H. Hardy, *Bertrand Russell and Trinity* (1942; rpt. Cambridge: Cambridge University Press, 1970).

45. E. M. Forster, *Howards End*, ed. Paul B. Armstrong (1910; rpt. New York: Norton, 1998), 56.

46. Virginia Woolf, "Modern Fiction," in *The Common Reader, First Series*, ed. Andrew McNeillie (San Diego: Harcourt, Brace, Jovanovich, 1984), 150.

47. For the press meeting, see Messinger, *British Propaganda and the State*, 36–38.

48. On the coopting of the press, see Sanders and Taylor, *British Propaganda*, 76–89. For Wells and Bennett, see Messinger, *British Propaganda and the State*, 184–212, 225–34.

49. John B. Thompson, *The Media and Modernity* (Stanford: Stanford University Press, 1995), 152–53.

50. On Masterman's elitism, see Messinger, *British Propaganda and the State*, 30–34.

51. The MoI was officially dissolved on December 31, 1918. It was not re-established until 1939.

52. See Cate Haste, *Keep the Home Fires Burning: Propaganda in the First World War* (London: Allen Lane, 1977), 5–20.

53. The flow of images was also regulated by Masterman's *War Pictorial*, a magazine published in twelve editions tailored to different nations. The first

number of the Canadian version underscored the necessity of reclaiming control over the pictures formerly snapped by officers with pocket cameras: "The days of indiscriminate photography on and behind our war-fronts passed long ago. . . . The task of making a pictorial record of the war rests now in the hands of a very limited number of Official Photographers"; *The Canadian War Pictorial*, no. 1 (London: Hodder and Stoughton, 1915), p 1.

54. *Third Report on the Work Conducted for the Government at Wellington House* (1916), 100. Hereafter cited in the text.

55. Minutes of interview (November 19, 1917) with W. M. Dixon, "Propaganda Inquiry; Evidence taken at Wellington House," 5. Public Record Office, Kew, England; INF 4/11.

56. According to Masterman, *Britain Prepared*, "specially taken to show the activities of the Navy and the Army, . . . has been exhibited in practically every country which possesses cinematograph facilities, and with very considerable success" (*Third Report*, 99).

57. See "*The Times* History and Encyclopedia of the War: British Propaganda in Enemy Countries," part 270, vol. 21 (December, 30, 1919). Ostensibly published in London by the Times Publishing Company, this is in fact a history produced by Wellington House.

58. "First Report of the War Office Cinematograph Committee," September 1918; Public Record Office at Kew, England; INF 4/1B.

59. L. Masterman, *Masterman*, 283.

60. Nicholas Hiley, "The British Cinema Auditorium," in *Film and the First World War*, ed. Karel Dibbets and Bert Hogenkamp (Amsterdam: Amsterdam University Press, 1995), 162.

61. For a thorough history, including information about administration, production, and the films themselves, see Nicholas Reeves, *Official British Film Propaganda During the First World War* (London: Croom Helm, 1986). My discussion is indebted to his scholarship.

62. Ibid., 259.

63. It should be pointed out, however, that British propaganda films became increasingly selective in their representation of scenes of death and destruction, out of the belief that by dwelling too much on the costs of war the films might undermine morale.

64. Minutes of a meeting on January 15, 1918, to discuss the use of film in propaganda; Public Record Office, Kew, England; HO 45/10960/340327.

65. Key excerpts from Zola's "Naturalism on the Stage" (1880) are reprinted in *Modernism: An Anthology of Sources and Documents*, ed. Vassiliki Kolocotroni, Jane Goldman, and Olga Taxidou (Chicago: University of Chicago Press, 1998), 169–74. The anthology also reprints excerpts from Arthur Symons's massively influential *The Symbolist Movement in Literature* (1899), which helped diffuse French symbolism through British culture (*Modernism*, 134–35).

66. Joseph Conrad, *Lord Jim* (Garden City, N.Y.: Doubleday, Page, 1924), 29. Hereafter cited in the text.

67. M. J. Van Den Heuvel, preface to Official Commission of the Belgian Government, *Reports on the Violation of the Rights of Nations and of the Laws*

and Customs of War in Belgium (London: Harrison and Sons, [1915–16]), v. Wellington House printed and circulated the Belgian reports as well as the Bryce Report. For a more detailed discussion of the Bryce Report, see chapter 3.

68. James Morgan Reid, *Atrocity Propaganda, 1914–1919* (New Haven: Yale University Press, 1941), 51–77.

69. Mary Poovey, *A History of the Modern Fact* (Chicago and London: University of Chicago Press, 1998), 1–28.

70. Other British practices intervened in the global flow of information in a more self-consciously manipulative way. For instance, Reuters distributed news throughout the world to affiliated agencies, and the DoI, noting that it was "essential" that Reuters's "independence . . . should be preserved," nonetheless financed a secret supplement to Reuters's ordinary service. "This supplementary service," according to a confidential memo, "carries all the news most favourable to the Allies which, in the opinion of the Chief Editor of Reuter's [*sic*] it is safe for an independent agency to circulate and which there is the likelihood of getting printed." Subscribers did not know about the information supplements, and the DoI memo acknowledges how difficult it was becoming to determine where information ended and propaganda began: the supplementary service "does not set out to be in any sense propagandist. The 'tendency' is very delicately introduced." Film was handled similarly, with "film tags" surreptitiously added to the newsreels that ran regularly in cinemas all over England, Europe, and the United States. Propagandists devised lists of suitable subjects for film tags—such as the need for economy in certain articles of food, and the recruiting needs of the various services—and they calculated various suitable lengths for what they determined were the four main genres of the tag: the story film (1,000–6,000 feet), "the moving cartoon film" (750 feet), "interest" films (which were essentially slice-of-life clips) (700 feet), and the topical tag, or "cinematic newspaper" (350–4,000 feet). See the Report on the News Section, from Earnest Perris to Mr. Donald, July 11, 1917; Public Record Office, Kew, England; INF 4/10; and "Cinematograph Propaganda in the United Kingdom," memo from the Cinematic Branch of the MoI, February 1918; Public Record Office, Kew, England; HO 45/10960/340327.

71. Wyndham Lewis, *Time and Western Man* (New York: Harcourt, Brace, 1928), 92.

72. Georg Lukács, *The Meaning of Contemporary Realism*, trans. John and Necke Mander (London: Merlin, 1963), 28.

73. Lippmann, *Public Opinion*, 15.

74. Quoted in Ronald Steel, *Walter Lippmann and the American Century* (New York: Vintage, 1980), 142.

75. Lippmann, *Public Opinion*, 25–26, 91–92.

76. See Jean Baudrillard, *Simulacra and Simulation*, trans. Sheila Faria Glaser (Ann Arbor: University of Michigan Press, 1994), 1–42.

77. For instance, Paul Virilio, who argues that "the First World War can be seen as the first mediated conflict in history," locates a comparable dialectic of derealization in a symbiotic relationship between war and cinema. What Virilio's theory lacks, however, is a place for the cultural work of propaganda, which gets lost in his tendency to invest media with a determining power independent of the

uses to which they are put. See Virilio, *War and Cinema*, trans. Patrick Camiller (London and New York: Verso, 1989), 58. Ellul offers the proper corrective: technology may make the man, who is indispensable to it, but "the process evolves though the 'con-naturality' of both." See Ellul, "An Aspect of the Role of Persuasion in a Technical Society," *Etc.: A Review of General Semantics* 36 (Summer 1979): 148.

78. See, for instance, Vanessa R. Schwartz, "Cinematic Spectatorship before the Apparatus: The Public Taste for Reality in *Fin-de-Siècle* Paris," in *Cinema and the Invention of Modern Life*, ed. Leo Charney and Vanessa R. Schwartz (Berkeley: University of California Press, 1995), 297–319.

79. J. David Bolter and Richard Grusin, *Remediation: Understanding New Media* (Cambridge, Mass.: MIT Press, 1999), 34, 54–59. Grusin and Bolter suggest that "at the end of the twentieth century, we are in a position to understand hypermediacy as immediacy's opposite number, an alter ego that has never been suppressed fully or for long periods," and they cite the modernist period as one in which the play between immediacy and mediation becomes particularly visible. This is true, but I want to stress that the oscillation between transparency and opacity that is so dramatic in digital technology only rose into cultural dominance in the early twentieth century, when an increasingly self-consciousness awareness of the inevitable mediation of experience emerged as a distinct sociological phenomenon. On this last point, see North, *Reading 1922*, 29.

80. D. H. Lawrence, foreword to *Women in Love* (New York: Penguin, 1995), 486.

81. J. A. Hobson, *The Psychology of Jingoism* (London: Grant Richards, 1901), 12.

82. Joseph Conrad, *Heart of Darkness*, ed. Robert Kimbrough (New York: Norton, 1988), 48. Hereafter cited in the text.

83. See Hunt Hawkins, "Conrad's Critique of Imperialism in *Heart of Darkness*," *Publications of the Modern Language Association* 94 (1979): 286–99, and Ellul, *The Technological Society*, 3–7.

84. Lionel Trilling, *Sincerity and Authenticity* (Cambridge, Mass.: Harvard University Press, 1971), 106.

85. Joseph Conrad, preface to *The Nigger of the "Narcissus,"* ed. Robert Kimbrough (New York: Norton, 1979), 147; emphasis added. Hereafter cited in the text.

86. Joseph Conrad, "A Glance at Two Books," in *Last Essays* (Garden City, N.Y.: Doubleday, Page, 1926), 132.

87. Compare Patrick Brantlinger: "[Conrad] knows that the 'will-to-style,' his own impressionism, points toward the production of novels that are hollow at the core—that can justify any injustice—and contain, perhaps, only an abyss, a Kurtz, the horror. Kurtz's devious, shadowy voice echoes Conrad's. It is just this hollow voice, eloquently egotistical, capable of both high idealism and of lying propaganda, which speaks from the center of the heart of darkness to sum up and to judge" (Brantlinger, *Rule of Darkness: British Literature and Imperialism, 1830–1914* [Ithaca and London: Cornell University Press, 1988], 271).

88. For an account of modernism and the late nineteenth-century romance revival as entwined responses to modernity, see Nicholas Daly, *Modernism, Romance and the Fin de Siècle* (Cambridge: Cambridge University Press, 1999), 1–29.

89. Joseph Conrad, "The Unlighted Coast," in *Last Essay*, 50. Hereafter cited in the text.

90. Conrad, "The Tale," in *Tales of Hearsay* (Garden City, N.Y.: Doubleday Page, 1925), 80. Hereafter cited in the text.

91. Typically attributed to the Prussian war strategist Carl von Clausewitz's *On War*, the proverbial phrase "the fog of war" never actually appears in the book. See Eugenia C. Kiesling, "*On War* Without the Fog," *Military Review* 81, no. 5 (September–October 2001):84–87.

92. Zdzisław Najder, *Joseph Conrad: A Chronicle* (New Brunswick, N.J.: Rutgers University Press, 1983), 424.

93. Conrad's eagerness to wrap himself in the mantle of Englishness, as he does in *A Personal Record* (1912), has more to do with projecting himself as an English author (as opposed to a Pole writing in English) than with a fundamentally political identification. Conrad's participation in the British war effort was very likely a direct consequence of his having written and presented to the British Foreign Office in August 1916 "a memorandum concerning the restoration of the Polish state as hereditary monarchy under the joint protectorate of England and France" (Najder, *Joseph Conrad*, 419). A month after writing the memo (later published as "Note on the Polish Problem" in *Notes on Life and Letters*), Conrad observed naval firing practice at Lowestoft, took a two-day trip on a minesweeper, and enjoyed a short flight on a patrolling biplane.

94. G. Jean-Aubry, *Joseph Conrad: Life and Letters* (Garden City, N.Y.: Doubleday, Page, 1927), 2:179; J. G. Sutherland, *At Sea with Joseph Conrad* (London: Grant Richards, 1922), 119, 137, 139.

95. See Ian Duncan, *Modern Romance and Transformations of the Novel* (Cambridge: Cambridge University Press, 1992), 1–19.

96. Conrad, "Travel," in *Last Essays*, 86. Hereafter cited in the text.

97. See John McClure, "Late Imperial Romance," *Raritan* 10, no. 4 (1991): 111–30.

98. Wireless in Britain at this time was largely controlled by the military. Though invented almost twenty years earlier, wireless had been made available to the public only two years earlier, in July 1914, and then only two months later, with the outbreak of war, all public licenses were withdrawn.

99. Sutherland, *At Sea with Joseph Conrad*, corroborates that Conrad learned how to work the wireless and decode messages, though one wonders how much to trust an account by someone whose first impressions are that Conrad was a man interested in "seeing only the bright side of things" and who judges their trip "the most memorable and exciting experience of [Conrad's] seafaring career" (12, 1).

100. Fredric Jameson, *The Political Unconscious* (Ithaca: Cornell University Press, 1981), 225–32, 241.

101. For an account of modernism as an attempt to reintegrate senses that have been disaggregated, or dis-integrated, under modernity, see Sara Danius, *The Senses of Modernism* (Ithaca: Cornell University Press, 2002).

102. Joseph Conrad, *The Secret Agent* (Garden City, N.Y.: Doubleday, Page, 1924), 260.

103. See Ivan Kreilkamp, "A Voice without a Body: the Phonographic Logic of *Heart of Darkness*," *Victorian Studies* 40, no. 2 (Winter 1997): 211–43.

104. Friedrich Kittler, *Gramophone, Film, Typewriter*, trans. Geoffrey Winthrop-Young and Michael Wutz (Stanford: Stanford University Press, 1999), 14.

105. For the inaugural version of this account of modernism, see Edmund Wilson, *Axel's Castle* (1931; rpt. New York: Norton, 1984), 1–25.

CHAPTER ONE
FROM CONRAD TO HITCHCOCK

1. Gary S. Messinger, *British Propaganda and the State in the First World War* (Manchester and New York: Manchester University Press, 1992), 35.

2. See Raymond Williams, "The Metropolis and the Emergence of Modernism," in *Unreal City: Urban Experience in Modern European Literature and Art*, ed. Edward Timms and David Kelley (New York: St. Martin's Press, 1985), 13–24.

3. For a groundbreaking intermedial approach to film, see Paul Young, *The Cinema Dreams its Rivals: Media Fantasy Films from Radio to the Internet* (Minneapolis: University of Minnesota Press, 2006). See also his "Media on Display: A Telegraphic History of Early American Cinema," in *New Media, 1740–1915*, ed. Lisa Gitelman and Geoffrey B. Pingree (Cambridge, Mass.: MIT Press, 2003).

4. Joseph Conrad, *The Secret Agent* (Garden City, N.Y.: Doubleday, Page, 1924), 81–82. Hereafter cited in the text. For "propaganda by the deed," see James Joll, *The Anarchists* (Cambridge, Mass.: Harvard University Press, 1980), 99–129.

5. Michael Balcon and Ivor Montagu produced *Sabotage*; Charles Bennett, Alma Reville (Hitchcock's wife), Ian Hay, and Helen Simpson all contributed to the screenplay, adaptation, and dialogue; Bernard Knowles directed the photography; Charles Frend edited. The cast: Sylvia Sidney (Mrs. Verloc), Oscar Homolka (Mr. Verloc), Desmond Tester (Stevie), John Loder (Ted), William Dewhurst (Mr. Chattman—Conrad's Professor). For treatments of *Sabotage* that focus on adaptation, see Michael Anderegg, "Conrad and Hitchcock: *The Secret Agent* Inspires *Sabotage*," *Literature/Film Quarterly* 3 (1975): 215–25; Paula Marantz Cohen, "The Ideological Transformation of Conrad's *The Secret Agent* into Hitchcock's *Sabotage*," *Literature/Film Quarterly* 22, no. 3 (1994): 199–209; and James Goodwin, "Hitchcock and Conrad: Secret Sharers," in *The English Novel and the Movies*, ed. Michael Klein and Gillian Parker (New York: Frederick Ungar, 1981): 218–27. See also note 34, below.

6. Poirier, "Pater, Joyce, Eliot," *James Joyce Quarterly* 26 (1988): 21–35.

7. Conrad, *The Secret Agent: Drama in Four Acts* (Canterbury: Goulden, 1921), 19.

8. Raymond Durgnat, *The Strange Case of Alfred Hitchcock* (London: Faber, 1974), 137.

9. Jonathan Crary, *Suspensions of Perception: Attention, Spectacle, and Modern Culture* (Cambridge, Mass.: MIT Press, 1999), 11–79. See also Crary's *Techniques of the Observer: On Vision and Modernity in the Nineteenth Century* (Cambridge, Mass.: MIT Press, 1990), which analyzes the shift from the classic, disembodied observer to the mobile, embodied observer characteristic of modernity.

10. For reflections on the way notes, marginalia, and other author-sponsored apparatuses operate in modernism, with special emphasis on Joyce, Woolf, and Pound, see John Whittier-Ferguson, *Framing Pieces* (New York: Oxford University Press, 1996).

11. On the relationship between early cinema and the "hyperstimulus" of urban life, see Ben Singer, *Melodrama and Modernity: Early Sensational Cinema and its Contexts* (New York: Columbia University Press, 2001).

12. Siegfried Kracauer, *Theory of Film* (London: Oxford University Press, 1960), 157–72.

13. Untitled document in the Records of the Metropolitan Police Office, Public Record Office, Kew, England; MEPO 2/1696.

14. See, for example, "The Lighting of Kinematograph Theatres," *Kinematograph and Lantern Weekly*, March 1, 1917, which reports on a discussion of a paper read by Dr. James Kerr of the Public Health Department before the Illuminated Engineering Society: "there was little doubt that kinema glare and flicker did have very bad effects upon children's eyesight, and it was not improbable that the moral instability that was so much feared might not follow in some measure from the instability set up through the effect on the eyesight" (24).

15. Interview with cinematographer Herbert G. Ponting, *Manchester Guardian*, September 11, 1914.

16. "First Report of the War Office Cinematograph Committee," September 1918; Public Record Office at Kew, England; INF 4/1B.

17. Meeting Minutes, Ministry of Information, January 15, 1918; Public Record Office at Kew, England; HO 45/10960/340327.

18. Hitchcock himself has written about the stabbing montage, perhaps setting the agenda for later critics. See his "Direction" (1937) in *Focus on Hitchcock*, ed. Edward J. LaValley (Englewood Cliffs, N.J.: Prentice-Hall, 1972). Slavoj Zizek has suggested in *Looking Awry: An Introduction to Jacques Lacan through Popular Culture* (Cambridge, Mass.: MIT Press, 1991) that Verloc virtually commits suicide in the stabbing sequence by thrusting himself onto his wife's knife, but I can find no corroboration in the film for this conjecture.

19. Hulme, *Speculations*, ed. Herbert Read (New York: Harcourt, Brace, 1924), 134. For a thorough investigation of the single film frame in relation to modernist fragmentation and continuity, see Garrett Stewart, *Between Film and Screen: Modernism's Photo Synthesis* (Chicago and London: University of Chicago Press, 1999).

20. Joseph Conrad, preface to *The Nigger of the "Narcissus,"* ed. Robert Kimbrough (New York: Norton, 1979), 147.

21. Quoted by Alex Ross in "Crying Shame," *New Republic* 208, no. 9 (March 1, 1993). Crowd control and a focus on the physiology of reception are related responses, as Crary helps us recognize, to a problem of attention.

22. Quoted in Peter Bogdanovich, *The Cinema of Alfred Hitchcock* (New York: Museum of Modern Art, 1963), 3.

23. *The Collected Letters of Joseph Conrad*, ed. Frederick R. Karl and Laurence Davies, 5 vols. (Cambridge: Cambridge University Press, 1983–96), 3:439–40. Hereafter cited in the text.

24. "I did not intend to make [the Professor] despicable," Conrad wrote to Graham: "In making him say 'madness and despair . . .' I wanted to give him a note of perfect sincerity" (*Letters*, 3:491). In the preface to *The Nigger of the "Narcissus,"* Conrad aspires to the same effect: "The task approached in tenderness and faith is to hold up unquestioningly, without choice and without fear, the rescued fragment before all eyes and in the light of a sincere mood"; Conrad, *The Nigger of the "Narcissus,"* 147. The Professor's words were used as the epigraph for the French translation of *The Secret Agent*, which until then had been Conrad's only nonposthumous book without an epigraph.

25. Conrad, "Autocracy and War," in *Notes on Life and Letters* (Garden City, N.Y.: Doubleday, Page, 1924), 90.

26. See Ford Madox Ford, *The Critical Attitude* (London: Duckworth, 1911), 113–29.

27. For Conrad's long description to Galsworthy of the difficulties of adapting his novel, see G. Jean-Aubry, *Joseph Conrad: Life and Letters*, 2 vols. (Garden City, N.Y.: Doubleday, Page, 1927), 2:257–59. Two years earlier he confessed to J. B. Pinker: "I cannot defend myself from the dread of the whole thing turning out repulsive to average minds and shocking to average feelings" (2:233). In the same letter he wrote about the stage in general: "Every rag of the drapery drops to the ground. It is a terribly searching thing" (2:234).

28. Conrad, *The Rescue* (Garden City, N.Y.: Doubleday, Page, 1924), xi. Having shelved it over twenty years earlier, Conrad finally finished *The Rescue* in 1920, the same year he wrote the dramatization of *The Secret Agent*.

29. Hitchcock was highly conscious that the audience he wished to master was composed largely of women. When Ted suggests jocularly to Verloc, who is pretending to head off for a trade show, that he select films with "plenty of murders" rather than the "love stuff," Verloc observes that "the women like it, though. After all, when you consider that 80 percent . . ." That women are the primary object of Hitchcock's manipulative designs becomes the self-consciously obsessive subject of *Vertigo* (1958). For the effects of cross-gender identification in Hitchcock, see Tania Modleski, *The Women Who Knew Too Much* (New York: Methuen, 1988). Conrad's letter to Graham (December 6, 1897) anticipates the erotic ambivalence of Hitchcock's cross-gender identifications by offering a textbook case of the process whereby the male subject establishes its autonomy by expelling the instability stigmatized in the elusiveness of a feminized object.

30. Compare the deeply felt need for a transparent representational order evident in Conrad's admiration for *The Spoils of Poynton* (1895): "The delicacy and tenuity of the thing are amazing. It is like a great sheet of glass—you don't know it's there till you run against it" (*Letters from Joseph Conrad, 1895–1924*, ed. David Garnett [Indianapolis, Ind.: Bobbs-Merrill, 1928], 89).

31. Ozick, *Metaphor and Memory* (New York: Knopf, 1989), 99. For an effort to theorize characters' relative freedom in polyphonic fiction versus their

constriction in monologic fiction, see Mikhail Bakhtin, *Problems of Dosto-evsky's Poetics*, ed. and trans. Caryl Emerson (Minneapolis: University of Min-nesota Press, 1984), 78–100.

32. Quoted from a 1922 letter to Alan Wade by Frederick R. Karl, *Joseph Conrad: The Three Lives* (New York: Farrar, Straus, and Giroux, 1979), 876.

33. Herbert Blau, *The Audience* (Baltimore: Johns Hopkins University Press, 1990), 1.

34. Though Anderegg, in "Conrad and Hitchcock: *The Secret Agent* Inspires *Sabotage*," explicitly discounts the influence of the play that other critics simply ig-nore (217), what Hitchcock saw at the Ambassadors Theatre immediately fore-grounds what the novel takes longer to make clear: the peculiar vulnerability of Ste-vie, who "would go through fire and water for Mr. Verloc" (Conrad, *The Secret Agent: Drama in Four Acts*, 1). The play also highlights how coercion and exploita-tion characterize virtually all the relationships in *The Secret Agent* (see Aaron Fogel, *Coercion to Speak: Conrad's Poetics of Dialogue* [Cambridge, Mass.: Harvard Uni-versity Press, 1985]). Possibly Hitchcock went to the play because he already knew the novel. No external evidence indicates when Hitchcock first read *The Secret Agent*, but tantalizing details suggest that he might have done so just before making his first important film, *The Lodger*, in 1926. A silent film based on Mrs. Belloc Lowndes's 1913 novel about a Jack the Ripper figure called the Avenger, *The Lodger* achieves brilliant visual stylization in part through a pattern of triangular shapes that recalls Conrad's insistent imagistic echoing of Verloc's code name, the Greek letter delta. Although in Lowndes's novel the Avenger's "calling cards" also feature a triangle, the image does not ramify as it does in Conrad and Hitchcock.

35. Rothman, *Hitchcock: The Murderous Gaze* (Cambridge, Mass.: Harvard University Press, 1982), 99–107.

36. For the historical and cultural contexts of Hitchcock's early career, see Tom Ryall, *Alfred Hitchcock and the British Cinema* (London: Croom Helm, 1986). For a valuable attempt to situate Rothman's work on Hitchcock in rela-tion to modernity's intensification of the reification process—specifically, "the fragmentation of the bodily sensorium and the 'reification' of sight itself" (126)—see Fredric Jameson, "Allegorizing Hitchcock," *Signatures of the Visible* (New York: Routledge, 1990), 99–127.

37. Donald Spoto, *The Dark Side of Genius: The Life of Alfred Hitchcock* (Boston: Little, Brown, 1983), 141, 154. Hereafter cited in the text. Bog-danovich, *Cinema of Alfred Hitchcock*, 6.

38. Eric Rohmer and Claude Chabrol, *Hitchcock: The First Forty-Four Films*, trans. Stanley Hochman (New York: Ungar, 1979), 47–48.

39. See, for example, R. A. Gekoski, *Conrad: The Moral World of the Novel-ist* (London: Elek, 1978), 150–51. Martin Price's attention to genre questions the fictional adequacy of Conrad's relentless irony ("Conrad: Satire and Fiction," *Yearbook of English Studies* 14 [1984]: 226–42).

40. Greene, *The Pleasure Dome: The Collected Film Criticism 1935–40*, ed. John Russell Taylor (London: Secker and Warburg, 1972), 122–23; Leonard J. Leff, *Hitchcock and Selznick* (New York: Weidenfeld and Nicolson, 1987), 23.

41. David Ragan, *Movie Stars of the '30s: A Complete Reference Guide for the Film Historian or Trivia Buff* (Englewood Cliffs, N.J.: Prentice-Hall, 1985), 161.

42. For a complementary study of the relationship between sadistic violence and cinematic self-assertion in Hitchcock, see David Mikics, "The Lesson of the Master: Violence and Authority in Hitchcock," *Gulf Coast* 4 (1991): 7–25.

43. Conrad, *A Personal Record* (Garden City, N.Y.: Doubleday, Page, 1924), 95, xv.

44. Jonathan Arac, *Critical Genealogies* (New York: Columbia University Press, 1987), 189.

45. See my *Joseph Conrad and the Fictions of Skepticism* (Stanford: Stanford University Press, 1990), 149–52.

46. This pattern, which includes Heat's inspection of Stevie's remains and Winnie's stabbing of Verloc with the carving knife, motivates the otherwise superfluous repetitions of roast beef in *Sabotage*: we first see Stevie removing a roast from the oven; Ted later orders roast beef for Mrs. Verloc and Stevie at Simpson's; Mrs. Verloc is carving a roast before she plunges the knife into her husband. Hitchcock returns to the cannibalism theme in more macabre fashion in *Frenzy* (1972), in which scenes of a killer breaking the clenched fingers of a corpse to remove an incriminating lapel pin are intercut with a dinner scene during which a woman serves her unhappy husband pig's knuckles; the crackling joints on the soundtrack amplify the grotesquerie.

47. I thank Rank Film Distributors Limited for providing me with copies of the full treatment (May 14, 1936) and the shooting script for *Sabotage*, and for kind permission to quote from the former (33–34).

48. There's a nice irony latent in the alternative etymology of "sabotage" offered by Thorstein Veblen in 1919: from the French *sabot*, or wooden shoe, the word suggests a calculated foot-dragging in order to impede efficiency ("On the Nature and Uses of Sabotage," *Dial* [1919]: 341–46).

49. Replaying his attraction to *The Secret Agent*, I would argue, Hitchcock told François Truffaut that "the thing that appealed to me and made me decide to do the picture [*Psycho*] was the suddenness of the murder in the shower, coming, as it were, out of the blue. That was about all" (Truffaut, *Hitchcock* [New York: Simon and Schuster, 1984], 268–69).

50. Compare Pascal Bonitzer, "Hitchcockian Suspense" in *Everything You Always Wanted to Know about Lacan (But Were Afraid to Ask Hitchcock)*, ed. Slavoj Žižek (London: Verso, 1992), 17–18.

51. At this point the viewer coming to *Sabotage* by way of *Blackmail* (1929) may remember Hitchcock's first extended cameo, in which he slaps at an annoying child on a bus.

52. Truffaut, *Hitchcock*, 109; Bogdanovich, *Cinema of Alfred Hitchcock*, 19.

53. The Hitchcockian suspense sequence normally moderates the experience of loss within an economy of recompense whereby the victim is understood to have asked for it. Janet Leigh did steal forty thousand dollars, after all. But Stevie's death forces viewers to face up to their ambivalent desires because it allows no such rationalization (See Mladen Dolor, "The Spectator Who Knew Too Much" in Žižek, *Everything You Always Wanted to Know about Lacan*, 129–36). Conrad's Stevie is also innocent, but the novel's disjunct narrative chronology does not follow an analogous logic of suspense: initially, readers are

led to believe that the bomb killed Verloc, not Stevie, whose death we experience after the fact from his sister's point of view.

54. Gunning, "The Cinema of Attraction[s]: Early Film, Its Spectator, and the Avant-Garde," *Wide Angle* 8, nos. 3–4 (1986): 64; see also Gunning, *D. W. Griffith and the Origins of American Narrative Film* (Urbana: University of Illinois Press, 1991), 41–42. For more on the material history of early spectatorship, particularly the context of projection, see Charles Musser, in collaboration with Carol Nelson, *High-Class Moving Pictures: Lyman H. Howe and the Forgotten Era of Traveling Exhibition, 1880–1920* (Princeton: Princeton University Press, 1991).

55. Ford Madox Ford, *Joseph Conrad: A Personal Remembrance* (London: Duckworth, 1924), 127.

56. Judith Mayne, "Mediation, the Novelistic, and Film Narrative," in *Narrative Strategies: Original Essays in Film and Prose Fiction*, ed. Syndy M. Conger and Janice R. Welsch (Macomb: Western Illinois University Press, 1980), 86–88.

57. Quoted by Dudley Andrew in his *André Bazin* (New York: Oxford University Press, 1978), 128. Andrew is quoting from an out-of-print French edition that includes passages, like this one, that were excised in later editions, but a related discussion of Welles's mise-en-scène can be found in André Bazin, *Orson Welles*, trans. Jonathan Rosenbaum (New York: Harper and Row, 1978), 77–81.

58. Aldous Huxley, *Brave New World* (New York: HarperCollins/Perennial Classics, 1998), 184. Pointing toward another nodal point in the shared space of modernism and propaganda, Huxley's critique is likely directed in part against the most influential technique ever devised to deal with the complexities posed by modernist literature, the emotive behavioralism of I. A. Richards's practical criticism. Aesthetician R. G. Collingwood took on Richards directly several years later for the same reason, objecting to his attempts "to estimate the objective merits of a given poem by tabulating the 'reactions' to it of persons from whom the poet's name has been concealed" (*Principles of Art* [Oxford: Clarendon Press, 1938], 35). For a complementary discussion of the historicity of Richards's concept of the pseudo-statement, see Vincent Sherry, *The Great War and the Language of Modernism* (New York: Oxford University Press, 2003), 70–74.

59. Walter Benjamin, "The Work of Art in the Age of Mechanical Reproduction" [1936], in *Illuminations*, ed. Hannah Arendt, trans. Harry Zohn (New York: Schocken, 1968), 226.

60. S. M. Eisenstein, "Literature and Cinema," in *Writings, 1922–1934*, ed. and trans. Richard Taylor, vol. 1 of *S. M. Eisenstein: Selected Works* (London: BFI; Bloomington: Indiana University Press, 1988), 96. For polyphonic montage and simultaneity, see "Vertical Montage" (1940), in *Towards a Theory of Montage*, ed. Michael Glenny and Richard Taylor, trans. Michael Glenny, vol. 2 of *S. M. Eisenstein: Selected Works* (London: BFI, 1991), 330.

61. See Gösta Werner, "James Joyce and Sergej Eisenstein," *James Joyce Quarterly* 27 (Spring 1990):495.

62. Eisenstein, "The Montage of Film Attractions" (1924), in Taylor, *Writings, 1922–1934*, 39.

63. S. M. Eisenstein, "Dickens, Griffith and Ourselves," in *Writings, 1934–47*, ed. Richard Taylor, trans. William Powell, vol. 3 of *S. M. Eisenstein: Selected Works* (London: BFI, 1996), 193–238.

64. For a more appreciative and ultimately more persuasive account of Griffith's parallel editing, see Miriam Hansen, *Babel and Babylon: Spectatorship in American Silent Film* (Cambridge, Mass.: Harvard University Press, 1991), 129–40, 202–17.

65. Miriam Bratu Hansen, "The Mass Production of the Senses: Classical Cinema as Vernacular Modernism," in *Reinventing Film Studies*, ed. Christine Gledhill and Linda Williams (London: Arnold, 2000), 335.

66. Durgnat, *The Strange Case of Alfred Hitchcock*, 139.

67. I am indebted here to Astradur Eysteinsson's account of a modernist aesthetics of interruption in his *The Concept of Modernism* (Ithaca: Cornell University Press, 1990), 197–241.

68. Ina Rae Hark, "Keeping Your Amateur Standing: Audience Participation in and Good Citizenship in Hitchcock's Political Films," *Cinema Journal* 29, no. 2 (1990):12–13.

CHAPTER TWO
THE WOOLFS, PICTURE POSTCARDS, AND THE PROPAGANDA
OF EVERYDAY LIFE

1. In her biography of Roger Fry, Woolf attributes to Fry a contrast between Mallarmé and English writers that resonates with her own view of literary modernism as the antithesis of propaganda. Where Mallarmé was able to treat words objectively the way a modern painter treats paint, English writers tend to be "moralists" and "propagandists," and "propaganda [she quotes Fry as saying] shuts off the contemplative penetration of life before it has found the finer shades of significance. It simplifies too much"; Woolf, *Roger Fry* (London: Hogarth, 1940), 240. Woolf gives no source for Fry's words, which are presumably cited from her conversations with him.

2. Virginia Woolf, *Three Guineas* (New York: Harcourt, Brace, 1938), 169–70. For an extended meditation on Woolf's complex negotiations between her roles as artist and propagandist that takes off from the horse-mule trope, see Jane Marcus, " 'No more horses': Virginia Woolf on Art and Propaganda," *Women's Studies* 4 (1977):265–90.

3. Virginia Woolf, *Diary of Virginia Woolf*, ed. Anne Olivier Bell and Andrew McNeillie, 5 vols. (San Diego: Harcourt, Brace, Jovanovich, 1982), 4:300. Hereafter cited as *Diary*.

4. For a more detailed discussion of the cultural proximity of modernism and propaganda, see the preface, above.

5. Virginia Woolf, "The Mark on the Wall," in *Women, Men, and the Great War*, ed. Trudi Tate (Manchester: Manchester University Press, 1995), 163.

6. Woolf rarely reviewed poetry, but she twice reviewed Sassoon's *The Old Huntsmen and Other Poems* (1917), both times very positively. See Woolf,

The Essays of Virginia Woolf, ed. Andrew McNeillie, 3 vols. (San Diego: Harcourt, Brace, Jovanovich, 1986–88), 2:119–22; 269–72. Hereafter cited in the text.

7. Virginia Woolf, *Mrs. Dalloway* (1925; rpt. San Diego: Harcourt, 1981), 93. Hereafter cited in the text.

8. Virginia Woolf, *To the Lighthouse* (1927; rpt. San Diego: Harcourt, Brace, Jovanovich, 1989), 133–34.

9. For the influence of Barbusse's novel on British war poets and the public, see Samuel Hynes, *A War Imagined: The First World War and English Culture* (New York: Atheneum, 1991), 203–6. Hynes points out that *Under Fire* was not realistic in any simple way, but its graphic imagery created more of a sensation than did its haunting surrealism and shifting points of view.

10. Roger Poole, picking up Paul Fussell's observation in *The Great War and Modern Memory* that the Field Service Postcard was the first widespread modern "form" (i.e., standardized document with blanks to fill in), has suggested that the brackets in "Time Passes" performed the same cultural function by reducing personal experience to mere statements of public fact. See Roger Poole, " 'We all put up with you Virginia': Irreceivable Wisdom about War," in *Virginia Woolf and War*, ed. Mark Hussey (Syracuse: Syracuse University Press, 1991), 84–85, and Paul Fussell, *The Great War and Modern Memory* (New York and London: Oxford University Press, 1975), 183–87.

11. Terry Eagleton, *The English Novel* (Malden, Mass.: Blackwell, 2005), 323.

12. Jacques Ellul, *Propaganda: The Formation of Men's Attitudes*, trans. Konrad Kellen (New York: Vintage, 1973), 174, 175.

13. Ibid., 64.

14. Virginia Woolf, *The Voyage Out* (1915; rpt. London: Penguin, 1992), 4. Hereafter cited in the text.

15. The golden age of the picture postcard in England is usually thought to begin in 1899, when changes in British postal regulations permitted the standard-sized card to circulate freely, and to end with World War I in 1918, when postal rates doubled and the exuberantly colored cards of the belle epoque gave way to the dull sepia tints of the bleak postwar years. See Anthony Byatt, *Picture Postcards and their Publishers* (Malvern, Eng.: Golden Age Postcard Books, 1978), 13–14.

16. John M. MacKenzie, *Propaganda and Empire: The Manipulation of British Public Opinion, 1880–1960* (Manchester: Manchester University Press, 1984), 16.

17. The Boer War sold papers for the new mass press at a time when "the locus of hero-worship" was moving "from Europe to the Empire"; with "colonial exploits . . . enthusiastically followed by the public," "war became a remote adventure in which heroism was enhanced by both distance and exotic locales"; MacKenzie, *Propaganda and Empire*, 6.

18. Ibid., 3.

19. In the course of a critique of British colonial ethnography in Sri Lanka, Bruce Kapferer singles out *The Village in the Jungle* for its unusual empathy with the Sinhalese and Tamil peoples while acknowledging Leonard's expected aloofness as a colonial administrator. I will return to these qualities of the novel later in my argument. See Bruce Kapferer, "From the Periphery to the Centre: Ethnog-

raphy and the Critique of Anthropology in Sri Lanka," in *Localizing Strategies: Regional Traditions of Ethnographic Writing*, ed. Richard Fardon (Edinburgh: Scottish Academic Press, 1990), 280–302.

20. See, for instance, Kathy J. Phillips, *Virginia Woolf against Empire* (Knoxville: University of Tennessee Press, 1994), 52–78.

21. Woolf, *Three Guineas*, 75, 64, 74, 70.

22. *Orlando* (1928) may come closest, but while Orlando's identity is shaped in part in opposition to racial and ethnic difference, the novel remains much more interested in gender, sex, and class.

23. LuAnn McCracken, who focuses on the maternal in relation to the formation of Rachel's identity, observes that Rachel's experience in the native village has received surprisingly little attention; Laura Doyle, one of the few critics to take up McCracken's challenge, persuasively links Rachel's "substitution of a man for a mother" to a corresponding substitution of "racial difference for gender solidarity," but her discussion focuses primarily on *Melymbrosia*, an earlier version of the novel, not on the much more developed scene in the published text of *The Voyage Out*. See LuAnn McCracken, " 'The synthesis of my being': Autobiography and the Reproduction of Identity in Virginia Woolf," *Tulsa Studies in Women's Literature* 9:1 (1990): 59–78, and Laura Doyle, *Bordering on the Body: the Racial Mix of Modern Fiction and Culture* (New York and Oxford: Oxford University Press, 1994), 148.

24. Although Woolf studies has devoted considerable attention to new media in recent years, postcards have gone unremarked. See, for instance, Diane Gillespie, " 'Her Kodak Printed at His Head': Virginia Woolf and Photography," in *Virginia Woolf: Themes and Variations*, ed. Vara Neverow-Turk and Mark Hussey (New York: Pace University Press, 1993), 90–109; Michele Pridmore-Brown, "1939–40: Of Virginia Woolf, Gramophones, and Fascism," *Publications of the Modern Language Association of America* 113 (May 1998): 408–21; and the essays in *Virginia Woolf in the Age of Mechanical Reproduction*, ed. Pamela L. Caughie (New York and London: Garland, 2000). For an intermedial approach to the shaping power of the tourist gaze, including a chapter on postcards in relation to early cinema, see Ellen Strain, *Public Places, Private Journeys: Ethnography, Entertainment, and the Tourist Gaze* (New Brunswick, N. J. and London: Rutgers University Press, 2003).

25. Frank Staff, *The Picture Postcard and its Origins* (London: Lutterworth Press, 1966), 56.

26. *Third Report on the Work Conducted for the Government at Wellington House* (London: Her Majesty's Stationery Office, 1916), 100.

27. All postcards described or reproduced here come from the Historical Postcard Collection or the African Postcard Collection, Manuscripts and Archives, Yale University Library. Some cards can be dated precisely via postmarks; the approximate dates of others can be inferred from their resemblance to other cards and from their design. All the cards used in this essay date from the first decade of the century. I thank the Yale Library for giving me access to the collections and William Massa in particular for his assistance in sorting through these massive holdings.

28. Richard Carline, *Pictures in the Post* (Bedford: Gordon Fraser, 1959), xv.

29. Howard Woody, "International Postcards: Their History, Production, and Distribution (Circa 1895 to 1915)," in *Delivering Views: Distant Cultures in Early Postcards*, ed. Christraud M. Geary and Virginia-Lee Webb (Washington and London: Smithsonian Institution Press, 1998), 43.

30. See, for instance, Rita Felski, *The Gender of Modernity* (Cambridge, Mass.: Harvard University Press, 1995), 66.

31. Ezra Pound, *Literary Essays of Ezra Pound*, ed. T. S. Eliot (New York: New Directions, 1968), 4.

32. Jerome Christensen, *Practicing Enlightenment: Hume and the Formation of a Literary Career* (Madison: University of Wisconsin Press, 1987), 188.

33. Susan Stewart, *On Longing* (Baltimore: John Hopkins University Press, 1984), 133–69.

34. See Woolf, *The Collected Essays of Virginia Woolf*, ed. Leonard Woolf, 4 vols. (New York: Harcourt, Brace, and World, 1966–67), 2:182. Compare Staff, *Picture Postcard*, 49.

35. For the text of the card, see Charles Saumarez Smith, "A Question of Fame: Virginia Woolf and the National Portrait Gallery," *Charleston Magazine* 12 (1995): 5–9.

36. Woolf, *Collected Essays*, 4:67.

37. Woolf, *The Waves* (New York: Harcourt, Brace, 1931), 60.

38. Woolf, *Jacob's Room* (New York: Harcourt, Brace, Jovanovich, 1960), 170.

39. For the history of the White City, see F. A. Fletcher and A. D. Brooks, *British and Foreign Exhibitions and their Postcards, Part 1 (1900–1914)* (Holborn: Fleetways Press, 1978), 21. For the ideological dimension of exhibitions, see Tony Bennett, *The Rise of the Museum* (London and New York: Routledge, 1995), 80–82, 169, 179; Anne McClintock, *Imperial Leather: Race, Gender and Sexuality in the Colonial Contest* (New York: Routledge, 1995), 56–61 and 207–31. In *Fair Representations: World's Fairs and the Modern World*, ed. Robert W. Rydell and Nancy Gwinn (Amsterdam: VU University Press, 1994), see Burton Benedict, "Rituals of Representation: Ethnic Stereotypes and Colonized Peoples at World's Fairs," 28–61, and Aram Yengoyan, "Culture, Ideology, and World's Fairs: Colonized and Colonizer in Comparative Perspectives," 62–83. See also Robert W. Rydell, *All the World's a Fair: Visions of Empire at American International Expositions, 1876–1916* (Chicago: University of Chicago Press, 1984), 2–8, 64–67, 160–63.

40. Paul Greenhalgh, *Ephemeral Vistas: The "Expositions Universelles," Great Exhibitions and World's Fairs, 1851–1939* (Manchester: Manchester University Press, 1988), 82.

41. Robert W. Rydell, "Souvenirs of Imperialism: World's Fair Postcards," in Geary and Webb, *Delivering Views*, 54.

42. Greenhalgh, *Ephemeral Vistas*, 82. Reconstructed native villages emerged as a new genre in international exhibitions at the 1878 Paris exhibition. For earlier English displays of cultural and racial others, see Richard Altick, *The Shows of London* (Cambridge, Mass.: Harvard University Press, 1978), 268–87. These traveling displays, affiliated with freak shows and cabinets of curiosities, typically lacked the totalizing impulse of the native villages that emerged from the exhibitionary complex in the second half of the nineteenth century.

43. *Daily Programme: Imperial International Exhibition, London, 1909* (Derby and London: Bemrose and Sons, 1909), 50–51. Hereafter cited in the text.

44. See Christopher Miller, "Hallucinations of France and Africa in the Colonial Exhibition of 1931 and Ousmane Socé's *Mirage de Paris*," *Paragraph* 18, no. 1 (March 1995): 39–63, and Meg Armstrong, " 'A Jumble of Foreignness': The Sublime Musayums of Nineteenth-Century Fairs and Expositions," *Cultural Critique* 21–23 (1992–93): 199–250. Miller, discussing the French Colonial Exhibition of 1931, uses the phrase *"state-sponsored hallucination"* to characterize colonial myth-making as an attempt to persuade the spectator that the "there" of colonial spaces are now the "here" (44, 51; italics in original). Cf. Armstrong: "Illusions of voyage, exotic objects displayed at exhibitions . . . encouraged the dreaming or hallucination of the exotic other and exotic places" (241).

45. If Woolf visited London's Imperial International Exhibition of 1909, her impressions of it are not extant. Yet in her account of the British Empire Exhibition, "Thunder at Wembley," Woolf observes that "At Earls Court and the White City, *so far as memory serves*, there was little trouble from [nature]" (*Essays*, 3:411; emphasis added). The White City was first built for the 1908 Franco-British Exhibition and then refurbished for the 1909 exhibition, the first international exhibition held in London since the Great Exhibitions of 1851 and 1861. Woolf also refers to the Earls Court Exhibition facilities in her letters and essays. See *Essays*, 2:290; *Letters*, 3:95; and Virginia Woolf, *Granite and Rainbow: Essays* (New York: Harcourt, Brace, 1958), 213–14. Woolf's attention to London's history of exhibitions registers in *Jacob's Room* as Clara and Bowley wander into Hyde Park (167).

46. Woolf may have read about the myth of the Amazon warrior in Elizabethan travel narratives, but the *Daily Programme*'s description of the Dahomey Village indicates how pervasive the myth was in popular culture: "It is a complete community, with its chief, warriors, and members of the tribe of Amazons, that band of women who guard their king in far-away Africa, and who are distinguished for their bravery in battle" (50).

47. A. W. Coysh notes, in *The Dictionary of Picture Postcards in Britain, 1894–1939* (Woodbridge, Suffolk: Baron Publishing, 1984) that "every exhibition resulted in a flood of postcards: souvenir cards, advertisers' cards and official cards" (90). Robert W. Rydell adds that by the time "the 1900 Exposition Universelle closed its gates in Paris, picture postcards had become as deeply ingrained in the exposition experience as Ferris wheels, the Eiffel Tower, and ethnological villages" (Rydell, "Souvenirs of Imperialism," in *Delivering Views*, 52). For reproductions of such postcards, see Fletcher and Brooks, *British and Foreign Exhibitions and their Postcards*.

48. Virginia Woolf, *Between the Acts* (San Diego: Harcourt, Brace, Jovanovich, 1969), 149, 153.

49. E. M. Forster, "The Birth of an Empire," in *Abinger Harvest* (New York: Harcourt, Brace, 1936), 47. Like Woolf's, Forster's account is informed by class distinctions. Often casting himself as a mildly dazed spectator, he also steps back from the imperial spectacle: paying customers exit an attraction "in little spouts,

NOTES TO CHAPTER TWO 293

like steam from an exhaust," implying that they, unlike the mocking highbrow journalist, are simply fuel for what Forster considers the "true denizens of Wembley," the machines (48, 47).

50. See Louise A. DeSalvo, *Virginia Woolf's First Voyage* (Totowa, N.J.: Rowman and Littlefield, 1980), 121, who makes the connection with Woolf's nickname and the goats, which are identified as Willoughby's cargo in earlier drafts.

51. Woolf's letters to Victoria Ocampo indulge her fantasies of South America as a land of pampas grass and butterflies. See *Letters*, 5:348–49, 395–96, 439.

52. The trope resonates with Woolf's critique of Jane Austen's "dominion of hedges," or the propagation of class hierarchies, as well as with Rachel's sense of Austen as too much like "a tight plait" (*The Voyage Out*, 49). Virginia Woolf, *The Moment and Other Essays* (San Diego: Harcourt, Brace, 1975), 151.

53. My reading is indebted to the only book to devote sustained critical attention to the representation of women in colonial postcards, Malek Alloula's pioneering study of Algerian postcards, *The Colonial Harem*, trans. Myrna Gozich and Wlad Godzich (Minneapolis: University of Minnesota Press, 1986). For more on colonial postcards, see the essays in Geary and Webb, *Delivering Views*. Given the usual gender dynamics of colonial figuration—male colonizer penetrates and masters the virgin territory—it is appropriate that apart from *Delivering Views*, the only other history of picture postcards to reproduce a series of colonial cards is William Ouellete and Barbara Jones's *Erotic Postcards* (New York: Excalibur Books, 1977), 108–11.

54. See Felix Bryk, *Dark Rapture: The Sex Life of the African Negro*, trans. Arthur J. Norton (New York: Walden Publications, 1939). Bryk's effort to refute the stereotype suggests how deeply entrenched it was. The book is intended "to demonstrate that the Negress is *naturally* endowed with sexual desires and capabilities, and with erotic emotions and sensations, that are in no way different from . . . those of the white woman" (27, emphasis in original). Sander Gilman's persuasive argument that nineteenth-century perceptions of racial otherness and inferiority were typically projected onto the image of the sexualized black woman provides a suggestive context for Rachel's journey upriver. On one hand, the longstanding link between untrammeled sexuality and blacks underscores through antithesis the domestic binding of female sexuality in Woolf's native village. On the other hand, late nineteenth-century representations of the sexualized black female as "the source of corruption and disease" suggest a submerged symbolic linkage between Rachel's entry into the village and the fever that kills her. See Sander Gilman, "Black Bodies, White Bodies: Toward an Iconography of Female Sexuality in Late Nineteenth-Century Art, Medicine, and Literature," in *"Race," Writing, and Difference*, ed. Henry Louis Gates, Jr. (Chicago: University of Chicago Press, 1986), 230.

55. Originally brought to the New World by West African slaves, the banjo entered into white urban culture in the mid-nineteenth century via minstrel shows and enjoyed a craze in England and America from about 1890 to 1930. The popularity of minstrel shows evidently transformed the banjo into a signifier of blackness, for by the late nineteenth century, as the banjo began to be incorporated into light classical music, Joel Chandler Harris (author of the Uncle

Remus tales) felt compelled to minimize the slave origins of the instrument in a controversial article in the *Critic* in 1883. See Jay Scot Odell, "Banjo," *New Grove Dictionary of Music and Musicians*, ed. Stanley Sadie, 20 vols. (London: Macmillan, 1980), 2:118–21.

56. Often it is impossible to tell whether a postcard was actually mailed or simply brought home as a souvenir; postmarks alone do not tell the story because some cards, particularly those featuring risqué pictures, were mailed in envelopes.

57. An inscription on the back of the West African card entitled "Motherhood" (figure 2.10) testifies to a related anxiety: "Dear Kath, Isn't this friccan nice. If they only stayed like this. Love Auntie Bell." Possibly the West African woman prompted Auntie Bell to bemoan the exhausting and largely female labor of child rearing. But the remark also bespeaks an English need to assert imperial control over subject races, here expressed as the desire to make Africa truly be, as Hegel claimed it was, "the land of childhood . . . lying beyond the days of self-conscious history." See G.W.F. Hegel, *Philosophy of History*, quoted in *The Post-Colonial Studies Reader*, ed. Bill Ashcroft, Gareth Griffiths and Helen Tiffin (London and New York: Routledge, 1995), 15. Nigeria would not be born for another sixty years, but already, with images of West African women and children flowing into England, boundaries between domestic and colonial spaces were eroding, and the casual ugliness of Auntie Bell's remark discloses British anxieties about what it would mean to let these subject people reproduce, in freedom.

58. See Louise A. DeSalvo, ed., introduction to *Melymbrosia: An Early Version of "The Voyage Out"* (New York: New York Public Library, 1982), xii–xliv; and idem, *Virginia Woolf's First Voyage*, 8, 75. Elizabeth Heine has also done extensive work on these revisions ("The Earlier *Voyage Out*: Virginia Woolf's First Novel," *Bulletin of Research in the Humanities* 82 (1979): 294–316; "New Light on *Melymbrosia*," in *Virginia Woolf Miscellanies: Proceedings of the First Annual Conference on Virginia Woolf, Pace University, New York, June 7–9, 1991*, ed. Mark Hussey and Vara Neverow-Turk [New York: Pace University Press, 1992], 227–30). Also invaluable is Heine, "Virginia Woolf's Revisions of *The Voyage Out*," in *The Voyage Out*, ed. Elizabeth Heine (London: Hogarth, 1990), 399–463. Often supplementing and correcting DeSalvo, Heine's edition prints important passages missing from *Melymbrosia* and others cut from late typescripts of *The Voyage Out*. For an attempt to theorize the relationship between *Melymbrosia* and *The Voyage Out*, see Susan Stanford Friedman, "Spatialization, Narrative Theory, and Virginia Woolf's *The Voyage Out*," in *Ambiguous Discourse: Feminist Narratology and British Women Writers*, ed. Kathy Mezei (Chapel Hill: University of North Carolina Press, 1996), 109–36. See also Rachel Blau DuPlessis, *Writing Beyond the Ending: Narrative Strategies of Twentieth-Century Women Writers* (Bloomington: Indiana University Press, 1985), 49–53.

59. Leonard Woolf, *Beginning Again* (New York: Harcourt, Brace, and World, 1963), 148. For Virginia's acknowledgment in November 1912 of having read *The Village in the Jungle*, see *Letters*, 2:12.

60. Although Mark Hussey observes that "the early fictions of Virginia Woolf (*Melymbrosia, The Voyage Out*, and *Night and Day*) and Leonard

Woolf (*The Village in the Jungle, The Wise Virgins*) create a complex structure of comments upon one another and upon the issues of affectivity, engagement, marriage, and passion in which their authors were themselves so caught up between 1906 and 1919," he is interested in *Night and Day* as a response to *The Wise Virgins*, not in *The Voyage Out* to *The Village in the Jungle* ("Refractions of Desire: The Early Fiction of Virginia and Leonard Woolf," *Modern Fiction Studies* 38 [1992]: 127). Both Natania Rosenfeld and Theresa M. Thompson compare *The Village in the Jungle* and *The Voyage Out*, but neither addresses the former's influence on the latter (Rosenfeld, *Outsiders Together: Virginia and Leonard Woolf* [Princeton, N.J.: Princeton University Press, 2000]; Thompson, "Confronting Modernist Racism in the Post-Colonial Classroom: Teaching Virginia Woolf's *The Voyage Out* and Leonard Woolf's *The Village in the Jungle*," in *Re: Reading, Re: Writing, Re: Teaching Virginia Woolf: Selected Papers from the Fourth Annual Conference on Virginia Woolf, Bard College, Annandale-on-Hudson, New York, June 9–12, 1994*, ed. Eileen Barrett and Patricia Cramer [New York: Pace University Press, 1995], 241–50). George Spater and Ian Parsons write as if the couple never read one another's work (*A Marriage of True Minds: An Intimate Portrait of Leonard and Virginia Woolf* [New York: Harcourt, Brace, Jovanovich, 1977]). Peter F. Alexander notes that when Leonard and Virginia were finishing their novels, they were living in the same house on Brunswick Square on separate floors; they "would each write about 500 words in the morning and spend the afternoon walking, sitting in parks and talking about their work." But he then argues that Virginia could only have influenced Leonard, not vice versa, because the "form and content [of *The Voyage Out*] were fixed long before Leonard entered her life" (*Leonard and Virginia Woolf: A Literary Partnership* [New York: St. Martin's, 1992], 72, 73). Lyndall Gordon writes in a similar vein: "Although she completed two drafts of *The Voyage Out* after her engagement, they were the last of numerous drafts and not much affected by the new relationship" (*Virginia Woolf: A Writer's Life* [Oxford: Oxford University Press, 1984], 109). Of all critics writing on *The Voyage Out*, only Heine acknowledges the possible influence of Leonard, remarking in passing that "Virginia Woolf's more sympathetic later portrayal of the native village probably also reflects her husband's first novel, *The Village in the Jungle*" ("Virginia Woolf's Revisions," 435). Although Heine does not explore intertextual relations between the two novels, she often shows how Woolf's relationship with Leonard can be felt in specific revisions (e.g., 402–3, 431, 434–35, 440).

61. See Woolf, "Mr Conrad: A Conversation," *Essays*, 3:378; "Mr. Conrad's Crisis," *Essays* 2:227; and "Mr Conrad's 'Youth,'" *Essays*, 2:158. Woolf took the phrase "moments of vision" from a passage in *Lord Jim*, which she cites in her 1917 review of the novel (*Essays* 2:142). See n. 70.

62. See Woolf, "Jane Austen," in *The Common Reader, First Series*, ed. Andrew McNeillie (San Diego: Harcourt, Brace, Jovanovich, 1984), 144. Hereafter cited in the text.

63. Elleke Boehmer discusses the Conradian qualities in Leonard's letters home from Ceylon between 1905 and 1911 and in his later short story, "Pearls and Swine," published in 1921 but drafted as early as 1912; see " 'Immeasurable

Strangeness' in Imperial Times: Leonard Woolf and W. B. Yeats," in *Modernism and Empire*, ed. Howard J. Booth and Nigel Rigby (Manchester: Manchester University Press, 2000), esp. 95–98, 104–6.

64. See Leonard Woolf, "Conrad's Vision: The Illumination of Romance," *English Literature in Transition* 36 (1993): 286–302. Leonard praised *Youth* (1902) in particular, the volume in which *Heart of Darkness* appeared, as exemplary of Conrad's ability to blend realism and romance. For commentary on the lecture and Leonard's interest in Conrad, see J. H. Stape, "The Critic as Autobiographer: Conrad under Leonard Woolf's Eyes," *English Literature in Transition* 36 (1993): 277–85.

65. E.F.C. Ludowyk, introduction to *The Village in the Jungle*, by Leonard Woolf (Oxford: Oxford University Press, 1981), ix. Subsequent quotations from the novel are from this edition and are cited in the text.

66. Hermione Lee speculates that Woolf must have felt threatened by the comparative ease with which Leonard finished *The Village in the Jungle*, published two years before *The Voyage Out* (Hermione Lee, *Virginia Woolf* [London: Chatto and Windus, 1996], 326). For Woolf's envy of Leonard's achievement, see *Letters*, 2:18–20.

67. For one of many examples, see the transformation of an incidental Conradian cadence into a complex allusion in Woolf's revision of the scene in which Helen reads aloud a letter from Rachel's father (*Melymbrosia*, 144; *The Voyage Out*, 180). Underlying the revised passage is the scene in *Heart of Darkness* in which Marlow first encounters the Company's chief accountant. See Joseph Conrad, *Heart of Darkness*, ed. Robert Kimbrough (New York: Norton, 1988), 21–22. Hereafter cited as *Heart of Darkness*.

68. Woolf's 1917 essay on *Lord Jim* suggests that such descriptions made a deep impression on her: "The sea and the tropical forests dominate us and almost overpower us" (*Essays*, 2:143).

69. Of Marlow's moment of revelation in response to the French lieutenant in *Lord Jim*, Woolf wrote: "That, so it strikes us, is the way in which Mr Conrad's mind works; he has a 'moment of vision' in which he sees people as if he had never seen them before; he expounds his vision, and we see it, too. These visions are the best things in his books" (*Essays*, 2:142). Oddly, T. S. Eliot, who wrote that removing the figure of the strong, isolated European male from Conrad's novels would yield the equivalent of Woolf's, missed this fundamental connection between the two: "Elle n'illumine pas par éclairs soudains mais répand une lumière douce et tranquille" [She does not illuminate with sudden flashes but casts a soft, gentle light] ("Les lettres anglaises: Le roman anglais contemporain," *Nouvelle revue française* 28 [1927]: 673).

70. Woolf, *A Room of One's Own* (New York: Harcourt, Brace, Jovanovich, 1957), 79. Hereafter cited in the text.

71. Lee, *Virginia Woolf*, surveys the key accounts and concludes that it was "not an a-sexual marriage" but was grounded in "affectionate cuddling and play" rather than in intercourse or other forms of explicitly sexual behavior (331–33).

72. See Roger Poole, *The Unknown Virginia Woolf*, 4th ed. (Cambridge: Cambridge University Press, 1995), 74–78; and Alexander, *Leonard and Virginia Woolf*, 73.

73. Douglas Kerr, "Stories of the East: Leonard Woolf and the Genres of Colonial Discourse," *English Literature in Transition* 41 (1998):272, 270, 273.

74. Compare Christine Froula, "Out of the Chrysalis: Female Initiation and Female Authority in Virginia Woolf's *The Voyage Out*," *Tulsa Studies in Women's Literature* 5, no. 1 (1986):76, and Susan Stanford Friedman, "Virginia Woolf's Pedagogical Scenes of Reading: *The Voyage Out, The Common Reader*, and her 'Common Readers,'" *Modern Fiction Studies* 38, no. 1 (1992): 109.

75. For a detailed reading of the lesbian subtext in this and other scenes, see Patricia Smith, "'The Things People Don't Say': Lesbian Panic in *The Voyage Out*," in *Virginia Woolf: Lesbian Readings*, ed. Eileen Barrett and Patricia Cramer (New York: New York University Press, 1997), 133–40.

76. D. H. Lawrence, *Women in Love* (London: Penguin Books, 1995), 12.

77. All references are much clearer in *Melymbrosia*: "The woman was sent to fetch biscuits drink and scented sweetmeats. She made a sign of reverence as she approached the strangers. Their hands felt strangely large and English as they took the food and their bodies well-nourished and formal, like soldiers in the midst of a crowd" (211).

78. The parallel between Rachel and the native women is anticipated earlier in the novel by a complex allusion to *Heart of Darkness* (see n. 67, above). Just as Conrad connects the imposition of domestic labor with large-scale colonial atrocities by linking the accountant to Kurtz, so Woolf insistently links micro- and macropolitics.

79. In "Souvenirs of Imperialism," Rydell (see n. 41, above) offers a related reading of exhibition postcards in which the smile suggests resistance to the dehumanizing frame of the reconstructed native village.

80. See Laura E. Donaldson, *Decolonizing Feminisms: Race, Gender, and Empire-Building* (Chapel Hill and London: University of North Carolina Press, 1992). Donaldson borrows the phrase "white solipsism" (1) from Adrienne Rich to characterize a privileging of white perspectives in some first-generation feminist criticism.

81. The full-blown emergence of racial treatments of modernism begins in 1994. See for instance, Michael North, *The Dialect of Modernism* (New York: Oxford University Press, 1994); the first two numbers of *Modernism/Modernity* 1, no. 1 (January 1994) and 1, no. 2 (April 1994), a two-part special issue on race and modernism; and Doyle, *Bordering on the Body* (1994).

82. Woolf played with racialized cross-dressing by touring the British battleship in black face at the very time she was expanding in revision the scene in the indigenous settlement. Quentin Bell reproduces a picture of the costumed and blackened pranksters in *Virginia Woolf* (New York: Harcourt, Brace, Jovanovich, 1972), between pp. 140 and 141. Jean E. Kennard points out that the conjunction of class and race in the hoax—they dress as royalty after all—complicates Kathy J. Phillips's claim that the African costume betokens Woolf's identification with oppressed groups. See Jean E. Kennard, "Power and Sexual Ambiguity: The *Dreadnought* Hoax, *The Voyage Out, Mrs. Dalloway* and *Orlando*," *Journal of Modern Literature* 20, no. 2 (1996):149–64, esp. 152. See also Phillips, *Virginia Woolf against Empire*, 248.

83. The tension between granting the women independent subjectivity and transforming them into natural objects is more pronounced in *Melymbrosia*. On one hand, the texture and feel of the English hands that receive sweetmeats from the natives is rendered from the native perspective. On the other hand, "their faces were an oily brown, and this perhaps explained why they did not look like faces; they seemed neither old nor young, neither clever malicious women, or sweet sympathetic women; they seemed more like fruit hung high up in their own forest trees. She owned that she knew nothing about them" (*Melymbrosia*, 211–12).

84. In one of the few essays on Woolf and race, the Jamaican writer Michelle Cliff corroborates my argument in her reflections on the Moor's head hanging from the rafters that Orlando stabs at in the opening of *Orlando*. Observing that "the European gaze was obsessed with the African head," Cliff works her way through Woolf's responses to sculpture from the Ivory Coast and Congo and through representations of racial difference in other English authors before concluding that the one issue to escape Woolf's impulse to rebuke "order, the expected, the inherited" was racial hierarchy. Despite Orlando's rejection of inherited orders, the Moor's head remains "mere device, curiosity; like the artists' whose work Woolf gazed at in the 1920 show" (102). One of the strengths of Cliff's essay is her ability to pursue a racial critique of Woolf without losing sight of all that remains valuable in her work. See Michelle Cliff, "Virginia Woolf and the Imperial Gaze: A Glance Askew," *Virginia Woolf: Emerging Perspectives*, ed. Mark Hussey and Vara Neverow (New York: Pace University Press, 1994), 91–102.

85. Compare Michael H. Levenson, *A Genealogy of Modernism: A Study of English Literary Doctrine, 1908–1922* (Cambridge: Cambridge University Press, 1984): "Vague terms still signify. Such is the case with 'modernism': it is at once vague and unavoidable" (vii).

86. See Bonnie Kime Scott, ed., *Gender of Modernism: A Critical Anthology* (Bloomington: Indiana University Press, 1990).

87. Sandra M. Gilbert and Susan Gubar, *No Man's Land: The Place of the Woman Writer in the Twentieth Century*, 3 vols. (New Haven, Conn.: Yale University Press, 1988–94).

88. Bonnie Kime Scott, *Women of 1928*, vol. 1 of *Refiguring Modernism* (Bloomington: Indiana University Press, 1995), xvi–xliii.

89. For a representative example, see Karen Lawrence, "Joyce and Feminism," in *The Cambridge Companion to James Joyce*, ed. Derek Attridge (Cambridge: Cambridge University Press, 1990), 237–58.

90. See Julia Kristeva, *Revolution in Poetic Language*, trans. Margaret Waller (New York: Columbia University Press, 1984).

91. Marianne DeKoven, *Rich and Strange: Gender, History, Modernism* (Princeton, N.J.: Princeton University Press, 1991), 4. Hereafter cited in the text.

92. In a particularly suggestive sequence, Rachel castigates Helen as "lazy" and "only half alive" when she balks at the idea of an expedition upriver (*The Voyage Out*, 248); then, as they walk side by side, an ambiguous pronoun reference introducing a sequence of free indirect discourse momentarily conflates the two women, as if the speculations of Helen-Rachel about the existence of a

"profound and reasonless law . . . moulding them all to its liking" were being enacted in the merging of their thoughts (ibid., 249).

93. Makiko Minow-Pinkney draws on Julia Kristeva's appropriation of Jacques Lacan's distinction between the semiotic and the symbolic to trace the emergence in Woolf of an *écriture féminine* dialectically engaged with the symbolic (*Virginia Woolf and the Problem of the Subject* [Brighton: Harvester, 1987]). Minow-Pinkney does not discuss *The Voyage Out*.

94. Suzette Henke, "Language, Memory, Desire," in *Virginia Woolf: Emerging Perspectives*, 107.

95. Virginia Woolf, "Professions for Women," in *The Death of the Moth, and Other Essays* (New York: Harcourt, Brace, 1942), 237; Woolf, *The Pargiters: The Novel-Essay Portion of "The Years,"* ed. Mitchell A. Leaska (London: Hogarth, 1977), xxix–xxx.

CHAPTER THREE
IMPRESSIONISM AND PROPAGANDA

1. The *OED* entry for "irreticence" lists only Woolf's *Night and Day* (1919); the sole citation in the entry for the plural "irreticences" is her collection of essays *The Captain's Death Bed* (1950). (In fact, Woolf also uses the plural in *Mrs. Dalloway.*) The entry for "irreticent" lists two citations, one from 1864, and the second from Woolf's "A Letter to a Young Poet" (1932).

2. Ford, "On Impressions" (1914), in *The Critical Writings of Ford Madox Ford*, ed. Frank MacShane (Lincoln: University of Nebraska Press, 1964), 54. Hereafter cited in the text as *Critical Writings*.

3. Peter Buitenhuis describes *Between St. Dennis and St. George* as perhaps "the most interesting propaganda book of the war" owing to its modernist narrative technique (what Ford in his collaboration with Conrad called "*progression d'éffet*"); *When Blood Is Their Argument* is equally modernist in this sense. See Buitenhuis, *The Great War of Words: British, American, and Canadian Propaganda and Fiction, 1914–1933* (Vancouver: University of British Columbia Press, 1987), 45.

4. In "Techniques" (1935), Ford declares that the impressionist "must render: never report"; *Critical Writings*, 67.

5. Robie Macauley, "The Good Ford," in *The Kenyon Critics*, ed. John Crowe Ransome (Cleveland: The World Publishing Company, 1951), 151. Although accounts of Ford as a liar are legion, particularly in biographies of his acquaintances, it should be pointed out that Macauley is here concerned with rescuing Ford from the oblivion into which he had fallen in the decade following his death.

6. Ford Madox Ford, *Ancient Lights* (London: Chapman and Hall, [1911]): "This book, in short, is full of inaccuracies as to facts, but its accuracy as to impressions is absolute. . . . I don't really deal in facts, I have for facts a most profound contempt" (xv). Ford here cites sincerity as the sole criterion of the truth of the impression.

7. The books were very well received. For excerpts of reviews in England, the United States, and France, see David Dow Harvey, *Ford Madox Ford,*

1873–1939: A Bibliography of Works and Criticism (Princeton: Princeton University Press, 1962), 322–33.

8. Michael H. Levenson, *A Genealogy of Modernism* (Cambridge: Cambridge University Press, 1984), 48.

9. C.F.G. Masterman, *Report of the Work of the Bureau established for the purpose of laying before Neutral Nations and the Dominions the case of Great Britain and her Allies*, June 7, 1915, p. 2. Public Record Office, Kew, England; INF 4/5.

10. Adolf Hitler, *Mein Kampf*, editorial sponsors John Chamberlain, Sidney B. Fay et al. (New York: Reynal and Hitchcock, 1939), 227–42. For the German debt to the British institutionalization of propaganda, see Phillip Knightley, *The First Casualty: From Crimea to Vietnam: The War Correspondent as Hero, Propagandist, and Myth Maker* (New York: Harcourt, Brace, Jovanovich, 1975), 79–112, 217–41. Perhaps it should not need saying, but the connection between Nazi and British propaganda is in no way meant to imply a moral equivalence.

11. Ivor Nicholson, "An Aspect of British Official Wartime Propaganda," *Cornhill Magazine*, series 3, vol. 70, no. 419 (May 1931):606.

12. Initially published as separate volumes in 1916 and 1917, Buchan's books were later reprinted in one volume as *The Battle of the Somme* (New York: George H. Doran, 1917). Apart from boosterish interjections about the "obtuseness that has always marked [Germany's] estimate of other races" (17) and passing references to the "discipline and courage and resolution" of "the flower of the manhood of the British Empire" (25), Buchan's account offers a reliable history of the battle.

13. On the government's failure to distance itself from fabrications and deceptions, see M. L. Sanders and Philip M. Taylor, *British Propaganda during the First World War, 1914–1918* (London: Macmillan, 1982), 264.

14. Mary Poovey, *A History of the Modern Fact* (Chicago and London: University of Chicago Press, 1998), 1–28.

15. James Morgan Reid, *Atrocity Propaganda, 1914–1919* (New Haven: Yale University Press, 1941), 51–77. Hereafter cited in the text.

16. Committee on Alleged German Outrages, *Report of the Committee on Alleged German Outrages* (London: His Majesty's Stationery Office, 1915), 4.

17. For more on this meeting, see the introduction, above.

18. Nevertheless, only the next year Ford was suspected of being responsible for the expulsion of D. H. Lawrence and his wife Frieda from Cornwall as German spies. That there is no credible evidence to back up such a claim did not prevent one of Lawrence's biographers, Jeffrey Meyers, from elaborating the charge, adding that Ford was also likely responsible for the suppression of *The Rainbow*. See Max Saunders, *Ford Madox Ford: A Dual Life*, 2 vols. (Oxford and New York: Oxford University Press, 1996), 1:476–78.

19. Violet Hunt, in collaboration with Ford Madox Ford, *The Desirable Alien at Home in Germany* (London: Chatto and Windus, 1913), x. Ford wrote a preface and two chapters for Hunt, whom he was hoping to marry at the time.

20. Ford evidently persuaded himself that his ploy had worked and referred in print to Violet as his wife, causing Elsie to sue. See Arthur Mizener, *The Saddest*

Story (New York: World Publishing, 1971), 201–22. The attempt to claim citizenship returned to dog him during the war when someone wrote to Scotland Yard claiming that "Mr. Hueffer [as he was still known] had obtained a divorce in the German courts *by suing as a German subject* and that he must therefore be either a German or a bigamist" (emphasis in original). Scotland Yard investigated Ford's nationality and came across an interview he gave to the *Daily Mirror* before the war in which he claimed to be a German citizen by virtue of being heir to a large estate in Prussia (he was not). M.I.5 consequently investigated Ford in 1918 and with the help of the Army General Staff Ford was exonerated in March of that year. For materials bearing on Ford's military record and the investigation, see WO339/37369 at the Public Record Office at Kew, England.

21. Ford Madox Ford, *When Blood Is Their Argument: An Analysis of Prussian Culture* (New York and London: Hodder and Stoughton, 1915), 213; Ford, *Between St. Dennis and St. George: A Sketch of Three Civilizations* (London, New York, and Toronto: Hodder and Stoughton, 1915), 66. Both hereafter cited in the text.

22. Thomas C. Moser, *The Life in the Fiction of Ford Madox Ford* (Princeton: Princeton University Press, 1980), 199.

23. For Ford's politics, see Robert Green, *Ford Madox Ford: Prose and Politics* (Cambridge: Cambridge University Press, 1981), esp. 53–79.

24. Saunders, *Ford Madox Ford*, 2: 25–26.

25. Virginia Woolf, *The Moment and Other Essays* (San Diego: Harcourt, Brace, 1975), 151.

26. Ford Madox Ford, *Henry James* (New York: Albert and Charles Boni, 1915), 121, 120.

27. Ford Madox Ford, *The Good Soldier*, ed. Martin Stannard (New York: Norton, 1995), 100. Hereafter cited in the text.

28. Ford Madox Ford, *The Critical Attitude* (London: Duckworth, 1911), 106. Hereafter cited in the text as *Critical Attitude*. For a horrific example of Kipling's war propaganda, see his story "Mary Postgate," in which the title character finds a dying German paratrooper in her garden and takes pleasure in letting him die.

29. Joseph Conrad, *Heart of Darkness*, ed. Robert Kimbrough (New York: Norton, 1988), 30.

30. The topic has a long history in Conrad studies. For a recent treatment, see John G. Peters, *Conrad and Impressionism* (Cambridge: Cambridge University Press, 2001).

31. *Letters from Joseph Conrad, 1895 to 1924*, ed. Edward Garnett (London: Nonesuch Press, 1928), 107.

32. Virginia Woolf, *Mrs. Dalloway* (1925; rpt. San Diego: Harcourt, 1981), 65. Ian Watt's term for the way Conrad dramatizes the lag between perception and understanding, "delayed decoding," gets at a key point in Conrad: there is always something there to be decoded, something with a thereness starkly independent of divergent modes of perception. See Ian Watt, *Conrad in the Nineteenth Century* (Berkeley and Los Angeles: University of California Press, 1979), 175–79.

33. Noam Chomsky, *Media Control: The Spectacular Achievements of Propaganda* (New York: Seven Stories Press, 1997), 20–21.

34. Ford to Scott-James, *Letters of Ford Madox Ford*, ed. Richard M. Ludwig (Princeton: Princeton University Press, 1965), 40.

35. See Walter Lippmann, *Public Opinion* (New York: Harcourt, Brace, 1922), 3–32.

36. John B. Thompson, *The Media and Modernity* (Stanford: Stanford University Press, 1995), 214.

37. Although Mizener, *The Saddest Story*, notes in passing that in Marburg on vacation in 1910 "Ford became an enthusiastic patron of the cinematograph" (202), Ford's one foray into writing about film, "The Movies," in *Outlook* (August 21, 1915), is notable mainly as a comic exercise in how to write a column when one has nothing to say. Ford holds off even mentioning the movies until the ninth paragraph of the ten-paragraph article, at which point he admits that "with the history of kinematography I am not well acquainted. Mr. H. G. Wells assured me the other day that this is a very ancient art, and, since Mr. Wells is our greatest censor of inventions, I take his word for it. He told me that the Writing on the Wall was the first of the Movies. I dare say it was. I am at any rate certain that this art has a very great future for it" (240). Ford's point is that with British theater being so awful, it may be that the movies can serve as a fitter place for disposing of actors and playwrights. Ford claims to have been paid for the rights to one of his books by a film company that proceeded by cutting out "nearly the whole of the book," the results of which Ford found "queerish" but "entirely satisfactory" (240). Ford may be referring to the sale earlier in 1915 of the film rights to *Romance*, his collaboration with Conrad, for which they received $500. A film of the novel was ultimately made and released in 1927, but the 1915 option expired without a film being made. See Gene M. Moore, Review of Saunders, *Ford Madox Ford*, in the *Conradian* 23, no. 2 (Autumn 1998), in a virtual annex to the *Conradian*, http://www.josephconradsociety.org\conradian_review_moore.htm.

38. For an historical account of the perceived decay in public discourse caused by the massification of journalism, see Alan J. Lee, *The Origins of the Popular Press in England, 1855–1914* (London: Croom Helm, 1976), 15–20, 213–33.

39. Here Ford seems to be describing the historical context that eventually would produce the appeal of a politician such as former U.S. President Bill Clinton, whose ability to persuade voters that he could "feel their pain" set him apart from the stereotype of the professional politician.

40. Levenson, *Genealogy of Modernism*, 108; the following discussion draws on Levenson's argument.

41. Ibid., 118, cites this well-known passage from David Hume's *A Treatise of Human Nature*.

42. See Jesse Matz, *Literary Impressionism and Modernist Aesthetics* (Cambridge: Cambridge University Press, 2001), 1–52. The following two paragraphs are indebted to these pages and enriched by my conversations with the author.

43. Ibid., 37.

44. Ibid., 156. Matz neatly distinguishes their politics: "whereas for Williams the structure of feeling makes art herald to new cultural formations, for Ford the compromised impression makes art look backwards, and try for a return to the

past" (160). To put it another way, one could say that both Ford and Williams are drawing on nostalgia for a more "organic" way of life, one rooted in the English countryside, but whereas Ford is invested in the lord of the manor, Williams idealizes the laborer. For Williams on structures of feeling, see his *Marxism and Literature* (New York: Oxford University Press, 1977), 132–33.

45. Jacques Ellul, "Information and Propaganda," *Diogenes* 18 (Summer 1957):77.

46. Of the many commentaries on the posthuman in postmodernism, the most relevant to my discussion here are Ihab Hassan, "Prometheus as Performer: Toward a Posthumanist Culture? A University Masque in Five Scenes," *Georgia Review* 31 (1977), and N. Katherine Hayles, *How We Became Posthuman: Virtual Bodies in Cybernetics, Literature, and Informatics* (Chicago: University of Chicago Press, 1999).

47. See Saunders, *Ford Madox Ford*, 1:476.

48. *When Blood Is Their Argument* alludes to *Henry V*, IV.i.142; *Between St. Dennis and St. George* to V.ii.207. The play was rushed into production a few months into the war; see Samuel Hynes, *A War Imagined: The First World War and English Culture* (New York: Atheneum, 1991), 39.

49. I should point out, however, that it is difficult to gauge the effect of propaganda so many years after the fact. While reviews in *The Times* (March 30, 1915) and the *New York Times* (June 6, 1915) applaud, as I initially did, Ford's treatment of the German educational system, a *Times Literary Supplement* review (September 30, 1915) singles out for praise Ford's commentary on Captain Marryat.

50. For a valuable account of Ford's propaganda books by an historian, see L. L. Farrar, Jr., "The Artist as Propagandist," in *The Presence of Ford*, ed. Sondra J. Stang (Philadelphia: University of Pennsylvania Press, 1981), 144–160. On the German educational system, Farrar (156) cites Gordon Craig's *Germany 1866–1945* (1978).

51. Dominick LaCapra, *Soundings in Critical Theory* (Ithaca: Cornell University Press, 1989), 24.

52. E. M. Forster, *Howards End*, ed. Paul B. Armstrong (New York: Norton, 1998), 47.

53. See John Reichert, "Poor Florence Indeed! Or: *The Good Soldier* Retold," *Studies in the Novel* 14 (1982): 82–96. Reichert provides a highly diverting demonstration of the degree to which Dowell's conjectural narration permits a wide range of redemptive against-the-grain readings by defending Florence against "Dowell's friends," which is to say all those critics who assume that Dowell and Leonora speak the truth about Florence's alleged (from Reichert's skeptical point of view) affair with Edward.

54. See *The Good Soldier* (ed. Stannard) for a good sampling of critical response, especially the essays by Mark Schorer, Samuel Hynes, Arthur Mizener, Grover Smith, Michael Levenson, and Paul B. Armstrong.

55. For a recent account corroborating Lippmann, see Arthur G. Miller, "Historical and Contemporary Perspectives on Stereotyping," in *In the Eye of the Beholder: Contemporary Issues in Stereotyping*, ed. Arthur G. Miller (New York: Praeger Publishers, 1982), 1–40.

56. Despite Lippmann's groundbreaking work, too often treatments of stereotyping lose sight of this historical dimension. See, for instance, Sander L. Gilman, *Difference and Pathology: Stereotypes of Sexuality, Race, and Madness* (Ithaca and London: Cornell University Press, 1985), who acknowledges that stereotypes are an inevitable aspect of our attempts to make sense of the world, only to lapse into the assumption that stereotypical thinking derives from a lack of information rather than an excess (242). Similarly, Russell A. Jones, "Perceiving Other People: Stereotyping as a Process of Social Cognition," in Miller, *In the Eye of the Beholder* acknowledges the relation between information flows and stereotyping without addressing the historical emergence of the information society (41–91).

57. The most often cited arguments in this vein include Samuel Hynes, "The Epistemology of *The Good Soldier*," *Sewanee Review* 61 (1961): 224–35; Paul B. Armstrong, "The Epistemology of the *The Good Soldier*: A Phenomenological Reconsideration," *Criticism* 22 (1980):230–51; and Michael Levenson, "Character in *The Good Soldier*," *Twentieth Century Literature* 30 (1984): 373–87. Matz takes a different tack by arguing that the novel dramatizes why what he calls impressionist collaboration—the impressionist's reliance on the "virgin mind" of an embodied other—is doomed to fail; Matz, *Literary Impressionism*, 169.

58. For a discussion of the scene of radical skepticism in *Lord Jim*, which lies behind Dowell's first sight of Edward, see my *Joseph Conrad and the Fictions of Skepticism* (Stanford: Stanford University Press, 1990), 107–14.

59. Mark Schorer, "*The Good Soldier* as Comedy," in *The Good Soldier*, Norton Critical Edition, ed. Stannard, 310.

60. Carol Jacobs, "The (Too) Good Soldier: 'A Real Story,' " *Glyph* 3 (1978): 42. Jacobs reprints the essay, lightly revised, in her *Telling Time* (Baltimore and London: Johns Hopkins University Press, 1993). It is also excerpted in the *The Good Soldier*, Norton Critical Edition, ed. Stannard.

61. For an alternative reading, see Vincent J. Cheng, "Religious Differences in *The Good Soldier*: the "Protest" Scene," *Renascence* 37 (1985), who probes the epistemological uncertainties of Dowell's narration in order to suggest that Ford may have wished to present Catholicism, through Leonora, as a moral foil for the "relativism and emptiness of a beleaguered, faithless work exemplified by the tale and its teller" (247).

62. For a history of the essay's revisions and reprintings, see the editorial note on p. 305 of the *The Good Soldier*, Norton Critical Edition, ed. Stannard. The Schorer quotation is on p. 308.

63. Michael Levenson, "Character in *The Good Soldier*," 386, 383.

64. See David Trotter, *Paranoid Modernism: Literary Experiment, Psychosis, and the Professionalization of English Society* (New York and London: Oxford University Press, 2001), 210.

65. Ford Madox Ford, "Dedicatory Letter to Stella Ford" (1927), in *The Good Soldier*, Norton Critical Edition, ed. Stannard, 4.

66. For West's review of *The Good Soldier*, as well as her positive review of *Between St. Dennis and St. George*, see *Ford Madox Ford: The Critical Heritage*, ed. Frank MacShane (London and Boston: Routledge and Kegan Paul, 1972),

44–46, 51–54. For Thomas Seccombe's review of *The Good Soldier* as contributing to "the cant of anti-militarism," see *The Good Soldier*, Norton Critical Edition, ed. Stannard, 229–30.

67. Ford must have found Rebecca West's review in the *Daily News and Leader* particularly gratifying: "And when one has come to the end of this beautiful and moving story it is worth while reading the book over again simply to observe the wonders of its technique." See MacShane, *Ford Madox Ford*, 46. The review is also reprinted in *The Good Soldier*, Norton Critical Edition, ed. Stannard, 222–24.

68. The phrase comes from Ford's "Dedicatory Letter to Stella Ford," Norton Critical Edition, *The Good Soldier*, ed. Stannard, 5.

CHAPTER FOUR
JOYCE AND THE LIMITS OF POLITICAL PROPAGANDA

1. James Joyce, *A Portrait of the Artist as a Young Man*, ed. Chester G. Anderson (New York: Penguin, 1968), 203. Hereafter cited in the text.

2. Vincent J. Cheng, *Joyce, Race, and Empire* (New York: Cambridge University Press, 1995) (unnumbered front matter). For Joyce's attitude toward Pearse, see G. J. Watson, "The Politics of *Ulysses*," in *Joyce's "Ulysses": The Larger Perspective*, ed. Robert Newman and Weldon Thornton (Newark: University of Delaware Press, 1987), and Watson's *Irish Identity and the Literary Revival: Synge, Yeats, Joyce and O'Casey* (New York: Barnes and Noble, 1979).

3. The first revisionary treatment of Joyce's politics is Richard Ellmann, *The Consciousness of Joyce* (New York: Oxford University Press, 1977). Ironically, Ellmann was aiming to revise a version of Joyce that his own biography, *James Joyce* (1959; rev. ed. New York: Oxford University Press, 1982), had done much to canonize. The main impetus for Ellmann's revision was the discovery of a list of Joyce's books in his Trieste library, which included many socialist and anarchist tracts. My approach in this chapter aims for a less utopian working out of Ellmann's claim in *The Consciousness of Joyce* that "*Ulysses* creates new Irishmen to live in Arthur Griffith's new state" (89)—that is, in the Irish Free State, founded in 1922, the same year *Ulysses* was published. For an extended treatment (also grounded in Joyce's Trieste library) of Joyce as a kind of libertarian, see Dominic Manganiello, *Joyce's Politics* (London and Boston: Routledge and Kegan Paul, 1980). For Joyce as "the very prototype of the postcolonial artist," see Colin MacCabe, "Broken English," in *Futures for English*, ed. Colin MacCabe (Oxford: Manchester University Press, 1988), 12; for the sociolinguistic theory underpinning such approaches as well as brief remarks on Joyce, see Gilles Deleuze, *Kafka: Toward a Minor Literature* (Minneapolis: University of Minnesota Press, 1986), 16–27. For a critical account of the wave of historicist treatments of Joyce that began not long after Franco Moretti proclaimed in 1983 that nothing of value had ever emerged from interpreting Joyce on the basis of Ireland (*Signs Taken for Wonders*, rev. ed., trans. Susan Fischer, David Forgacs, and David Miller [London and New York: Verso,1988], 190),

see my "Joyce in the Postcolonial Tropics," *James Joyce Quarterly* 39 (Fall 2001): 69–92.

4. Declan Kiberd, "Anglo-Irish Attitudes," Field Day Theatre Company, in *Ireland's Field Day* (London: Hutchinson, 1985), 83.

5. James Joyce, *Ulysses: The Corrected Text* (New York: Random House, 1986), 17.1769–73. Hereafter cited in the text by episode and line number.

6. For a discussion of Reuters, see the introduction and x, note 70 thereto, above.

7. Cheryl Herr, *Joyce's Anatomy of Culture* (Urbana: University of Illinois Press, 1986), 112–14.

8. James Joyce, *Letters of James Joyce*, ed. Richard Ellmann, 3 vols. (New York: Viking Press, 1966), 3:22.

9. Claude Gandelman, *Reading Pictures, Viewing Texts* (Bloomington: Indiana University Press, 1991), 33.

10. Sontag, "Posters: Advertisement, Art, Political Artifact, Commodity," introduction to Dugald Stermer, *The Art of Revolution* (New York: McGraw-Hill, 1970), vii, x.

11. Given that most analytic models of postcolonialism are grounded in the breakup of empire following World War II, it may not be appropriate to use the same models to discuss Ireland's quite different historical circumstances. The alternative approach I undertake here is influenced by James Clifford's understanding of modern ethnographic subjectivity in terms of "discrepant cosmopolitanisms." See his "Traveling Cultures," in *Cultural Studies*, ed. Lawrence Grossberg, Cary Nelson, and Paula A. Treicher (New York: Routledge, 1992). Like Clifford, I wish to strip the term of its connotations of worldly leisure and to avoid invoking the history of socialism associated with "internationalism."

12. Frantz Fanon, *The Wretched of the Earth*, trans. Constance Farrington (New York: Grove Press, 1963), 247–48. Fanon's argument is directed against nationalists who encourage insularity and Marxists/socialists who argue for skipping over national consciousness in order to arrive more quickly at a utopian international order.

13. Quoted in Manganiello, *Joyce's Politics*, 151.

14. Extensive war poster collections in Manuscripts and Archives, Yale University Libraries, in Trinity College, Dublin, and in the National Army Museum, London, do not contain any poster meeting Bloom's description. Available evidence indicates that though some pictorial posters were in use as early as 1780, and though their use became widespread beginning in 1890, it was not until World War I that the image came to dominate the poster's simple slogan. Earlier posters showing uniforms showed only one style of uniform per poster and therefore would not have featured "soldiers of all arms on parade." I am indebted to Michael B. Ball of the National Army Museum for this information. Thanks also to Charles Benson, Keeper of Early Printed Books, Trinity College Library, Dublin.

15. For two valuable exceptions, see Robert E. Spoo, "'Nestor' and the Nightmare: The Presence of the Great War in *Ulysses*," *Twentieth Century Literature* 32, no. 2 (Summer 1986): 137–54, and James Fairhall, *James Joyce and the Question of History* (Cambridge: Cambridge University Press, 1993). Spoo's essay is reprinted, lightly revised, in *Joyce and the Subject of History*, ed.

Mark A. Wollaeger, Victor Luftig, and Robert Spoo (Ann Arbor: University of Michigan Press, 1996).

16. See Jennifer Wicke's pioneering exploration of the interrelation of discourses of advertising and fiction in her *Advertising Fictions: Literature, Advertising, and Social Reading* (New York: Columbia University Press, 1988), especially pp. 120–69. Many have since taken up the conjunction; see the special issue of the *James Joyce Quarterly* 30–31 (Summer/Fall 1993) on "Joyce and Advertising."

17. Ellmann, quoting from the diary of Joyce's language pupil, Georges Borach, for August 1, 1917, in his *James Joyce*, 416. Frank Budgen, *James Joyce and the Making of "Ulysses"* (New York: Oxford University Press, 1989), 15.

18. Ellmann, *James Joyce*, 417, commenting on the Borach diary (see note 17, therein); the description of Bloom is Ellmann's on page 5. Both the diary and Budgen's version in his *James Joyce and the Making of "Ulysses,"* 15–18, refer to recruiting officers. Joyce made these remarks to Borach and Budgen around the same time he was drafting "Lotus Eaters," the episode in which the recruiting poster appears.

19. Although during these years Joyce remained in Zurich (itself bombarded with propaganda from all sides), his mock-heroic battle with Henry Carr and the British Consulate over a pair of trousers acted out his resistance to the British Empire while transforming his neutral haven into a litigious war zone, complete with threat of conscription from Consul-General Bennett. See Ellmann, *James Joyce*, 440–41, and *Selected Letters of James Joyce*, ed. Richard Ellmann (New York: Viking, 1975), 215, 231–32.

20. Budgen, *James Joyce and the Making of "Ulysses,"* 17.

21. Ibid., 196. Jean-Michel Rabaté, *James Joyce, Authorized Reader* (Baltimore: Johns Hopkins University Press, 1991), has Joyce responding "proudly": "I have written *Ulysses*. And you?" (8). Rabaté's wording, which probably derives from Tom Stoppard's *Travesties*, captures my sense of the tone perfectly. Stoppard's Joyce responds to the question, "And what did you do in the Great War?" with a tart "I wrote *Ulysses* . . . What did you do? Bloody nerve" (65). Stoppard very likely invented the counterquestion. The *differences* between Stoppard and Rabaté probably result from the latter's retranslation from his own French: "*J'ai ecrit Ulysses. Et vous?*" I thank Thomas Whitaker for the Stoppard connection and the translation conjecture.

22. O'Brien, *"Dear, Dirty Dublin": A City in Distress, 1899–1916* (Berkeley: University of California Press, 1982), 243–44. The ideological arguments: high recruitment was a consequence of Irish infantilization owing to English education, a "damnable conspiracy against Irish manhood"; others claimed that many recruits were members of the Anglo-Irish Ascendancy, who hated Ireland, or members of the middle class, who wanted a commission.

23. See the *Spark*, May 2, 1915, which prints the complete ballad, reworked. Evidence suggests that economic, social, and political factors (such as the 1916 Rising) probably influenced enlistment more than any particular recruiting technique. See Patrick Callan, "Recruiting for the British Army in Ireland during the First World War," *Irish Sword* 17, no. 66 (Summer 1987): 42–56.

24. For bibliography and illustrated commentary on the history of the poster, see, in addition to the sources cited elsewhere in this essay, Maurice Rickards, *The*

Rise and Fall of the Poster (New York: McGraw-Hill, 1971) and his *Posters of the First World War* (New York: Walker, 1968). John Barnicoat's *A Concise History of Posters: 1870–1970* (New York: Harry N. Abrams, 1972) is beautifully illustrated, wide-ranging, and authoritative. For the influence on posters of the art of the "silhouette" and Japanese prints, and for the enabling technologies of lithography and the high-speed printing press, see Harold E. Hutchinson, *The Poster: An Illustrated History from 1860* (New York: Viking, 1968), 10–12. For an informative early study, see Charles Hiatt, *Picture Posters* (London: George Bell, 1896).

25. Alexandre Arsène and others, *The Modern Poster* (New York: Scribners, 1895), 23, 24. The OED first records "postermaniac," "one who has a mania for collecting posters," in 1895.

26. William Edward David Allen, *David Allens: The History of a Family Firm, 1857–1957* (London: John Murray, 1957), 137. Allen includes a useful chapter on billsticking during World War I.

27. Ibid., 134–37.

28. When I taught at Yale University, traces of the continuing regulation dynamic were inscribed all over campus in university signs prohibiting unauthorized posting. The attempt to restrain the spread of posters over all available public surfaces was visible as well in the installation of sidewalk kiosks and in huge notice boards located outside the university post office. In a meeting of Yale's Committee on Undergraduate Organizations a letter from the head of custodial services was read aloud decrying the loss of money and man-hours spent cleaning up after "the poster devil." We weighed withdrawing student funding for poster production and the merits of free speech (a university lawyer was present), the aesthetics of the campus, and the possible efficacy of more kiosks; we also noted the logic of transgression whereby the most effective poster is placed where it is most prohibited, learned that the average half-life of a poster on campus is forty-five minutes and that posters must be defaced when posted in order to discourage students from collecting them as dorm room decor. We adjourned for lunch, taking no action.

29. Rickards, *Rise and Fall of the Poster*, recounting that Sir John Millais initially became "apoplectic" (18) when Thomas Barratt, manager of Pears' Soap, asked permission in 1885 to use a Millais painting as a commercial poster, offers one example of resistance and its fate. The resulting poster is reprinted in Alexandre, *The Modern Poster*.

30. These examples are culled from the OED.

31. See Donald Spoto, *The Dark Side of Genius: The Life of Alfred Hitchcock* (Boston: Little, Brown, and Co., 1983), 89.

32. See Marie Seton, *Sergei M. Eisenstein* (New York: A. A. Wyn, 1952), 37

33. E. M. Forster, *Howards End*, ed. Paul B. Armstrong (New York: Norton, 1998), 61; Wyndham Lewis, *Tarr: The 1918 Version* (Santa Rosa: Black Sparrow, 1990), 198.

34. Sontag, "Posters," vii. She also notes on the same page that the force of the poster partly derives from its "form," which "depends on the fact that many posters exist—competing with (and sometimes reinforcing) each other."

35. E. M. Forster, *Anonymity: An Enquiry* (London: Hogarth Press, 1925), 10, 11.

36. Conrad, preface to *The Nigger of the "Narcissus,"* (1897), ed. Robert Kimbrough (New York: Norton, 1979), 147. Conrad's typographic emphasis falls only on "see."

37. For a provocative treatment of "the congruity between the modern city and the printed book" in Joyce, see Hugh Kenner, *The Mechanic Muse* (New York: Oxford, 1987), who observes that cheap single-volume novels became available only with the invention of linotype in 1884 (61–82). The mass production of modern posters became possible only with the conjunction of lithography and high-speed presses around 1848.

38. Hutchinson, *The Poster*, notes that with World War I pictorial posters became "essential weapons of mass persuasion in the new science of psychological warfare" and that many "distinguished academic painters [were] eager to lend their talents to the war effort" (70).

39. Quoted in Allen, *David Allens*, 220.

40. O'Brien, *"Dear, Dirty Dublin,"* 243.

41. The quotation from *The Billposter*, and the Conan Doyle, also from *The Billposter*, are from Allen, *David Allens*, 224.

42. See Stephen Watt, *Joyce, O'Casey, and the Irish Popular Theater* (Syracuse: Syracuse University Press, 1991), 62. Don Gifford,*"Ulysses" Annotated* (Berkeley: University of California Press, 1988), quotes from the leaflet and notes how the issue was revived (86).

43. That many recruiting posters also suggest collage techniques underscores the point that politics do not inhere in a particular form of representation but in the uses to which those forms are put. Walter Benjamin, like Sergei Eisenstein on montage, claimed an intrinsically liberating power for collage and other strategies of aesthetic dislocation at a time when technically advanced art could still seem revolutionary simply by virtue of being advanced; prior, that is, to the media saturation of postindustrial society. See Fredric Jameson's afterword to *Aesthetics and Politics*, esp. 207–8. For Benjamin, see "The Author as Producer" (1937), in *The Essential Frankfurt School Reader*, ed. Andrew Arato and Eike Gebhardg (New York: Continuum, 1988), 266–67.

44. David Cairns and Shaun Richards, *Writing Ireland: Colonialism, Nationalism and Culture* (Manchester: Manchester University Press, 1988), 50–51, 66–67, 71, 85–86. For less polemical treatments, see the essays in *Views of the Irish Peasantry, 1800–1916*, ed. Daniel J. Cassy and Robert E. Rhodes (Hamden, Conn.: Archon Books, 1977). For a more recent reappropriation of the World War I peasant woman, this time as the incarnation of Ulster, see the color reproduction of a 1988 mural in Bill Rolston, *Politics and Painting: Murals and Conflict in Northern Ireland* (Cranbury, N.J.: Associated University Presses, 1991), between pages 32 and 33.

45. A writer in the *Spark* (March 5, 1916) has great satiric fun with Redmond's claim that one minutely detailed map used a four-inch scale by pointing out that if four inches equaled one mile, the map would have been twenty-nine by twenty-five yards and thus of sufficient size, once removed from the Prussian pocket, to provide sleeping accommodations for two hundred, including tents, ground cloths, and a marquee.

46. See L. Perry Curtis, *Apes and Angels: The Irishman in Victorian Carica-ture* (Washington, D.C.: Smithsonian Institution Press, 1971). For a more wide-ranging treatment of colonial misrepresentation, see Richard Ned Lebow, *White Britain and Black Ireland: The Influence of Stereotypes on Colonial Policy* (Philadelphia: Institute for the Study of Human Issues, 1976).

47. By producing poster-mannequins that effectively sublate the history of Irish-English misrepresentation, posters featuring the commodified attractiveness of the hero perfectly execute the homogenizing function that Seamus Deane, eliding the differences between *Ulysses* and the discourse of advertising it en-gages, attributes to *Ulysses*. See Deane, "Heroic Styles: the Tradition of an Idea," in *Ireland's Field Day*.

48. Sontag, "Posters," vii.

49. See Hayman, "James Joyce, Paratactician," *Contemporary Literature*, 26, no. 2 (1985):165–66.

50. For the influence of Picasso and Braque on verbal montage, see Marjorie Perloff, *The Futurist Moment: Avant-Garde, Avant Guerre, and the Language of Rupture* (Chicago: University of Chicago Press, 1986), 44–79. Joyce's *Scissors and Paste*–like attention in *Ulysses* to the circulation and transformation of in-formation through the mass media belies Fredric Jameson's claim that in the "great village which is Joyce's Dublin" gossip dominates the networks of com-munication to the virtual exclusion of modern forms of mass communication. See his *"Ulysses* in History," in *James Joyce and Modern Literature*, ed. W. J. McCormack and Alistair Stead (London: Routledge and Kegan Paul, 1982).

51. See Francis Phelan, "A Source of the Headlines of 'Aeolus'?" *James Joyce Quarterly* 9 (Fall 1971):146–51.

52. Ironically, though it was "Sirens" that prompted Ezra Pound's laconic ad-vice that "a new style per chapter not required," Pound's own doctrine of the im-age, substituting rhythm for syntax and fragmentation for pictorial unity, in ef-fect authorizes that episode's narrative mode. Pound's letter of June 1918 is quoted by Ellmann, *James Joyce*, 459.

53. Joyce makes comparable use of Ireland's storehouse of traditional symbols in *Dubliners*, though the harp in "Two Gallants," as observed by Lenehan, dis-plays its subjection to foreign political power more openly as a form of ravish-ment. Accompanying a melancholy song of liberation deferred, the harp, "heed-less that her coverings had fallen about her knees, seemed weary alike of the eyes of strangers and of her master's hands." Even apart from the harp's status as an emblem of Ireland's past glories, the proximity of "master" and "strangers"—both code words for the English in Ireland—catalyzes the colonial resonance sus-tained in Lenehan's compliant response: "The air which the harpist had played began to control his movements. His softly padded feet played the melody while his fingers swept a scale of variations idly along the railings after each group of notes." Lenehan's *incorporation* of the harp's notes—he is played as he plays—epitomizes the subject rendered perfectly passive before the interpellative designs of the recruiter (James Joyce, *Dubliners* [New York: Penguin, 1968], 54, 56).

54. As G. A. McCoy has put it, "we may speak of the Irish struggle of modern times as one to remove the crown from above the harp and to place the harp it-self on a green field instead of a blue"; quoted from Hayes-McCoy's *A History of*

Irish Flags in Rolston, *Politics and Painting*, 71. For useful information on the production, distribution, and print-run of posters, as well as specific commentary on a few posters, see Mark Tierney, Paul Bowen, and David Fitzpatrick, "Recruiting Posters," in *Ireland and the First World War*, ed. David Fitzpatrick (Dublin: the Lilliput Press and Trinity History Workshop, 1988).

55. See Slavoj Žižek, *The Sublime Object of Ideology* (London: Verso, 1989), 87–97.

56. According to notes in Trinity College Library (Dublin), the Proclamation later became the proud possession of a Major Tamworth, whose widow sold it to Trinity in 1970.

57. See Louis Althusser, "Ideology and Ideological State Apparatuses," in *Lenin and Philosophy and Other Essays*, trans. Ben Brewster (New York: Monthly Review Press, 1971), 121–73.

58. Herr, *Joyce's Anatomy of Culture*, 205–6.

59. The implication, of course, is that someone with the clap wants pills sent for relief. As usual, Joyce's selection of detail invokes broader historical currents: the British government imposed only one new control on advertising during the war, the Venereal Diseases Act of 1917, which banned advertising connected to "any condition associated with sexual indulgence." See T. R. Nevett, *Advertising in Britain: A History* (London: Heinemann, 1982), 143. The composition history of *Ulysses* suggests that Bloom is remembering rather than imagining the transgression: Joyce inserted the phrase, "Some chap with a dose burning him" just after "POST 110 PILLS," as if to indicate Bloom's surmise about the perpetrator of this *détournement*. Ironically, Joyce himself had to correct the inscribed revision of the prohibition in proofs. See *The James Joyce Archive*, ed. Michael Groden, 49 vols. (New York: Garland, 1978), 18:90, 98.

60. See Thomas E. Lewis, "Aesthetic Effect/Ideological Effect," *Enclitic* 7, no. 3 (Fall 1983):4–16, who analyzes the problem of preserving the aesthetic in Althusser, Lukàcs, Macherey, and Eagleton before arguing that the only solution for a rigorous Marxism is to abandon the distinction altogether.

61. Jay, "Hierarchy and the Humanities: The Radical Implications of a Conservative Idea," *Telos* 62 (Winter 1984–85):144. It is worth noting that this argument does not always sit well with oppositional critics. An earlier version of my argument in this chapter was almost rejected by a scholarly journal precisely for its invocation of Jay's defense of hierarchy. Years later, a colleague in a discussion group objected so vociferously to Jay's argument that conversation was effectively shut down. In a conversation with me some time ago Jay expressed surprise over the vehement resistance his article has elicited over the years.

62. See Bürger, *Theory of the Avant-Garde*, trans. Michael Shaw (Minneapolis: University of Minnesota Press, 1984), esp. 53, 80–82.

63. Ellmann, *James Joyce*, 513.

64. See Pierre Bourdieu, *Distinction: A Social Critique of the Judgement of Taste*, trans. Richard Nice (Cambridge, Mass.: Harvard University Press, 1984), 5.

65. Ellmann, *James Joyce*, 697.

66. For a critical overview of the issue as well as essays bearing on it, see my *James Joyce's "A Portrait of the Artist as a Young Man": A Casebook* (New York: Oxford University Press, 2003).

67. In a letter to Harriet Shaw Weaver (August 6, 1919), Joyce used "initial style" to designate the narrative mode for which floundering readers of "Sirens," including Weaver and Pound, would feel nostalgic (*Selected Letters of James Joyce*, ed. Ellmann, 242). My characterization of this mode is indebted to Hugh Kenner's discussion in *Joyce's Voices* (Berkeley: University of California Press, 1978), 15–38. For a more extensive reading of Joyce's critique of Stephen's fantasies of autonomy, see my "Stephen/Joyce, Joyce/Haacke: Modernism and the Social Function of Art," *English Literary History* 62 (1995):691–707.

68. Moretti, *Signs Taken for Wonders*, 194–95; Umberto Eco, *The Aesthetics of Chaosmos: The Middle Ages of James Joyce*, trans. Ellen Esrock (Cambridge, Mass.: Harvard University Press, 1989), 43. I write that Moretti selectively invokes Eco because the Italian edition Moretti consulted, *Le Poetiche di Joyce* (1966), includes the qualification I cite here from *The Aesthetics of Chaosmos*, as does the earlier *Opera Aperta* (1962). Though in a more recent treatment Moretti describes Bloom's absentmindedness as "an active tool" for coping with city stimuli, he ultimately misconstrues Bloom's stream of consciousness as a kind of passivity by comparing it with radio reception (Moretti, *The Modern Epic*, trans. Quintin Hoare [London: Verso, 1996], 137–38, 271–72).

69. For a sustained exploration of the foregrounding of textuality in "Penelope," see Derek Attridge, "Molly's Flow: The Writing of 'Penelope' and the Question of Women's Language," *Modern Fiction Studies* 35 (Autumn 1989):543–65, who also draws attention to the typographic display of numerals and crossed-out letters as contributing to the textualized quality of Molly's voice.

70. Patrick Brantlinger, "The Nineteenth-Century Novel and Empire," in *The Columbia History of the British Novel*, ed. John Richetti (New York: Columbia University Press, 1994), 560.

71. See D. A. Miller, *The Novel and the Police* (Berkeley: University of California Press, 1988). Conduct books are invested with a similarly coercive and insidious power in some studies of the eighteenth-century novel. See, for instance, Nancy Armstrong, *Desire and Domestic Fiction: A Political History of the Novel* (New York: Oxford University Press, 1987).

72. See O'Brien, "*Dear, Dirty Dublin*," 180.

73. Lord Morely is quoted in Dorothy Macardle, *The Irish Republic: A Documented Chronicle of the Anglo-Irish Conflict and the Partitioning of Ireland, with a Detailed Account of the Period 1916–1923* (London: Victor Gollancz, 1937), 53. Macardle's description of the Castle is on page 319.

74. Budgen, *James Joyce and the Making of "Ulysses,"* 123–25.

75. Ellmann, *James Joyce*, 438.

76. For the arranger, adopted by Hugh Kenner and others, see David Hayman, *"Ulysses" and the Mechanics of Meaning* (rev. ed. Madison: University of Wisconsin Press, 1982) 88–104. For the extradiegetic narrator, see Gerard Genette, *Narrative Discourse: An Essay in Method*, trans. Jane E. Lewin (Ithaca: Cornell University Press, 1980), 228.

77. See Foucault, "The Subject and Power," in *Art After Modernism: Rethinking Representation*, ed. Brian Wallis (New York: The New Museum of Contemporary Art, 1984).

78. Andreas Huyssen, *After the Great Divide: Modernism, Mass Culture, Postmodernism* (Bloomington: Indiana University Press, 1986), 23.

79. See Macardle, *The Irish Republic*, 376.

80. Earnan P. Blythe, "The D.M.P.," *Dublin Historical Record* 20, nos. 3/4 (June/September 1965):122–23. Though Blythe always invents excuses for hostility to the police, he acknowledges a political motivation for that friction only when observing that the nationalism of the Dublin Corporation denied municipal employment to police pensioners. Between attempts to downplay the problem, Blythe notes that "some landlords were prepared to reduce rent for constables, but others would not let houses to constables at all"; he also admits that "the public at large wouldn't cooperate with the police" (122, 123).

81. See *Intelligence Notes, 1913–16*, ed. Breandàn MacGiolla Choille (Dublin: Government Publication Sale Office, 1966), xvii–xix, and Leon O Broin, *Dublin Castle and the 1916 Rising* (London: Sidgwick and Jackson, 1970), 141.

82. See Patrick Farrelly, " 'Come Forward' Appeal to Blackmail Victims," *Irish Times* (September 8, 1990).

83. See Gifford, *"Ulysses" Annotated*, 472–74.

84. David Cannadine, "The Context, Performance, and Meaning of Ritual: The British Monarchy and the 'Invention of Tradition,' c. 1820–1977," in *The Invention of Tradition*, ed. Eric J. Hobsbawm and Terence Ranger (Cambridge: Cambridge University Press, 1983), 122, 123, 125.

85. Bodley, *The Coronation of Edward the Seventh* (London: Methuen, 1903), 307, 322.

86. See Gifford, *"Ulysses" Annotated*, 474; his translation.

87. Bodley, *The Coronation of Edward the Seventh*, 306–7.

88. See F. L. Radford, "King, Pope, and Hero-Martyr: *Ulysses* and the Nightmare of Irish History," *James Joyce Quarterly* 15 (Summer 1978): 310.

89. Quoted in Colin MacCabe, *James Joyce and the Revolution of the Word* (London: Macmillan, 1978), 117.

90. Budgen records Joyce's famous remark that if Dublin were destroyed, it could rebuilt from the pages of his novel. See *James Joyce and the Making of "Ulysses,"* 69.

91. Joyce, "Fenianism," in *The Critical Writings of James Joyce*, ed. Ellsworth Mason and Richard Ellmann (Ithaca: Cornell University Press, 1959), 190.

92. A "strategy" operates within existing structures of power by utilizing the circuitry already laid out; a "tactic" functions oppositionally within the interstices of existing systems by productively exploiting the potential for contingency within otherwise hegemonic structures of determination. See Michel de Certeau, *The Practice of Everyday Life*, trans. Steven Rendall (Berkeley: University of California Press, 1984), xviii–xx.

93. Hume R. Jones, *The Policeman's Manual* (Dublin: Alexander Thom, 1908), seventh edition, 2.

94. Quoted from *James Joyce: The Critical Heritage*, ed. Robert H. Deming, 2 vols. (London: Routledge and Kegan Paul, 1970), 1:253. The other reviews quoted in this paragraph are excerpted in the same volume, pp.193, 208, 189, 232.

95. C. C. Martindale in the *Dublin Review* (1922), in Deming, *The Critical Heritage*, 1:205.

96. Benedict Anderson, *Imagined Communities: Reflections on the Origin and Spread of Nationalism* (London: Verso, 1983), 28–40.

97. Compare Clifford, "Traveling Cultures," 108.

CHAPTER FIVE
FROM THE THIRTIES TO WORLD WAR II

1. National Archives of Ireland web site, "James Joyce and *Ulysses*," Commentary no. 10, http://www.nationalarchives.ie/topics/JJoyce/ccinema.htm (viewed February 25, 2006).

2. Rebecca West, *The Return of the Soldier* (New York: Penguin, 1998), 5. Hereafter cited in the text. For frame enlargements of the famous "over the top" sequence, see Nicholas Reeves, *Official British Film Propaganda During the First World War* (London: Croom Helm, 1986), between pages 128 and 129, and his discussion of the debate over the sequence's authenticity (101–3, 160–61).

3. For Lawrence's views on the counterfeit as the epitome of technological modernity, see "A Propos of 'Lady Chatterly's Lover,' " in *Phoenix II*, ed. Warren Roberts and Harry T. Moore (New York: Penguin, 1978), 487–515; quotation on p. 493, where he also observes that "radio and film are mere counterfeit emotion all the time."

4. D. H. Lawrence, *Women in Love* (New York: Penguin, 1995), 485.

5. D. H. Lawrence, "Men Must Work and Women as Well," *Assorted Articles* (New York: Knopf, 1930), 168.

6. For a provocative exploration of film as modernism, see Garrett Stewart, *Between Film and Screen: Modernism's Photo Synthesis* (Chicago: University of Chicago Press, 1999).

7. Henri Bergson, *Creative Evolution*, trans. Arthur Mitchell (1907; rpt. Westport, Conn.: Greenwood Press, 1975), 332.

8. An anonymous reviewer of Joyce's *Portrait* in the *New Age*, for instance, complains about Joyce's "wilful cleverness, his determination to produce kinematographic effects instead of a literary portrait," and H. G. Wells, also commenting on *Portrait*, felt that Joyce's use of dashes instead of quotation marks produced "the same wincing feeling of being flicked at that one used to have in the early cinema shows" (*James Joyce: The Critical Heritage*, ed. Robert H. Deming, 2 vols. [London: Routledge and Kegan Paul, 1970], 1:110, 87).

9. For a detailed investigation of the effectiveness of cinematic propaganda, see Nicholas Reeves, *The Power of Film Propaganda: Myth or Reality* (London and New York: Cassell, 1999). Undertaking case studies of Britain, the Soviet Union, Germany, and Italy, Reeves concludes that World War II films produced by Britain and Nazi Germany were most effective but that their relative success demonstrates "not the power of film propaganda, but rather the powerful constraints within which such propaganda operates" (240).

10. See, for instance, Jean-Louis Baudry, "Ideological Effects of the Basic

Cinematographic Apparatus," and Jean-Louis Comolli, "Technique and Ideology: Camera, Perspective, Depth of Field," both in *Narrative, Apparatus, Ideology*, ed. Philip Rosen (New York: Columbia University Press, 1986).

11. Baudry, "Ideological Effects of the Basic Cinematographic Apparatus," 296.

12. Miriam Bratu Hansen, "The Mass Production of the Senses: Classical Cinema as Vernacular Modernism," in *Reinventing Film Studies*, ed. Christine Gledhill and Linda Williams (London: Arnold, 2000), 332–50.

13. Radio was the other. See *Film and Radio Propaganda in World War II*, ed. K.R.M. Short (Knoxville: University of Tennessee Press, 1983), and Siân Nicholas, *The Echo of War: Home Front Propaganda and the Wartime BBC, 1939–1945* (Manchester and New York: Manchester University Press, 1996). The most notorious instance of World War II radio propaganda was William Joyce, "Lord Haw Haw," the so-called English voice of Nazi Germany. See Peter Martland, *Lord Haw Haw* (Kew: National Archives, 2003).

14. Peter Buitenhuis, *The Great War of Words: British, American, and Canadian Propaganda and Fiction, 1914–1933* (Vancouver: University of British Columbia Press, 1987), xviii; see also 148–78; 170 (Kipling quotation).

15. Michael Stenton, *Radio London and Resistance in Occupied Europe* (Oxford and New York: Oxford University Press, 2000), 3. Hoare is quoted on the same page. John Buchan briefly ran the DoI in 1917, but his autobiography fails to mention the British propaganda campaign, let alone his own role in it. See John Buchan (Lord Tweedsmuir), *Pilgrim's Way* (Cambridge, Mass.: Houghton Mifflin, 1940).

16. Susan A. Brewer, *To Win the Peace: British Propaganda in the United States during World War II* (Ithaca and London: Cornell University Press, 1997), 24–25.

17. Ibid., 11–54.

18. For the use of writers, including Somerset Maugham and J. B. Priestly, to draw the United States into the war despite the "no propaganda" policy, see Robert Calder, *Beware the British Serpent: The Role of Writers in British Propaganda in the United States, 1939–1945* (Montreal: McGill-Queen's University Press, 2004).

19. For the scaling back of British propaganda between the wars, see Philip. M. Taylor, *The Projection of Britain: British Overseas Publicity and Propaganda, 1919–1939* (Cambridge: Cambridge University Press, 1981), 11–43, 83–124.

20. Quoted in ibid., 111.

21. Quoted in Margaret Dickinson and Sarah Street, *Cinema and State* (London: BFI, 1985), 19; for film quotas, see 5–33.

22. Reeves, *The Power of Film Propaganda*, 149.

23. For a detailed comparison of the two, see ibid., 83–204. See also James Chapman's informative article, "Cinema, Propaganda and National Identity: British Film and the Second World War," in *British Cinema, Past and Present*, ed. Justine Ashby and Andrew Higson (New York: Routledge, 2000), 193–206.

24. A 1994 Paramount documentary, *It's All True*, directed by Norman Foster, Bill Krohn, Myron Meisel, Orson Welles, and Richard Wilson, includes the reconstructed short, "Four Men on a Raft," as well as parts of the Carnaval footage shot in Rio, and parts of "My Friend Bonito," shot in Mexico.

25. George Orwell, *The Collected Essays, Journalism and Letters of George Orwell*, ed. Sonia Orwell and Ian Angus, 4 vols. (New York: Harcourt, Brace, and World, 1968), 2:335. Hereafter cited in the text.

26. Orwell did not require a rationalization for his own World War II propaganda work. He saw England and its allies (with the problematic exception of the Soviets) as the best hope for preserving a measure of freedom in the world and wanted to do his part.

27. Various circumstantial connections also exist. Both Hitchcock and Welles tried to use Joseph Conrad to establish themselves in Hollywood, Hitchcock by adapting *The Secret Agent* as *Sabotage* while still with Gaumont in England, Welles by attempting to adapt *Heart of Darkness* as his first Hollywood film and later by borrowing Conrad's characteristic narrative structures for *Citizen Kane* (1941). Once in Hollywood, they also came to have film people in common. When John Houseman, who suffered through a contentious though productive relationship with Welles in New York, finally broke with Welles in Hollywood, he was hired by David O. Selznick, who assigned him to work with Hitchcock. For the lead actor in *Shadow of a Doubt* (1943), Hitchcock hired Joseph Cotten, famous after his role in *Citizen Kane*, after watching a pre-release copy of *The Magnificent Ambersons*. And when Hitchcock was finally able to exercise complete control over his scores, he turned to a composer who first became famous through his work with Welles, Bernard Hermann.

28. Frank Brady, *Citizen Welles* (New York: Scribner's, 1989), 303–4.

29. Robert L. Carringer notes the connections with *Rebecca* in *The Making of Citizen Kane* (Berkeley: University of California Press, 1985), 20.

30. Patrick McGilligan observes that in *Saboteur* the name of Robert Cummings's character was changed after Hitchcock's first script sessions with Houseman (McGilligan, *Alfred Hitchcock* [New York: HarperCollins, 2003], 301).

31. For a sustained examination of Hitchcock's cinematic response to Welles, with particular attention to *Psycho*, see John W. Hall, "Touch of Psycho? Welles' Influence on Hitchcock," *Bright Lights Film Journal*, http://www.brightlightsfilm.com/14/psycho.html (viewed February 24, 2006).

32. In his interviews with Truffaut, for instance, Hitchcock notes that he was "determined to break with the traditional way of handling dream sequences through a blurred and hazy screen" (*Hitchcock* [New York: Simon and Schuster, 1984], 163).

33. The sequence Dalí originally planned was longer than the two and a half minutes that ultimately survived the cutting-room floor, perhaps by a minute or so. It was never as long as the twenty minutes Ingrid Bergman erroneously remembered when interviewed by Donald Spoto (see note 58, below). For the fullest account of the making of the sequence, see the narrative based on James Bigwood's research in the Criterion Collection DVD of *Spellbound* (2002).

34. For Welles's reflections on radio, see Brady, *Citizen Welles*, 164. For German radio propaganda, see Julian Hale, *Radio Power* (Philadelphia: Temple University Press, 1975), 1–16.

35. Welles's typed notes are in the Orson Welles Collection, Lilly Library, Indiana University, Bloomington, Indiana (Box 14, File 8), and are quoted here with the kind permission of the Lilly Library. The notes are unpaginated and uncor-

rected. I have silently emended Welles's many consistent misspellings, such as "propoganda," and have sometimes supplied missing punctuation.

36. Brady, *Citizen Welles*, 80.

37. For a comparison of the U.S. and British movements, see Stuart Cosgrove, "From Shock Troupe to Group Theatre," in *Theatres of the Left, 1880–1935*, ed. Raphael Samuel, Ewan MacColl, and Stuart Cosgrove (London: Routledge and Kegan Paul, 1985), 259–79.

38. Daniel Friedman, "A Brief Description of the Workers' Theatre Movement of the Thirties," in *Theatre for Working-Class Audiences in the United States, 1830–1980*, ed. Bruce A. McConachie and Daniel Friedman (Westport, Conn.: Greenwood, 1985), 111.

39. Ibid., 113.

40. Ibid., 115.

41. The phrase "first person singular" is closely associated with Welles's interest in medium-specific experimentation. In the same year Welles wrote these notes, his Mercury Theatre began a weekly series of radio dramas entitled *First Person Singular*, and Welles announced to the newspapers that "we plan to bring to radio the experimental techniques which have proved so successful in another medium, and to treat radio itself with the intelligence and respect such a beautiful and powerful medium deserves" (quoted in Barbara Leaming, *Orson Welles* [New York: Limelight Editions, 1995], 153). This is precisely the attitude Welles took to Hollywood a year later when he proposed to make *Heart of Darkness*, which he had already adapted for the radio.

42. Orson Welles, Revised Estimating Script, September 30, 1939, for *Heart of Darkness*. The quotation is from the title page of Welles's introductory sequence to the film proper. Held in the Orson Welles Collection, Lilly Library, Indiana University, Bloomington, Indiana (Box 14, File 16). Subsequent references to the introduction will be cited in the text by page number.

43. For the phrases from Conrad, see the preface to *The Nigger of the "Narcissus,"* ed. Robert Kimbrough (New York: Norton, 1979), 147.

44. See Henry James, *Notes on Novelists, with Some Other Notes* (New York: Scribner's, 1914), 345, 346.

45. Eric Gill, "All Art is Propaganda," in *Modernism: An Anthology of Sources and Documents*, ed. Vassiliki Kolocotroni, Jane Goldman, and Olga Taxidou (Chicago: University of Chicago Press, 1998), 530.

46. R. G. Collingwood, *The Principles of Art* (Oxford: Clarendon Press, 1938), 32.

47. The first view is R. Miller-Budnitskaya's in a 1938 article on Joyce in *Dialectics: A Marxian Literary Journal*; the second is Harry Levin's in his 1939 review of *Finnegans Wake* in *New Directions*. See Deming, *James Joyce: The Critical Heritage*, 2:658, 694.

48. The Motion Picture Production Code of 1930 (Hays Code), http://www.artsreformation.com/a001/hays-code.html (viewed February 24, 2006).

49. David Bordwell, Janet Staiger, and Kristin Thompson, *The Classical Hollywood Cinema* (New York: Columbia University Press, 1985), 79.

50. See Brady, *Citizen Welles*, 199–201.

51. McGilligan, *Alfred Hitchcock*, 75–76.

52. Leonard Leff, *Hitchcock and Selznick* (New York: Weidenfeld and Nicolson, 1987), 35.

53. Reproduced in the Criterion Collection DVD of Hitchcock's *Rebecca* (2001).

54. Cited in McGilligan, *Alfred Hitchcock*, 327.

55. Ibid., 256. A scheduling conflict prevented Hitchcock from directing his segment of *Forever and a Day*, but *Foreign Correspondent* (1940) also skirted the Neutrality Act. The film ends with a dramatic radio address that uncannily anticipates Edward R. Murrow's famous broadcasts from London during the Blitz, but it cleared nervous Hollywood censors by suppressing any reference to Germany.

56. Quoted in Leff, *Hitchcock and Selznick*, 99.

57. Ibid., 121–22.

58. The cable exchange makes for amusing reading. Though Bernstein ultimately mollifies him, Selznick cannot resist adding that "I think I was justified in resenting the possibility of Hitchcock going to England to make a short with my enthusiastic endorsement and this co-operation boomeranging on us through [Bernstein's] utilizing this trip for his own selfish purposes and against our interests" (Telegram, David O. Selznick to Jenia Reissar, October 12, 1944. The Papers of Lord Sidney Bernstein, Department of Documents, Imperial War Museum, London). Though Donald Spoto claims otherwise (*The Dark Side of Genius* [Boston and Toronto: Little, Brown, 1983], 271), there is little reason to think that Bernstein was lying when he claimed that he had no plans to go into business with Hitchcock. Although later they did become partners, forming Transatlantic Pictures in 1947, they probably did not begin speaking in earnest about such an enterprise until the late spring of 1945, when Hitchcock returned to London to work with Bernstein on a documentary about German concentration camps and the extermination of Jews. See Caroline Moorehead, *Sidney Bernstein* (London: Jonathan Cape, 1984), 170–71, and McGilligan, *Alfred Hitchcock*, 365–66. Spoto might have been thinking of conversations during Hitchcock's 1944 London visit in which Bernstein tried to interest Hitchcock in filming stage plays as part of the British war effort to communicate an appealing sense of Englishness to their new allies in America. See John Russell Taylor, *Hitch: The Life and Times of Alfred Hitchcock* (New York: Pantheon, 1978), 206.

59. Brady, *Citizen Welles*, 87–88.

60. One way to make the distinction is to stipulate that cinematic propaganda records events that were designed in order to be filmed, while documentary records unstaged events. Riefenstahl's *Triumph of the Will* accordingly falls into the category of propaganda, though it has often been defended as a documentary, because the Nazi Party Congress was staged for the camera, whereas *It's All True*, part documentary footage of Carnaval, part recreation of an historical journey, part fiction, falls into a gray area. The distinction is rarely clear-cut, in any case, since the open presence of a camera can have a scripting effect on the events being filmed.

61. Jorge Luis Borges, *"Citizen Kane"* (1945), in *Focus on Citizen Kane*, ed. Ronald Gottesman (Englewood Cliffs, N.J.: Prentice-Hall, 1971), 128.

62. Quoted in David Bordwell, *"Citizen Kane,"* in *Perspectives on Orson Welles*, ed. Morris Beja (New York: G. K. Hall, 1995), 96. The article was originally published in *Film Comment* 7 (Summer 1971): 38–47.

63. Laura Mulvey points out that the script was begun just after Hitler invaded Poland in September 1939 and went into production during "the bleakest moments of the war"; she also discusses the film's anti-isolationism (*Citizen Kane* [London: BFI, 1992], 15, 38–39).

64. For an excellent account of the controversy over the film, see "The Battle Over *Citizen Kane*," originally shown on television as part of the American Experience series (WGBH Educational Foundation) and now part of Warner Home Video's digitally remastered release of *Citizen Kane* on DVD (2001).

65. For discussion and bibliography, see Ina Rae Hark, " 'We Might Even Get in the Newsreels': The Press and Democracy in Hitchcock's World War II Anti-Fascist Films," in *Alfred Hitchcock: Centenary Essays*, ed. Richard Allen and S. Ishii Gonzalès (London: BFI, 1999), 339.

66. Bordwell, *"Citizen Kane,"* in *Perspectives on Orson Welles*, ed. Beja, 90–93. Bordwell points out, for instance, that the dreamlike imagery of the film's opening sequence, culminating in the falling paperweight and the nurse's distorted reflection in the glass, recalls "the fantasy of Mèliés," and the abrupt switch to "News on the March" draws on "the reportage of Lumière."

67. Stam, "Orson Welles, Brazil, and the Power of Blackness," in Beja, *Perspectives on Orson Welles*, 219–44. As Stam puts it, Welles was trying to make "a generic synthesis of city symphony film (about Rio de Janeiro), Flaherty-style documentary (the *jangadeiro* episode), musical, travelogue, social consciousness film, and cinematic essay" (219), but RKO only saw black people jumping up and down. As David Thomson remarks, it probably came as a shock to Rockefeller and the studio that blacks and whites often danced together in Brazil: "There was only so much Inter-American understanding the United States could take" (Thomson, *Rosebud: The Story of Orson Welles* [New York: Knopf 1966,] 213).

68. Ibid., 240, 239.

69. Brady, *Citizen Welles*, 342.

70. Stam, "Orson Welles, Brazil, and the Power of Blackness," 227.

71. See, for example, Brady, *Citizen Welles*, who calls it "perhaps one of the great feature documentaries never made" (349), and Stam, "Orson Welles," who argues that the film anticipated many of the best qualities of Brazil's Cinema Novo (227–28).

72. It is worth mentioning that Welles did not edit any of these sequences. He left notes about the general contours but not for microlevel assembly. The journey itself suffers from slow pacing that Welles undoubtedly would have improved in a final cut.

73. Quoted in Brady, *Citizen Welles*, 380.

74. Letter from Director Habib, Office Français d'Information Cinematographique, August 31, 1994. Held in the Papers of Lord Sidney Bernstein, Department of Documents, Imperial War Museum, London. Unless otherwise noted, all the other original documents relating to the production of *Bon Voyage* and *Aventure Malgache* come from this collection.

75. A few film historians have suggested that one or both had a limited release, but MoI records indicate that Bernstein's superiors found Habib's letter persuasive and felt that neither film should be shown. What is certain is that *Bon Voyage* was shown at least once as a special sneak preview in October 1944 at Cinema Radio Cité Bastille. François Truffaut told Hitchcock that he thought he saw the film in late 1944; in the same interview Hitchcock expresses the opinion that *Aventure Malgache* was never released. So either Truffaut was present at the preview of *Bon Voyage* or the film did indeed have a limited release. See Truffaut, *Hitchcock*, 160–61.

76. Rod Lurie, review of *Bon Voyage* and *Aventure Malgache*, *Los Angeles Magazine* 39, no. 6 (June 1994): 113.

77. Undated Central Office of Information document, Film and Video Archive, Imperial War Museum, London.

78. See Sidney Gottlieb, "The Unknown Hitchcock: *Watchtower Over Tomorrow*," *Hitchcock Annual* (1996–1997):117–30. The film is available only in the Library of Congress.

79. See Elizabeth Sussex, "The Fate of F3080," *Sight & Sound* 53, no. 2 (1984):92–97. In contrast to Welles's *It's All True*, the German atrocity film was abandoned because it made its point about German war crimes *too* effectively, and it was decided that, in the interests of friendly postwar relations between the Allies and Germany, the German people should not be subjected to the film's horrifying images.

80. Truffaut, *Hitchcock*, 176. One critic erroneously quotes Goebbels as describing *Foreign Correspondent* as "a masterpiece of propaganda," but the only authority for Goebbels's response to the film is Truffaut, who simply reports a rumor that Hitchcock heard as well.

81. Hark, " 'We Might Even Get in the Newsreels,' " 344.

82. Jakobson discusses the "focus on the message for its own sake," as contrasted with expressive or conative uses of language, as the dominant function of poetic language: "This function, by promoting the palpability of signs, deepens the fundamental dichotomy of signs and objects" (Roman Jakobson, "Linguistics and Poetics," in *The Structuralists: From Marx to Lévi-Strauss,* ed. Richard T. de George and Fernande M. de George [Garden City, N.Y.: Anchor, 1972], 93).

83. For an alternative explanation of Hitchcock's growing interest in media in the forties, see Ina Rae Hark, "Keeping Your Amateur Standing: Audience Participation and Good Citizenship in Hitchcock's Political Films," *Cinema Journal* 29, no. 2 (1990):8–22. For a quirky take on the prominence of media in Hitchcock's propaganda films, see James M. Vest, "Phones as Instruments of Betrayal in Alfred Hitchcock's *Bon Voyage* and *Aventure Malgache*," *French Review* 72, no. 3 (1999):529–42.

84. "Have You Heard?", *Life* (July 13, 1942), 68. The story is credited as "suggested by" Stephen Early, directed by Hitchcock, and photographed by Eliot Elisofon.

85. Jane E. Sloan, *Alfred Hitchcock: A Guide to Reference and Resources* (New York: G. K. Hall, 1993), 200. Sidney Gottlieb, "Hitchcock's Wartime Work: *Bon Voyage* and *Aventure Malgache*," *Hitchcock Annual* (1994):163.

86. See Truffaut, *Hitchcock*: "We used to work on the screenplay in my room at Claridge's, and there was a whole group of French officers," including one "who never agreed to anything the others suggested. We realized that the Free French were very divided against one another, and these inner conflicts became the [film's] subject" (161).

87. *Rapport de la Presentation Publique du Film "Bon Voyage,"* October 1944. Held in the Papers of Lord Sidney Bernstein, Department of Documents, Imperial War Museum, London.

88. Letter from the OFIC Director to Sidney Bernstein, August 31, 1944. Held in the Papers of Lord Sidney Bernstein, Department of Documents, Imperial War Museum, London.

89. For a provocative account of the way war-time propaganda and commercial radio in the United States contributed to "the expansion of a corporate-led, consumer-oriented ideology and the construction of a new—and increasingly privatized—public sphere," see Gerd Horten, *Radio Goes to War: The Cultural Politics of Propaganda during World War II* (Berkeley: University of California Press, 2002), 4.

CODA

1. Congressional Record: February 2, 2005 (U.S. Senate), Page S896.

2. GAO, Report B-305368, Department of Education—Contract to Obtain Services of Armstrong Williams, September 30, 2005 (http://www.gao.gov/decisions/appro/305368.htm) (viewed February 23, 2006).

3. Ford Madox Ford, *The Critical Attitude* (London: Duckworth, 1911), 115.

4. It was reported in November 2005, for instance, that the United States has secretly paid newspapers in Iraq to circulate positive stories about the war effort. True to the Wellington House model, "though the articles are basically factual, they present only one side of events and omit information that might reflect poorly on the U.S. or Iraqi governments, officials said." Although Foreign propaganda is not covered by the "Stop Government Propaganda Now" Bill, it is illegal for the military to carry out psychological operations or plant propaganda through American media outlets. Nonetheless, according to an article in the *Los Angeles Times*, "the Pentagon's efforts were carried out with the knowledge that coverage in the foreign press inevitably 'bleeds' into the Western media and influences coverage in U.S. news outlets." See Mark Mazzetti and Borzou Daragahi, "U.S. Military Covertly Pays to Run Stories in Iraqi Press," *Los Angeles Times* (November 30, 2005).

5. British television seems not to have a comparable homegrown show, but the *Daily Show* is broadcast on a one-day delay, and at least one British blogger with access to the American broadcast sometimes relays Stewart's coverage of breaking news in advance of the British rebroadcast. See, for instance, S. J. Howard's entry on U.S. Vice President Dick Cheney's shooting of his seventy-eight-year-old friend in the face with a shotgun while hunting quail (http://www.sjhoward.co.uk/) (viewed February 27, 2006). Still, More 4, the free digital channel that airs the *Daily Show*, is relatively obscure, and cable television itself in Britain has penetrated far less of the market than it has in the United States.

6. Roland Barthes, *S/Z*, trans. Richard Miller (New York: Hill and Wang, 1974), 3–5.

7. Virginia Woolf's devaluing of satire in 1935 indexes a general modernist distrust of univocal satiric modes: "The more complex a vision the less it lends itself to satire: the more it understands the less it is able to sum up and make linear"; Woolf, *A Writer's Diary*, ed. Leonard Woolf (New York: Harcourt, Brace, Jovanovich, 1954), 238–39.

8. For a range of attempts to articulate the contemporary literary and political relevance of Conrad, see *Conrad in the Twenty-First Century*, ed. Carola M. Kaplan, Peter Lancelot Mallios, and Andrea White (New York: Routledge, 2005).

For the music soundtrack to *Modernism, Media, and Propaganda*, consult my personal webpages, currently linked to the English Department pages at Vanderbilt University.

INDEX